Understanding and Interaction in Clinical and Educational Settings

Studies in Communication in Organisations and Professions
Series Editors: Christopher N. Candlin† and Srikant Sarangi, Aalborg University, Denmark

This series aims to build bridges between communication and discourse studies and a broad range of professional, organizational, and workplace sites by foregrounding authoritative analyses of real-life practice – in collaborative, informed and explanatory ways. The series provides an interdisciplinary and interprofessional forum for dialogue between academic researchers and professional/workplace communities and organisations. Examples of appropriate fields of inquiry include: social and community welfare, medicine and healthcare, counselling and therapy, education, law, media, management and business, policy and government and development studies. Coherence among books in the series is achieved through their common concern with cross-over concepts such as power, diversity, identity, agency, decision-making, expertise, risk, appraisal and evaluation.

Published:
Dialogue in Focus Groups: Exploring Socially Shared Knowledge
Ivana Markova, Per Linell, Michele Grossen, Anne Salazar Orvig

Writing the Economy: Activity, Genre and Technology in the World of Banking
Graham Smart

Forthcoming:
Discourse and Responsibility in Professional Settings
Edited by Jan-Ola Östman and Anna Solin

Morality in Practice: Exploring Childhood, Parenting and Schooling in Everyday Life
Edited by Jakob Cromdal and Michael Tholander

Team Talk: Decision-making across the Boundaries in Health and Social Care
Edited by Srikant Sarangi and Per Linell

Interpreter Mediated Healthcare Consultations
Edited by Srikant Sarangi

Language and the Job Interview
Celia Roberts

Understanding and Interaction in Clinical and Educational Settings

Barry Saferstein

SHEFFIELD UK BRISTOL CT

Published by Equinox Publishing Ltd.
UK: Office 415, The Workstation, 15 Paternoster Row, Sheffield, South Yorkshire S1 2BX
USA: ISD, 70 Enterprise Drive, Bristol, CT 06010

www.equinoxpub.com

First published 2016

British Library Cataloguing-in-Publication Data
A catalogue record for this book is available from the British Library.

ISBN-13 978 1 84553 435 6 (hardback)
978 1 84553 436 3 (paperback)

Library of Congress Cataloging-in-Publication Data
Names: Saferstein, Barry, author.
Title: Understanding and interaction in clinical and educational settings / Barry Saferstein.
Description: Sheffield, UK; Bristol, CT: Equinox Publishing Ltd, [2016] | Series: Studies in Communication in Organisations and Professions | Includes bibliographical references and index.
Identifiers: LCCN 2015031001| ISBN 9781845534356 (hb) | ISBN 9781845534363 (pb)
Subjects: LCSH: Cognition and culture | Communication in medicine | Communication in education | Discourse analysis—Social aspects | Social interaction | Organizational sociology | Sociolinguistics.
Classification: LCC BF311 .S26 2016 | DDC 404/.41—dc23
LC record available at https://lccn.loc.gov/2015031001

Typeset by S.J.I. Services, New Delhi
Printed and bound by Lightning Source Inc. (La Vergne, TN), Lightning Source UK Ltd. (Milton Keynes), Lightning Source AU Pty. (Scoresby, Victoria).

Contents

Introduction: Interpretation Activities, Information Resources, and Understandings

This book examines how the interplay of interpretation activities, settings, and professional culture affects understandings. It is based on studies of interventional radiology consultations and genetics education activities in high school biology classes. Analysis of video and audio recordings shows how the interpretation activities of organizing information to create *process narratives*, *grey boxes*, and *discourse frameworks* are central to understanding explanations and concepts.

Part One shows that understandings involve people developing brief chains of information, which express various types of relationships among linguistic terms, physical objects, images, and actions. It examines how those *process narratives* distill information and concepts into a memorable form. Process narratives are a nexus of individual or collaborative interpretation activities, information resources, and culturally shaped patterns of interaction. The category, 'process narrative', pertains to the processes of interpreting human interaction and environmental information resources that result in any type of understanding. Studying process narratives emphasizes the relationships among the various types of interpretation activities and information resources that lead to understandings – during the initial production of the understandings and during their subsequent recall and application. Analysis of the development and use of process narratives exposes the social and individual interpretation activities that sustain beliefs and ideologies. It clarifies aspects of understanding that have been considered in terms of categorical distinctions such as context and content, tacit knowledge, functional fixedness, and oracular reasoning.

Part Two examines the ways that people often develop placeholders for missing information – referred to here as *grey boxes* – in order to produce process narratives. The professional cultures of teachers and clinicians feature routine communication patterns that often restrict access to pieces of information needed to create coherent, recallable process narratives. Grey boxes connect the pieces of information that suggest, but do not clearly depict a relationship. They take various forms, such as pointing or gesturing at objects or graphics, using linguistic terms that have vague meanings, or using tables that replace missing scientific information with computations of probable outcomes. Grey boxes reduce the interpretive contingencies of seeking missing information. Part Two explains grey boxes and their relationship to the interpretation activities and information resources of genetics learning activities. Although grey boxes help people to interact and complete tasks in a specific setting, they can hinder the transfer of knowledge between settings, because they are linked to the environment in which they were formed.

Part Three examines how the activities of creating process narratives and grey boxes also produce *discourse frameworks*, which affect the nature and recall of understandings. Discourse frameworks incorporate individual and social interpretation activities, particular material resources in a setting, and the constraints affecting the use of those resources. Discourse frameworks function as components of understandings, because recall of process narratives also involves recall of the interpretation activities that led to them. Examining the relationship of discourse frameworks to process narratives and grey boxes reveals how the interaction that creates and reproduces a professional culture also affects understandings.

Part Four explains how the patterns of expression specific to professional cultures often restrict access to information in ways that affect the quality and recall of understandings. Comparing the genetics and radiology data shows why understanding does not simply result from presenting well-designed explanations. Strategies intended to support comprehension may feature interpretive contingencies that restrict understanding. However, data related to the interventional radiology consultations show how patterns of interaction involving visual resources can replace commonplace restrictive patterns of interaction in medical consultations, and help patients develop recallable understandings of useful medical information.

Appendix A describes the research methods. Chapter 12 presents ethnographic information concerning the participants and settings.

Cognitive Approaches to Understanding

The representation, memory, and recall of information have been key concerns of research proposing models of how information is organized in the minds of individuals (e.g., Bauer and Johnson-Laird, 1993; Bobrow and Norman, 1975; D'Andrade, 1989; Johnson-Laird, 2006, 2010; Penington and Hastie, 1992; Rumelhart and Norman, 1978, 1981; Schank and Abelson, 1995; Simon, 2004; Simon, Stenstrom, and Read, 2015; Thagard, 1989, 2006; Vendetti et al., 2014; Winograd, 1975). These studies have presented useful findings and inferences about the complexities of reasoning, learning, and recalling concepts. However, their focus on individual mental processes also deemphasizes or neglects the extent to which the resources in a setting, the social structures of a setting, or the cultural constraints of a setting meld with mental and linguistic processes during the creation of understandings.

Much of the cognitive science and cognitive psychology research related to understanding has applied experimental approaches that investigate reasoning about predetermined variables. In contrast, the data analyzed throughout this book show that the study of understanding in commonplace settings provides a richer set of data, which increases the range of relevant activities and information resources that contribute to understandings. The analysis of process narratives, grey boxes, and discourse frameworks throughout this book expands on cognitive explanations of understanding. It also expands on the author's previous research examining the effects of interpretation activities on producing understandings and ideology (Saferstein, 1992, 1994, 2007, 2010). It examines the construction and components of understanding by analyzing the activities of creating process narratives and comparing them with individuals' recall and explanation of information and concepts. This approach provides concrete naturalistic data that display relationships between tangible information resources, interpretation activities and the creation of recallable understandings. It clarifies or replaces ambiguous categories, such as retrieval, segment linkage, story grammars, and cognitive systems, which have resulted from an emphasis on mental operations. The findings relocate key complexities of understanding from an individual's mental operations to interactions with resources in settings and with other people.

The Ecology of a Cognitive System: Cognition, Setting, and Culture in the Production of Process Narratives

The clinical and classroom data discussed in this book show how a cognitive system of understanding extends beyond both an individual's mental processing and the communication between individuals related to that processing. The analysis of radiology consultations and genetics learning activities provides ecologically valid real-world data that explicate and expand on the findings of jury experiments discussed by Simon (2004) and others (e.g., Holyoak and

Simon, 1999; Pennington and Hastie, 1992; Simon, Snow, and Read, 2004). For example, students deciding how to interpret and explain the inheritance of traits presented by a computer simulation display what Simon describes as the central finding of coherence-based reasoning research:

> … the cognitive system *imposes* coherence on complex decision tasks. Throughout the decision-making process, the mental representation of the considerations undergoes gradual change and ultimately shifts toward a state of coherence with either one of the decision alternatives. (Simon, 2004: 517)
>
> … the ultimate state of coherence is essentially a byproduct of the cognitive system's drifting toward either one of two skewed mental models. Within each of these models, the initially complex and incoherent mental model has been spread into two subsets, one of which dominates the other, thereby enabling a relatively easy and confident choice. This skewed representation reflects an artificial polarization between the inflated representation of the variables that support the chosen conclusion and the deflated ones that support the rejected conclusion; it differs considerably from the way the task variables were perceived before the decision-making process got underway, and it differs also from the way they will be perceived some time after the completion of the task. (Simon, 2004: 522–523, fn. 34)

Analysis of how people develop and apply process narratives reveals the specific interpretation activities that are part of a cognitive system. This expands the concept of 'cognitive system' from an emphasis on mental calculations, logic-based choices between predetermined decision options, or mental models. Unlike models of memory and understanding that emphasize mental processes, the process narrative model accounts for the role of resources in settings, professional culture, and organizational arrangements, as well as both the social and individual aspects of cognition.

Stories and Narratives

Various models of understanding have considered how interpreting and organizing information affect perception of meaning. An early example of such concern with how the presentation of information affects understanding is the Aristotelian framework of drama, expressed in *The Poetics* (Golden and Hardison, 1968). *The Poetics* discusses *plot* as an arrangement of incidents that affects the interpretation and understanding of a dramatic representation. It presents the idea that the various meanings interpreted from a set of information relate to the particular ways that the pieces of information in the set are linked. A particular arrangement of incidents must make sense in some way to an audience or the plot will inhibit the perception of a story or theme. An unbelievable plot is one in which the arrangement of certain incidents leaves out information needed to infer a credible relationship among them (in terms of cause-effect, analogy, temporality, etc.).

However, *The Poetics'* model of dramatic meaning also presents the enduring tension between artifact and process that has complicated and limited the reach of explanations of reasoning and understanding. Aristotle applied a referential correspondence approach to meaning, focusing on how a particular arrangement of certain pieces of information in a dramatic artifact produces specific predictable interpretations – categorized as tragedy, melodrama, or comedy. Research in linguistics, sociolinguistics, linguistic anthropology, cognitive sociology, cognitive psychology, cognitive anthropology, discourse analysis, pragmatics, cognitive science, and other disciplines has shown the limitations of such referential rhetorical explanations of understanding.[1] In that context, the process narrative model of understanding emphasizes the interpretation activities and information resources that produce recallable understandings.

Many contemporary studies of reasoning and understanding have continued to emphasize the role of the artifacts resulting from interpretation activities (e.g., solutions to logic problems, expressed stories, or verdicts of juries) as keys to reasoning and understanding, while deemphasizing or neglecting the effects of the interpretation activities that produced those artifacts. For example, a number of studies of cognition and language have discussed the role of stories in the understanding, recall, and application of information (e.g., Eggly, 2002; Polanyi, 1985; Schank and Abelson, 1995). These studies have considered the symbolic and analogical value of themes, settings, and expository styles of stories as key components of the cognition involved in categorizing new information and relating it to relevant background knowledge. In a provocative monograph, Schank and Abelson argued that memory is based on stories (Schank and Abelson, 1995).[2] Their discussion of the cognitive role of stories emphasized the expression of experiences and information more than the initial creation of the expressed memories.

Process narratives differ from such story-based conceptions of understanding and memory in that they do not require a connecting of information to themes, characterizations, or emotional significance in order to contribute to understanding and recall of information. The production of process narratives combines the activities of interpreting information with the mental operations of organizing and recalling understandings. Both the administrative and creative aspects of interpretation are embedded in a process narrative. The data analysis throughout this book shows how the recalled components of prior experiences (e.g., process narratives, grey boxes, and frames of reference) are shaped by the initial interpretation activities that produced them.

Contingencies and Coherence. Approaches to cognition that contribute to models of understanding have investigated reasoning through experimental studies involving formal logic problems (e.g., D'Andrade, 1989, Bauer and Johnson-Laird, 1993, Johnson-Laird *et al.*, 2000), thought experiments (e.g., Johnson-Laird, 2002, 2006), computer modeling (e.g., Ranney and Thagard, 1989; Thagard, 1989) or experimental situations involving simulated juries (e.g., Pennington and Hastie, 1992; Simon, 2004; Simon and Holyoak, 2002). Those studies have emphasized two factors, which are also relevant to the production of process narratives: contingencies and coherence (discussed in detail in Chapters 4, 6, 8, and 11).

The data analysis throughout this book reconfigures earlier concepts of contingencies. It shifts emphasis from the complex mental operations of managing logical propositions to the activities of interpreting tangible information resources and linking them as process narratives. For example, jury experiments, which apply the perspectives of coherence based reasoning and constraint satisfaction theory, have suggested that understandings result from a variety of reasoning processes that contribute to narrative explanations – e.g., deduction, analogy, causal connections, linguistic constructs, and schemata (Pennington and Hastie, 1992; Simon and Holyoak, 2002; Simon, 2004; Simon, Stenstrom, and Read, 2015; Vendetti *et al.*, 2014). They also point out that the fitness of an explanation is related to the explanatory system in which it is applied. However, in regard to explanatory or cognitive systems, those studies emphasize the individual mental processes of organizing the various types of information as stories or explanations.

In contrast, the present study shows how the individual and social activities related to linking information intertwine with the constraints presented by professional culture and a setting's information resources. Such activities include developing grey boxes to contend with the aspects of professional cultures that restrict the information needed to produce recallable process narratives. Analysis of the interpretation activities that produce process narratives explicates and expands on findings of constraint satisfaction research. For example, drawing on findings of experiments featuring decisions by simulated juries, Simon (2004) mentions the reciprocal effects of reasoning and information resources:

> In complex decisions, the initial mental representation of the task is naturally incoherent. Constraint satisfaction processes force the task

> variables to change toward a better fit with the gradually emerging state of coherence....
>
> This reversed induction gives coherence-based reasoning its bidirectional character: while the strength of supporting variables determines the conclusion, the variables themselves are transformed by the cognitive process so as to provide considerably stronger support for the conclusion. (Simon, 2004: 522–523)

Such findings are consistent with studies in cognitive sociology and other phenomenological research approaches, which emphasize the interrelationship of interaction, cognition, and social organization (e.g., Cicourel, 1973, 1987; Frake, 1980; Gumperz, 1982; Hymes, 1986, Knorr-Cetina, 1999; Ochs, 1992; Saferstein, 1994, 2007). This interrelationship is rooted in the ongoing interpretation activities applied to making sense of interaction and communication. Actions, utterances, and interpretations influence each other as people develop a communication format, develop interpretive frames of reference, and recall or seek additional information relevant to the immediate circumstances. Those interpretation activities help people to organize the great amount of information that they perceive at every instant.

Reading the Book

This book is intended for readers who have different areas of interest, including clinical communication, patients' understandings of medical information, classroom interaction, students' understandings of science, cognition and reasoning, and discourse analysis. Many of the chapter and section titles refer to the three main research areas: clinical settings, educational settings, and cognitive science. I urge readers who are more interested in one of those areas than the others to jump to the chapters and sections that focus on their area of interest.

The chapters include extensive transcripts of continuous interaction. Some chapters analyze complete sequences of the interpretation activities related to creating particular understandings – rather than presenting a few examples of key events. They present such detail in order to emphasize a key theme of the research – that the processes rather than the artifacts of interpretation activities are fundamental to explaining understanding. Presenting a complete set of interpretation activities clarifies how, during particular moments of interpretation activity, participants often recall and apply information resources and interpretations that they encountered developed and much earlier – i.e., the creation of understandings is not simply a result of the linear contiguity of interaction. However, I have also summarized and quoted key parts of the transcripts in the text. I urge readers who are not interested in details of the discourse analysis and do not want to read the entire transcript segments to skip through the detailed transcript extracts. If the subsequent text piques your interest in the preceding transcripts, there will be no disadvantage in backtracking to examine them.

Acknowledgments

My thanks to the patients, students, clinicians, and teachers who participated in the three research projects that contributed to this book. They remain anonymous in order to maintain the privacy of the participants who were recorded. I am grateful to the clinicians, teachers, and school administrators for permitting access to the clinical and classroom settings. The teachers featured in the data examples analyzed throughout the book were highly committed to their students' educational success and to advancing pedagogy and curriculum for biology education. They demonstrated that commitment in their willingness to participate in the research projects that produced the data presented here – and in their courage to be recorded over weeks and months during routine and sometimes difficult classroom situations in which students often did the unexpected, requiring teachers to cope by improvising. None of the teachers' interactions with students were planned specifically for the research analyzed in this book – they occurred for the education of the students. The data featuring two teachers' interactions with students are representative examples of activities that occurred in the classes of all seven of the biology teachers whose classes were studied. The discussion of restrictive communication patterns in regard to learning activities, the Mendelian curriculum, and the professional culture of biology teachers applies to the teaching of genetics in general, and is not directed at the quality of specific teachers' expertise.

I want to recognize the significant contribution of Nancy Oiye in regard to research and editorial activities, which included cataloging classroom video, co-recording some classroom data, participating in my follow-up discussions with students in the second classroom study, transcribing some of the educational and clinical data, and consultation on manuscript draft revisions. She initially brought to my attention the interventional radiology practice's use of images during consultations, and facilitated my initial contact with the clinicians. I also want to acknowledge the work of research assistants, Dominic Payne and Elizabeth Kangles, who contributed to the transcription of the first classroom study's recordings of genetics learning activities. I am grateful for the contributions of Lynn Furnald and Ross Christensen to accomplishing the clinical research project. Many thanks to Kemi Nevins, Patrick and staff for a creative atmosphere, helpful questions, and letting me write long past closing time. I want to acknowledge the valuable comments on the prospectus by Chris Candlin, and on the manuscript by Srikant Sarangi, co-editors of the series. Tia DeNora and Douglas Tudhope offered helpful comments on the book's figures.

Above all, I thank members of my family, here and gone, both for moral support during the writing of the book, and for inspiring my interest in the nature of understanding through their own experiences in clinical and educational settings. I dedicate this work to all of them.

PART ONE
PROCESS NARRATIVES

Process narratives are recallable units of meaning presenting a brief chain of information. They can be expressed by a combination of language and gesture related to objects or images. Process narratives are not stories. They do not necessarily feature a beginning and end of a series of events or actions. They are narrative only in the sense that they link a few pieces of information to indicate a relationship among them.

Interpretation activities applied to interaction and information resources select and link pieces of information in ways that produce the recallable units of meaning I categorize as process narratives. I first used the term when noticing how people link information about genetic or biological processes in my recorded clinical and classroom data (Saferstein, 2007). Further data analysis has shown that process narratives do not always describe a process of how things operate. Rather, 'process' refers to the activities of interpreting and linking information. Process narratives simply express a grouping of information that has relevance to a particular setting or activity.

For the people who participate in creating them, process narratives index particular interpretation activities and resources that were applied to their production. As research data, process narratives also point toward particular interpretation activities of organizing information for recall. The relationship of process narratives to specific interpretation activities and information resources is central to their analytical value for showing how people develop or fail to develop transferable understandings of new information. The following explanation of process narratives emphasizes the relationship between interaction, cognition, and setting in producing and applying understandings.

1 Process Narratives in a Clinical Setting

Chapter One examines how patients interpret, understand, and recall verbal and visual information encountered during interventional radiology consultations concerning the symptoms and treatment of uterine fibroid tumors. The chapter presents analysis of interaction during two clinical consultations and a post-consultation discussion with each patient. These representative examples of a larger recorded data set show that communication patterns including gestures and pointing affect which pieces of information patients link as process narratives and understandings. During each consultation, a patient and a nurse view and discuss a set of images on a computer screen in order to help the patient understand a medical procedure she is considering. The data show how the patterns of interaction related to the use of visual and verbal information support the patient's creation of process narratives, which she recalls days after the consultation.

The clinical data presented here and in subsequent chapters derive from recordings of interventional radiology consultations and post-consultation discussions with the patients recorded four to eleven days after each consultation.[3] During the consultations, a nurse presented and explained a set of medical images about the uterine fibroid embolization procedure (UFE) for treating uterine fibroid tumors.[4] In a consultation room, following discussion of a patient's medical history, the patient and nurse observed and discussed images and text presented on the screen of a laptop computer. The radiology clinicians' objective in using the set of images during the consultations was to provide the patients with information and explanations about fibroid tumors and UFE that would help the patients decide if UFE was an acceptable alternative to more invasive surgical procedures.

The following analysis of recorded consultations shows that discussion of the medical images triggers patients' questions about diagnosis, treatment, and prognosis. Such interpretation activities provide clinicians and patients with a common focus for discussion. The pictures and text provide a framework for the clinician's explanations, which feature pointing at features of the images on the computer screen. The data show that patients respond by asking additional questions and stating their concerns in order to further clarify the pictures or text in the presentation. This prompts additional explanation by the clinician. These interpretation activities contributed to the recallable process narratives patients subsequently expressed in telephone discussions, which revealed their understandings of medical information about uterine fibroid tumors, their symptoms, and options for treatment.

Filling Information Gaps

The radiology practice developed the set of images for use during patient consultations, because the way that the UFE procedure treats the symptoms of uterine fibroid tumors is more complex than the alternative treatments, myomectomy and hysterectomy, which surgically remove the fibroid tumors or the uterus. As explained during the recorded consultations, UFE involves the insertion of a catheter through a small incision in the femoral artery of the right leg. The radiologist moves the catheter through the arterial system until it reaches the uterine arteries, which supply the blood that supports growth of the uterine fibroid tumors. Minuscule particles, called the 'embolizing agent', pass through the catheter, and the radiologist deposits them in the uterine arteries supplying blood to the tumors.[5] This blocks the blood supply to the tumors. In most cases, the fibroid tumors shrink within a few months, alleviating the symptoms that had troubled the patient.

The patients who participated in the recorded consultations had encountered some information about UFE prior to the radiology consultations. However, they all mentioned that the discussion of explanatory images at the consultation contributed to their understandings of various aspects of the UFE procedure, preparations for it, recovery, or potential complications. Comparison of each patient's post-consultation telephone discussions with the interpretation activities during her radiology consultation shows that patients' understandings derived from the communication patterns during discussion of the visual information, rather than from the visual information alone. The communication patterns that result from a patient and clinician discussing explanatory images during the radiology consultations provided opportunities for patients to interpret and link information as process narratives that contributed to recallable understandings.

For example, during the radiology consultations it was common for patients to refer to images of blood vessels as 'veins'. The nurse, N1, would correct them by mentioning that the blood vessels in the pictures are arteries. This occurred in the consultation of patient, P3, during discussion related to an image titled, 'What Is Embolization?' which displayed before-and-after x-rays of an embolization of a brain artery (Transcript Extract 1.1).

Transcript Extract 1.1[6]

2. P3: (Raises arm and points toward screen with right index finger) Does anything (looks at N1) happen to the vein. (N1 looks toward screen; then P3 looks toward screen) when you (P3 makes chopping gestures with hands) stop the blood flow?
3. N1: These are all (N1 and P3 look at each other) arteries
4. P3: Art/eries/
5. N1: /that/ (N1 looks toward screen. Then P3 look toward screen) we're talk/ing about/

N1 explains to P3 that all of the blood vessels displayed in the image and in their discussion of UFE are arteries. P3 repeats the word, 'arteries', as soon as N1 says it (Transcript Extract 1.1, lines 3, 4). During a post-consultation telephone interview five days later, P3 corrects herself, changing 'vein' to 'arteries', while explaining some of the information from images discussed during the radiology consultation that she had recalled and found useful:

> I knew they had gone into through the groin area and they y'know put a catheter in there and everything, but to actually see the catheter in the vein and in the y'know in the what's that, vein I guess – it's going through arteries. (Endnote 9, in lines T38, T40)

During the consultation, the nurse's explanation was not merely a linguistic definition. She linked her comments about arteries to images showing blood vessels. As the consultation proceeded, the nurse explained other x-ray images and diagrams showing arteries and a catheter placing the embolizing agent near fibroid tumors. The interactive discussion of visual information during the radiology consultations provided opportunities for the clinician and the patient to verbally compare and conform their use of medical terms with the visual images of uterine fibroid tumors and their effects on physiology.

The distinction between veins and arteries is significant in regard to patients understanding how the direction of blood flow affects placement of the embolizing agent in the uterine arteries during the UFE procedure in order to stop blood supply to the fibroid tumors. For example, in two telephone discussions

I conducted with another patient, P1, four days after her clinical consultation, she expressed the following process narrative as she recalled and explained information she had encountered at the consultation while viewing one of the images and asking the nurse a question about it:

> … the particles that were going to be permanently in my body. How they don't come back out because you know the blood flow in the arteries is one-way, something I forgot. Yeah we discussed that (Figure 1.1, Row C, Column 2, lines 1.4.3, 1.4.5)

P1's process narrative connects the functioning of the embolizing agent during the UFE procedure with a diagram P1 observed during her radiology consultation and a question she had asked the nurse. The process narrative linked the information provided by the nurse and the diagram with P1's concern about the potential for dangerous movement of the embolizing agent within her body. Analysis of the recorded consultation shows that P1's process narrative combined the talk, image, and gestures that were part of the interpretive interaction at the consultation. It is an example of how process narratives condense information into a form that is recallable.[7]

In the following pages, comparison of the interpretation activities and visual information of the radiology consultation with the process narratives that the patient expressed four days later shows how the consultation activities led to her new understandings of the UFE procedure.

Linking Verbal and Visual Information Expressed during the Radiology Consultation

During the radiology consultation, the patient and nurse viewed a drawing that showed a cross-section of a uterus, a fibroid tumor, and uterine arteries containing embolizing agent particles represented as small spheres (called 'beads' or 'particles' by the nurse and P1). The drawing displayed a catheter in the artery placing embolizing agent particles that block blood flow to the tumor (Figure 1.1, Row A, Column 1). P1 looked at the image while the nurse explained the UFE procedure. Pointing at the embolizing agent in the diagram, P1 asked, 'Now what keeps those little particles there instead of coming back into my – and giving me a blood clot' (Figure 1.1, Row B, Column 1, line 2).

Figure 1.1: N1 Presents New Information[8]

[Highlighted text indicates activities at the consultation that correlate with understandings P1 expressed during the telephone discussion. Bold text indicates verbal information that correlates. Italics indicate closely matching expressions of information. R1 is the author.]

	P1 Clinical Consultation	**P1 Telephone Discussion 4 Days Later**
A	Image Viewed During This Part of the Consultation* 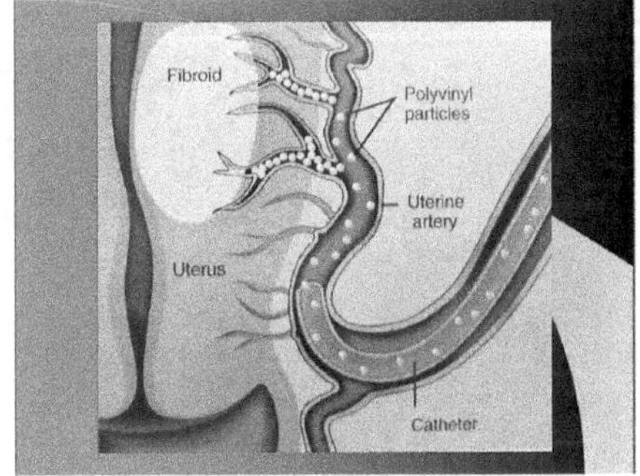 	[After researcher asked if P1 recalled details of a diagram she mentioned, showing embolizing particles in uterine arteries.] 2.1.1 P1: I don't know. **I guess I saw them moving toward their *end destination*, and then *just stayin' there*.** And then I asked a question you know 2.1.2 R1: Yeah 2.1.3 P1: So, that's what helped me
B	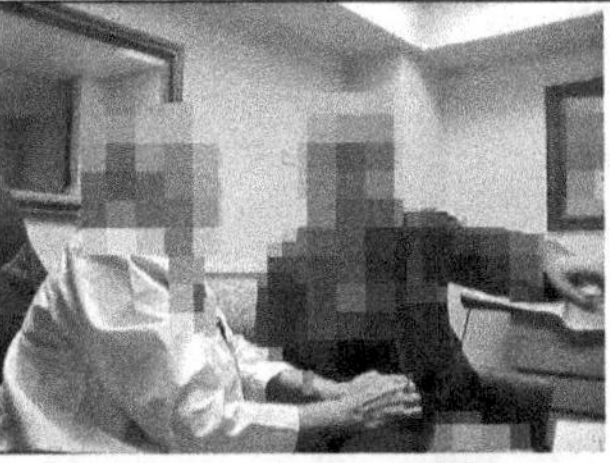 2. P1: (P1 leans toward screen and points with left hand at the diagram, moving hand to point at different parts of the diagram. N1 looks toward screen following P1's pointing.) **Now what keeps those little particles there instead of coming back into my** (P1 moves left hand back to her side, leaning back partially)—**and giving me** (points right hand at middle of her chest) **a blood (moves hand back to side) clot or something?**	1.3.1 R1: Any specific parts of it [the set of images] that uh come to mind that uh? 1.3.2 P1: Yeah, **the diagram of the uh parti—the uh particles that are gonna be in my arteries.** That was (chuckles) duh huh—that wa--that reminded me yeah I wanted to find out how—how **those weren't gonna come back and give me a clot.**

Figure 1.1 (continued)

<table>
<tr>
<td>C</td>
<td>3. NI: Good question. Well (NI moves right hand in front of her) first of all blood only flows in (NI moves hand in forward direction) one direction
4. PI: Okay
5. NI: (Clears throat) Nch nch and (still holding hand out, points at the screen with index finger) these are arteries, (moves hand in forward direction again)

so it's going that direction, (leans forward to point at a part of the diagram on the screen) /up to/
6. PI: /?Oh yeah?/
7. NI: those (PI laughs. NI leans away from screen and moves arm to her side) yeah (chuckles) up to those little blood vessels and-and you see how (NI looks at PI) they're not connected to anything else?
8. PI: Yeah. (nods head)</td>
<td>[Responding to researcher's question about consultation information that she discussed with her husband]
1.4.3 PI: /The particles/ the particles that were going to be permanently in my /body./
1.4.4 II: /Yeah/
1.4.5 PI: How they don't come back out because you know . the blood flow in the arteries is one-way, something I . forgot.</td>
</tr>
</table>

Figure 1.1 (continued)

D	9. N1: (Turns head toward screen) **Those are called** (Looks at P1) **end blood vessels (P1 nods,** N1 looks at screen) **that's real common in lots of kinds** (looks at P1) **of tumors.** 10. P1: **Okay.** (Nods and sits up in chair) 11. N1: **Even** (gestures with both hands) **some cancer** (P1 looks at N1) **tumors.** (Both look at screen)  **So** (N1 points toward screen with right hand) **when s— those beads go there,** (N1 moves hand back to her side) **they're** (N1 looks at P1) **stuck there. They can't go any place else.** 12. P1: (Nods) **Okay.**	2.1.1 P1: I don't know. **I guess I saw them moving toward *their end destination, and then just stayin' there.*** And then I asked a question you know 2.1.2 I1: Yeah 2.1.3 P1: So, that's what helped me

* Diagram in Row A Copyright David Klemm and Society of Interventional Radiology. Reprinted with their permission. All rights reserved.

The diagram showed that none of the spheres moved past the arteries leading to the fibroid tumor. However, the diagram's top border limited the presentation of information about the destination of another artery, which could carry the spheres to other parts of the body. Thus, the diagram alone did not answer P1's question. Nor did it present all of the information in the process narratives P1 expressed four days later during the post-consultation telephone discussion. During that discussion, P1 recalled the combination of visual information and interpretation activities at the consultation, which had contributed to understanding of why the embolizing agent particles do not move to other parts of the body.

During the radiology consultation, the nurse's answer to P1's question had linked gestural and verbal information to the screen image. The nurse gestured toward the image that P1 mentions during the post-consultation telephone discussion (Figure 1.1, Rows C, D, Column 1). The image showed the spheres conglomerating in the blood vessels near the tumor and 'then just stayin' there', as P1 said in the telephone discussion (Figure 1.1, Row D, Column 2).

Figure 1.2: Sequence of Images Concerning the UFE Procedure*

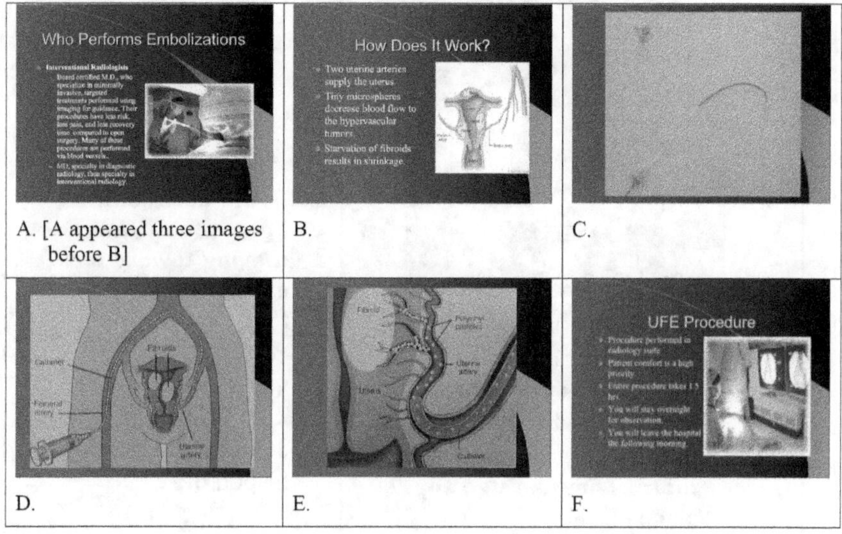

A. [A appeared three images before B] B. C. D. E. F.

* Image in B Copyright John Yesko. Images in D and E Copyright David Klemm and Society of Interventional Radiology. Reprinted with their permission. All rights reserved.

The preceding images (Figure 1.2, Images A-D) also presented information relevant to the interpretation of the image that P1 remembered (Figure 1.2, Image E) and to the nurse's explanation. Those images presented an anatomical context for the image and explanation:

- Image A contains a photograph of a radiologist holding a catheter inserted into a patient during an actual embolization procedure. It also contains text arranged as bullet points, which express a process narrative:

    UFE decreases blood flow from the two uterine arteries to the fibroid tumors, and starves the fibroids, which shrinks them.

It appeared three images prior to B, among images related to explaining the role and expertise of an interventional radiologist in regard to the UFE procedure.

- Image B contains a drawing of the uterus and uterine artery system, with textual labels for the uterus, uterine arteries, and fibroids. It is more anatomically detailed than image (E), which P1 mentions during the telephone discussion. It also includes text that presents linguistic terms indexing the more detailed visual information.
- Image C is a photo of a catheter, the instrument inserted into the artery to deliver the embolizing material.
- Image D is a cross-section drawing of a body from waist to thigh, showing a catheter containing particles of embolizing agent (dots) inserted through femoral arteries to the uterine arteries. Textual labels identify the catheter, femoral artery, uterine artery, and fibroids. The drawing of a catheter resembles the catheters shown in the preceding photographs (A, C). Like Image D, Image E contained dots or spheres, labeled as polyvinyl particles, in the arteries leading to a fibroid tumor.

Images B, D, and E (Figure 1.2) progressively presented more detailed information about the female anatomy or embolization, including medical terms, labeling parts of the drawings (i.e., *catheter, femoral artery, uterine artery, polyvinyl particles*). Images A-D provided information that supported inferences about the particulars of the embolization procedure (using a catheter to deposit the embolizing agent particles in certain arteries) and its purpose (blocking blood supply to the tumor).

During the post-consultation telephone discussion, P1 recalls and expresses process narratives based on visual and verbal information she had encountered four days earlier during the consultation. Those process narratives contribute to her understanding of why the embolizing agent particles do not move away from the uterine fibroids to other parts of the body where they might block vital blood supply. For example, during the post-consultation telephone discussion, she recalls that Image E (Figure 1.2) showed the particles 'moving toward their end destination' (Figure 1.1, Row D, Column 2, line 2.1.1). P1 links the visual information showing the catheter and embolizing agent with the verbal information that the nurse had expressed.

At the radiology consultation, P1 often looked at the text and images on the screen, which displayed information about a particular topic, while the nurse was commenting on that topic. P1 would also point, gesture, or look toward the screen when interested in an image or the nurse's explanation of it (Figure 1.3).

Figure 1.3: Pointing at Image E

<table>
<tr><td colspan="3">[Still frames are from synchronized simultaneous recordings of computer screen images and consultation interaction] *</td></tr>
<tr><td>A</td><td>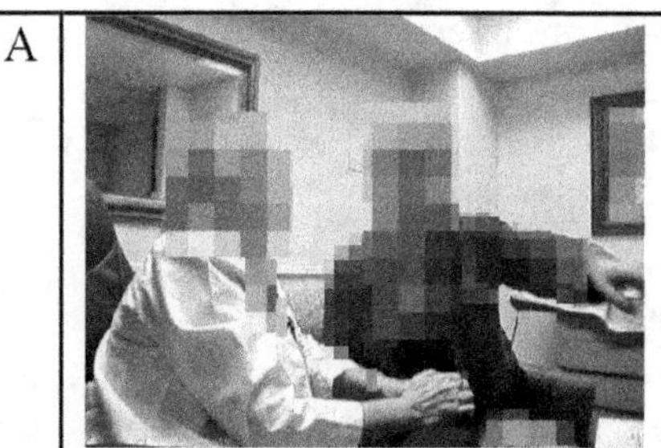</td><td>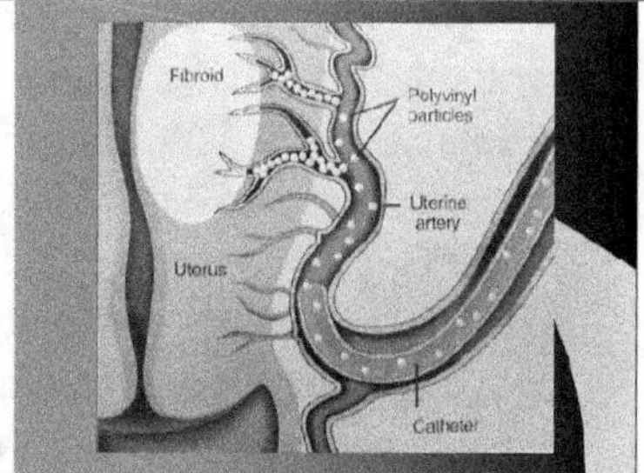
</td></tr>
<tr><td>B</td><td colspan="2">2 [partial]. P1: (P1 leans toward screen and points with left hand at the diagram, moving hand to point at different parts of the diagram. N1 looks toward screen following P1's pointing.) Now what keeps those little particles there instead of coming back into my (P1 moves left hand back to her side, leaning back partially)—and giving me (points right hand at middle of her chest) a blood (moves hand back to side) clot or something?</td></tr>
<tr><td>C</td><td>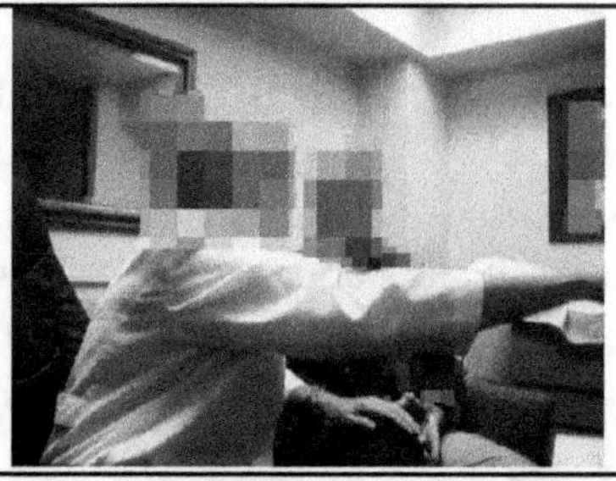</td><td>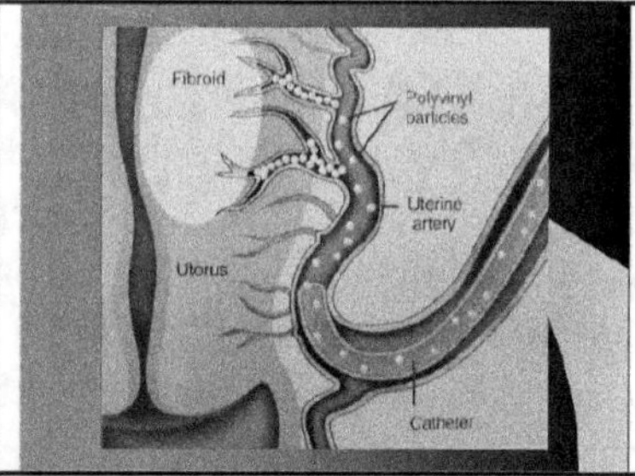
</td></tr>
<tr><td>D</td><td colspan="2">5 [partial]. N1: (still holding hand out, points at the screen with index finger) these are arteries, so it's going that direction, (leans forward to point at a part of the diagram on the screen) /up to/
6. P1: /?Oh yeah?/
7. N1: those yeah (chuckles) up to those little blood vessels
8. P1: Yeah.
9. N1: Those are called end blood vessels that's real common in lots of kinds of tumors.</td></tr>
</table>

When P1 viewed the drawing of a catheter placing the embolizing agent particles in the blood vessels leading to fibroid tumors, she pointed at the drawing and then gestured toward her chest, while asking the nurse about the potential for the embolizing agent to travel through the blood vessels to other parts of the body (Figure 1.3, Rows A, B). The nurse responded by presenting process narratives that combine verbal explanation, gestures, and pointing at specific parts of the image displayed on the computer screen (Figure 1.3, Rows C, D). She reminded P1 that blood flows in only one direction. That information augmented the image, which showed the embolizing agent particles in the uterine artery and the smaller blood vessels leading to the fibroid tumor.

The discussion fostered by P1's response to the diagram provided information, which she had linked as the process narratives that she expressed four days later during the telephone discussion, when I asked her about aspects of the radiology consultation she had recalled or used:

> *The particles the particles that were going to be permanently in my body. How they don't come back out because you know the blood flow in the arteries is one-way* (Figure 1.1, Row C, Column 2, lines 1.4.3, 1.4.5)
>
> *... I guess I saw them moving toward their end destination, and then just stayin' there.* (Figure 1.1, Row D, Column 2, line 2.1.1)

P1's use of the phrase, 'moving toward their final destination', during the post-consultation telephone discussion displays an understanding of the embolization procedure in regard to placement of the embolizing agent particles and their function of blocking blood flow to the fibroid tumors. The video recordings of P1's radiology consultation show specific images, gestures, and verbal comments that relate to 'moving toward their final destination', i.e.:

- The preceding images (Figure 1.2, images A-D) had presented information about the setting and practice of the actual UFE procedure, including a catheter entering a body through a femoral artery, and traveling to blood vessels connecting to a fibroid tumor.
- P1 and the nurse had gestured and pointed at specific parts of the image, which showed the embolizing agent particles in blood vessels leading to a fibroid tumor (e.g., Figure 1.3, Rows A and C).
- The nurse had mentioned 'end blood vessels' as she explained the image (Figure 1.3, row D, line 9).

Transcript Extract 1.2

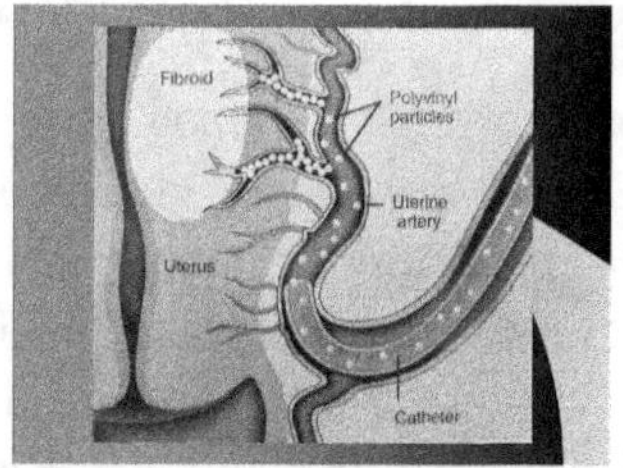

Image Displayed on Computer Screen*

13. NI: (NI looks toward screen) Now can the beads go some place else? Sure they could .if whoever's (NI looks at PI) putting those (PI looks at NI) beads in doesn't put 'em in the right place, (PI nods; NI looks at screen) they (NI gestures with hands) could go (NI stops gesturing) elsewhere and that's not good. (NI looks at PI) It's called non-target embolization.
14. PI: /And that would be awful/
15. NI: /So if they went/ (NI moves eyes away from PI) to your (NI gestures with left hand toward her own abdomen) . bowel or your bladder or something like that, that causes death of that tissue. (NI looks toward screen)
16. PI: (PI looks up to ceiling rolling her eyes, and moves upper body forward /(laughs nervously)/
17. NI: /Have we ever encountered (looks toward PI) it?/ No.
18. PI: Okay.
19. NI: (Looks away from PI) Have we even read about (PI looks at NI) it in the literature? – Only that it's theory not that it's (NI nods head) happened.
20. PI: (Nods head and looks toward screen) Okay.
21. NI: (NI looks toward screen) So, in other words, (NI looks toward PI) you trust your
22. PI: Your /radiologist/
23. NI: /your/doc/tor/
24. PI: /Yeah/ (clears throat)
25. NI: to be doing it (NI looks toward screen) properly.
26. PI: Okay.
27. NI: So (moves forward pointing right hand at screen diagram) yes if you put it in . let's say if you put the beads in – start putting 'em here, they could go to that (moves hand away from screen, leans back, and looks at PI) blood vessel, (gestures with both hands) wherever that blood vessel goes. (PI nods) But (gestures with both hands) he knows where to –

Transcript Extract 1.2 (continued)

28. P1: /(raises both hands in front of her as if holding something) (?and that?)/
29. N1: /(raises both hands mirroring P1) and that's/ why he's looking
30. P1: (P1 looks at N1) Yeah (nods and moves right hand to scratch beneath her right eye and looks at screen, while moving left hand to her side).
31. N1: while he's (looks toward screen)doing it
32. P1: Right. (P1 moves right arm to her side.)
33. N1: (N1 nods and looks at P1) Is that starting to come together
34. P1: (Nods) /Yeah/
35. N1: /a little bit?/ (looks toward and moves arm toward computer)
36. P1: That makes sense
37. N1: /Okay/
38. P1: /because/ that was the something (N1 looks at P1) I was just thinking about /(??)/
39. N1: /(Looks toward computer) yeah/ sure. (Looks at screen and advances presentation to next image) It's a common question.

The verbal and visual information about *end blood vessels* provided a link with the previously encountered information about the UFE procedure, which P1 mentioned in her question (e.g., the 'particles' used to block blood flow [Figure 1.3, Row B, line 2]). The nurse continued her response to P1's question about the potential movement of the embolizing agent particles, which she called 'beads', to other parts of the body, by explaining how the radiologist's actions and expertise in regard to the UFE procedure relate to a safe outcome (Transcript Extract 1.2, lines 13–23). The visual information and nurse's comments did not present all details of the radiologist's actions during a UFE procedure. However, they presented P1 with enough information for her to link some of it as coherent process narratives, which describe how the embolizing agent particles are contained in order to avoid the blood clot that she had mentioned at the consultation.

During the post-consultation telephone interview, P1 links the diagram's visual information picturing the catheter and particles with the nurse's verbal information about the shrinkage of fibroids and the radiological procedure.

P1 also links that visual and verbal information with information presented earlier in the consultation (e.g., the visual information displayed in Figure 1.2, images A-D) as a process narrative expressing the lack of danger that the 'particles' would move to other parts of the body:

> *the particles that were going to be permanently in my body ...* ***don't come back out, because you know the blood flow in the arteries is one-way,*** *...* (Figure 1.1, Row C, Column 2, lines 1.4.3, 1.4.5)

During the radiology consultation, the patterns of verbal and gestural information triggered by P1's question had contributed to a process narrative that animated the static diagram. In conjunction with the images, the pattern of gesturing and verbal communication contributed to P1 interpreting and linking terms such as 'end blood vessels' and 'moving to their final destination' in a way that produced recallable process narratives explaining the UFE procedure.

P1 simultaneously developed an interpretive frame of reference and focused on certain information that became relevant for linkage with other information to form coherent process narratives. She was able to recall and express those process narratives during the telephone discussion, when she did not have access to the visual information or the nurse's comments. The effects of the medical images on the patterns of interaction and patients' creation of process narratives are further detailed in Part Three, Discourse Frameworks.

The Intertwining of Interpretation Activities, Information Resources, and Process Narratives

The preceding example emphasized the effects of communication patterns related to visual information on the creation of process narratives. While interpreting an image, the patient had asked a question related to the nurse's explanation of the image. The question informed the nurse of the patient's misconception or lack of information about the direction of blood flow. The nurse provided additional information. Process narratives the patient expressed during her subsequent follow-up telephone discussion mentioned not only interpretations of the information she had encountered at the radiology consultation, but also the activities by which she had interpreted that information.

The next example shows how the absence of certain information in an initial verbal explanation by the nurse to another patient, P3, led to a patient-prompted discussion that resulted in a recallable understanding of medical information. During a post-consultation telephone discussion five days after her consultation, P3 expressed a process narrative that reflected the activities at her consultation by which she had prompted and interpreted information about the appearance of the materials used during a UFE procedure. That information was ancillary to the nurse's initial verbal explanation and the computer screen image to which the nurse had referred. That ancillary information about the size of the embolizing agent particles was not central to the nurse's immediate explanation of how an interventional radiologist used a catheter to place the embolizing agent and block blood flow to the fibroid tumors.

P3's post-consultation process narrative presented her understanding of the effects of the embolizing agent:

> *as much as it wasn't a natural substance that's gonna go into the body, it's it's as tiny and minute minute as possible y'know anything that's smaller than that wasn't gonna do anything. So It made me realize that okay this isn't such a bad procedure and these things going into my body don't look harmful at all whatsoever.* (Figure 1.4, Row C, line T70)

The combination of the verbal, gestural, and pictorial information P3 had encountered during the consultation contributed to her comment that the embolizing particles are 'as minute as possible'. In that context, she concluded that fibroid embolization 'really isn't such a bad procedure'.

P3's understandings of UFE did not derive simply from the presence of the visual and verbal information, but from particular interpretation activities applied to that information. Those activities included the nurse's gestures augmenting the screen images, P3's unelicited brief utterances acknowledging certain comments by the nurse about the images, P3's and the nurse's comments about the embolizing agent, and P3's action of inspecting vials of the embolizing agent (Transcript Extract 1.3).

Transcript Extract 1.3: P3 Acknowledging Information about UFE Procedure*

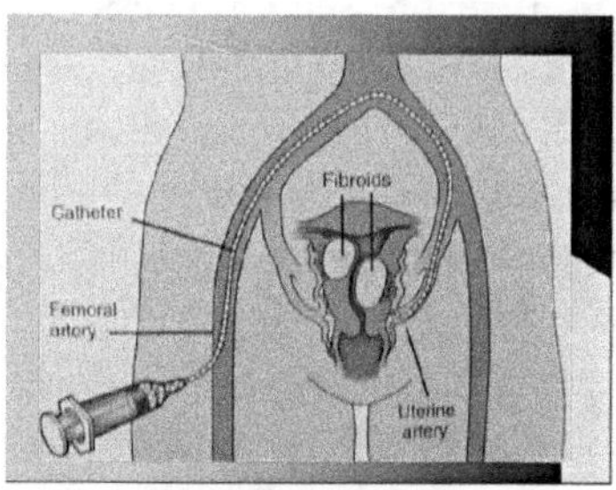

C51. N1: (N1 and P3 looking at screen) And then this is just another diagram. (N1 moves both hands to her own upper right thigh to demonstrate) We go into the groin (N1 looks at P3. P3 looks at N1's hands; closes eyes; nods head; then looks at screen) right here. It's right in the crease of your leg. And it's you've had an I.V. started /in your hand/
C52. P3: /(nods head) Yes./
C53. N1: before? Well (N1 looks at P3) actually this is (P3 looks at N1) just a little bigger than an I.V.
C54. P3: (Nods head) Okay.
C55. N1: (N1 raises right arm, holding thumb and index finger together. P3 looks at her) So it's not really even an incision (N1 moves right hand in front of her face moving thumb and index finger apart slightly. P3 looks at N1's hand). It's y'know yea (N1 lowers arm and looks toward screen. P3 looks toward screen) big.
C56. P3: Okay.
C57. N1: (Moves right arm and points at various areas of screen) So (moves right hand to follow picture of catheter in artery) thread the catheter around to the left side. Embolize. (Moves right hand across screen to point at right side of pictured body) Bring the catheter back around to the right side. Embolize. Bring the catheter out (Moves hand away from screen. Moves right hand in front of her, holding thumb and index finger slightly apart. Looks at her hand. Turns head toward P3.). You have a little bandage about yea big (P3 looks at N1 and nods head), and that's it.
C58. P3: (P3 looks toward screen.) Wow.

Transcript Extract 1.3 (continued)

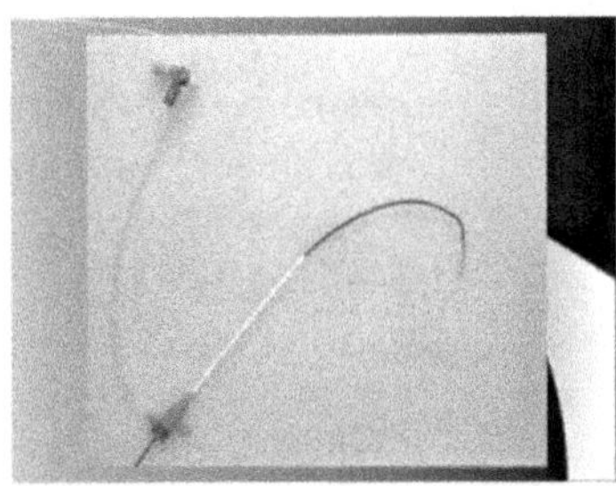

C59. N1: (Looks at screen. Moves right hand to keyboard; advances to next image) So that's the size of the catheters they use.

C60. P3: (Nods head) Umhmm.

C61. N1: (Advances to next image) And then uum this is just a close-up diagram of . (N1 moves right arm to point at screen) when he puts the beads in.

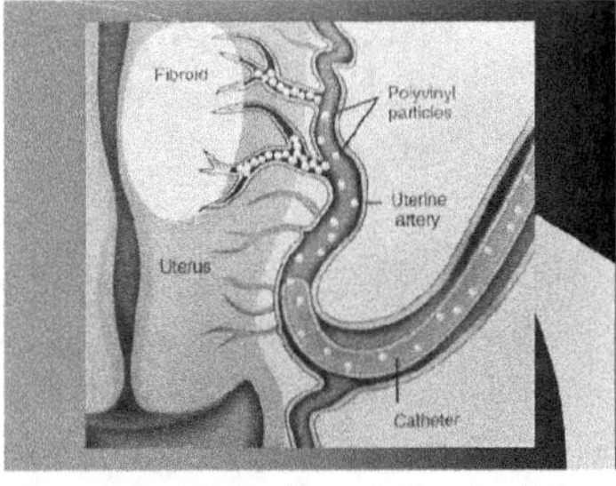

C62. P3: (Nods head) Umhmm.

C63. N1: The the blood (moves right hand upward) only flows one direction (rests right hand on computer) in your artery of course so it--and it's (moves right hand in circle) fast. It goes that (N1 moves right hand close to screen; moves hand upward on screen) that this direction up. And then umm the fibroids are real greedy. They like (N1 clinches right hand) a blood supply; like estrogen, progesterone.

C64. P3: (Nods head) Umhmm

C65. N1: So (N1 moves hand across screen) the beads just go directly to those fibroids. (P3 nods; smiles) A few of the beads will go to the (N1 moves right arm toward screen, pointing with index finger) to the normal regular uterus, but (N1 moves right hand away from screen; moves hands in front of her as if holding something) the uterus (N1 moves hands together and apart) is getting a blood (P3 looks at N1) supply from the rest of the abdomen (P3 nods; looks at screen). So the uterus survives, but the fibroids don't.

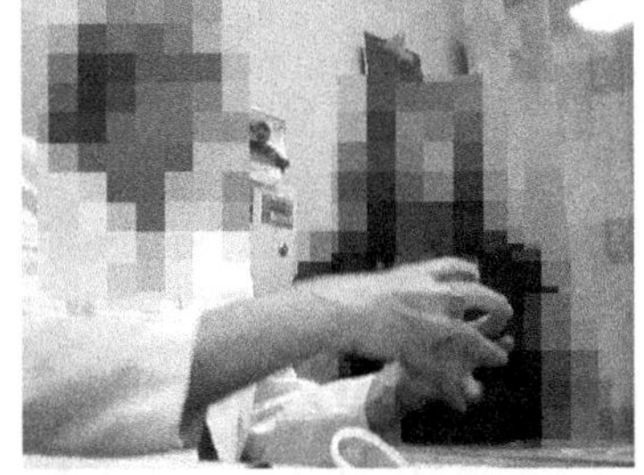

C66. P3: (Nods) Okay.

Transcript Extract 1.3 (continued)

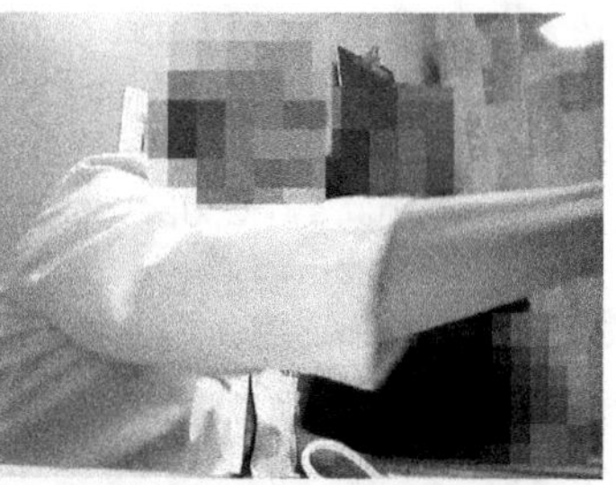

C67. N1: (N1 moves right hand toward screen, pointing index finger) And you can see these are called end (N1 moves hand around screen) blood vessels. They just go (N1 moves right arm to her side) to the fibroid. They don't (N1 moves left hand in front of her face and then away from her body; looks at P3) connect to any other blood vessels. (N1 moves right arm toward screen) So they just stop there.
C68. P3: Got it. Okay.
C69. N1: So as the fibroid (N1 moves hands together in front of her chest, clenches right hand and cups it with left hand) shrinks down (N1 makes shaking motion with clasped hands), those beads stay right with it. (P3 nods) And these (N1 moves right hand in front of her face with thumb and index finger slightly apart. N1 looks at P3.) are microscopic /size. (N1 looks at screen; moves hand toward computer) They d (N1 points at the screen) they're not (N1 moves right hand away from screen) that big/
C70. P3: /Umhmm. Is it the size of (P3 looks at N1) a sand/ (P3 looks at screen) particle or something like that?
C71. N1: Yyeah yeah. Actually (reaches down to get sample vials of the beads and gives one to P3. P3 holds it in front of her face with left hand) hold that up to the light. (P3 holds vial up toward light) See 'em?
C72. P3: Oh yeah. Wow.
C73. N1: (Chuckles)
C74. P3: (Chuckles) Ha ha okay. (P3 gives vial to N1. N1 takes the vial and hands her another vial. P3 holds second vial up to the light. N1 looks toward P3) These are them dry?
C75. N1: Um hmm . .
C76. P3: Wow. (P3 gives vial to N1. Both look toward vial) That's not (?) Okay.
C77. N1: Yeah. (N1 puts away vial. P3 looks at screen. N1 looks at screen; moves right hand to computer; N1 advances image.)

* Diagrams in Lines C51, C61 Copyright David Klemm and Society of Interventional Radiology. Reprinted with their permission. All rights reserved.

During the consultation, P3 expressed a concern about the size of the embolizing agent particles that would remain in her body after the UFE procedure (Transcript Extract 1.3, line 70). Prior to P3 inquiring about the size of the embolizing particles, the nurse, N1, had explained computer images showing how a catheter is inserted into the femoral artery and travels to the uterine artery where it deposits the embolizing agent in the blood vessels leading to the uterine fibroid tumors (Transcript Extract 1.3, lines C51-C67; and Figure 1.4).

Figure 1.4: Linking Visual and Verbal

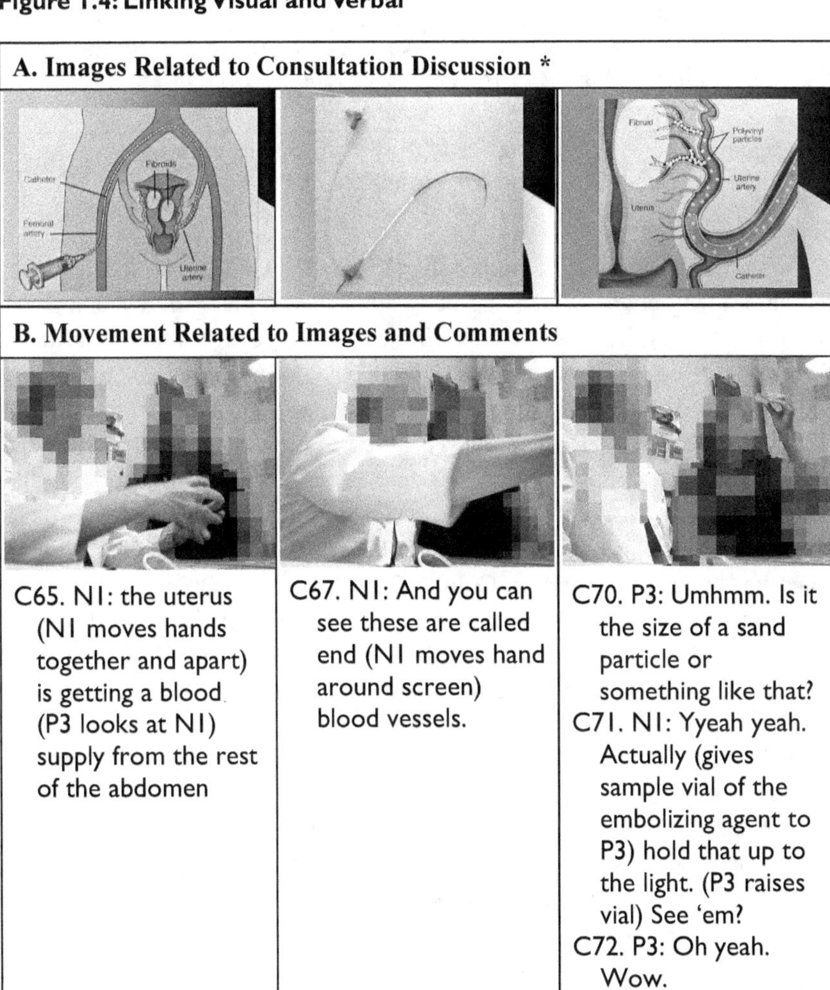

Figure 1.4 (continued)

C. Process Narratives Expressed Five Days Later	
T68. P3:	In in viewing the-the the material used, it was um . . . it helped me realize that you know it w-**it wasn't like these little black plastic balls that they were sticking in this to embolize the /th/**
T69. I1:	/Ah/
T70. P3:	**the . arteries.** It was truly just it-it it as much as it wasn't a natural substance that's gonna go into the body, **it's it's as tiny and minute minute as . possible y'know anything that's smaller than that wasn't gonna do anything. So it made me realize that okay this isn't such a bad procedure and these things going into my body don't look harmful at all whatsoever.**

* Diagrams in Row A Copyright David Klemm and Society of Interventional Radiology. Reprinted with their permission. All rights reserved.

As the nurse continued to explain the embolization procedure, she described the embolizing agent, which she had called 'beads', as 'microscopic size', while positioning her right hand in front of her face with thumb and index finger slightly apart (Transcript Extract 1.3, lines C69). Then she pointed at the picture on the screen (Fig 1.4, Row A, Column 3) as she said, 'they're not that big' (line C69). At that point, P3 asked a question about the size of an embolizing agent particle, 'is it the size of a sand particle or something like that?' (Transcript Extract 1.3, line C70). The nurse then handed P3 sample vials of the embolizing agent, which P3 held up toward the ceiling light and examined (Figure 1.4, Row B, Column 3).

During her post-consultation telephone interview, P3 expressed process narratives that combined this information encountered during the consultation with information she had found prior to it:

> *In in viewing the-the the material used, it was um it helped me realize that you know it w-it wasn't like these little black plastic balls that* ***they were sticking in this to embolize the th the arteries****. It was truly just it-it it as much as it wasn't a natural substance that's gonna go into the body, it's it's as* ***tiny and minute minute as possible*** *y'know* ***anything that's smaller than that wasn't gonna do anything****. So It made me realize that okay this really isn't such a bad procedure and* ***these things going into my body don't look harmful at all whatsoever****.* (Figure 1.4, Row C, lines T68, T70)

The activity of inspecting the vials of the embolizing agent contributed to P3 linking information about the catheter, the blood vessels, and fibroid tumors with information about the embolizing agent (bold text). However, the linking of the information occurred in the context of the activities of the preceding nine minutes, which featured the patient's questions, comments, and gestures, as well as the screen images, the nurse's verbal explanations, and the nurse's gestures.

During the post-consultation telephone discussion, P3 describes the shift in her understanding of the embolizing agent from a vague notion, expressed as 'little black plastic balls,' to a process narrative describing or indexing particular images, gestures, and verbal information, which relate to the embolization procedure. Although the phrase, 'little black plastic balls', describes the illustration of embolizing agent particles as spheres in the heuristic diagrams, it is inconsistent with the actual sample of the embolizing agent in the vials provided by the nurse.[9] When P3 explains how viewing the vials of the actual embolizing agent had affected her understanding of the UFE procedure and her decision concerning it (Figure 1.4, Row C, line T68), she refers to the embolizing agent as 'the material used' and further describes it by saying, 'it's as tiny and minute, minute as possible' (Figure 1.4, Row C, line T70).

The information resources and interpretation activities of the consultation triggered P3's inference about the approximate size of unnatural particles introduced into the body that would make them dangerous to her health. During the telephone discussion she justifies the risk of having the embolizing agent particles permanently inside of her body by saying, 'anything that's smaller than that wasn't gonna do anything .... and these things going into my body don't look harmful at all whatsoever' (Figure 1.4, Row C, line T70). Her explanation links the information she encountered at the consultation: i.e., the extremely small size of the embolizing agent particles ('tiny and minute,' line T70), the vascular system leading to the fibroid tumors, and the location and nature of the fibroid tumors ('they were sticking in this to embolize arteries,' lines T68, T70). For example, her use of the phrase, 'embolize the th the . arteries', to create context for mention of the particles correlates with her comments, 'yes,' 'okay,' 'wow,' 'umhmm,' and 'got it,' acknowledging N1's verbal and gestural explanation of the images about UFE at the consultation (Transcript Extract 1.3, lines C51-C68). The combination of visual information and N1's explanation featuring gestures toward the pictures led to P3 replacing 'beads' and 'little black balls' with 'material as tiny and minute as possible'.

Even though P3 did not need to know the precise size of the embolizing agent in order to understand embolization, the presentation and clarification of visual information filled an information gap and led to her process narrative concerning the size of the particles. When linked as process narratives, the information about the UFE procedure as a method of shrinking fibroid tumors and the information about the size of the embolizing agent amplified each other.

P3 developed an explanation addressing her concern about risk to her health, which consisted of process narratives emphasizing the information discussed during the consultation. These led to her conclusion that nothing harmful happens when the embolizing agent is placed in the uterine arteries: “these things going into my body don’t look harmful at all whatsoever” (Figure 1.4, Row C, line T70).

P3 does not construct a detailed scientific explanation of the danger or safety of the embolizing agent. Her process narratives do not express a technical understanding. Rather, they are a practical risk assessment linking her concerns about the size or amount of the foreign substance that UFE would place in her body with the variety of information she interpreted at the consultation.

Such process narratives do not include all the information an individual encounters. The recorded data show that communication patterns including gestures and pointing affect which pieces of information a patient links when forming understandings (further examined in Chapter 9). Those patterns contribute to the concurrent creation of process narratives and an interpretive frame of reference.

Chapter 1 has presented an introduction to the complexities of creating process narratives and understandings. The discussion of medical images during the radiology consultations optimized patients’ opportunities to seek and clarify information. Many settings in which people attempt to interpret information and produce understandings do not present such straightforward support for the production of process narratives. The classroom information ecology examined in Chapters 2 and 3 provides examples. Those chapters show the effects on understandings of more difficult interpretation activities, which involve concurrently interpreting multiple modes of information, culling interpretations, and developing relevant frames of reference, while producing process narratives.

2 Process Narratives in an Educational Setting

The discussion of classroom data in Chapter Two provides a counterpoint to the clinical data examined in Chapter One. It presents a type of commonplace situation in which the creation of process narratives is complicated by the absence of explanatory information. The chapter details the intricate interpretation activities that organize information as process narratives when high school biology students learn about the genetic inheritance of traits by using a computer simulation, which shows the breeding of generations of rabbits. The classroom interaction displays the interpretive contingencies that students contend with as they create process narratives from newly encountered information. Those contingencies include the concurrent activities of interpreting visual information and developing frames of reference for determining what information is relevant to the activity. The contingencies also include the constraints on seeking and applying information that are part of the conventional Mendelian curriculum concerning trait inheritance.

Genetics Education: Understanding the Inheritance of Traits

Chapters Two and Three present a very detailed analysis of biology students engaged in learning activities concerning the inheritance of traits across generations. The intricacy of the analysis derives from the complexity of the interpretation activities that lead to understandings. It demonstrates that an accurate model of understanding requires recognition of process, rather than a focus limited to the linguistic or neural artifacts that result from interpretation activities. A comprehensive model of understanding does not just show *that* certain interpretation activities occur or *what* interpretation activities and information resources are involved. Rather, it shows *how* those interpretation activities mobilize certain information resources to produce understandings.

The Textual and Pictorial Resources

The classroom learning activities analyzed here involve students using a computer software program that provides examples of genetic inheritance by simulating the breeding of generations of rabbits, some of which have straight ears, and some of which have floppy ears.[10] The teacher has prepared the curriculum so that students work together in groups of two to four to complete a series of learning tasks that require interpreting and explaining the results of increasingly complicated aspects of genetic inheritance. Each group uses one computer.

The computer simulation features linguistic, pictorial, and alphanumeric information, which the students collaboratively interpret in order to develop understandings of the Mendelian approach to genetic inheritance. The students examine visible physical characteristics (i.e., straight or floppy ears) of pictures of rabbits displayed on the computer screen. In order to complete the assigned tasks, the students must also learn to use the computer simulation software.

The tasks are presented in the form of text on paper in file folders at each workstation (Figure 2.1). The text includes prompts directing the students to use the computer simulation in particular ways and questions about the results displayed on the screen of the computer monitor. The tasks proceed from breeding rabbits having the same ear shape, to breeding rabbits having different ear shapes, to breeding rabbits having the same ear shapes whose parents had different ear shapes. In each case, the printed task prompt instructs the students to create a series of generations by breeding two offspring from the most recent generation. The students must examine and explain the visual images depicting the series of rabbit generations in regard to the ear shapes that occur across them (Figure 2.2).

Figure 2.1: Partial Text of Printed Task Prompt (WINGS for Learning, 1991, adapted for classroom use by T1 [Formatting is that of the original document])

Investigation 8.2. A Living Puzzle

☞ Purpose: Learn how to interpret the results from crossing two pure-breeding strains or pure strains.

Unexpected surprises often stimulate scientific discovery. In this activity, you will explore one such surprise recognized by Gregor Mendel in his studies of peas.

To begin, open the following lab under the file in the Menu: *Investigation* 8.2.

a. Click on "Clear Screen" button,

b. Click on the "Add Couple #1" and "Add Couple *#2"* buttons.

Now both sets of parents will be present in the "Bank" or screen. You will now simulate the mating of the male from Couple #1 with the female from Couple #2.

c. Place these individuals in the mating box.

Before you run the simulation, make a prediction.

☞1. What trait variation or variations (for ear position) do you think will appear in the F1 generation?

Geneticists often use the term cross to describe when two different individuals mate to produce offspring. Often the cross is written in an abbreviated form using the letters to represent the individuals and the letter "x" between the letters to show that they will be mated with each other.

☞ 2. How many different ear position(s) you expect to see in the offspring? [sic]

d. Now run the P x P (read "P crossed with P" or "mating P with P") by clicking on the RUN tool.

☞ 3. How many different ear position(s) you see in the offspring? [sic]

☞ 4.How are the F1 offspring different from their parents?

The teacher had studied and applied a Socratic approach to pedagogy. Rather than providing students with declarative explanations when they asked questions related to genetics concepts, he asked the students to describe and explain the results of their use of the computer simulation. The video data show the students interpreting the task prompt questions, using the computer simulation software, developing written answers to the task prompt questions, and verbally answering the teacher's questions. The examples analyzed here are representative of interpretation activities applied by other students in the classes studied. The video provides detailed evidence of the students' production of coherent process narratives that function as understandings of the inheritance of traits.

The example discussed in the following pages features a task group of three students developing a mistaken understanding of the visual information they interpret.[11] Analysis of the interpretation activities that produce and reinforce the mistake is particularly revealing in regard to the creation of process narratives and understandings. Furthermore, the students' interaction as they re-examine visual resources while correcting their mistake shows the endurance of process narratives.

Interpreting the Pictorial and Textual Resources

As the students encounter new information presented on the computer screen, they begin the interpretation activity that leads to linking the textual and pictorial information as process narratives. The video data show the students expressing recognition of a pattern of straight-eared and floppy-eared rabbits in the generation displayed after breeding a floppy-eared rabbit and a straight-eared rabbit. This activity involves verbal descriptions and questions, reading of task prompts, manipulation and interpretation of computer images, as well as selective attention to certain details of those images.

Figure 2.2: Software Interface

The students first develop an understanding of the software's organization of the screen representations of rabbits as it relates to the ear shapes of groups of offspring. Following directions in a printed task prompt, the students begin to operate the software by using the computer mouse to drag images of a male and a female rabbit into a square box at the top right corner of the screen and then mouse-clicking on a symbol of a person running. This produces changes to the screen, which include more rabbits appearing as rows and columns within a rectangular border accompanied by alphanumeric characters, such as (e.g., *F1.1*, Figure 2.2). The software indicates a relationship among representations of rabbits by redrawing the screen to show two rabbits appearing as parents in a row, and their offspring appearing in rows beneath them. The information presented on the screen visually represents generations through the proximity of rows of offspring to their parents and by thick borders that create separate boxes around each set of parents and offspring.

The printed task prompt then instructs the students to describe the ear shapes of the images of rabbits that appear on the computer screen. At the beginning of their work with the computer simulation, the students display a lack of knowledge or understanding of genetics terms such as *dominant* and *recessive*. The collaborative interpretation of the text and visuals involves the students developing a communication format that becomes part of the discourse framework for interpreting and discussing the pictorial and textual resources of the learning activities. This communication format includes verbal description and pointing at the screen images (Saferstein, 2004: 205–209). As the students apply it, they both express and shape their interpretations of the task prompt, the screen images, and their understandings of genetic inheritance (Saferstein and Sarangi, 2010).

During the interpretation activities, B21 and G21 mention both the nature and configuration of the images of rabbits on the screen as influences on their interpretations or inferences. This includes types of information that fit the following categorical distinctions:

Pictures

- Images of rabbits
- Floppy ears
- Floppy-eared rabbits
- Straight ears
- Straight-eared rabbits

Organization of Pictures

- Columns
- Parent groups
- Offspring groups
- Rows
- Parent boxes
- Generation boxes

Characteristics of Organized Groupings of Pictures

- Heterogeneous floppy and straight-eared columns and rows
- Homogeneous floppy-eared columns and rows
- Homogeneous straight-eared columns and rows

The recorded data show that the students' interpretations and inferences are also influenced by the task prompt's request for a prediction of an outcome (WINGS for Learning, 1991, adapted for classroom use by T1):

Before you run the simulation, make a prediction.
☞ 1. What trait variation or variations (for ear position) do you think will appear in the F1 generation?
Geneticists often use the term ***cross*** to describe when two different individuals mate to produce offspring. Often the cross is written in an abbreviated form using the letters to represent the individuals and the letter 'x' between the letters to show that they will be mated with each other.
☞ 2. How many different ear position(s) you [sic] expect to see in the offspring?

The students interpret certain images and words in relation to the activities required by the task prompt in order to create written and verbal explanations, which the teacher will grade. The students develop shared interpretive frames of reference about the task and the information by engaging in a process of collective cognition that helps them to cope with the constraints of perceiving and organizing the large amount of information presented by the computer screen, the task prompt, and each other (cf. Saferstein, 1992).

Concurrently Creating Interpretive Frames of Reference and Process Narratives: Looking for a Pattern

As the students start to operate the computer simulation, their talk and pointing note aspects of the screen images (Transcript Extract 2.1, lines B9-B23). The students express and conform their perceptions and interpretations of the screen images by linking them as process narratives. Such interpretation activities begin the creation of an understanding. These foundational interpretation activities and their products affect both the form and content of later activities. This is due to the reciprocal effects of interpreting information and developing frames of reference – both individually and socially. The students' interaction displays the complexities of interpreting new information as they interact with each other and the task resources. Their interpretation activities resemble those of people involved in the collaborative interpretation of visual and linguistic information, during which individuals express and discuss various interpretations of new information in order to develop shared descriptive terms and interpretive frames of reference (Saferstein, 1992, 1994).

Transcript Extract 2.1 [Added rectangle marks discussed columns]

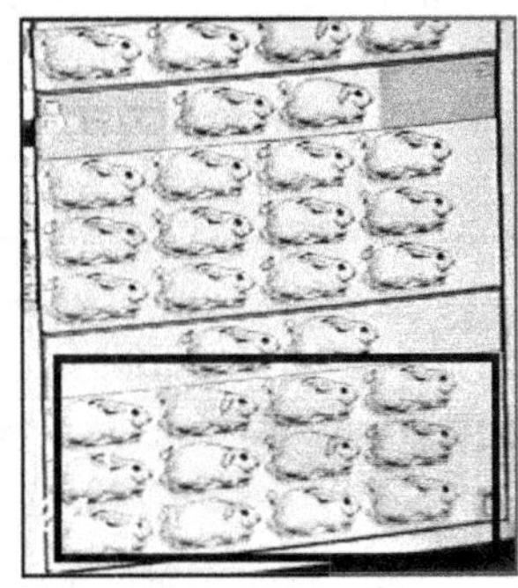

B9. G21: Ou! . . Oh look! (points pen at rabbits on computer screen) How interesting. What-what? . .
B10. B21: So first three that way. Second three that way then 1, 2, 3 and then (points at lower right side of screen near set of offspring rabbits) fourth goes in a pattern so the next one should be all floppy. Then it should be /straight floppy straight (??) / . and so (points at lower right side of screen near set of offspring rabbits) goes in a pattern so the next one should be all floppy. Then it should be /straight floppy straight ?????/
B11. G21: /(Pointing at screen) No. But it . but look. No no/ look
B12. B21: (2 second pause) Yeah see. (points at 1st column in set of rabbits demarcated by box in lower portion of screen) See how the first
B13. G21: Yeah
B14. B21: starts off like that. (points at 3rd column of rabbits) See this be the end of their like little cycle
B15. G21: Umm Hmm
B16. B21: (Pointing at 4th column of rabbits) and it's starting over again so the next one would be floppy.
B17. G21: (Points at 1st or 2nd column of rabbits) The end of that cycle?
B18. B21: Yeah. (pointing at columns of rabbits on the screen) 1, 2, 3, (pointing at side of monitor as if columns continued off screen) 1, 2, 3. You know like that.
B19. G21: (Pointing at a floppy-eared rabbit in 3rd column) No, but did you see the one with that one like that?
B20. B21: That
B21. G21: No I said the one like that. It's all down (pointing at a floppy-eared rabbit).
B22. B21: (Pointing at the same rabbit) (?"Those" or "Oh"?)
B23. G21: (Pointing at two straight-eared rabbits) An these two are up. . (The next 9 seconds are inaudible. G21 pauses to look at the task prompt. B21 looks at the computer screen. After 2 seconds, B21 points his pen at the F2 parents, with no audible utterances, except for the barely audible word 'generation'. He then looks at the task prompt for 2 seconds, until G21 continues the discussion.) Wait. Look. . (pointing at the parents of the rabbits in the columns) How come the ears are the same?

The interrelationship of the students' attention to particular modes of representation and their interpretations of certain images is evident in B21's development of a process narrative to organize his encounter with the visual and linguistic resources of the task. Interpretation at the level of recognizing information (e.g., the configuration of rabbits as columns and the different ear shapes) is interwoven with interpretation of the symbolic or indexical meanings of the information. For example, B21 demonstrates a search for coherence among the textual and visual information by finding patterns relevant to the ear shapes of the images of rabbits and the configuration of those images. He expresses an interpretation of the screen that links the format and quality of the visual information. He links descriptions and interpretations of the visual information as a process narrative by combining description with pointing at the specific screen images:[12]

> *(Using computer mouse pointer to point out images) So first three that way. Second three that way then 1, 2, 3 and so (points at lower right side of screen near set of offspring rabbits) goes in a pattern so the next one should be all floppy. Then it should be /straight floppy straight ...* (Transcript Extract 2.1, Line B10)

In the context of the images displayed, B21's descriptions and gestures toward the screen express process narratives, which can be paraphrased as:

> *In the F2 generation box, the first column contains three rabbits which all have straight ears, the second column contains only floppy-eared rabbits, and the third column contains only straight-eared rabbits. This presents a pattern based on columns arranged across the width of the screen.*
>
> *Since the fourth column has all straight-eared rabbits, it appears that the cycle has begun again. Therefore, I predict that the fifth column, which is not shown on the screen, would contain only floppy-eared rabbits like column two.*

G21 contests B21's process narrative in a way that expresses a different interpretation of the images. She points out the different ear shapes of the rabbits within the third column as if B21 had not noted them:

> (Pointing at a floppy-eared rabbit in the third column) No but did you see the one with that one like that? No I said the one like that. (pointing at a floppy-eared rabbit) It's all down. (pointing at two straight-eared rabbits) An these two are up. (Transcript Extract 2.1, lines B19, B21, B23)

Her pointing and verbal description present the process narrative:

There is no straight-floppy-straight pattern of columns, because the third column contains a straight-eared rabbit and two floppy-eared rabbits.

In response to G21's correction, B21 stops discussing the pattern (Transcript Extract 2.1, lines B19-B21). He studies the screen, points his pen at the parents of the rabbits in the columns he had mentioned, and then looks at the task prompt (lines B22, B23). G21 looks at the task prompt, then mentions the ear shapes of the parent rabbits. At this point, the students shift the discussion away from the pattern of offspring ear shapes. However, they have introduced a frame of reference emphasizing offspring generations as a key component of a pattern of inherited traits. That frame of reference will reemerge later in the students' interpretation activities.

B21's gestures and comments indicate that he was looking for a pattern or cycle within the generation boxes by attributing meaning to the characteristics of the rabbits in each column as he looked from left to right across the columns. He had just encountered the software interface, and his inferences were incorrect regarding how the configuration of the images related to the actions specified by the task prompt (i.e., using the software to produce images representing generations of rabbits) and to the genetics terminology (e.g., 'trait', 'variation', 'offspring', 'cross'). Operating the software to breed rabbits would not increase the number of columns that appear horizontally across the screen within a generation box. Thus, there would not be a relevant pattern repeated within the generation box that B21 mentioned. The operation of the software shows that the vertical configuration of boxes of rabbit images is significant for discerning patterns of inheritance – not the horizontal configuration of columns as B21 initially infers.[13]

Moreover, the inference B21 expressed related to the arrangement and characteristics of the screen images, not to genetic causes of the pattern of ear shapes that he noticed. However, the students' expression of process narratives introduced the terms and concepts, 'pattern' and 'cycle', as approaches to interpreting and expressing the relevance of visual information (Transcript Extract 2.1, lines B10 and B14). Although incorrect as answers to the questions posed by the task prompt, the early expression of terms to describe and organize the screen images contributes to the frame of reference that the students eventually develop for proceeding with the task. Their expressions of and responses to candidate interpretations of information affect the understandings and the answers to questions that they produce as they continue to work on the genetic inheritance learning task. For example, focusing on the configuration of offspring rabbits within a specific generation box leads to a particular interpretation of the task prompt question, 'What trait variation or variations (for ear position) do you think will appear in the F1 generation?' (Figure 2.1, Question 1). B21's approach to discerning a pattern presents an interpretation of 'in the F1 generation' that concentrates on the set of offspring images demarcated by dark borders, rather than examining the vertical configuration of parents and their offspring within each generation.

As the students continue their work on the learning task and are tested by the teacher, that interpretation of pattern – focusing mainly on the offspring generation boxes – becomes problematic. It shapes process narratives that produce an incorrect understanding of genetic inheritance when the students answer the teacher's questions. Subsequently, it complicates the teacher's efforts to help them produce a satisfactory model of genetic inheritance.

Interpretive Frames of Reference and Coherence

By attempting to create and express process narratives, the students begin to organize information in ways that seem coherent in regard to the framework of the task prompt and visual resources. The students display different interpretations of the screen images. B21's description of a three-part cycle emphasizes the differences among the columns of offspring rabbits moving horizontally from left to right within the box marking the offspring generation. He focuses on the homogeneity or heterogeneity of the ear shapes among the offspring within a generation. In contrast, G21's interpretive frame of reference emphasizes the vertical organization of the screen images. She notes the differences in ear shape among offspring rabbits within a column, and then points at the homogeneous straight ears of parent rabbits above the offspring box (Transcript Extract 2.2, lines B19, B21, B23).

Transcript Extract 2.2

B16. B21: (Pointing at 4th column of rabbits) and it's starting over again so the next one would be floppy.
B17. G21: (Points at 1st or 2nd column of rabbits) The end of that cycle?
B18. B21: Yeah. (pointing at columns of rabbits on the screen) 1, 2, 3, (pointing at side of monitor as if columns continued off screen) 1, 2, 3. You know like that
B19. G21: (pointing at rabbits on the screen) No, but did you see the one with that one like that?
B20. B21: That
B21. G21: No I said the one like that. It's all down (pointing at a floppy-eared rabbit).
B22. B21: (pointing at the same rabbit) (?) those
B23. G21: (pointing at two straight-eared rabbits) An these two are up. (The next 9 seconds are inaudible. G21 pauses to look at the

Transcript Extract 2.2 (continued)

task prompt. B21 looks at the computer screen. After 2 seconds, B21 points his pen at the F2 parents, with no audible utterances, except for the barely audible word 'generation'. He then looks at the task prompt for 2 seconds, until G21 continues the discussion.) Wait. Look. How come the ears are the same?

B24. B21: Hm?
B25. G21: Is it? This is it . couple two (3 second pause) That's the female
B26. B21: One's a female. (looks down toward paper on which he is writing)
B27. G21: and that that's the male (pointing at screen with pen).
B28. B21: (Clicks mouse on the male showing a number) The male's number three. (5 second pause)
B29. G21: You know number one? (referring to the question on the assignment sheet)
B30. B21: Hmmm?
B31. G21: Oui or no?
B32. B21: Umm female number one, male number tu – three, male number three.
B33. G21: (Reading aloud from task prompt) "How many types of ears do you see in the (points at the F2 generation on the screen) F2 generation?"
B34. B21: (Points at column 3 of the F2 generation) Two.
B35. G21: F2 generation, okay. (7 second pause while they silently read task prompt) (reading aloud from task prompt) "What is really puzzling about this?"
B36. B21: (Pointing pen at screen) Because it skipped a generation. (4 second pause while they write answers to prompts)

Figure 2.3: Students Concurrently Using Talk, Gesture, Graphics, and Text

G21 points at the parent rabbits of the F2 generation box as she says: 'Wait. Look. (pointing at the parents of the rabbits in the columns) How come the ears are the same?' (Transcript Extract 2.2, line B23). 'The same' will eventually be replaced by words indexing phenotype (e.g., 'straight' and 'floppy'), and genotype, (e.g., 'dominant' and 'recessive').[14] However, at this point in the interpretation activity, the students have not yet decided how noticing rabbits with the same types of ears helps them to develop a response to the task prompt. They do not link the information that they have already noticed as a coherent process narrative relevant to creating that response.

When the students do not develop a shared description of a pattern, they pause to examine both the prompt and the screen (Transcript Extract 2.2, line B23). They hold and look at the task prompt as they work with the computer simulation software (Figure 2.3). After examining the prompt, they backtrack to complete activities that the prompt had described as precursors to running the simulation and producing generations of offspring (Figure 2.4, Rows e, f.):

Figure 2.4: Task Prompt Instructions for Using the Simulation Software to Produce a Second Generation of Rabbits [Immediately following instructions in Figure 2.1]

e. Next, you will simulate the Fl x Fl cross. To do this, use the ARROW tool to choose one male and one female from the Fl offspring.

f. Record the Fl identification (ID) number of each individual. (Do this by clicking with the ARROW tool on the chosen individual. The individual's ID number will appear.) Place these parents in the mating box.

☞ 5. id number of F1 male:

id number of F1 female:

g. Simulate the Fl x Fl cross by clicking on the RUN tool. To help observe the offspring, click on the zoom box on the F2 subwindow.

☞ 6. How many types of ears do you see, in the F2 generation?

☞ 7. What is really puzzling about this?

Could it be that your surprising result in the F2 generation is a result of the specific Fl parents you chose?

h. To test this hypothesis, repeat steps e, f and g with different pairs of Fl offspring as parents. Record your results in the table below

The students note the gender and identification number of the each of the rabbits they had selected earlier as parents for the generation whose pattern they had discussed (Transcript Extract 2.2, lines B25-B32):

B25. G21: Is it? This is it . couple two (3 second pause) That's the female
B26. B21: One's a female. (looks down toward paper on which he is writing)
B27. G21: and that that's the male (pointing at screen with pen).
B28. B21: (Clicks mouse on the male showing a number) The male's number three. (5 second pause)
B29. G21: You know number one? (referring to the question on the assignment sheet)
B30. B21: Hmmm?
B31. G21: Oui or no?
B32. B21: Umm female number one, male number tu – three, male number three.

By consulting each other and the screen images, the students belatedly conform their use of the software to the task prompt. For example, G21 reads the task prompt aloud as she points at the F2 generation on the screen, 'How many types of ears do you see in the F2 generation?' and B21 responds by pointing at a column of the F2 generation rabbits while saying, 'two' (Transcript Extract 2.2, lines B33, B34). The task prompt did not structure the students' activities. This was not simply a lack of effort or attention. It is a common consequence of the cognition related to using technology (cf. Brown and Duguid, 2000; Suchman, 1987). After providing basic instructions about how to use the software, the task prompt stated, 'Before you run the simulation, make a prediction. What trait variation or variations (for ear position) do you think will appear in the F1 generation' (Figure 2.1, Question 1). However, while the students expressed a very general concern with the inheritance of ear shape across generations of rabbits, they did not verbally predict or discuss the results of crossing two rabbits until after B21 had run a simulation and they had described certain aspects of the screen display. Rather than following the sequence of the instructions provided by the prompt, the students worked to develop a shared frame of reference about what particulars of the screen image were relevant to the task (Transcript Extract 2.1, lines B9-B19). The students interpreted the prompt, the images on the screen, and the nature of the task in relation to one another and in the context of their background knowledge of high school learning activities, using computers, and social realities such as families.

Following the inconclusive discussion of pattern, the examination of the screen images, and the review of the task prompt, B21 shifts his focus for interpreting the images from the horizontal arrangement of columns to the vertical arrangement of offspring generation boxes. B21 answers the prompt question, 'What is *really* puzzling about this?' by saying 'Because it skipped a generation' (Figure 2.5, line B36). This addition to the evolving task discourse has great significance for subsequent process narratives that the students develop to explain how the simulation software depicts trait inheritance. B21 begins to emphasize a particular type of pattern. He observes that the absence of floppy ears in the F1 generation (which includes the F2 generation's parents) appears on the screen as the skipping of a generation. This contributes to a frame of reference emphasizing description of screen images. That frame of reference eventually supports process narratives stating that floppy ears automatically skip a generation, which the students apply to answering questions posed by the task prompt and the teacher.

Figure 2.5: Students' Responses to Task Prompt

Task Prompt Directions and Questions

g. Simulate the Fl x Fl cross by clicking on the RUN tool. To help observe the offspring, click on the zoom box on the F2 subwindow.

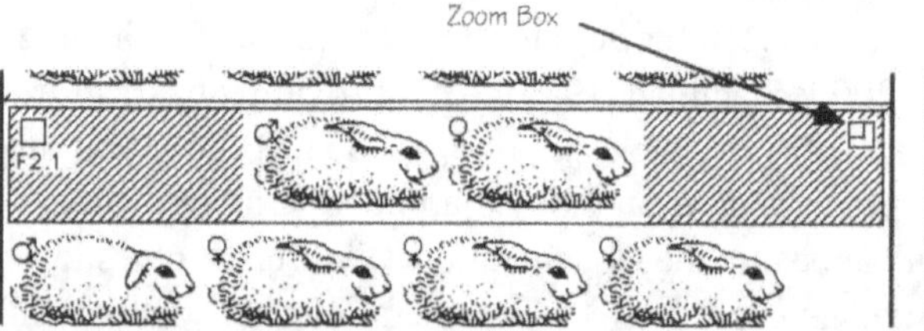

6. How many types of ears do you see, in the F2 generation?
7. What is *really* puzzling about this?

Students' Responses

B33. G21: (Reading aloud from task prompt) "How many types of ears do you see in the (points at the F2 generation on the screen) F2 generation?"
B34. B21: (Points at column 3 of the F2 generation) Two.
B35. G21: F2 generation, okay. (7 second pause while they silently read task prompt) (reading aloud from task prompt) "What is really puzzling about this."
B36. B21: (Pointing at screen) Because it skipped a generation. (4 second pause while they write answers to prompts)

The Complexity of Interpretation Activities that Create Coherent Process Narratives

The work that G21 and B21 do to conform their interpretations of the screen and each other's utterances both creates and contends with multiple interpretive contingencies. Those contingencies include concurrently developing a communication format and a frame of reference for making sense of the screen images in relation to the task prompt. This complicates the students' attempts to create process narratives that identify and link the relevant particulars of genetic inheritance.

For example, the interpretation of a relevant pattern in the configuration of screen images is intertwined with understanding and applying the conventional Mendelian nomenclature that applies to explanations of genetic inheritance (Saferstein and Sarangi, 2010: 168–173). The students display a trial and error process of linking linguistic terms and pictorial symbols: e.g., 'parents', 'F2', 'generation', images of rabbits having different ear shapes, and the configuration of the screen images in boxes and rows.

Shortly after B21 said, 'Because it skipped a generation' (Figure 2.5, line B36), as a response to the task prompt's question about what is puzzling about the simulation, G21 reread the prompt question aloud (Transcript Extract 2.3, line B41). Then B21 began to explicate 'it skipped a generation' in terms of the screen images and the relevant genetics terminology (line B42):

- B21 points at particular screen images with his pen before he says 'That their parents the okay. The F2's parents,' (Figure 2.6, Row B, line B42).
- G21 challenges B21's accuracy in correlating the screen images with the genetics nomenclature and the task prompt by pointing at the F1 generation box as she says 'F1' (Row C, line B43).
- B21 rejects her challenge by saying 'No', as he points at the F2 offspring box (Row C, line B44).
- By saying 'Oh oh okay. Sorry,' as she points at the F2 offspring box, G21 conforms her interpretation of B21's utterance to his interpretation of the relation between the nomenclature, 'F2', and the screen images (Row D, line B45).

Figure 2.6: Pointing at Visual Information[15]
(B21 pointing from right of screen, G21 pointing from left of screen)

A		B41. G21: (Reading aloud from the task prompt) "What is really puzzling about this?"
B	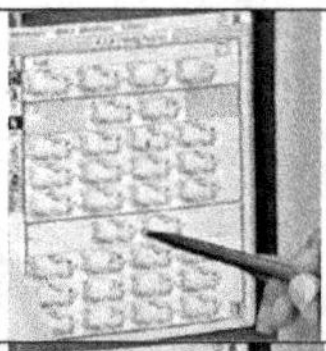	B42. B21: (Pointing pen at screen) That their parents . the okay. The F2's parents
C		B43. G21: (Points pen at screen) F1 B44. B21: No
D		B45. G21: Oh oh okay. Sorry.

As they combine talk with pointing, the students express complete or partial process narratives, which link information as usable knowledge: e.g.:

- *The horizontal arrangement of boxes of images of rabbits shows a sequence of generations (Transcript Extract 2.3, lines B46-B50);*
- *The F2 generation is demarcated by the box around the rows of rabbits in the lower portion of the screen (Transcript Extract 2.3, line B50);*
- *The parents of a generation appear in a row above the box demarcating their offspring (Transcript Extract 2.3, lines B42, B46, B50).*

Transcript Extract 2.3

[In lines B37-B40, B21 and G21 quibble off-topic]

B41. G21: Quiet! (laughs) (Reading aloud from the task prompt) 'What is really puzzling about this?'
B42. B21: (Pointing pen at screen) That . their parents . the okay. The F2's parents
B43. G21: (Points pen at screen) F1
B44. B21: No
B45. G21: Oh oh okay. Sorry.
B46. B21: the the parents for the F2 generation (points pen at F2 parents)
B47. G21: Uhuh.

Transcript Extract 2.3 (continued)

B48. B21: (points pen at F1 offspring) both of their ears are straight . but then
B49. G21: There's a pattern . /The – there's two types (????)/
B50. B21: /(points pen at F2 parents) their parents also are straight but then/. . Okay . . So (points finger at the F2 parents) these two couples are from (circles finger around F1 offspring) this block right here. (points finger at F2 parents) So that means their parents . (points finger at F1 parents) their mom . . /and . /

Such linking of linguistic and pictorial information as process narratives or incomplete process narratives affects the students' emphasis on the relevance of particular screen images to discovering a pattern that would be useful for explaining the rabbits' inheritance of different ear shapes. The students conform their understandings of *pattern* to the preceding interpretation activities and to the immediate resources and constraints:

B49. G21: There's a pattern . /The – there's two types (????)/
B50. B21: /their parents also are straight but then/. Okay (Points at screen) . . So these two couples are from this block right here. So that means their parents . their mom . . /and . /

G21 mentions that the array of individual rabbits with either straight or floppy ears has something to do with recognizing a pattern (Transcript Extract 2.3, line B49). B21 examines the images on the computer screen in order to describe the particular ear shapes of parent rabbits and the position of those parents within a preceding generation of offspring (line B50). The ways that the students resolve the interpretive contingencies affect the process narratives they eventually develop to explain the screen images in regard to the inheritance of traits.

Coherence and Process Narratives

The data show how process narratives and interpretive frames of reference develop concurrently and influence each other. In this case, they combine to shape the students' interpretation of 'pattern'. For example, when B21 and G21 write and verbalize their answers to the task prompt, they question and interrupt each other in order to address linguistic ambiguities and their confusion about how to explain the computer simulation's pattern of ear shapes across generations of rabbits (Transcript Extracts 2.3, 2.4). In the process, they apply and express two interpretive frames of reference emphasized by their respective observations and comments: i.e., (1) describing what the screen shows, or (2) making inferences, based on the screen images, about the effects of hidden genes. This recognition of potentially useful frames of reference takes place as the students' adopt the nomenclature and terminology related to the screen and the task prompt (e.g., 'the parents are a couple of two F2,' Transcript Extract 2.5, line B67).

The students begin to emphasize the observation that the appearance of floppy ears 'skipped a generation' (mentioned by B21 in Transcript Extract 2.2, line B21, and by G21 in Transcript Extract 2.5, line B76). They consider whether that observation is an adequate answer to the task prompt's request, 'Describe the "living puzzle" you have observed, and summarize, in terms of the parents (p) and the F1 and F2 generations, what happens when two pure-breeding strains are crossed or mated' (WINGS for Learning, 1991: 8.2).

B21 and G21 sort out the meanings of linguistic terms and the screen images as they work on the task. For instance, B21 begins to explain 'it skipped a generation' by mentioning that the parents of the F2 generation have straight ears (Transcript Extract 2.3, lines B42, B46, B48, B50). He describes the screen image presenting arrays of rabbits showing that a straight-eared parent and a floppy-eared parent have produced an F1 generation of straight-eared offspring. However, his description falters in regard to the portion of the screen image showing that parents selected from the F1 offspring produce an F2 generation, which includes both floppy-eared and straight-eared rabbits. B21 says only, 'But then', (Transcript Extract 2.3, lines B48, B50). G21 links the interpretation of a pattern to the two shapes of ears, saying, 'There's a pattern. The – there's two types' (Figure 2.7, row B, line B49).

As the students work on the task, they construct coherence by emphasizing certain pieces of information and ways of communicating about them. The emerging communication format and frame of reference, which emphasize particular visual information, influence each other. B21 begins to emphasize ear shape, but hesitates and shifts his emphasis. He points his pen at the F2 parent box. Then, he moves the pen from a rabbit in the F2 parent box up to the F1 offspring box as he says, 'the the parents for the F2 generation both of their ears are straight . but then' (Figure 2.7, Rows A-B, lines B46, B48). He pauses, and moves the pen away from the screen.

B21 tries to incorporate the relevance of ear shape, location on the screen, and kinship. However, he has not sorted out a relationship among those factors that will help answer the task prompt question, 'What is *really* puzzling about this [the appearance of two ear shapes in the F2 generation having straight eared parents]?' In both of B21's attempts to map ear shape to position on the screen and to kinship, he follows his verbal and gestural description of ear shape by saying, 'but then', without completing the formulation (lines B48, B50). He has not found information that he can link with ear shape to create a coherent process narrative relevant to the task prompt question.

Figure 2.7: Pointing and Talking to Resolve Interpretive Contingencies

A		B46. B21: the the parents for the F2 generation (points pen at F2 parents) B47. G21: Uhuh.
B		B48. B21: (points pen at F1 offspring) both of their ears are straight . but then B49. G21: There's a pattern . /The—there's two types (????)/ B50. B21: /their parents also are straight but then (moves pen away from screen)/. .
C		Okay. . So (points finger at the F2 parents) these two couples
D		are from (circles finger around F1 offspring) this block right here.
E		(points finger at F2 parents) So that means their parents .
F		(points finger at F1 parents) their mom . . /and . / B51. G21: /Recessive genes./
G		B52. B21: (moves hand away from screen) . . and uh . B53. G21: Recessive genes. B54. B21: What the hell does that mean? . .

After moving his pen away from the screen and pausing, B21 says 'Okay', as if restarting his explanation. He points with his finger as he again offers an interpretation of the relationship between the rabbits in different sectors of the screen (Figure 2.7, Rows C-F, line B50). His emphasis shifts from ear shape to a relationship between generations of rabbits. B21 attempts to link the screen location of the rabbits to their kinship (Figure 2.7, Rows C-F, line B50). He points at rabbits in the F1 offspring generation box directly above the F2 parent rabbits, saying, 'So these two couples are from this block right here' (Figure 2.7, Rows C, D).[16] He continues, 'So that means their parents . their mom,' while moving his finger from the F2 parents to the pair of rabbits in the F1 parents box near the top of the screen – i.e., the grandparents of the rabbits at which he has just pointed (Figure 2.7, Rows E, F). Again, he does not find information to complete a process narrative that answers the task prompt question. He just pauses, then says, 'and', before pausing again.

However, the students have verbally and gesturally interpreted both the layout of the images on the screen and the preceding use of the simulation software, which reconfigured the screen images to produce that layout, as meaning that the two rabbits at which he first pointed have some relationship to the demarcated sets of rabbits above and below them. Their talk and pointing also have indicated that such information was relevant to discovering a pattern as specified by the task prompt.

This evolving approach to coherence limits the information that the students emphasize and how they interpret it. The students have begun to focus on the particular linguistic, visual, and gestural components of their interpretation activities, which they will eventually apply to the creation of process narratives explaining the computer simulation in regard to the inheritance of traits.

Difficulties Producing Process Narratives: The Case of Recessive Genes

Organizing Information and Constructing a Frame of Reference

At this point in the interpretation activity, describing and sorting aspects of the screen images in regard to patterns and ear shapes of offspring have not led the students to a coherent process narrative that would link their interpretations of the pieces of information they encountered as an explanation of trait inheritance. As B21 haltingly suggests that he is about to express some relationship among the screen images that is relevant to the task prompt, G21 twice says, 'recessive genes' (Transcript Extract 2.4, lines B50-B53). In response, B21 shifts from trying to explain 'it skipped a generation' to inquiring about the meaning and relevance of 'recessive genes'. B21's response, 'What the hell does that mean?' (line B54) shows that he does not recall relevant background knowledge, which he might use to connect the new information (the term, 'recessive genes') to the preceding interpretations of the screen images and the task prompt (Saferstein and Sarangi, 2010: 171–176).

Transcript Extract 2.4: Difficulty Linking Information to Explain 'Recessive Genes'

B50. B21: /their parents also are straight but then/. . Okay (Points finger at screen) . . So (pointing at the F2 parent rabbits) these two couples are from (pointing at the F1 offspring) this block right here. So that means their parents . their mom . . /and . /
B51. G21: /Recessive genes./
B52. B21: . . and uh .
B53. G21: Recessive genes.
B54. B21: What the hell does that mean? . .
B55. G21: It's inside you know (points at floppy and straight-eared rabbits on screen with pen) like . look, (points at the F1 female floppy-eared parent) that one . and (moves the pen across the F1 generation box) none of them (again points the pen at the F1 female floppy-eared parent) got that gene.
B56. B22: (Arriving late) Hello my fellow partners.
B57. G21: (Pointing at screen; moves pen around the F1 generation box) But each of them has has it in them (moves pen to F2 parents). Then (moves pen around the F1 generation box) when they didn't and (moves pen to F2 generation box, pointing at floppy-eared rabbits) whatever . you know
B58. B21: that's what it's called, recessive genes?
B59. G21: Well I don't know that's what I hear I think . /(???)/

In the absence of an expressed process narrative linking B21's previous utterances, G21's emphasis on 'recessive genes' briefly becomes the topic of discussion. However, as the interpretation activity continues neither of the students has information that would link the screen images with 'recessive genes' to form a process narrative that would help answer the task prompt question. G21 responds to B21 by saying, 'It's inside you know like', and then briefly pausing. This exchange takes place while the students are looking at the screen images (Figure 2.8, Row A). G21 continues by pointing with her pen at the floppy ear of the female parent of the F1 generation of offspring (Figure 2.8, Row B). By pointing, she links the uttered phrase, 'It's inside', with a representation of a physical characteristic and a specific rabbit, neither of which she identified linguistically. In the context of the preceding utterances, her pointing also links *recessive genes* with floppy ears.

G21's gestures and comments link pictorial and linguistic information as a process narrative that she does not express verbally i.e.:

> *Genes inside of the parents are related to the ear shape of the parents and are passed on to their offspring even if the offspring do not show the trait.* (Transcript Extract 2.4, lines B51-B55, and Figure 2.8)

She expresses this process narrative by pointing at the F1 floppy-eared parent rabbit as she says, 'look, that one' (Figure 2.8, Row B) which emphasizes that floppy ears constitute information relevant to the task. She then presents an inference about the link between the parent rabbits' ear shapes and the ear shape of their offspring. She suggests an unseen biological relationship, which is not represented by the screen images, between the ear shape of the F1 floppy-eared parent and something inside the F1 offspring: 'It's inside you know like . look, that one (F1 floppy-eared parent) . and none of them (F1 offspring) got that gene (points at the floppy ear of the parent)' (Figure 2.8, Rows A-D).

However, the students do not express a process narrative that clearly links the screen images to the term, 'recessive genes' (Saferstein and Sarangi, 2010: 174–176). G21 moves the pen around the various images of rabbits without stopping to point at any particular image:

- First, as she says, 'But each of them has has it in them', she moves her pen over images of rabbits showing straight ears, including the F1 generation parents and offspring as well as the parents of the F2 generation (Figure 2.8, Row E).
- Next, as she says, 'And then when they didn't', she moves her pen over the images of the F1 generation rabbits showing straight ears (Figure 2.8, Row F).
- Then, as she says, 'and whatever', she moves her pen over the images of the F2 generation rabbits, which include some floppy-eared rabbits (Figure 2.8, Row G).
- Finally, she moves her pen away from the screen and says, 'you know' (Figure 2.8, Row H).

Figure 2.8: Linking Visual and Linguistic Information[17]
(From Transcript Extract 2.4, lines 55, 57)

A		B55. G21: It's inside you know like .
B	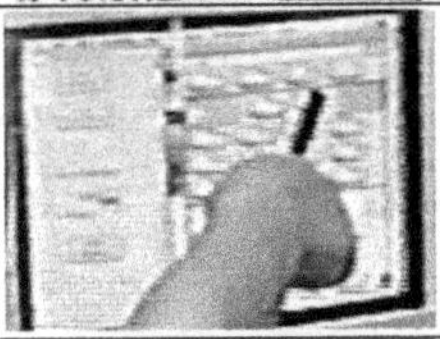	(points pen at floppy ear of F1 female floppy-eared parent) look, that one
C		(pointing pen in circular motion around the rows of F1 offspring) and none of them got
D		(points at F1 floppy-eared parent again) that gene.
E		B57. G21: (Pointing at screen; moves pen around the F1 generation box) But each of them has has it in them (moves pen to F2 parents).
F	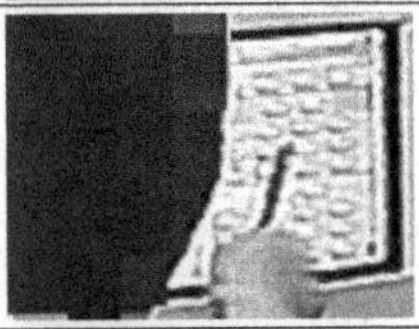	And then (moves pen around the F1 generation box) when they didn't
G		(moves pen to F2 generation box, pointing at floppy-eared rabbits) and whatever .
H		(moves pen away from screen) you know

G21's pointing and utterances display a gap in the information needed to explain how the term, 'recessive genes', relates to the appearance of floppy ears on the screen. Her utterance, 'But each of them has has it in them' began to present a description that would link 'it', the cause of floppy ears, with the presence of the recessive genes inside the offspring ('in them', Figure 2.8, Row E). However, G21 does not find the words or the screen images to express what happens next and complete the process narrative. Her utterance, 'And then when they didn't', suggests that she is about to mention some relationship between the appearance of floppy ears in the F2 generation and the absence of floppy ears in the F1 generation (Figure 2.8, Row F). However, she just utters the words, 'whatever . you know', while moving her pen over the F2 generation rabbits, and then moving it away from the screen (Figure 2.8, Rows G, H).

The Influence of Task Resources on Process Narratives

The students' ensuing interpretation activities lead them to discard the frame of reference involving inferences about dominant and recessive genes. Instead, they emphasize a descriptive frame of reference emphasizing particular features of the screen images. The students' emphasis on particular screen images by pointing at them contributes to the descriptive frame of reference that eventually supports a process narrative expressing a mistaken 'automatically skips a generation' explanation of the inheritance of ear shapes.

Merely noting images and stating Mendelian genetics terminology did not support an inferential frame of reference that would contribute to an explanation of trait inheritance incorporating the concept of recessive genes. For example, G21's pointing and her utterance, 'none of them got' (Figure 2.8, Row C), expressed a concern with the offspring rabbits inheriting from their parents something inside their bodies, which caused the different ear shapes, but was not shown on the screen. G21 clarified what was inherited by again pointing at the floppy ear of the parent rabbit as she said, 'that gene' (Figure 2.8, Row D). However, since the screen images did not show genes, she could not describe or point at them. Although this was a problem in regard to completing her process narrative emphasizing inferences about the effects of hidden genes, it contributed to developing a frame of reference that emphasized description of the screen images.

G21 introduced information, the term, 'recessive genes', and attempted to link the screen images to the task prompt – i.e., to explain what is puzzling about traits disappearing and reappearing. However, neither the screen images nor the task prompt presented information she could use to explain the pattern of ear shapes across generations and how the genes that the F1 generation rabbits had 'in them' affected the ear shapes of the F2 generation rabbits. Thus, G21 did not link 'recessive genes' to the characteristics of the F2 rabbits or to her linguistic-gestural process narrative about the F1 generation offspring inheriting unexpressed genes from their parents (Figure 2.8). At this point in their interpretation activities, the students have not developed process narratives that deal with the effects of genes on ear shape. In the absence of recallable explanatory process narratives, the students emphasize the descriptive frame of reference. They develop a selective emphasis in regard to the particular screen information that is useful for creating process narratives. In so doing, they disregard other information (such as the ear shapes of the parent generations and the need to operate the software in a way that shows entire generations of offspring), other frames of reference (such as inferring a role of unseen dominant and recessive genes in the appearance of straight or floppy ears), and alternative interpretations (such as a pattern that would account for the relationship between the ear shapes of parents and their offspring in addition to ear shapes across offspring generations). Consequently, as the work proceeds the students interpret and link visual and verbal information in a way that produces process narratives explaining that floppy ears automatically skip alternating generations.

For example, B21 reinforces the emphasis on generations as significant information by mentioning the alphanumeric nomenclature, 'F2', which is a form of the conventional genetics discourse displayed on the screen and in the task prompt (Transcript Extract 2.5, line 67):

> Hold on. (taps the screen image of floppy-eared F2 rabbits) Oh ... (both students writing at the same time) The .... the parents . are a couple .... of F2

However, the students' emphasis on describing the screen images in terms of the rectangles grouping rabbits as a vertical sequence of offspring generations becomes problematic later. It contributes to a descriptive frame of reference and to process narratives supporting a mistaken answer to the prompt questions. Ultimately, the emphasis on skipping generations in the process narratives that the students create diminishes their attention to the parent boxes as they explain the pattern of screen images.

At this point, the students have established a degree of coherence in their interpretations of information relevant to comprehending and completing the task. Their interpretation activities included developing a frame of reference by eliminating certain interpretations of the screen images and the task prompt. Those activities also included using certain linguistic terms and pointing at specific parts of the screen images in order to reduce the interpretive contingencies they encountered as they worked with the computer program, the task prompt, and each other.

As they restate the descriptions of the screen images in order to write answers to the task prompt, their answers begin to resemble an explanation, i.e., one or more process narratives that suggest some causal, temporal, or conceptual relationship among pieces of information. Augmenting B21's earlier descriptive utterance noting that floppy ears skipped a generation (Transcript Extract 2.2, line B36), the students link visual, verbal, and textual information describing the functioning of the breeding simulation (Transcript Extract 2.5).

The computer screen continues to show the first couple selected as parent rabbits when the students initially ran the simulation. One of those rabbits has straight ears and the other has floppy ears. The screen also shows their offspring, all having straight ears. Thus, the screen presents a vertical sequence of images in which heterogeneous rabbits produce homogeneous offspring, which in turn produce heterogeneous offspring. In that context, the students' utterances suggest a descriptive process narrative: *Floppy ears skip a generation, since F1 parents that both have straight ears produce straight-eared and floppy-eared offspring* (Transcript Extract 2.5, lines B67-B76).

However, the ensuing interaction shows that the way the students emphasize or disregard information as they concurrently develop an interpretive frame of reference and create coherent process narratives leads to an unsatisfactory result. When they present the written and verbal explanations of their work to the teacher, he does not accept their explanation of the simulation, which asserts that the floppy ears automatically skip every other generation.

Transcript Extract 2.5: Sorting Out Frames of Reference

B67. B21: There (or 'their' or 'they're'). (pointing pen at the F2 parents) Hold on. (taps the screen image of floppy-eared F2 rabbits) Oh . . . (both students writing at the same time) The . . . . the parents . are a couple . . . . of F2
B68. G21: Generation?
B69. B21: have yeah have . ssstraight have straight ears. . . .
B70. G21: Their offspring right?
B71. B21: Umm. But . their . offspring
B72. G21: have two types of ears
B73. B21: has two types (9 second pause while writing) floppy and
B74. G21: pointy
B75. B21: straight pointy (3 second pause) But (2 second pause)
B76. G21: They skipped a generation an so (??)

The Reciprocal Effects of Culling Information, Developing Interpretive Frames of Reference, and Creating Process Narratives

The interpretation activities that lead to the mistaken explanation highlight how the concurrent creation of the process narratives and a particular interpretive frame of reference (descriptive rather than inferential) emphasizes certain components of the screen image at the expense of others. This constitutes a belief system, which complicates the students' subsequent attempts to correct their mistake. As the students interpreted the screen images and the task prompt questions, they eliminated interpretive contingencies by sorting and culling information. When they subsequently link the remaining information, their expressed process narratives not only present the selected results of that culling, but also restrict the students' subsequent attention to the visual information presented by the computer simulation. This limits the students' interpretive frames of reference, resulting in tunnel vision regarding the meaning of the screen images.

For example, twenty minutes into their work with the computer simulation, the students continue to interpret the screen images in order to answer the task prompt's final request:

> Discussion: Describe the 'living puzzle' you have observed, and summarize, in terms of the parents (p) and the F1 and F2 generations, what happens when two pure-breeding strains are crossed or mated. (WINGS for Learning, 1991: 8.2)

Another student, B22, who arrived 15 minutes earlier (Transcript Extract 2.3, line B56), participates with B21 and G21 in discussing the information they have interpreted from the screen as they write their answers to the task prompt. The students also consult the teacher regarding the task prompt's directions for using the simulation software to answer the question (Transcript Extract 2.6, lines B349-B364). He directs them back to the computer simulation. As the students develop and express process narratives linking their interpretations of information, they incorporate particulars of their earlier talk and pointing, which emphasized certain aspects of the screen images.

Figure 2.9: Examples of Students' Process Narratives

A	'So first three that way. Second three that way then 1, 2, 3 and so (points at lower right side of screen near set of offspring rabbits) goes in a pattern so the next one should be all floppy. Then it should be straight floppy straight . . .' (B21: Transcript Extract 2.1, Line B10)
B	'So (pointing finger at the F2 parent rabbits) these two couples are from (pointing finger at the F1 offspring) this block right here.' (B21: Transcript Extract 2.3, line 50)
C	'Recessive genes. It's inside you know (points pen at F1 straight-eared rabbits on screen) like . look (points pen at floppy ear of the F1 female floppy-eared parent) that one . and (pointing pen in circular motion around the rows of F1 offspring) none of them got (again points the pen at the F1 female floppy-eared parent) that gene.' (G21: Transcript Extract 2.3, lines B53-B55) [*Genes inside of the parents are related to the ear shape of the parents and are passed on to their offspring even if the offspring do not show the trait.*]
D	B21: There (or 'their' or 'they're'). (pointing pen at the F2 parents) Hold on. (taps the screen image of floppy-eared F2 rabbits) Oh . . . (both students writing at the same time) The . . . . the parents . are a couple . . . . of F2 G21: Generation? B21: have yeah have . ssstraight have straight ears. . . . G21: Their offspring right? B21: Umm. But . their . offspring G21: have two types of ears B21: has two types (9 second pause while writing) floppy and G21: pointy B21: straight pointy (G21 and B21: Transcript Extract 2.5, lines B67-B74) [*Floppy ears skip a generation, because parents that have straight ears produce offspring having straight or floppy ears.*]

During their preceding work with the simulation the students had expressed explanatory process narratives through their comments and pointing at the screen (Figure 2.9). These process narratives addressed:

- The relevance of the rabbits' ear shape to the task (e.g., 'But their offspring has two types floppy and straight pointy,' Figure 2.9, Row D)
- The relevance and meaning of the demarcated areas of the screen (e.g., 'The the parents are a couple of F2', Figure 2.9, Row D)
- An unseen mechanism of trait inheritance (e.g., 'Recessive genes. It's inside you know', Figure 2.9, Row C)
- The emphasis on terms identifying gender and kinship as components of the communication format for the task (e.g., 'parents', 'F2', 'generation', 'offspring'; Figure 2.9, Row D).

The students' production of process narratives had functioned as a sorting and culling mechanism. The resulting process narratives served as interpretive anchors that removed the need to repeatedly sort and cull the information as the interpretation activity continued. Process narratives are necessary components of understandings, but are not self-contained understandings. They function as prompts for recalling and sustaining the frames of reference and the selective emphasis on particular pieces of information that have reduced interpretive contingencies.

For instance, B21 describes the results of a new running of the simulation with comments and gestures:

> Ooohh (Pointing at a straight-eared mail rabbit in the F1 generation) the dominant (moving finger up to point at the straight-eared female parent rabbit) trait is in (sliding his finger down the screen toward the same male straight-eared offspring) in the male. (Transcript Extract 2.6, line B366)

Figure 2.10: Linking Visual and Linguistic Descriptions

B21 Pointing and Talking (Transcript Extract 2.6, Line B366)			
A	B	C	D
		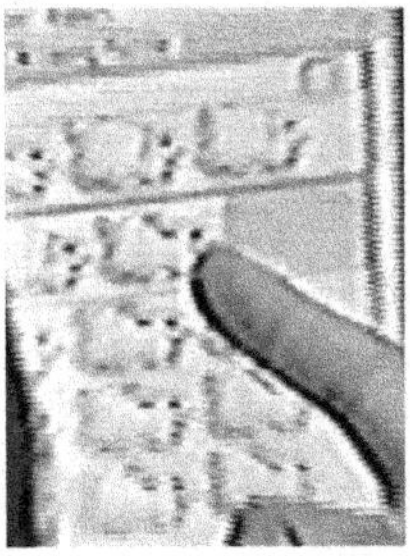	
Ooohh	the dominant	trait is in	in the male.

B21's pointing at specific rabbits displayed on the screen shows that when he comments that 'the dominant trait is in in the /male' (Figure 2.10), he points at the female parent rabbit. During the work on the task, B21 consistently confused the gender symbols that were displayed for each rabbit on the screen. However, in this case, despite his error regarding the straight-eared parent's gender, his pointing and comments express two process narratives that link the term, 'dominant', to the trait, straight ears, and to the homogeneous straight-eared generation of offspring, which resulted from mating the straight-eared and floppy-eared parents (Transcript Extract 2.6, lines B357-B366):

Mating a straight-eared male and a floppy-eared female produces a generation of straight-eared offspring.

So, the dominant trait is straight ears, and 'is in' the male parent.

B21 applies 'dominant trait' as an indexical expression for straight ears. His pointing as he says, 'the dominant trait is in in the male', indicates an emphasis on the visible similarities between the straight-eared parent and the F1 offspring. As he says, 'the dominant', he points at a straight-eared offspring rabbit (Figure 2.10, Column B). Then, as he says, 'trait is in', he moves his finger to the straight-eared parent rabbit (Figure 2.10, Column C). Finally, he moves his finger back to the straight-eared offspring rabbit (Figure 2.10, Column D).

B21's gesture and statement are not simply descriptions of a particular instant in the use of the computer simulation. They are based on process narratives derived from the preceding interpretive work to make sense of the images, their organization, and the term, 'dominant', in regard to the inheritance of traits across generations. B21 links the terms, 'dominant' and 'trait', to specific images.

B21 verges on expanding his interpretive frame of reference to include making inferences based on the pattern of screen images about genetic causes of the reappearance of floppy ears. His use of 'is in' ambiguously suggests a location of some relevant factor and implies a process by which something inside the rabbits can affect their ear shapes. The utterance could lead to an inference about the effects of genes.

However, B21 does not mention genes. 'Is in' is a placeholder, a grey box, for missing information: i.e., something that is not shown on the screen *is in* the male and results in pointy ears showing (Part Two discusses grey boxes in detail). Instead of discussing genes, he mentions traits – dominant traits. Once more, his utterance is descriptive. He has adopted the genetics vocabulary term, 'dominant trait', and applied it to the previously developed descriptive frame of reference for finding coherence that he developed earlier. He does not make inferences about how genes affect the pattern of visible traits. G21's and B22's utterances, 'Yeah' and 'Oh yeah it does it', show agreement with

B21's interpretation, and add emphasis on a descriptive frame of reference. (Transcript Extract 2.6, lines B367-B368).

Transcript Extract 2.6: Dealing with New Information

B349. T1: F go back and clear the screen
B350. B22: Puzzling
B351. B21: Okay clear.
B352. B23: Which one?
B353. T1: Yeah
B354. B22: Oh eight two
B355. T1: Add couple one (B21 is using the mouse to operate the simulation; a straight-eared female rabbit and a straight-eared male rabbit appear on the screen to the right of the straight-eared rabbits.)
B356. G21: Take take.
B357. T1: Add couple two. (B21 uses the mouse to operate the simulation; a floppy-eared female rabbit and a floppy-eared male rabbit appear on the screen.) Now take now instead take the female from couple one.
B358. G21: Yeah.
B359. B21: This one? (3 second pause in talk as B21 moves the straight-eared female rabbit to the mating box)
B360. G21: Yeah.
B361. T1: And then take the male from couple two
B362. G21: (B21 hesitates moving the mouse to grab one of the rabbits) Arrow (2 second pause in talk as B21 moves the floppy-eared male rabbit to the mating box)
B363. B21: Let's see.
B364. G21: Run.
B365. B22: Let's get some children.
B366. B21: Ooohh (Pointing at a straight eared mail rabbit in the F1 generation) the dominant (moving finger up to point at the straight-eared female parent rabbit) trait is in (sliding his finger down the screen toward the same male straight-eared offspring rabbit) in the /male./ [B21 confuses the symbols for male and female often during the task]
B367. G21: /Yeah/
B368. B22: So yeah it does it
B369. G21: Dominant and recessive.
B370. B21: Well hold on. (using mouse to set up another mating) Let's let's try it again with the .. with the male here. Male? (2 second pause) Is this the male right?

In contrast to B21's descriptive use of 'dominant trait', G21's utterance, 'Dominant and recessive', again presents the inferential frame of reference (Transcript Extract 2.6, line B369). She continues to index unseen internal factors that influence the visible traits. Her utterance expresses her inference that the F1 rabbit, at which B21 was pointing would carry the genes for both the dominant and recessive traits, even though all of the F1 rabbits have straight ears. Since the recessive trait, floppy ears, does not appear in the F1 generation offspring, the relevance of 'recessive' to the task is based on inferring that some information, which is not displayed on the screen, affects the information that is displayed. However, the students do not express a process narrative linking the pattern of visible ear shapes to the role of genes hidden inside the rabbits. Instead, they resort to the descriptive frame of reference, simply asserting that floppy ears skip generations.

The students' interpretation activities show how understanding is produced by concurrently developing indexical expressions for information, culling information, and linking information as process narratives. The students' subsequent activities (Transcript Extract 2.7, lines B383-B395) move them toward favoring the *'automatically skips a generation'* process narrative as a framework for finding coherence among the information presented by the screen, the prompt, and their own interpretation activities.

Interpretive Drift

The cause of this interpretive drift toward the descriptive frame of reference is the students' difficulty in addressing how genes influence the development of traits. This difficulty results from the absence of information in the task prompt and the computer simulation about such cellular, biochemical processes (Saferstein and Sarangi, 2010). In accordance with the traditional Mendelian curriculum, the printed prompt (Figure 2.1, Lab 8.2), and the computer interface do not present even a symbolic gloss of such information.

The 'automatically skips a generation' explanation avoids the interpretive contingencies related to finding information about dominant and recessive genes. For example, G21 mentioned the terms, *recessive* or *recessive genes*, five times during the learning activities discussed in this chapter (Transcript Extract 2.3, lines B51, B53; Transcript Extract 2.6, line B369; Transcript Extract 2.7 lines B384, line B393). However, when she tried to apply the term to an explanation, she displayed difficulty expressing a process narrative that would link information concerning the meaning and function of recessive genes. After B21's mention that the dominant trait *is in* the rabbits (Transcript Extract 2.6, line B366), she said, 'dominant and recessive' (line B369). When B21 ran another simulation, mating a floppy-eared and a straight-eared rabbit, which also resulted in all offspring having straight ears, G21 elaborated on 'dominant and recessive' by saying, 'But they have recessive genes with floppy ears' (Transcript Extract 2.7, line B384).

At this point, G21 begins to apply 'recessive' to a process narrative. However, when she tries to link it to the screen images or to the interpretations of the screen already expressed, she does not succeed. Instead, she says, 'So if they . whatever do you think they will . like you know' (Transcript Extract 2.7, line B384). Her utterance, 'they have recessive genes with floppy ears', has the potential to expand the explanation of the screen images to include the word 'recessive' and the genetic processes it indexes. However, as in her earlier uses of 'recessive', G21 does not find the words to complete a process narrative that would contribute to organizing, remembering, and applying information relevant to recessive genes. Her utterance simply describes the screen images.

In contrast to G21's ambiguous mention of recessive genes, B21 indexes descriptive process narratives expressed during the earlier discussion and pointing related to certain screen images. His comment, 'maybe it skipped a generation' (Transcript Extract 2.7, lines B385, B387), recycles the phrase, *skipped a generation*, which he and G21 had mentioned earlier (Transcript Extract 2.2, line B36; Transcript Extract 2.5, line B76).

Transcript Extract 2.7

B383. B21: Well let's run these.
B384. G21: But they have recessive genes with floppy ears. So if they . whatever do you think they will . like you know
B385. B21: Well let's see, and maybe it /skipped a/
B386. G21: /Then take/
B387. B21: generation. (Begins using mouse to select rabbits to breed another generation)
B388. G21: I think (points at the F1 generation rabbits) they would have um a mixture . if none of them (??) (8 second pause while they attend to the screen. Software produces another generation showing straight and floppy-eared rabbits)
B389. B22: Nope.
B390. B21: Ah!
B391. G21: Yeah /. see/
B392. B21: /See/ . look! They skipped. (B21 points at floppy-eared F2 rabbit. Then skips his finger up the screen, pointing at another floppy-eared F2 rabbit, a straight-eared F1 rabbit, and, finally, a floppy-eared parent of the F1 generation.)

Transcript Extract 2.7 (continued)

B393. G21: No, you know why? .. Because (points at the F1 generation of rabbits all having straight ears, then at the straight ear of the female parent of the F1 generation) the they they carry this gene, the dominant, but they have recessive genes in these ones (points at the floppy-eared parent, then at the F1 generation, then at the floppy-eared parent) so they have that that trait (placing her thumb and index finger over the male F1 parent in a position that suggests placing an object in or withdrawing an object from a container – as if she were going to grab the male F1 parent rabbit's floppy ear between her fingers) in them (moves her hand to the image of a straight-eared rabbit in the set of F1 generation offspring, then away from screen, and then back to the screen moving it from the F1 to the F2 rabbits) so I guess /if they they get that one ?/

B394. M21: /(moving the mouse pointer to the straight ear of the F1 generation female parent) So the dominant gene/ is in the male, but then in some like like some some of their (moving the mouse pointer to the floppy ear of the F1 generation male parent) offspring these traits come out.

B395. G21: Yeah

Emphasis on process narratives related to floppy ears 'skipping' generations reinforces the descriptive frame of reference. Those process narratives and the descriptive frame of reference eventually lead to more descriptive process narratives, which express the explanation that: *The information on the screen shows a pattern of inheritance in which floppy ears automatically appear in alternate generations* (Transcript Extract 2.7, line B392; Transcript Extract 3.2, lines B419-B422; Transcript Extract 3.2, lines B430-B433; Transcript Extract 3.4, lines B442-B451).[18]

B21's utterance, 'maybe it skipped a generation', circumvents the interpretive contingencies related to the absence of visual or linguistic information about dominant and recessive genes. Consequently, the ongoing concurrent development of an interpretive frame of reference and process narratives favors the 'automatically skips a generation' explanation of the screen images. The process narratives serve as anchors and signposts indexing an emphasis on particular information, a frame of reference for selecting information, and a particular way of organizing relevant information.

Coping with Missing Information by Expressing a Descriptive Frame of Reference

The students' ensuing interpretation activities display their route toward an understanding of the screen images and the task prompt based on the 'automatically skips a generation' process narratives and the descriptive interpretive frame of reference. By applying previously expressed process narratives to emphasize description of the screen images, they reduce the interpretive contingencies of seeking information that would replace grey boxes such as 'trait is in' and 'recessive'. Consequently, they deemphasize and eventually abandon both the frame of reference based on inferring the effects of hidden genes and the development of process narratives that mention dominant or recessive genes.

As B21 runs another generation of the computer simulation and says, 'Well let's see, and maybe it skipped a generation' (Transcript Extract 2.7, lines B385, B387), G21 shows attention to the screen and the task prompt, which asked, 'What trait variation or variations (for ear position) do you think will appear in the F1 generation?' (Figure 2.1, WINGS for Learning, 1991: 8.2). She uses gestures and talk to predict the ear shapes that would appear in the F1 generation, saying, 'I think (points at the F1 generation rabbits) they would have um a mixture' (Transcript Extract 2.7, line B388). Her utterances and pointing at the screen present a process narrative based on a frame of reference, which involves inferring that mixtures of unseen dominant and recessive genes within the rabbits cause the appearance of floppy or straight ears.

When the software produces another heterogeneous generation of rabbits on the screen, both G21 and B21 indicate that the resulting images of F2 generation rabbits support their respective earlier predictions and process narratives. G21's utterance, 'Yeah see' (Transcript Extract 2.7, line B391), emphasizes that her prediction of a mixture of ear shapes was correct. B21 specifies that his earlier focus on floppy ears skipping alternating generations was correct ('See look! They skipped,' Transcript Extract 2.7, line B392).

Rather than expressing agreement with B21 that the screen information shows the floppy-ears skipping a generation, G21 again directs attention to an inferential explanation of why the floppy ears show up in the F2 generation:

> No, you know why? . . Because (points at the F1 generation of rabbits all having straight ears, then at the straight ear of the female parent of the F1 generation) the they they carry this gene, the dominant, but they have recessive genes in these ones (points at the floppy-eared parent, then at the F1 generation, then at the floppy-eared parent) so they have that that trait (placing her thumb and index finger over the male F1 parent in a position that suggests placing an object in or withdrawing an object from a container – as if she were going to grab the male F1 parent rabbit's floppy ear

between her fingers) in them (moves her hand to the image of a straight-eared rabbit in the set of F1 generation offspring) so I guess if they get that one. (Transcript Extract 2.7, line B393; Figure 2.11, Rows A-D)

Figure 2.11: Interrelationship of Gesture, Talk, and Meaning

A		B393. G21: No, you know why? Because the they they carry this gene, the dominant,
B		but they have recessive genes in these ones so they have .
C		that . that trait
D		in them so I guess /they get that one ?/
E	[Ellipse added to note B21 pointing mouse arrow at floppy ear trait]	B394. B21: /So the dominant gene/ is in the male but then in some like like some some of their offspring these traits come out?

G21 explains her inferences about the role of dominant and recessive genes in producing the pattern of inheritance by mapping terms and concepts to the computer screen images and to the interpretations and understandings of the task previously expressed through talk and pointing at the screen (Figure 2.11). However, G21's gestures toward the screen images are more precise and detailed than her verbal description (Saferstein and Sarangi, 2010: 177–178). Using the visual resources of the computer simulation, G21 gesturally and linguistically expresses both a notion of recessiveness and the role of recessive genes in the inheritance of traits. Her gestures elaborate on the vague use of the linguistic grey boxes, 'they carry this gene' and 'they have recessive genes in', which cover gaps in information about the genes within the rabbits and their distribution across generations (Figure 2.11, Rows C, D).

She changes her hand gesture from pointing with her index finger to placing her thumb and index finger over the male F1 parent rabbit's floppy ear (and, in conjunction with her preceding utterances, the unseen recessive gene) in a position that suggests placing an object in or withdrawing an object from a container – as if she were going to grab the floppy ear/recessive gene between her fingers (Figure 2.11, Row C). Concurrently, she says, 'That . that trait' (part of the utterance 'they have that . that trait in them so I guess they get that one'). Then, she maintains the grabbing-lifting gesture of her thumb and index finger, while moving her hand to the image of a straight-eared rabbit in the set of F1 generation offspring.

In conjunction with her utterance, 'in them', G21's gesture portrays the act of taking the recessive (floppy-eared) gene from the parent and placing it within the offspring (Figure 2.11, Row D). During her ensuing utterance, G21 again gestures toward the screen. She moves her hand from the F1 to the F2 rabbits as she says, 'so I guess/if they they get that one', and then stops speaking.

When G21 moves her hand away from screen after making the gesture of placing the gene for floppy ears in the F1 rabbit, B21 moves the computer's mouse pointer toward the F1 straight-eared parent, and begins to speak, overlapping G21's utterance, 'they get that one'. His utterance and his use of the mouse pointer combine as a process narrative presenting his interpretation of G21's preceding gestures and talk (they also show that B21 continues to disregard or misinterpret the symbols indicating male and female rabbits):

> *(moving the mouse pointer to the straight ear of the F1 generation female parent) So the dominant gene is in the male, but then in some like like some some of their (moving the mouse pointer to the floppy ear of the F1 generation male parent) offspring these traits come out.* (Figure 2.11, Row E, line B394)

B21 links the picture of a trait, straight ears, to the term, 'dominant'. He links his interpretation of G21's explanation with his description of the screen images to form a process narrative suggesting a causal connection between dominant genes and straight ears: 'So the dominant gene is in the male'. However, he immediately notes contradictory information by saying, 'but then in some like like some some of their offspring these traits come out', while moving the mouse pointer to the floppy ear of the F1 generation male parent (Figure 2.11, Row E, line B394). 'But then' and 'come out' are substitutes for missing information that would link 'dominant gene is in the male', to the appearance of some floppy-eared rabbits in the F2 generation.

B21's use of the phrases, 'dominant gene is in' and 'traits come out', suggests an unspecified functional relationship between genes and traits. Resolving the ambiguity of that relationship would require emphasizing an inferential frame of reference that involved seeking and interpreting information that the screen and the text of the task prompt do not present.

B21 applies the information, which G21 had expressed by her gestures and verbal references concerning the ear shapes of particular images of parents and offspring (Figure 2.11, Rows A-D, line B393), to a descriptive process narrative explaining the relative positioning of screen images. He applies the form of expression and descriptive particulars featured in G21's pointing at the screen, rather than her inferences about genes that are not displayed by the screen images. In conjunction with his use of the mouse pointer to emphasize a particular screen image, B21's utterances, 'the male', 'some of their offspring', and 'these traits' contribute to the frame of reference emphasizing descriptions of visible screen images rather than inferences about unseen genes (Figure 2.11, Row E, line B394).

The Interrelationship of Process Narratives and Frames of Reference

As the students coped with the interpretive contingencies prompted by the absence of information about genes, their process narratives drifted toward the descriptive frame of reference. When G21 dealt with the lack of textual, or visual information about the functioning of genes, she used a combination of gesture and talk to express her inferences about the rabbits 'carrying' dominant and recessive genes within them. This reinforced an emphasis on describing the pictorial images. By linking linguistic and pictorial representations through gesture, G21 showed that she was trying to form a process narrative, which included the terms *dominant* and *recessive*. However, while helping to express her point that something inside the rabbits moves from parents to offspring and affects ear shape, her gestures and the images at which she directed them also constrained both the communication format and the resulting process narratives.

Paradoxically, G21's gesturing at the screen when she attempted to express inferences about the effects of unseen genes reinforced the descriptive frame of reference and eventually supported the acceptance of the mistaken 'automatically skips a generation' process narrative, which de-emphasized the link between genes and traits. Collective cognition during collaborative interpretation activities often includes such paradoxes in which the form or connotation of utterances presented as examples of one viewpoint unintentionally contributes to a frame of reference and process narratives favorable to another viewpoint (cf. Saferstein, 1994). The students' ensuing task activity continues to display the interrelationship of process narratives and frames of reference as the students de-emphasize inferences about the genetic factors inside of the rabbits and emphasize a descriptive frame of reference supporting the explanation that floppy ears automatically skip every other generation.

These data show how a communication pattern featuring both talk and gestures is interrelated with the concurrent development of process narratives and an interpretive frame of reference. Once developed, the process narratives and embedded frame of reference affect subsequent interpretation activities and the resulting understandings. While the students' interpretation activities are more hesitant than those of the patients and nurse in Chapter One's radiology consultation examples, the types of interpretation activities that produce process narratives are similar. Examining the production of the process narratives explains how such interpretation activities affect understandings.

3 Understandings and Beliefs

By continuing analysis of Chapter Two's genetics learning activities, Chapter Three examines how coherent understandings evolve, the endurance of process narratives and frames of reference, and the difficulties of modifying process narratives. The biology students' initial process narratives and their interpretive drift toward a descriptive frame of reference have led to a mistaken understanding of the computer simulation's pattern of trait inheritance. The cognitive intertwining of process narratives and interpretation activities is why recall of a particular process narrative triggers recall of relevant frames of reference, and particular information resources – all of which combine to constitute an understanding or a belief. The data show how the students' interpretation activities and resulting process narratives produce a belief system that is difficult to change. One of the students adheres to the 'automatically skips' process narratives and frame of reference – even when the teacher rejects them and running another simulation provides counterevidence.

How Coherence Evolves

Figure 3.1 shows the different frames of reference that G21 and B21 have developed. It displays the concurrent interrelated activities of interpreting information. These activities include expressing process narratives that coherently link linguistic terms with pictorial information, and expressing particular interpretive frames of reference for sorting and culling information. Despite using the same words, 'dominant' and 'genes', and pointing at the same images, B21 and G21 have not matched their developing frames of reference for interpreting the pictorial and textual information of the computer simulation and task prompt.

Figure 3.1: Expressing Inferential and Descriptive Frames of Reference
(From Transcript Extracts 2.7, 2.8)
[Bold type indicates utterances expressing a frame of reference]

	1	2
	Attempts to Create Inferential Process Narratives Concerning Recessive Genes	Emphasis on Describing Screen Images
A	B384. G21: **But they have recessive genes with floppy ears. So if they . whatever do you think they will . like you know**	B385, B387. B21: **Well let's see, and maybe it skipped a generation (Begins using mouse to select rabbits to breed another generation).**
B	B393. G21: No, you know why? Because (points at the F1 generation of rabbits all having straight ears, then at the straight ear of the female parent of the F1 generation) the they **they carry this gene**, the **dominant**, but **they have recessive genes in these ones (points at the floppy-eared parent, then at the F1 generation, then at the floppy-eared parent) so they have that that trait** (placing her thumb and index finger over the male F1 parent in a position that suggests placing an object in or withdrawing an object from a container—as if she were going to grab the male F1 parent rabbit's floppy ear between her fingers) **in them** (moves her hand to the image of a straight-eared rabbit in the set of F1 generation offspring) **so I guess /if they they get that one** (?)**/**	B394. B21: **/(moving the mouse pointer to the floppy ear of the F1 generation female parent) So the dominant gene/ is in the male but then in some like like some some of their offspring these traits come out (moving the mouse pointer to the floppy ear of the F1 generation male parent).** [They agree to run another simulation.] B397. B21: /So hold on/ **let's see.** B398. G21: **Let's do /it/**
C		[B21 hypothesizes about outcomes.] B405. B21: Look . if if it skips a gene **then it'll most likely be like this (points at floppy-eared rabbit), but if not, then it would be like this (points at straight-eared rabbit).**

Column 1 shows G21 trying to develop explanatory process narratives linking internal genetic factors to ear shape (e.g., 'But they have recessive genes with floppy ears,' Figure 3.1, Row A, Column 1; 'They have recessive genes in these ones,' Figure 3.1, Row B, Column 1). However, when she attempts to link the screen images of floppy ears in a particular offspring generation with an inference about undisplayed recessive and dominant genes, she confronts the interpretive contingencies related to missing information. Images and words fail her:

> 'So if they . whatever do you think they will . like you know' (Figure 3.1, Row A, Column 1)
>
> 'they carry this gene, the dominant, but they have recessive genes in these ones so I guess if they they get that one' (Figure 3.1, Row B, Column 1)

These echo G21's earlier incomplete attempts to create inferential process narratives that applied the terms 'dominant' and 'recessive' (Transcript Extract 2.4, lines B51-B59; Transcript Extract 2.6, line B369).

In contrast, B21 attempts to develop process narratives by describing and pointing at the specific images on the computer screen (Figure 3.1, Column 2). He responds to G21's incomplete inference concerning 'recessive genes with floppy ears' (Figure 3.1, Row A, Column 1) by using the simulation to produce more visual information, saying 'Well let's see, and maybe it skipped a generation' (Figure 3.1, Row A, Column 2). Then, B21 emphasizes the gestural, descriptive aspects of G21's subsequent incomplete attempt at a process narrative (i.e., her gestures directed at the screen images, Figure 3.1, Row B, Column 1). By using the mouse pointer as he expresses the term, 'dominant gene' (Figure 3.1, Row B, Column 2), B21 links those terms to specific images on screen:

> So the dominant gene is in the male but then in some like like some some of their offspring these traits come out.

B21's use of the mouse pointer also shows that he links the word, 'skips', to floppy ears. He uses the mouse pointer to emphasize specific ear shapes on the screen while formulating a process narrative, 'if it skips a gene then it'll most likely be like this, but if not, then it would be like this' (Figure 3.1, Row C, Column 2). In order to contribute to the interpretive work on the task, he does not need to know or infer the missing information about the operation of genes. He merely points at the different ear shapes on the screen and refers to the previously expressed process narratives by saying 'if it skips a gene then it'll most likely be like this' (Figure 3.1, Row C, Column 2).[19]

Process Narratives and Frames of Reference as Emergent Constraints on Interpretation

At this point in the task activity, the students have expressed a sense of coherence by recognizing and linking certain information as process narratives they can recall and communicate while they continue their work. They have developed and expressed two frames of reference that could shape ensuing work: G21's 'carry the genes' model which considers the effects on inherited traits of inferred dominant and recessive genes within their bodies, and B21's 'skips a generation' model which describes the visible pattern of ear shapes in the screen images.

In the activity discussed below (Transcript Extracts 3.1, 3.2), the students follow the task prompt instructions and the teacher's suggestions to run the simulation again and produce another example showing the result of mating a floppy-eared rabbit with a straight-eared rabbit. The descriptive and inferential interpretive frames of reference that B21 and G21 developed during the earlier work are still evident. However, as the students continue their work, they eliminate the inferential approach, and develop an understanding based on process narratives stating that the pattern of inheritance features floppy ears automatically skipping a generation – i.e., floppy ears appear in every other generation. The data show how the process narratives and the descriptive frame of reference that the students have created support selective attention to certain information. This affects the subsequent interpretation activities, delimiting the resulting understandings.

Summarizing the students' preceding interpretation activities: G21 has expressed a verbal and gestural explanation of her inferences about the cause of the pattern of trait inheritance displayed on the computer screen (Figure 3.1, row B, Column A, line B393). It is more detailed and specific than her earlier attempts to introduce dominant and recessive genes into the interpretation activities. However, the conclusion to her inference dwindles into an incomplete formulation, 'so I guess if they they get that one'. G21's combination of talk and gesture suggest process narratives on the order of:

> *The simulation shows that the F2 generation offspring includes both floppy-eared and straight-eared rabbits, and that the F1 parents also were floppy-eared and straight-eared. I infer that the homogeneous straight-eared F1 offspring must carry the floppy-eared trait without showing it. So I guess if they get the cause of the floppy-eared trait.* (Based on Figure 3.1, Column A)

B21 then articulated his interpretation of G21's utterances and gestures. His talk and use of the mouse pointer suggest process narratives on the order of:

> *Since the F1 offspring all have straight ears, the gene for straight ears is dominant over the gene for floppy ears. However, since the F2 generation has both straight-eared and floppy-eared rabbits, the cause of the floppy-eared trait in the F1 parent exists in the floppy-eared F2 offspring.* (Based on Figure 3.1 Column B)

Like G21's explanation, B21's interpretation of it also lacked specificity regarding how floppy-ears reappear in the F2 generation. As B21 subsequently develops an explanation of trait inheritance, he turns to other components of the communication format that the students have developed, i.e., the computer simulation software and pointing at the screen images. He returns to the existing screen images that show two generations of rabbits, which resulted after initially mating a floppy-eared male and a straight-eared female. The screen shows the original parents, the straight-eared F1 generation and the F2 generation containing five floppy-eared offspring and seven straight-eared offspring.

With input from G21 and B22, B21 selects a floppy-eared female rabbit as a parent (Transcript Extract 3.1, line B399). Then he begins to select a straight-eared male as a parent, but he stops, saying, 'Hold on let's take an arrow [referring to the male gender symbol] with floppy ears', while selecting a floppy-eared male (Transcript Extract 3.1, lines B403, B405).

Transcript Extract 3.1

B396. B22: It's just a /(??)/
B397. B21: /So hold on/ let's see.
B398. G21: Let's do /it/
B399. B21: /Here/ (points at female floppy-eared F2 generation rabbit on the screen) let's take one of these then. (4 second pause as B21 moves the rabbit to mating box with mouse; then moves mouse pointer over other rabbits)
B400. G21: Arrow [arrow indexes an earlier part of the discussion and refers to the arrow on the male gender symbol]
B401. B21: (moves mouse pointer to straight-eared male F2 rabbit) This one?
B402. G21: Mm-hmm
B403. B21: Hold on let's take /an arrow/
B404. G21: /Yes/

Transcript Extract 3.1 (continued)

B405. B21: with floppy ears. Is there an arrow with floppy ears? Right here. See what happens? (uses mouse to move floppy-eared F2 rabbit to mating box) Look . if if it skips (points at straight-eared F2 rabbit with left hand and floppy-eared F2 rabbit with right hand) a gene then it'll most likely be like this (points with right hand at floppy-eared rabbit in row of possible parents at the top of screen), but if not, then it would be like this (points with left hand at straight-eared rabbit near bottom of screen. Then uses mouse to run the mating) ... They both have floppy ears remember.
B406. G21: Hmm.
B407. B21: Ah see (points at floppy-eared F3 rabbit)
B408. G21: Now /they all have the ears/
B409. B21: /(points at floppy-eared F3 parents, then at F3 offspring) there it has/ both. (points at floppy-eared F3 parents, then at F2 generation box) Now hold on let's go back up to here (uses mouse to select F2 rabbits to breed a second set of F3 offspring.)
B410. B22: get a old man.
B411. B21: (The size of the box for the F2 generation limits visibility of some rabbits' ears, and does not show a floppy-eared male that would comply with B22's suggestion) We need a floppy ear. We need a floppy ear (????). Where do I go up? (B21 does not know how to enlarge the generation box)
B412. B22: Click on that box (???)
B413. B21: (B21 closes the F1 box, revealing all of the F2 and F3 rabbits. B21 then uses the mouse to move the pointer around the F2 and F3 boxes on the screen.) There . okay (4 second pause as B21 uses the mouse to select a straight-eared male F2 rabbit for breeding). Straight ears (B21 points at the straight-eared rabbit that he had selected.) (10 seconds without talk as B21 selects a floppy-eared F2 female rabbit for breeding, then produces a second F3 generation, F3.2. The simulation replaces the F3.1 generation box with smaller adjacent F3.1 and F3.2 generation boxes.)
B414. B22: They all have . / floppy ears/
B415. G21: /(?see?)/ No no-no here (points at a straight-eared F3.2 rabbit at the bottom of the screen)
B416. B22: Oh
B417. G21: Pointy and floppy
B418. B21: But

A key point in the development and acceptance of the descriptive frame of reference is the activity beginning with B21's speculation about the potential outcomes of the mating and his concurrent pointing at the floppy-eared F2 rabbit and its floppy-eared female grandparent (Figure 3.2).

Figure 3.2: B21 Pointing as Part of Communication Format (Line B405)

A	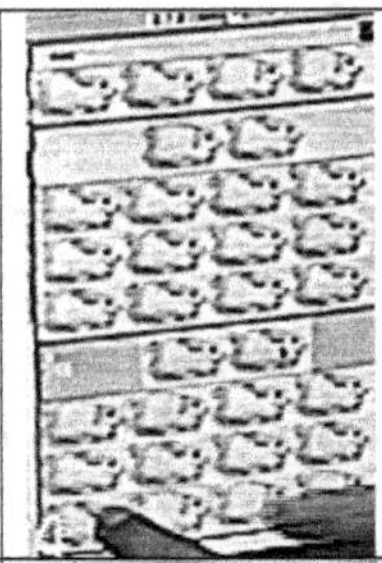	Line B405. B21: See what happens? (uses mouse to move floppy-eared F2 rabbit to mating box) Look . if if it skips (points at straight-eared F2 rabbit with left hand and floppy-eared F2 rabbit with right hand) a gene then it'll most likely
B	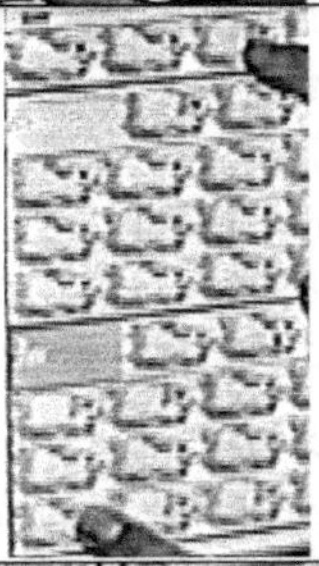	be like this (points with right hand at floppy-eared rabbit in row of possible parents at the top of screen),
C		but if not, then it would be like this (points with left hand at straight-eared rabbit near bottom of screen. Then uses mouse to run the mating) . . . They both have floppy ears remember.

B21's words and gestures display his emphasis on the visible screen images rather than inferences about causes of inheritance hidden within the rabbits. His pointing at rabbits in different sectors of the screen amplifies this emphasis. B21's pointing is descriptive, in contrast to G21's earlier pointing and gesturing to convey the idea of some internal factor moving from parents to offspring. B21's pointing illustrates the types of ear shape he mentions verbally, but it does not express a relationship of dominant and recessive genes to the ear shapes of the rabbits at which he points. Instead, B21 expresses process narratives, which hypothetically relate 'automatically skips a generation' to the appearance of the offspring, and suggest a way to corroborate the 'skips' explanation (Figure 3.2):

> *Look if if it skips (points at straight-eared F2 rabbit with left hand and floppy-eared F2 rabbit with right hand) a gene then it'll most likely be like this (points with right hand at floppy-eared female grandparent rabbit in row at the top of screen),*
>
> *but if not, then it would be like this. (points with left hand at straight-eared rabbit near bottom of screen. Then uses mouse to run the mating)*
>
> *They both have floppy ears remember.*

B21 combines the descriptive frame of reference, based on interpreting the images produced by the computer simulation, with the inferential frame of reference expressed by G21's incomplete process narratives about dominant and recessive genes (Figure 3.1, Column A). However, B21's comments emphasize the images on the screen, not the unseen recessive or dominant aspect of genes. B21's utterance, 'They both have floppy ears remember' (Figure 3.2, Row C), suggests that he is considering the possibility of some unseen factor causing the inheritance of floppy ears as a potential component of an explanatory process narrative. However, the 'automatically skips a generation' explanation that the students ultimately express does not suggest or state how the ear shapes in a generation are biologically linked to the ear shapes of its grandparents. The students' neglect of the dominant and recessive aspects of genes derives from the interrelated process narratives and interpretive frame of reference that they create as they deal with the contingencies of missing information about cellular genetic processes.

As the students develop and accept the 'automatically skips a generation' explanation, they provide an example of how the activities of interpreting information and constructing coherent process narratives purge certain frames of reference and interpretations of information, while favoring others. The students begin to interpret and comment on the screen images in the context of the 'automatically skips' process narratives developed during the preceding task activities. For example, B21 and B22 did not attend to the presence of heterogeneous offspring in the F3.2 box, which G21 had pointed out (Transcript Extract 3.1, line B415).[20]

Such selective emphasis on particular information – an emphasis both contributing to and shaping the expressed process narratives – eventually leads the students to develop a mistaken explanation of the inheritance of physical characteristics. B21's and B22's mistakes or oversights in regard to accurately recognizing the pattern of screen images were not simply lack of concern or sloppy thinking. All three of the students were high achievers, who took the assignment seriously, were engaged with the objective of learning about trait inheritance, and wanted to earn high grades. They were applying the interpretation activities of many people – adults and experts, not just high school students – when encountering information that is new to them in both form and content, and then confronting an absence of ancillary information that would help them to link the new information in coherent process narratives. The students' interpretations of the screen images were influenced by the concurrent development of process narratives and an interpretive frame of reference, in the context of an absence of information about genes.

Transcript Extract 3.2: Emphasizing the 'Skips' Frame of Reference

B419. B22: It looks like every generation it's skipping
B420. R1: It's skipping a generation?
B421. B21: It did on the first time.
B422. B22: And then it did on the second time too. But we put
B424. B21: (Clears the screen and starts the task over using the computer to pick and breed rabbits) We have one here and one here. Took one of these (selects female straight-eared rabbit).
B425. R1: Ah
B426. B21: and then this one (selects male floppy-eared rabbit).
B427. R1: Yeah.
B428. B21: Then it's gonna come out pointy. I think it does in the male (runs the simulation, producing F1 generation of straight-eared offspring). . See. But then I took one of these (selects straight-eared F1 rabbit) . . . and then took one of these (selects straight-eared F1 rabbit). Then it's gonna have a mixture (runs simulation producing F2 generation with floppy-eared and straight-eared rabbits) . .

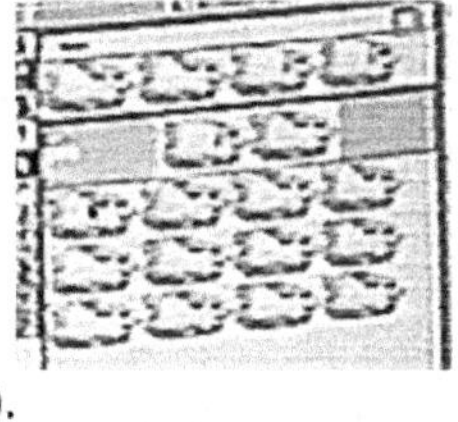

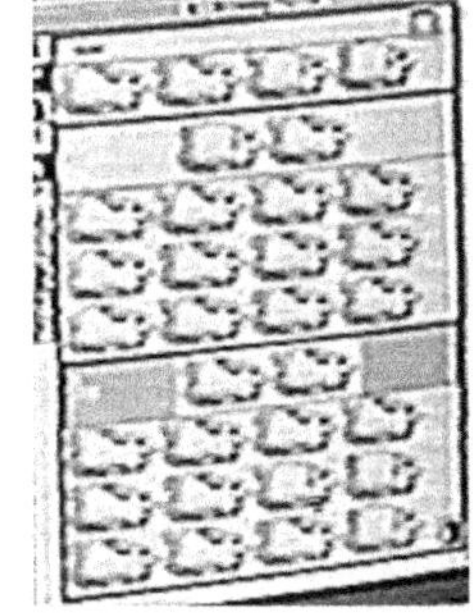

B429. B22: Nuh
B430. B21: It skipped.
B431. B22: It skipped a generation.
B432. R1: Oh you mean it doesn't show up in the firs-in that
B433. B22: In the first one it won't show up and then the second one will.
B434. B21: Yeah so from here from this generation from these two, it came out straight ears (??)

The nascent 'automatically skips' process narratives affect the development of subsequent process narratives and the ultimate understanding of trait inheritance that the students present to the teacher. For example, in order to verify the pattern in which floppy ears skip a generation and reappear, B21 clears the screen and runs the simulation again (Transcript Extract 3.2, lines 424–431). He narrates his operation of the simulation by referring to the previous outcomes, expressing process narratives that feature the past tense and predict what the outcomes of the matings will be:

> *Took one of these (selects female straight-eared rabbit)* (line B424)
>
> *Then it's gonna come out pointy* (line B428)
>
> *But then I took one of these (selects straight-eared F1 rabbit) and then took one of these (selects straight-eared F1 rabbit). Then it's gonna have a mixture (runs simulation producing F2 generation with floppy-eared and straight-eared rabbits)* (line B428).

Then both B21 and B22 reiterate 'skipped' as a description of the outcome over two or more generations when the simulation begins with the mating of rabbits having different ear shapes:

B430. B21: It skipped.
B431. B22: It skipped a generation.
B432. R1: Oh you mean it doesn't show up in the firs-in that
B433. B22: In the first one it won't show up and then the second one will.

The students' interpretation activities make 'skipped' or other forms of 'skip' indexical for a particular series of actions in the operation of the computer simulation (selecting and mating rabbits from successive generations) and for an explanation of trait inheritance related to the task prompt questions (Figure 3.3).

The students' emphasis and re-emphasis on variations of 'skipped a generation' to refer to their use of the computer simulation and their interpretations of the results supplants other possible linguistic formulations and interpretations that could apply, such as expressions based on inferring the relevance of dominant and recessive genes (Figure 3.3). Process narratives and beliefs emerge, change, and solidify through such interpretation activities.

Figure 3.3: Development of the 'Skips a Generation' Explanation Regarding the Presence of Floppy Ears
(From Transcript Extracts 2.2, 2.5, 2.7, 3.1, 3.2)

A	B35. G21: F2 generation, okay. (7 second pause while they silently read task prompt) (reading aloud from task prompt) "What is really puzzling about this?" B36. B21: (Pointing pen at screen) Because **it skipped a generation**.
B	B71. B21: Umm. But . their . offspring B72. G21: have two types of ears B73. B21: has two types (9 second pause while writing) floppy and B74. G21: pointy B75. B21: straight pointy (3 second pause) But (2 second pause) B76. G21: **They skipped a generation** an so (??)
C	B385. B21: Well let's see, and **maybe it /skipped a/** B386. G21: /Then take/ B387. B21: **generation**.
D	B392. B21: /See/ . look! **They skipped**. (B21 points at floppy-eared F2 rabbit. Then **skips his finger up the screen**, pointing at another floppy-eared F2 rabbit, a straight-eared F1 rabbit, and, finally, a floppy-eared parent of the F1 generation.)
E	B405. B21: **Look . *if if* it skips** (points at straight-eared F2 rabbit with left hand and floppy-eared F2 rabbit with right hand) a gene then it'll most likely be like this (points with right hand at floppy-eared rabbit in row of possible parents at the top of screen), but if not, then it would be like this (points with left hand at straight-eared rabbit near bottom of screen).
F	B419. B22: It *looks like* every generation **it's skipping** B420. R1: It's skipping a generation? B421. B21: **It did on the first time**. B422. B22: **And then it did on the second time too**. But we put--both of 'em have straight.
G	B430. B21: **It skipped**. B431. B22: **It skipped a generation.** B432. R1: Oh you mean it doesn't show up in the firs-in that B433. B22: In the first one it won't show up and then the second one will.

Reducing Interpretive Contingencies: Coherence by Elimination

Early in the students' interpretation activity, 'skipped a generation' refers to the absence of floppy-eared rabbits in the F1 generation after mating a straight-eared parent with a floppy-eared parent. Later, the students apply it to an explanation indicating that floppy ears skip every other generation. As they establish coherence among pieces of information by emphasizing the process narratives that describe the patterns of ear shapes presented on the screen, all three of the students – even G21 – stop considering and making inferences to explain what happens biologically inside of the rabbits to affect the inheritance of traits. By expressing, recalling, and repeating process narratives, they reinforce a particular frame of reference, i.e., the emphasis on describing the screen images.

As B21 continues using the software to produce a sequence of generations in order to investigate whether the 'skips' model stands up, his actions and words emphasize both the 'skips' explanation and the descriptive frame of reference (Transcript Extract 3.3). That frame of reference supports a mistake he makes when using the software, which then reinforces the 'skips' explanation. The screen shows that the software was set to produce and display 12 offspring in each generation, formatted as three rows, each containing four rabbits. When the software produced an F3 generation, it automatically reduced the size of all of the generation boxes so that they could all appear on the screen. This caused the top row of rabbits in each box to be hidden and the middle row to be partially obscured (lines B437-B440). However, upon close examination, enough of each rabbit in the middle row showed to reveal floppy ears, if they were present. Only the bottom row was entirely visible.

In order to see the top row of a particular generation, the operator of the software must close one of the other generation boxes by using the mouse to click a button in that generation box. Doing that enlarges the remaining generation boxes. B21 was using the computer's mouse to operate the software. Since the parent rabbits he selected were a heterozygous straight-eared rabbit and a homozygous floppy-eared rabbit, the software algorithm would have produced at least one floppy-eared rabbit in the F3 generation. Coincidentally, the visible bottom row and the partially visible middle row of the F3 generation did not contain any of those floppy-eared rabbits (Transcript Extract 3.3, line B437, second image). Thus, the floppy-eared rabbits would have appeared in the hidden top row. However, B21 did not enlarge the F3 offspring box to show the top row.

Transcript Extract 3.3: 'Automatically Skips' Process Narratives Override Attention to Software Constraints

B435. R1: The only thing is that (???) this whole thing is supposed to do is (???) to find out (??????)

B436. B21: Well let's see what happens here. (Uses mouse to breed F2 floppy and straight-eared rabbits).

B437. R1: I'm going to get out of your way (7 second pause in talk, while students look at simulated generations of rabbits on screen. The screen shows that the number of rabbits in each generation is set for 12, formatted as 3 rows of 4 rabbits. As the software produces an F3 generation, it automatically reduces the size of all of the generation boxes so that they will all fit on the screen. This causes the top row of rabbits in each box to be hidden. Thus, the ears are not visible)

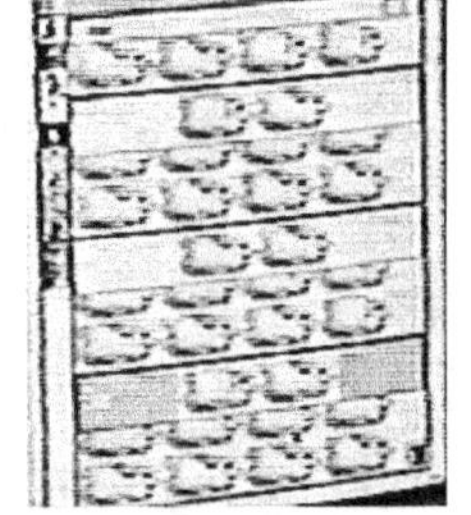

B438. B21: Look .

B439. B23: (B21's first name)'s /right/

B440. B21: /look/ they're straight (uses mouse pointer to point out two rabbits) . they're straight.

B441. G21: How about the top one?

B442. B21: (B21 does not reveal the top row.) So then. Then now . they're gonna be floppy. Watch. (7 second pause in talk as he creates another generation from the F3 parents.) See. /Floppy/ (The production of the F4 box further reduces all of the generation boxes, revealing only one row of rabbits in each box. B21 refers to the mixture of floppy and straight-eared rabbits in the visible row of the F4 box.)

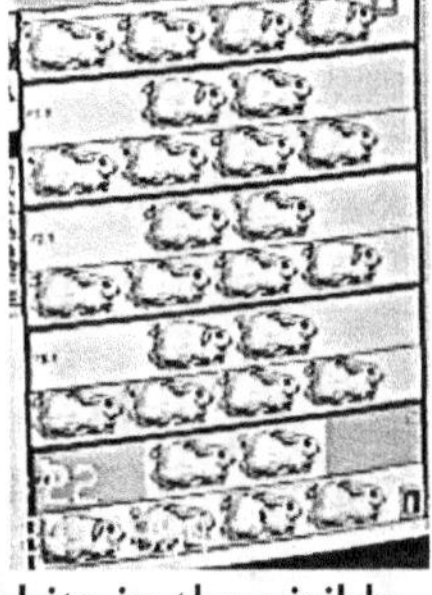

B443. G21: /One./ (May refer to the one floppy-eared rabbit visible in the new generation)

G21 suggests the possibility of floppy-eared rabbits being hidden by the configuration of the screen images when she says, 'How about the top one?' (Transcript Extract 3.3, line B441). This may refer to the top row of the rabbits in the F3 generation box, which is completely hidden. B21 neglects G21's utterance as he attends to the visual information presented on the screen and to operating the software to produce that information. Rather than responding to G21's question, he says, 'So then. Then now . they're gonna be floppy. Watch. See. Floppy.' (line B442). Those comments show his focus on the previously created process narratives. His concern with verifying the 'skips a generation' process narratives leads him to interpret the incompletely inspected F3 generation as evidence that the appearance of floppy ears would automatically alternate generations. This descriptive interpretive frame of reference continues to affect the development of the 'automatically skips' process narratives as B21 continues to run the simulation.

The complexity of the cognition related to using the software and interpreting the screen, which included recall and application of the previously created process narratives and descriptive frame of reference, increased the potential for the students to miss or disregard some information, including comments of other participants. In this case, B21 did not act to expand the windows showing the generation of rabbits, and he did not attend to G21's comment (Transcript Extract 3.3, lines B441, B442).[21]

When the screen shows the F4 and subsequent generations, the generation boxes are further reduced showing only one row of each generation, i.e., only four of the 12 offspring in that generation. The students examine those images without expanding the generation boxes to examine all of the offspring. The 'skips a generation' process narratives are shaped by the combined constraints of the visual information (i.e., the software design contributes to the students' failure to view all rows of rabbits in each generation), the immediate interaction among the students, and the curriculum design expressed by the task prompt (the teacher chose not to inform the students about a feature of the software that represents each rabbit's genes for ear shape).[22] In that context, G21 does not reiterate her comment about the hidden row. Instead, like B21, she attends to the information on the screen and B21's comments. G21 does not talk during the B21's seven-second pause while they wait for the software to show the results of B21's latest mating of the rabbits. When she does speak, like B21, she focuses on the visual information, seeming to point out the one floppy-eared rabbit in the new generation by saying 'one' (Transcript Extract 3.3, line B443). Whatever G21's intention in saying 'one', the utterance is compatible with the emphasis on describing the visual information as displaying a 'skips a generation' explanation of the appearance of heterogeneous ear shapes.

Thus, both B21, and G21, contribute to interpreting the visual information provided by the simulation as showing that floppy ears skip generations. B22 inserts that interpretation into a broader proposition communicated by a sequence of utterances that express the process narrative:

> *It just automatically skips a generation. It doesn't matter which one you put in there. It's always gonna skip a generation.* (expressed in Transcript Extract 3.4, lines B447, B451)

This describes the displayed images, not the biology of trait inheritance.

Without addressing the missing information about how dominant and recessive genes operate, the use of 'automatically' links the boxes on the screen representing different generations of rabbits and the different ear shapes of the rabbits that B21 has just described. The evolving discourse framework, which included the 'skips' process narratives and the interpretations of partially visible offspring generations, has contributed to the meaning and use of 'automatically'.

The activity preceding B22's 'automatically skips a generation' explanation shows how this happened. After the appearance of the F3 generation, B21 had predicted the outcome of mating two straight-eared F3 rabbits from the visible row: 'they're gonna be floppy. Watch' (Transcript Extract 3.4, line B442). The students refer to an offspring generation as being 'floppy' when it contains at least one floppy-eared rabbit. When the screen showed the resulting F4 generation box, which was reduced to display only one of its three rows, B21 said, 'See. Floppy', referring to the one floppy-eared rabbit in the row (Transcript Extract 3.4, line B442). Then, preparing to mate the floppy-eared F4 rabbit with a straight-eared F4 rabbit – again selecting both from the one visible row of the generation box – B21 predicted, 'now they're gonna go back' (Transcript Extract 3.4, line B444). When all four of the offspring in the one visible row of the F5 generation box had straight ears, B21 excitedly said, 'I told you! They skip generations.' (Transcript Extract 3.4, line B444). B22 affirmed that interpretation, saying, 'They skipped a generation' (Transcript Extract 3.4, line 445) and then, responding to a question I asked, he introduced the grey box, 'automatically', saying, 'No it doesn't make a difference cause it just automatically skips a generation' (Transcript Extract 3.4, line 447).

Transcript Extract 3.4: The Tipping Point

B442. B21: (B21 does not reveal the top rows of the F3 generation box.) So then. Then now . they're gonna be floppy. Watch. (7 second pause in talk as he creates another generation from the F3 parents.) See. /Floppy/ (The production of the F4 box reduces all of the generation boxes again, revealing only one row of rabbits in each box. B21 refers to the floppy-eared rabbit at the left side of the visible row of the F4 box.) 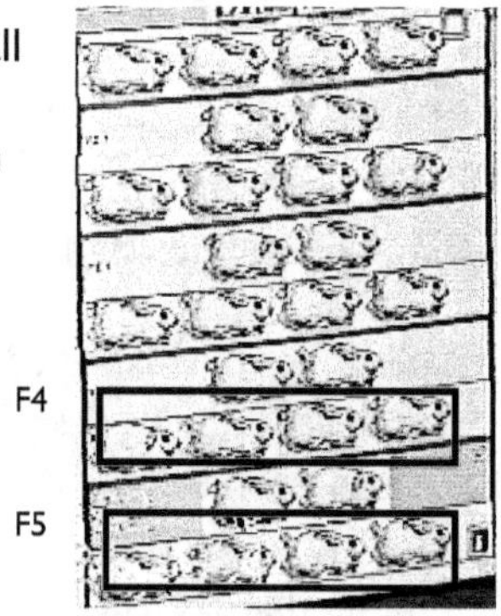
B443. G21: /One./ (May refer to the one floppy-eared rabbit visible in the new generation)
B444. B21: But watch, now they're gonna go back (7 second pause in talk as B21 creates another generation of rabbits). Go back. (4 second pause in talk while they pause wait for the computer to create a new generation) I told you! They skip generations.
B445. B22: They skipped a generation.
B446. R1: Does it ah (?????)
B447. B22: No it doesn't make a difference cause it just automatically skips a generation.
B448. B21: Why though?
B449. B22: (questioning) Hmmm?
B450. G21: So it's no?
B451. B22: It's no, because it doesn't matter which one you put in there. It's always gonna skip a generation.
B452. B21: So we started off with sss floppy and straight--ended up with straight. And then we took two of those, mated them, and then it came out straight and floppy. We took two of those (hand movements) opposite ears
B453. B22: They came out
B454. B21: came out /straight./
B455. B22: /straight./ . . The only thing we didn't--forgot was a full floppy family. (4 second pause)
B456. B21: But (pointing at the monitor) if we take two straights . . if we take two floppy's it is gonna be (? 'a' or 'all' ?) floppy.
B457. B22: Well yeah, but we never took two floppies.
B458. B21: We tried it before already.

B21 momentarily voiced a concern about causes of the automatic pattern when he asked, 'Why though?' (Transcript Extract 3.4, line B448). However, G21 and B22 diverted the discussion from that topic, when they emphasized answering a task prompt question:

B450. G21: So it's 'no'?
B451. B22: It's 'no', because it doesn't matter which one you put in there. It's always gonna skip a generation.

G21's question (line B450) addresses prompt question 13, '*Did you get different results using the opposite sets of parents in the p x p cross?*' She focuses on the relation of the visible images to the task prompt despite her previously expressed concern about the top row of offspring being obscured (Transcript Extract 3.3, line B441). The yes/no format of G21's utterance, 'So it's "no"?' (Transcript Extract 3.4, line B450), correlates with the prompt question. It inserts that dichotomizing frame of reference as a constraint on the interpretation activity. B22 reinforces that frame of reference by saying, 'It's "no"'. He then emphasizes a model of prediction based on the observable screen information by saying, 'because it doesn't matter which one you put in there. It's always gonna skip a generation' (Transcript Extract 3.4, line B451). B22 expresses the answer as an unambiguous process narrative describing use of the computer simulation. In the context of the preceding comments, 'skip a generation' clearly indexes the images appearing on the screen, rather than missing information about biological processes.

In this context, the frame of reference that G21 supports with her question about how to answer the task prompt (Transcript Extract 3.4, line 450) contributes to overriding the frame of reference she expressed earlier, (i.e., an emphasis on inferences about the rabbits carrying recessive genes). Such attention to creating an answer to the task prompt in the form of a summative process narrative diverts the students from G21's earlier concern that counter-evidence might exist in the hidden top row of the F3 generation box (Transcript Extract 3.4, line B441). Her question seeking verification of the answer to the task prompt ('So it's "no"?' Transcript Extract 3.4, line B450) results in an emphasis on the descriptive frame of reference rather than inferences about the genetic causes of the rabbits' ear shapes. The descriptive frame of reference also reduces the interpretive contingencies of the inferential frame of reference, such as the absence of information about genes that led to the term, 'recessive', functioning as a grey box (Transcript Extract 2.4, lines B53-B59 and Transcript Extract 2.7, line B384, discussed in Chapter Two).

The students contend with both the creative and administrative aspects of the learning task (cf. Saferstein, 1992). In addition to dealing with the creative contingencies of interpreting and linking the visual information presented by the computer simulation, they cope with the administrative contingencies of managing the output of their interpretation activity, such as writing answers to the task prompt questions. The creative and administrative contingencies affect the emphasis on certain information and the culling of other information. Such determinations of relevance and irrelevance contribute to the shared interpretive frame of reference. The descriptive frame of reference reduces both the creative and administrative contingencies the students had encountered earlier when attempting to apply an inferential frame of reference in the absence of the cellular process information needed to link the screen information with terms such as 'recessive' and 'genes' to form process narratives.

For example, B21 drops his question about causation in regard to floppy ears skipping a generation ('Why though?' Transcript Extract 3.4, line B448), and returns to a frame of reference that focuses on describing the observed visual information rather than making inferences about causes. B21 and B22 express a process narrative related to particular screen images, which supports the 'skips a generation' explanation (Transcript Extract 3.4):

B452. B21: So we started off with sss floppy and straight – ended up with straight. And then we took two of those, mated them, and then it came out straight and floppy. We took two of those (hand movements) opposite ears
B453. B22: They came out
B454. B21: came out /straight./

The 'automatically skips a generation' process narratives address what is observable on the screen. They do not address genetic processes. The students reiterate and reinforce those process narratives and the descriptive frame of reference as they continue the learning activities. For example, 11 minutes later, while writing answers to the task prompt without using the computer simulation, the students apply their recall of the earlier outcomes of the simulation (Transcript Extract 3.5).

Transcript Extract 3.5

B550. B22: They like like like floppy ears and straight ears. /Then you'll get/
B551. B21: /Or do you ?/
B552. B22: floppy ears . . and you'll get both
B553. B21: No, but remember when we did that for our first generation? It came out straight.

Transcript Extract 3.5 (continued)

B554. B22: I know, but every other you'll get you'll get a . a difference every other generation. (eleven second pause, while B22 and G21 write their answers)
B555. G21: In every what? In every two generations?
B556. B22: In every other generation.

The students' utterances present the process narratives:

> *When you mate a parent having floppy ears with a parent having straight ears the first generation of offspring will have straight ears.* (Based on Transcript Extract 3.5, lines B550-B553)
>
> *When you mate the offspring of the ensuing generations, you'll find floppy-eared rabbits in every other generation.* (Based on Transcript Extract 3.5, lines B554-B556)

The students' comments display the intertwining of the visual resources with the process narratives and the descriptive frame of reference that the students had created earlier in order to link and recall information. When they wrote their answers to the task prompt without using the computer simulation, the process narratives substituted for the absent visual information. The process narratives not only emphasized particular information and particular interpretations of information, but also functioned to deemphasize or eliminate from consideration potentially confounding or conflicting information. The process narratives were the tangible product of the preceding social and individual interpretation activities. For the students, they also indexed those interpretation activities.

The Endurance of Frames of Reference and Process Narratives: Correcting a Mistake

The students' complex interpretation activities produced a frame of reference and process narratives supporting a particular understanding of the computer simulation's depiction of trait inheritance. That understanding was mistaken. It did not explain trait inheritance in a way that matched the scientific model, initially developed by Gregor Mendel – which the teacher had anticipated would result from the students' operation of the computer simulation to answer the task prompt questions. However, as an explanation of the simulation's screen images, the students' answer was not entirely false – it was reasonable as a description of certain aspects of particular outcomes of the simulation (cf. Saferstein, 2014). In the context of the descriptive frame of reference and the concept of 'pattern' that the students applied as they developed the process narratives, the 'automatically skips a generation' explanation had coherence. Analysis of the students' responses to the teacher's rejection of their explanation shows how the concurrent activities of interpreting and linking information embedded certain frames of reference within process narratives, and led to an enduring belief in a particular understanding.

The students' 'automatically skips a generation' explanation of the software simulations were challenged ten minutes after the activity in Transcript Extract 3.5, when the teacher read their written answers and verbally responded to them (Transcript Extract 3.6). The teacher did not accept B22's statement that after the F1 generation, floppy ears would appear in every other generation (Transcript Extract 3.6, line B600). The teacher then told B21 and G21 to help B22 rewrite the answer (lines B629-B631). Their difficulty correcting the mistake displays the function of process narratives in forming recallable understandings.

Transcript Extract 3.6: T1 Rejects Explanation of Skips Model

B600. T1: (While reading the group's answers to the task prompts) You need a little bit more. You need to tell me what happened in the breeding experiment that you were doing.
B601. B22: I did.
B602. B21: It was harder though
B603. B22: The puzzling the puzzling thing /the puzzling/
B604. T1: /Mmmhm/
B605. B22: I did
B606. B21: that it we told him that
B607. B22: that that it skips a generation. It skips its every other generation
B608. T1: What skips?
B609. B21: The the
B610. B22: /the ears/
B611. B21: /the parents' traits/
B612. B22: their ears
B613. B21: It doesn't matter what the parents look like, /but in/
B614. B22: /Yeah/
B615. B21: the first generation we took opposite looking parents the ears
B616. B22: and the ears /are/
B617. B21: /and then the F the F1 they all had pointy ears
B618. B22: Yeah
B619. B21: and then we took /two of those/
B620. T1: /Is that what you say/ where uh do you say that here?

Transcript Extract 3.6 (continued)

B621. B22: Yes
B622. B21: and then we took two of th/ose/
B623. T1: /Wa/it wait I'm r I'm r reading his here
B624. B21: I'm answering the question.
B625. T1: No, I'm not asking you a question, I'm looking to see if it's in your conclusion… (reading B22's explanation of the 'living puzzle' aloud) but if the
B626. B22: /(looks at the explanation and says something not clearly audible, perhaps reading along)/
B627. T1: /parents' ears are/ different, then every other generation will (stops reading) What?
B628. B22: That's what I'm saying right. . I'm not very good with words, but that's what I'm /trying to say/
B629. T1: /Wel/llll uummm (to B21 and G) go hey go help (B22's first name) rewrite his conclusion.
B630. B21: Okay
B631. T1: He needs help. He needs help on it.

The students' mistake provides an example of how the concurrent social interpretation activities and the mental organizing of interpreted information affect each other. When B21 and B22 rewrite the answer, their recall and description of the previously encountered screen images presents the interpretation that resulted from their earlier mistake of failing to expand the generation boxes when the production of a series of generations hid rows of offspring (discussed above in regard to Transcript Extract 3.3, lines B440-B442). The alternating homogeneous and heterogeneous generations of rabbits were an artifact of the students' mistake of not expanding the boxes to inspect them and the coincidence of the floppy-eared rabbits occurring in the hidden rows. The reiteration, as process narratives, of the students' experiences using the software and the interpretations they expressed at that time, contributed to their continuing emphasis on the 'automatically skips a generation' explanation and the descriptive frame of reference. Those process narratives also functioned to reduce interpretive contingencies by disregarding contradictions and confounding information.

After the teacher told B21 and G21 to help B22 rewrite his answer to the task prompt question, B21 walked back and forth while recalling and reconstructing the earlier simulation as he dictated the answer to B22, who was writing (Transcript Extract 3.7). They did not use the computer. B21 recalled the previous work with the computer simulation:

... when we started our experiment ... the parents had different looking ears. (part of line B645, Transcript Extract 3.7)

... in F1, the children of those parents ... all had the same pointy ears. (part of line B652, Transcript Extract 3.7)

Transcript Extract 3.7: Recalling the Computer Simulation

[Bold text indicates utterances expressing recalled process narratives.]

B645. B21: Then . okay . so . just say that when we started our experiment we bo the the parents had different looking ears. Right?
B646. B22: Hold on hold on.
B647. B21: The parents have different ears ... but then
B648. B22: Hold on hold on ...
B649. B21: Are you done with that part yet? ...
B650. B21: Alright
B651. B22: Yeah. Got it.
B652. B21: Now, in F1 the children of those parents .. the F1 they all had the same pointy ears.
B653. B22: (speaking as he writes) the . children
B654. B21: F1 had the same pointy ears.
B655. B22: (speaking as he writes) the . same
B656. B21: and then when we breeded the next two
B657. B22: Hold on hold on.
B658. B21: **with pointy ears .. their children had mixed ears** ... Say "their children had mixed ears."
B659. B22: (mumbling as he writes. 15 second pause as he writes)
B660. B21: The children had mixed ears
B661. B22: (writing) ?? Is that it?
B662. B21: And then when we took two of those .. their children had pointy ears again ... So it's like a pattern. The pattern is .
B663. B22: (writing) (?)
B664. B21: straight ears pointy ears straight ears pointy ears
B665. B22: Every other one
B666. B21: Straight ears yeah (gesturing for ear shapes) straight ears and floppy mix. **Straight then mixed straight mixed straight mixed. That's how the pattern ends.**

The students often expressed process narratives, which described the simulations that they had run in order to answer questions the teacher asked during verbal testing or when he reviewed the written answers to the task prompt questions. In this case, B21 presents a process narrative linking the following information about earlier activities (lines B645, B652):

just say that when we started our experiment we bo the the parents had different looking ears. Right?

Now, in F1 the children of those parents . . the F1 they all had the same pointy ears.

These combine as a process narrative:

When we started the experiment, we bred a straight-eared parent and a floppy-eared parent, which resulted in an F1 generation in which all the rabbits had straight ears.

B21 then adds another descriptive comment:

then when we breeded the next two with pointy ears their children had mixed ears. (lines B656, B658)

In the context of the previous task activities, this forms another process narrative:

Following the first mating, we bred two of the straight-eared F1 rabbits, producing offspring, which included individuals with straight ears and individuals with floppy ears.

B21 continues to recall the previous work at the computer by expressing process narratives that emphasize the descriptive frame of reference:

And then when we took two of those their children had pointy ears again. (line B662)

The pattern is straight then mixed straight mixed straight mixed. That's how the pattern ends (lines B664, B666)

These comments link with the information the students' encountered during the previous activities as a longer process narrative:

We bred two of the F2 rabbits, resulting in a generation of straight-eared offspring. We continued breeding rabbits in this way until we had produced six generations of rabbits. The screen images showed a pattern of ear shapes across generations. The pattern was a straight generation, a mixed generation, a straight generation, a mixed generation, a straight generation, and a mixed generation. The pattern did not change.

The students' process narratives accurately describe what they had observed on the computer screen 36 minutes earlier – with the exception that

B21 had produced five, rather than six, generations of rabbits, which followed the pattern he describes.

Figure 3.4 compares B21's utterances immediately after running the computer simulation and his utterances when dictating a revision of the written answer to B22 later. Neither B21 nor B22 reevaluates their earlier inference, which was based on the descriptive frame of reference. Instead, they treat the teacher's rejection of their written answer as a prompt to express a more detailed version of 'it just automatically skips a generation'. This is an example of the interlocking of the concurrently developed interpretive frame of reference and the inferences supported by that frame of reference.

Figure 3.4: Comparison of Recalled Process Narratives
[Bold indicates process narratives that correlate across columns]

Just After Using the Computer Simulation	**When Revising the Written Explanation** (34 Minutes Later)
B452. B21: So **we started off with sss floppy and straight--ended up with straight.**	B645. B21: Then . okay . so . just say that **when we started our experiment we bo the the parents had different looking ears.** Right? B647. B21: The parents have different ears . . . but then B652. B21: Now, **in F1 the children of those parents . . the F1 they all had the same pointy ears.**
And **then we took two of those, mated them, and then it came out straight and floppy.**	B656. B21: and **then when we breeded the next two** B658. B21: **with pointy ears . . their children had mixed ears.** . . Say "their children had mixed ears."
We took two of those (moves right hand up and down) **opposite ears** B453. B22: **They came out** B454. B21: **came out /straight./**	B662. B21: **And then when we took two of those . . their children had pointy ears again**

The previous interpretation activities of the students that led to B21's subsequent extemporaneous description of the simulation without using the computer included:

- Producing, observing, and interpreting the screen images that constituted five generations of rabbits;
- Discussing their respective interpretations of the screen images in the context of the task prompt's questions and vocabulary;
- Discussing and writing answers to the task prompt questions while retrospectively recalling their activities using the simulation software to produce certain screen images;
- Verbally recalling and reconstructing the screen images and interpretations of them.

Each of these activities involved the students expressing progressively more coherent process narratives to link information. The later process narratives coalesce descriptive interpretations of the screen images (e.g., generations of offspring, cognizance of ear shapes within those generations), emphasis of certain aspects of the screen images developed through talk and pointing, genetics vocabulary presented by the task prompt or the screen (e.g., *F1, generation*), and complete or partial process narratives the students had expressed earlier. The ultimate process narratives reduce the contingencies of recalling and coordinating such interpretation activities. In all of them, the terms 'children', 'generation' and 'F1' index and link specific configurations of images on the screen: i.e., the rows and columns of rabbits, and the vertical array of boxes demarcating succeeding generations.

The ways that the students develop, recall, and apply the process narratives show that the indexicality of such linguistic terms is developed concurrently with the process narratives – i.e., indexicality is a function of the activities related to linking information as process narratives. In that context, the students' reiterate the process narratives developed during their earlier use and discussion of the computer simulation – incorporating both the descriptive frame of reference and the linkage of particular aspects of the screen images.

Analyzing the creation of process narratives shows how understandings develop from interpretation activities that intertwine environmental information resources with individual and social aspects of cognition. The production of understandings does not result from individuals simply applying formal logic or considering rhetorical fallacies. Rather, it involves the production and reproduction of particular process narratives that result from spontaneous inferences related to managing interpretive contingencies.

Revising Understandings: The Difficulties of Modifying Process Narratives

As they attempted to correct their mistake, the students further demonstrated how process narratives incorporate recall of interpretation activities, frames of reference, and particular information resources. As a consequence, changing the mistaken understanding was not a matter of simply abandoning process narratives and replacing them with different ones. The students' rewritten answer did not satisfy the teacher. In response, the students insisted that their answer was based on the simulation. They then used the computer simulation to demonstrate their findings to the teacher (Transcript Extracts 3.8–3.10). However, the pattern of alternating homogeneous and heterogeneous generations did not reappear. Analysis of the video data provides an explanation for the discrepancy. After B21's earlier use of the simulation to produce the 'automatically skips' sequence of generations, he had learned how to use the software to expand the generation boxes when he did not immediately see rabbits with both types of ears. Subsequently, when he tried to demonstrate the 'skips' model to the teacher, he expanded the generation boxes to reveal all of the rabbits in each generation. Thus, there were no hidden rows containing unnoticed floppy-eared rabbits as there had been in the earlier interpretation activities when the students reinforced the 'automatically skips' explanation.

The students' process of reinterpreting this unexpected screen information and dealing with the cascade of interpretive contingencies that it triggers begins when they observe that the visual information displayed on the screen presents a sequence of four generations (F2.1-F5.1), each containing both floppy-eared and straight-eared rabbits (Transcript Extract 3.8, lines B703, B732-B737, B749, B754,; also Figure 3.5, columns 1, 2, discussed below). B21's response to the images shows that reorganizing interpretations of the screen information is more complicated than just substituting new information for old information. The failure of the new simulation to show homogeneous and heterogeneous sets of offspring alternating every other generation does not lead B21 to abandon the 'automatically skips a generation' process narratives. This is due to the interrelationship of the previously developed process narratives, interpretive frames of reference, and interpretation activities.

Transcript Extract 3.8: Demonstrating the 'Skips' Model to the Teacher

[Bold font indicates utterances in which the students attempt to reconstruct the 'automatically skips a generation' process narrative by explaining the new visual information. Grey shading indicates the production of new generations of offspring.]

B672. B21: (using the software, expecting to demonstrate skipping) **Couple 1** /(???)/
B673. T1: /(?)/ 1
B674. B21: **Couple 2**
B675. T1: (Calls out B22's first name), you're gonna show me this. Ri/ght?/
B676. B21: /Get/ over here (B22's first name)... **Okay. Now we take . the female**
B677. T1: Mm hmm
B678. B21: **from couple 1**
B679. T1: Mm hmm
B680. B21: Put it in the bank.
B681. T1: Mm hmm
B682. B21: **and the male from couple 2**
B683. T1: Mm hmm
B684. B21: **We run 'em and they're the same** (F1.1 generation of offspring rabbits appears on screen).
B685. T1: As what?
B686. B21: The same as (mistakenly points at the floppy-eared male parent in the top row) the male.
B687. B21: Look. (Pointing at the floppy-eared male parent)
B688. T1: As the male?
B689. G21: **As the female.**
B690. B22: **As the female.**
B691. B21: **As the female.**
B692. T1: Does the (??) follow the parent wherever the female is?
B693. B21: No.
B694. G21: No.
B695. B22: Not always.
B696. B21: **Now watch.**
B697. B22: Oooh.
B698. G21: Just just just just
B699. B21: **We'll take we'll take the male . . and the female (moves rabbits into the mating box).**

Transcript Extract 3.8 (continued)

B700. T1: Uh huh.
B701. B21: **And notice their ears are the same.**
B702. T1: Uh huh.
B703. B21: **We run' em. (mouse clicks the run icon) Now they're going to be different.** (pointing at the F2.1 generation added to the screen image) See.
B704. B22: /See/
B705. B21: /(pointing at the new generation) They have/
B706. T1: Uh huh. Then what?
B707. B21: **And now we kept going.**
B708. T1: Okay so if I take the
B709. B21: You take a /male/
B710. B22: /Floppy ear/ female
B711. B21: /No, it's a male./
B712. T1: /So I took two/ floppy ears?
B713. B21: You take two floppy ears then th
B714. B22: They'll (??)
B715. B21: The are no two the same. We can't run with these can we?
B716. B22: We can't run two. Yeah. You can't do that.
B717. B21: But if we take two
B718. B22: There's no lesbian ah running here.
B719. B21: Yeah.
B720. G21: (laughs)
B721. B21: **(Breeding another generation) So we take the opposite . . .**
B722. Male student from another group: (To B22 about another course assignment) Dude, the plane's all messed up.
B723. B21: **and we run'em . . /???/** (F3.1 generation is added to the screen image)
B724. B22: /(Talking to line B720 student about another assignment) I know . ./ I still got full credit/ for it. So who cares. It's not messed up only the uh only /the dimensions are./
B725. B21: **/(using mouse pointer to point to rabbits in new generation box, which reveals only one of 3 rows of rabbits completely) They're all floppy./ [This is a mistake. Close inspection of one of the partially hidden rabbits shows it has straight ears.]**

Transcript Extract 3.8 (continued)

B726. T1: Is that right?

[Four lines omitted, in which B22 and T1 talk off topic to students from other groups. During lines B727 and B728, B21 uses the computer mouse to close the F3.1 generation window, which results in the screen showing only the F1.1 and F2.1 generations of offspring]

B731. G21: /What's this? Look, (pointing at F2.1 rabbits) floppy/ pointy

B732. B21: See they're /mixed./

B733. T1: /(To a student outside of the group) Put it/ in with your folder (T1 now returns his attention to the group) Huh?

B734. B21: See /how they're mixed./

B735. G21: /They're mixed/ floppy and pointy

B736. T1: Oh well they're still mixed.

B737. B21: /Yeah./

B738. T1: /So you/ took some and and they're still mixed

B739. B21: **See (using the cursor to point to the generations) they're mixed straight mixed now we'll take /this/**

B740. T1: /(Using a pen to point at the generations represented on the screen) There's/ mixed . all /straight/

B741. B21: **/Mixed/ straight mixed.**

B742. T1: Right okay.

B743. G21: Str . mixed /straight/

B744. T1: /(Pointing at generations of rabbits with pen) Well/ you've mixed two. Okay now they're they're straight. Now they're they're mixed. And th-this is oh. But that's the one . (leans closer to the screen) that's the old one. This one here right? (5 second pause as T1 or B21 reopens the F3.1 generation box, and then expands it to reveal all of the rabbits, closing the F1.1 and F2.1 boxes) Okay /so they're/

B745. B21: /They're all floppy./ They're all mixed.

B746. T1: Oh. (6 second pause as B21 moves a straight-eared male to the mating box)

B747. B21: (As B21 moves the mouse pointer over a floppy-eared female) Then . .

B748. T1: You're gonna mix 'em? (As B21 moves the floppy-eared rabbit to the mating box) Okay. Then what should I get? (F4.1 generation appears with both straight and floppy-eared rabbits)

Transcript Extract 3.8 (continued)

B749. B21: You should get . .
B750. B22: (???)
B751. B21: But what if we take two of the same though?
B752. T1: Okay. (8 second pause while B21 mates two straight-eared rabbits and the software produces F5.1 generation having both straight and floppy-eared rabbits
B753. B22: Then /they come out mixed./
B754. B21: /They're mixed/ . (B21 moves mouse pointer to a floppy-eared rabbit) right here.
B755. T1: (???)
B756. B22: Once the genes get started they won't stop.
B757. B21: Just keep going. They're still inside.

B21's perseverance in supporting the 'automatically skips' explanation, despite the evidence refuting it, reflects the earlier interpretation activities, which were embedded in the incorrect process narratives. For example, during their earlier work leading to the 'automatically skips' process narratives, the students emphasized the boxes of rows containing offspring. After the teacher had rejected the 'automatically skips' explanation, B21 persisted in this emphasis. During his demonstration of the simulation for the teacher, B21 did not emphasize the parents' ear shapes along with those of their offspring as components of the pattern of traits that appeared across generations. Even when he pointed out the different ear shapes of the parents that he would select to produce the F2.1 generation, he emphasized the continuing sequence of heterogeneous offspring generations:

> We'll take we'll take the male and the female (moves rabbits into the mating box). And notice their ears are the same. We run 'em. (mouse clicks the run icon) Now they're going to be different (pointing at the F2.1 generation added to the screen image). (From Transcript Extract 3.8, lines B699, B701, B703)

He treated the choice of parents with particular ear shapes as a way to affect the ear shapes of offspring generations, but not as information to be included in the explanatory process narratives.

After the heterogeneous F4.1 generation again disproved the process narratives stating that floppy ears skip every other generation, B21 again briefly considered parents' ear shapes. He said, 'But what if we take two of the same though?' (Transcript Extract 3.8, line B751), and mated two straight-eared parents. However, when the result was another heterogeneous generation, B21 and B22 just described it, reemphasizing the descriptive interpretive frame of reference:

B753. B22: Then /they come out mixed./
B754. B21: /They're mixed/ . (B21 moves mouse pointer to a floppy-eared rabbit) right here.

B21's description of the confounding results of the new computer simulation shows that he does not adjust his explanation of the visual information to include both the pattern of parent ear shapes and the pattern of offspring ear shapes. Instead he continues searching for a pattern of repetition by counting the number of homogeneous offspring generations between the offspring generations containing heterogeneous offspring (Transcript Extract 3.9, lines B769-B777, B795).

Transcript Extract 3.9

B758. T1: Th – They – after the after the first generation they keep they keep mixed?
B759. B21: Yeah.
B760. T1: They keep staying mixed huh?
B761. B21: Yeah . . . (using the computer) 'cause look
B762. B22: This time they do .
B763. B21: (?) . . and (4 second pause while B21 selects parents to breed another generation of rabbits) run these (4 second pause as software produces F6.1 generation)
B764. B22: (???)
B765. T1: They're all mixed?
B766. B21: Nope (10 second pause as B21 uses the mouse to expand the F6.1 box to show all rabbits)
B767. ?: We're seeing like a (???)
B768. T1: (6 second pause as B21 breeds another generation) There (or 'they're' or 'their') – (A student from another group calls T1's name, but T1 focuses on the screen and does not respond.)
B769. B21: (?) not – /what'd they do?/
B770. T1: /Next./
B771. B21: Jump back and forth? They're not /after/
B772. T1: /Next/
B773. B21: every
B774. G21: Every other gen/eration./
B775. B21: /Wait wait wait/. (breeding another generation) No no no. After . how many? We went down to five right?

Transcript Extract 3.9 (continued)

B776. T1: Six.
B777. B21: Went down /to six/
B778. T1: /You're in/ your sixth genera/tion./
B779. B21: /Okay/ hold on. Wait wait wait wait. (breeds another generation) This . . . (???)
[1 line omitted featuring a student outside of group asking T1 about lab rats' names]
B781. B21: /(As the F7.1 generation of rabbits appears) They're mixed. Okay if we/
B782. G21: The same kind.
[2 lines omitted featuring a student from another group and T1 talking about lab rats' names]
B785. B21: Wait wait wait.
B786. G21: (referring to B21's use of the software to breed another generation) /Put the same kind in/
[5 lines omitted featuring students outside of group talking with T1 about lab rats' names]
B792. B21: No. I think /(??)/
[2 lines omitted featuring students outside of group talking about lab rats' names]
B795. B21: (continuing to breed rabbits) After every six generations. (As F8.1 generation appears) That's gonna be mixed... Okay wait. (Moving mouse pointer over the software interface) Is there some way we can?
B796. T1: (B21 reaches for mouse. To B21) Yeah you can just close it (uses mouse to close windows for all but the F8.1 generation).
B797. B21: Down tuh . .
B798. T1: Okay now what?
B799. B21: (As B21 uses the mouse to select a floppy-eared male rabbit as a parent of the next generation) Down to here.
B800. T1: Uh huh.
B801. B21: (??) (Breeds F9.1 generation) . . . .
B802. T1: What do you get when you mix again huh?
B803. B21: Can I open it? [(?'See mixed' or 'Same mix'?)] (bell rings to end the class) Is it every six generations /that they/
B804. T1: /I don't/ know. I don't know . . (B21 uses mouse to enlarge the last generation window to show all of the rabbits) I don't know.
B805. B21: Yeah you do, you're just not telling. (Selects F9.1 straight-eared rabbit as parent for next generation)

Transcript Extract 3.9 (continued)

B806. T1: (In a louder voice) I don't know.
B807. B22: (Joking) Yes you do. You're just not telling . because you're mean and nasty.
B808. B21: Watch (using the computer to create another generation of rabbits) . It's gonna be mixed 'cause this is number 10 (referring to the F10.1 generation appearing on the screen).

Another example of the endurance of interrelated components of understandings (process narratives, interpretive frame of reference, and discourse framework) occurred when the confounding evidence prompted B22 and B21 to mention briefly and vaguely the role of genes inside the rabbits. After the computer simulation displayed two generations that matched the 'skips a generation' pattern the students had noted earlier (Figure 3.5, Column 1), the ensuing generations diverged from that pattern. Responding to the appearance of three consecutive heterogeneous generations (F2.1-F5.1), B22 commented, 'Once the genes get started they won't stop' (Figure 3.5, Column 2, line B756). B21 then said, 'Just keep going. They're still inside.' (Figure 3.5, Column 2, line B757). B21's comment, 'They're still inside', echoed G21's earlier visual and linguistic process narrative about the rabbits 'carrying' genes ('It's inside you know like . look that one . and none of them got that gene. But each of them has has it in them,' Transcript Extract 2.4, lines B55, B57, discussed in Chapter Two).

Figure 3.5: Noticing Confounding Visual Information

	1	2
Screen Images	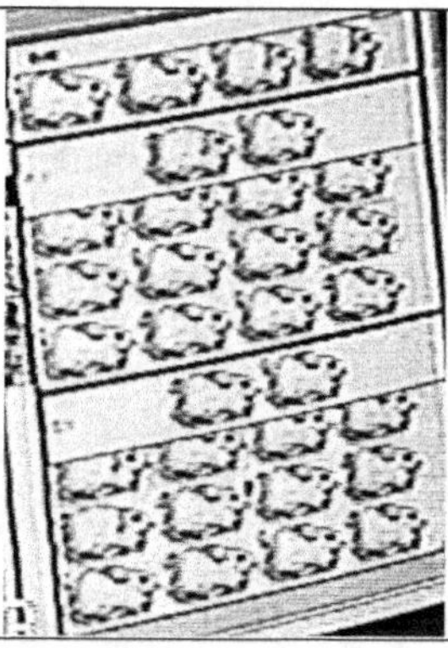	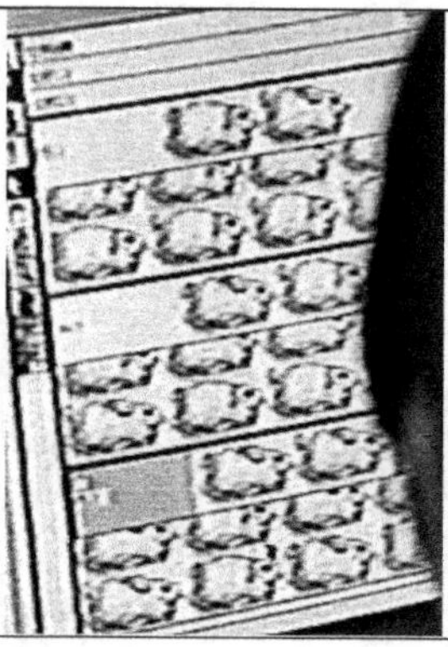
Generation and Trait Information Displayed	Parents: Mixed F1: Straight Ears F2: Mixed	F3-F5: All mixed
Students' Interpretations of the Information	B740. B21: See they're mixed straight mixed (Transcript Extract 3.8)	B756. B22: Once the genes get started they won't stop. B757. B21: Just keep going. They're still inside. (Transcript Extract 3.9)

Although B22 and B21 referred to genes inside the rabbits, they put that information in the service of the describing new visual information presented by the simulation. B22's comment that the genes 'won't stop' and B21's comment, 'just keep going' (Figure 3.5, column 2), describe the operation of the computer simulation that resulted in a sequence of consecutive generations of offspring containing both floppy-eared and straight-eared rabbits. B21's utterance, 'they're still inside' (Figure 3.5, column 2), could have led the students toward inferences about dominant and recessive genes. However, making such inferences would involve dealing with the same interpretive contingencies that short-circuited G21's earlier attempts at creating inferential process narratives – particularly the absence of additional information about dominant and recessive genes. In contrast, the 'automatically skips' process narratives and descriptive interpretive frame of reference provided them with an alternative that did not present those contingencies. They had created a discourse framework for interpreting and discussing the screen images, which helped them to establish coherence by excluding certain information from consideration. The students had developed an interpretation of 'pattern' that selectively attributed relevance to some screen images and not others.

Reconfiguring Belief: The Endurance of Process Narratives and Frames of Reference

The students' attempts to reconstruct coherence when interpreting the outcome of the simulation are constrained by the descriptive frame of reference (i.e., their attention to certain information at the expense of other information), and the process narratives that they had developed through their earlier activities. However, in the context of the descriptive frame of reference, the new information on the screen is not coherent with the old process narratives. As the students acknowledge the unexpected results of the simulation, B21 displays a slow reconfiguring of process narratives and understandings. He attempts to revise them rather than reject them. Figure 3.6 displays the sequence of generations and B21's comments as he encounters evidence that contradicts the 'skips' model.

He continues to apply the 'automatically skips' process narratives and the descriptive frame of reference. He merely adjusts the expression of coherence among the visual information from the automatic appearance of homogeneous offspring in every other generation to the automatic appearance of homogeneous offspring after a different fixed number of generations (Transcript Extract 3.9, lines B775, B777, B795, B803).

Figure 3.6: Coping with Confounding Information (From Transcript Extracts 3.8, 3.9, 3.10)

A.	B.	C.	D.	E.
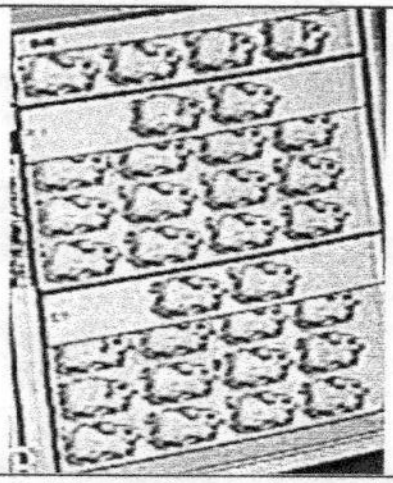	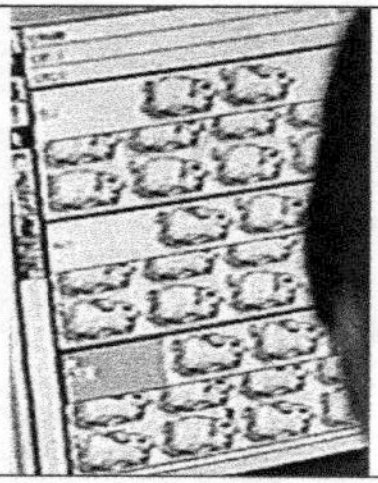	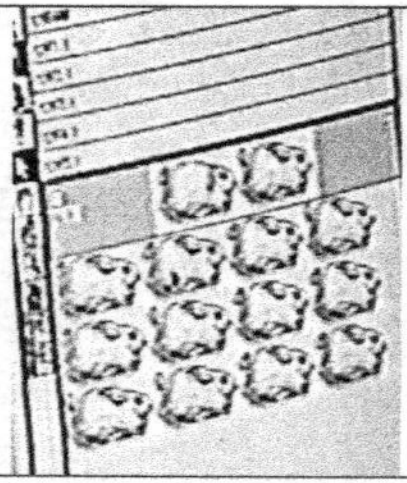	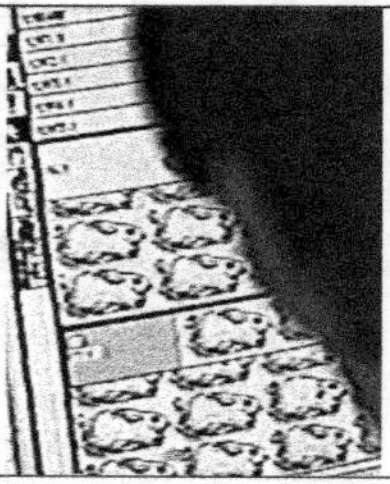	
F1.1-F2.1: Straight, mixed	**F3.1-F5.1: All mixed**	**F6.1: Straight**	**F6.1-F7.1: F7.1 Mixed**	**F8.1-F9.1: Mixed**
B21: See they're mixed straight mixed (line B739)	B22: Once the genes get started they won't stop. (line B756)	B21: Went down to six (line B777)	B21: They're mixed [F7.1] (line B781)	B21: Is it every six generations? (line B803)

F.	G.	H.	I.	J.
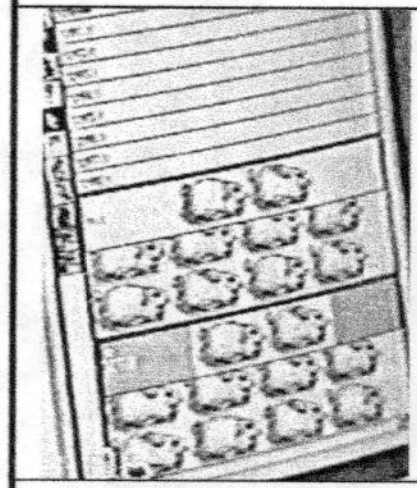	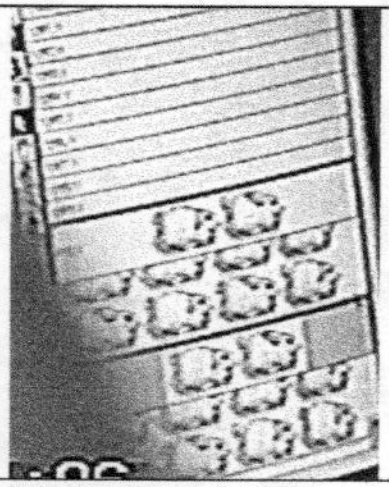	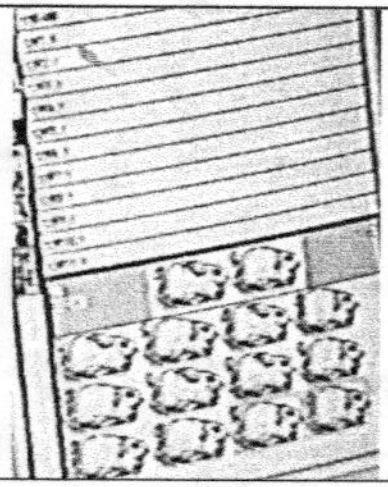	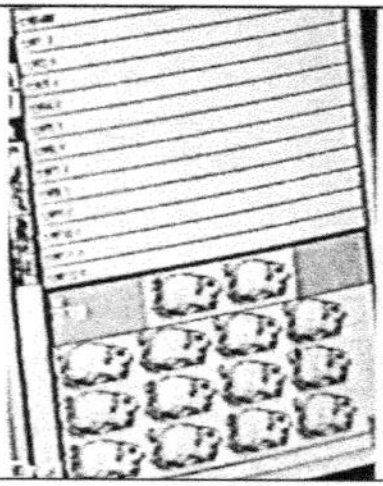	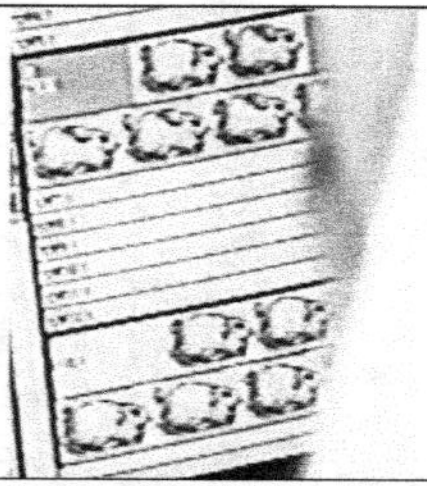
F9.1-F10.1: Mixed	**F10.1-F11.1: Mixed**	**F12.1: Mixed**	**F13.1: Floppy**	**F6.1: Straight/F13.1: Floppy**
B21: It's mixed (line B814)	B21: It's gonna be mixed again. This is gonna be eleven (line B820)	T1: maybe it was the next one (line B828)	B21: They're the same. Was it every sixth--every sixth to seventh generation that are the same, but are they gonna alternate? (line B842)	B21: so they alternate (line B847)

B21's effort to revise rather than abandon the 'skips' explanation provides another example of the endurance of process narratives and related frames of reference. Despite the visual evidence that the original findings are not replicated, he does not consider other explanations, such as inferences about dominant and recessive genes. The previously constructed process narratives, interpretive frame of reference, discourse framework, and the activities that constructed them combine to constitute a belief that ear shape is an automatic result of producing a particular number of generations. That belief affects B21's interpretation of the differences between the new visual information and the information that the students had encountered earlier. G21 contributes to this enduring belief in the 'automatically skips' process narratives by participating in the counting of offspring generations ('The sixth', Transcript Extract 3.10, line B843).

Transcript Extract 3.10

B842. B21: They're the same. (produces **F13.1** generation of floppy-eared rabbits) Was it every sixth every sixth to every seventh generation that are the same, but are they /gonna alternate/ (?)
B843. G21: /The sixth/
B844. T1: Okay, now how is this compared to the one – the sixth one was the one that was the same right /before (?)/
B845. B21: /(opening the screen window for the F6.1 generation: Floppy-eared and straight-eared parents; straight-eared offspring showing in top row – partial window) Yeah./ . . They're different.
B846. T1: (uses the mouse pointer to point at the F6.1 floppy-eared and straight-eared parents) But they were different. (uses the mouse pointer to point at the F13.1 floppy-eared parents) These are the same .
B847. B21: (points to the floppy-eared and straight-eared F6 parents) These are the same. So they alternate.
B848. T1: (uses the mouse pointer to point at the F13.1 floppy-eared parents) But see these are the same. . These
B849. B21: Oh.
B850. T1: are different (uses the mouse pointer to point at the F6.1 floppy-eared and straight-eared parents).
B851. B21: Oh! . Hold on. How do I open it back up? . . (??).

B21 stipulates that a set of homogeneous offspring automatically appear every sixth or seventh generation (Figure 3.6, I). However, he adds a concern about noting whether those homogeneous generations would alternate between floppy and straight ears: 'Was it every sixth – every sixth to seventh generation that are the same, but are they gonna alternate?' (Transcript Extract 3.10, line B842) and 'so they alternate' (B847). B21 suggests the process narrative:

> *Rather than a sequence of generations in which every other generation shows homogeneous or heterogeneous ear shapes, six out of every seven generations show heterogeneous ears and every sixth generation alternates between homogeneous floppy or straight-eared rabbits.*

B21 modifies the earlier 'automatically skips a generation' process narrative to include the alternating of homogeneous straight-eared offspring and floppy-eared offspring in every sixth or seventh generation. He holds on to the descriptive interpretive frame of reference emphasizing a pattern of rows of offspring across generations. He continues to produce generations of offspring until a homogeneous generation appears – either floppy-eared or straight-eared. He counts the number of heterogeneous generations between homogeneous generations. Then, he adjusts the meaning of 'skip' and 'alternate' so that the appearance, disappearance, and reappearance of traits across generations remained automatic and the pattern continued to involve 'skipping' a particular number of generations between sets of homogeneous offspring.

Shifting the Interpretive Frame of Reference: A Disruptive Intervention

This case displays the strength of process narratives as components of understandings. Analysis of B21's attempt to integrate new, contradictory information into the 'automatically skips a generation' explanation of trait inheritance shows how process narratives intertwine with the interpretation activities that contributed to them. The teacher intervenes in B21's attempts to redefine the pattern of screen images and retain the 'automatically skips' aspect of the process narrative. He recognizes a particular component of B21's interpretation of the simulation that has contributed to a problematic concept of the pattern of traits across generations – B21 and the other students had developed selective attention only to the pattern of offspring generations, excluding the images of the parents of each generation. The teacher expresses comments and questions that draw attention to aspects of the screen images that the students had eliminated from the interpretive frame of reference embedded in the 'automatically skips a generation' process narratives.

When B21 described the screen images, his inattention to the sequence of parent boxes and their relationship to the pattern of offspring across generations was noticed by the teacher. B21's anomalous choice of two floppy-eared parents for the F13 generation (Figure 3.6, Image I, line B842) provided an opportunity for the teacher to emphasize that the parents' boxes contain information relevant to the answer he wants (Transcript Extract 3.10, lines B846, B848, B850). This revisits information that the students had previously deemphasized.

The teacher uses the mouse pointer to note the difference between the heterogeneous parents of the F6 offspring and the homogeneous floppy-eared parents of the F13 offspring:

> (Pointing at the F6.1 parents) But they were different. (Pointing at the F13 parents) These are the same. (Transcript Extract 3.10, line B846)

When B21 responds by merely describing the difference ('So they alternate', Transcript Extract 3.10, line B847), the teacher again uses the mouse pointer to indicate that both of the F13 parents have floppy ears ('But see these are the same', Transcript Extract 3.10, line B848), while the F6 parents are heterogeneous, a floppy-eared male and a straight-eared female ('These are different', line B850). B21 acknowledges that information by saying 'oh' after the teacher points to each set of parents (Transcript Extract 3.10, lines B848-B851):

B848. T1: (uses the mouse pointer to point at the F13.1 floppy-eared parents) But see these are the same. . These
B849. B21: Oh.
B850. T1: are different (uses the mouse pointer to point at the F6.1 floppy-eared and straight-eared parents).
B851. B21: Oh! .

Prior to this, B21 had been focusing on the offspring boxes. His modifications to the initial 'automatically skips' process narratives had sustained the frame of reference based on describing the offspring generations. However, when the teacher repeats the point that the parents of the F6 and F13 generations respectively differ in ear shapes (Transcript Extract 3.10, lines B848, B850), he draws B21's attention to the parents' boxes on the screen. This is an example of explaining by expanding the set of information to which the students attend. In this way, the teacher emphasizes that the visual information regarding the difference between the two sets of parents is important in regard to satisfactorily answering the task prompt question and learning about the topic. B21 considers how to coherently combine the new and old information by continuing to examine the images on the screen. In order to deal with the new information, he must again determine which aspects of the screen images are relevant to new process narratives.

B21's attempt to adapt rather than replace the 'automatically skips' process narrative is an example of the endurance of understandings that results from the interrelationship of interpretation activities, frames of reference, and process narratives.[23] Detailed analysis of the creation of process narratives uncovers the components of interpretation activities that are embedded in understandings. Examining the complex and concurrent linking of interpretation activities, information resources, and process narratives reveals why formal logic does not explain understandings or their endurance in the face of confounding information. Due to the cognitive intertwining of process narratives with interpretation activities, recalling a particular process narrative also triggers recall of relevant frames of reference, particular information resources, and related process narratives – all of which combine to constitute an understanding or a belief.

4 Process Narratives and Models of Cognition

Chapter Four examines information constraints in the production of understandings and beliefs. It considers how the process narrative approach relates to and expands on Johnson-Laird's mental models, Rumelhart and Norman's typology of schema formation in learning, Schank and Abelson's story approach to memory, D'Andrade's discussion of contentful sense of contingency in reasoning, as well as the categories of mental operations, functional fixedness and oracular reasoning. Unlike approaches to memory and understanding that emphasize mental operations, the process narrative approach accounts for both the material and mental components of understandings.

Going Beyond Categories of Mental Operations

Research that has considered the cognition related to explanations and understandings in terms of mental models or cognitive schemata has focused on operations of reasoning within the mind (Bauer and Johnson-Laird, 1993; Johnson-Laird, 2006, 2010; Rumelhart and Norman, 1978, 1981).[24] In contrast, the process narrative approach emphasizes a persistent linkage of recalled information, interpretation activities, resources in settings, frames of reference, and culturally influenced patterns of expression. In that regard, the data analysis presented here shows how the creation and expansion of mental models or schemata take place.

Rumelhart and Norman (1978) have approached such complexities of memory and learning by describing three categories of cognition (accretion, tuning, and restructuring) that correlate with the degree to which new information differs from an individual's existing understanding. Those categories emphasize mental operations, which contribute to cognitive schemata. That approach can lead to treating recallable concepts as complete sets of information stored in memory. However, it also opens the door to a model of understanding based on the endurance of an initial outline as a functional component of memory or understanding.

The clinical and classroom data presented here show that accretion, tuning, and restructuring are actually aspects of the concurrent creation of process narratives and interpretive frames of reference. Each of those categories occurs during all of the interpretation activities of developing the recallable process narratives that function as understandings. The ease or difficulty of producing understandings does not correlate respectively with the separate types of mental operations categorized as accretion, tuning, or restructuring. Rather, those categories reflect the different types and quantities of interpretive contingencies that individuals encounter when they attempt to link pieces of information as process narratives.

For example, during the patients' and students' interpretation activities, *accretion* resembles the initial interpretation activity, which emphasizes developing a communication format in order to begin producing a process narrative – i.e., expressing process narratives that describe images and explanations, and then attempting to incorporate new information as additional process narratives. *Tuning* correlates with developing frames of reference that contribute to culling linguistic terms, information, or candidate process narratives. *Restructuring* correlates with responses to interpretive contingencies (e.g., restrictions on information or encountering new information), which challenge the coherence of previously developed process narratives or the organization of available information as process narratives.[25]

Analysis of the creation and application of process narratives emphasizes that the interpreting, perceiving, and organizing of perceptions affect each other. Organizing information as process narratives coalesces and congeals perceptions and interpretations into manageable units. However, process narratives are not mental models or cognitive schemata – although they may serve as the skeletons or components of the larger groupings of recalled information that have been categorized as mental models or schemata.

Analysis of process narratives, grey boxes, and discourse frameworks emphasizes the details of interpretation activities. Such emphasis is important, because it is during the process of interpreting information that people contend with social, cultural, and environmental resources and constraints to develop the understandings, which underlay the decisions and actions that create or reproduce forms of social organization.

Contingencies and Content

The data show that process narratives function by concisely linking information. Creating process narratives requires the recognition of a few pieces of information that can be coherently linked. For example, in the previously discussed learning activities, the computer simulation and task prompt did not present linguistic or pictorial information concerning the functioning of genes, which the students could use to link dominant and recessive genes to the screen images showing the appearance, disappearance, and reappearance of floppy-eared rabbits across generations. The interpretive contingencies presented by this absence of information increased the difficulty of forming coherent explanatory process narratives, and led to the students' emphasis on describing the way the screen simulation software organized images as a sequence of generations, rather than inferring the operation of genes, which the screen did not display. That emphasis on description supported the 'automatically skips' explanation.

The descriptive interpretive frame of reference and related 'automatically skips' process narratives that reduce such interpretive contingencies function similarly to the *contentful sense of contingency* that D'Andrade (1989) finds useful for solving formal logic problems (cf. Bauer and Johnson-Laird, 1993; Johnson-Laird, 2006). The contentful context is the students' immediate experience of the collective cognition related to interpreting the visual information – even when the relevant content is a socially shared interpretation based on a mistake, as in the case of the 'automatically skips' process narratives. In that regard, the students' interpretation activities do not simply draw on prior experience. Rather, they present an example of the basic components of the production and reproduction of understanding and belief through interpretation activities. The 'automatically skips' process narratives simplify interpreting and linking the information presented by the screen and the task prompt by reducing the interpretive contingencies of considering visual and linguistic information while simultaneously making inferences about the internal biological processes that the simulation does not display.

The radiology consultation data present a different approach to providing context that is useful for explaining new information to patients. The medical images and the nurse's explanations are organized in a way that reduces each patient's interpretive contingencies. The interaction at the radiology consultations is oriented toward filling information gaps. The images prompt the patient's questions and comments, and the nurse answers and elaborates on them until the patient indicates that missing medical information has been supplied.

Such information – providing technical detail that can function as a link between more general information – was missing from the classroom genetics explanations. During the UFE radiology consultations, the organization of the visual and verbal information presented by the images and accompanying discussion removed some of the interpretive contingencies that the biology students had faced – and which patients also face in many conventional clinical consultations. The nurse's verbal explanations provided cues to the patient that helped to resolve ambiguities related to multiple meanings or multiple frames of reference suggested by the images. The images did the same for ambiguities or confusion related to interpreting the verbal communication – for both the clinician and the patient. Thus, the patient's interpretive contingencies were reduced by the way that the visual information presented on the computer was composed, organized, and discussed.

During the consultations, patients progressively applied the process narratives they had developed as they elicited explanations of images they subsequently encountered. As they received new explanations from the nurse, the patients created additional process narratives. That pattern of communication reduced the interpretive contingencies of seeking or noting absent information. It dealt with such contingencies before they challenged the patient's interpretation activities and creation of process narratives. The post-consultation telephone discussions show that the patients used the interpretation activities of the radiology consultations to organize the new information they encountered there as recallable process narratives (Chapters 1, 8).

In clinical consultations lacking the radiology consultations' discussion of visual information, the analysis of the creation of process narratives presented in this book indicates that, in order to formulate and ask a question to obtain requisite information, a patient contends with various concurrent interpretive contingencies. These would include the cognitive effort of remembering confusing terms, while continuing to interact, continuing to interpret additional information, and dealing with organizational and cultural constraints, such as time limits and authority, expressed through patterns of talk. For example, patients would have to remember each of the unfamiliar medical terms expressed by a clinician (e.g., femoral artery, catheter, uterine artery, and blood vessels), and either ask questions, try to recall relevant information, or anticipate that clarifying information would ensue. This is the type of interpretation activity that has been glossed as *contentless sense of contingency* (cf. D'Andrade, 1989). Such interpretive contingencies can lead to a situation that is familiar to many patients: i.e., not knowing what questions to ask of clinicians during a consultation, thinking of the questions after the consultation has concluded, and not recalling or understanding medical information that were discussed during the consultation.

In contrast, the radiology patients' production of process narratives shows that discussion of visual information during the consultations reduced patients' interpretive contingencies by creating communication patterns that provided missing pieces of information before their absence increased the load on a patient's memory during the ensuing consultation interaction. For example, during the telephone discussion with patient, P1, four days after her radiology consultation, she mentions, in the absence of the images viewed at the consultation, that a particular image contributed to her questioning of the nurse concerning the mobility of the embolizing agent within the body:

> the diagram of the uh parti – the uh particles that are gonna be in my arteries. That was (chuckles) duh huh – that wa – that reminded me yeah I wanted to find out how – how those weren't gonna come back and give me a clot. (Figure 1.1, line 1.3.2)
>
> I don't know. I guess I saw them moving toward their end destination, and then just stayin' there. And then I asked a question you know. So, that's what helped me. (Figure 1.1, lines 2.1.1, 2.1.3).

The opportunity to discuss and gesture toward visual information supported both the patients' questioning of clinicians and the clinicians' answering of patients' questions. The images and the related discussion provided pieces of information that patients linked with previously encountered information as coherent recallable process narratives.

Visual information can function to reduce interpretive contingencies, but may not always do so – as the classroom data have shown. This is an important difference between the radiology consultations and the trait inheritance learning activities. The traditional Mendelian curriculum that shapes genetics assignments intentionally omits key information, i.e., the cellular genetic processes by which genes affect traits. It restricts students' attempts to find information that would complete process narratives. It emphasizes nomenclature and Punnett squares as placeholders, grey boxes, substituting for missing information.

Understandings and Beliefs: Effects of the Production of Process Narratives

Process Narratives and the Reduction of Interpretive Contingencies

In response to the interpretive contingencies related to missing cellular process information the biology students' interpretive interaction had deemphasized or eliminated certain information from consideration. During the development of the 'automatically skips a generation' process narratives and the descriptive frame of reference, reduced the cognitive contingencies of considering visual and linguistic information while simultaneously making inferences about the internal biological processes that the computer simulation did not display. This reduction in the amount of information to consider as relevant supported the creation of process narratives. It simplified the students' interpreting and linking of the information presented by the screen and the task prompt. In that context, the explanation with fewest interpretive contingencies was one based on describing the screen images, while minimizing inferences about unseen causes.

This is why the students eliminated searching for information concerning dominant and recessive genes from the interpretation activities that developed their explanatory process narratives – and why they did not develop process narratives related to an inferential frame of reference. The shift away from G21's inferential interpretive perspective to the descriptive frame of reference and the 'automatically skips a generation' process narratives was not an explicitly stated or preconceived strategy based on minimizing effort. The students' intricate examining and discussing of the screen images showing their willingness to work on the task. However, during interpretation activities, ambiguity increased the contingencies related to linking pieces of information. Consequently, as the students worked to establish coherent linkages among the visual, gestural, textual, and verbal information they encountered, they concurrently developed process narratives and an interpretive frame of reference that emphasized certain aspects of the screen images while neglecting others. The biology students' interpretation activities show how the 'automatically skips a generation' process narratives and the descriptive frame of reference functioned as Occam's Razor – i.e., in the context of the various linguistic terms and images that the students found unclear, ambiguous, or confusing, they eventually emphasized the simplest explanation that seemed to fit the task prompt and minimize interpretive contingencies.

However, when the teacher and a subsequent run of the computer simulation challenged the 'automatically skips a generation' process narratives, changing the process narratives and the descriptive frame of reference would involve revisiting those interpretive complexities and contingencies. B21 avoided this by seeking a way to acknowledge the new information and make it coherent with the results of the previous interpretation activities and the resulting process narratives. He persistently applied the 'automatically skips' process narratives despite encountering both the teacher's negative response and confounding visual evidence after rerunning the computer simulation (Chapter 3). He treated the change in the information presented by the computer simulation and the teacher's emphasis on the relevance of the new information as new interpretive contingencies. However, he contended with them in the context of the previously developed process narratives and descriptive frame of reference. The video of B21 considering counterevidence to the 'automatically skips a generation' explanation presented by the computer simulation provides an example of this (Transcript Extract 3.9):

B771. (partial). B21: They're not /after/
B772. T1: /Next/
B773. B21: every
B774. G21: Every other gen/eration./
B775. B21: /Wait wait wait/. (breeding another generation) No no no. After . how many? We went down to five right?
B776. T1: Six.
B777. B21: Went down /to six/
B778. T1: /You're in/ your sixth genera/tion./
B779. B21: /Okay/ hold on. Wait wait wait wait. (breeds another generation) This ... (???)
[1 line omitted featuring a student outside of group asking T1 about lab rats' names]
B781. B21: /(As the F7.1 generation of rabbits appears) They're mixed. Okay if we/
B795 (partial). B21: (continuing to breed rabbits) After every six generations. (As F8.1 generation appears) That's gonna be mixed.

B21 repeatedly used the computer simulation to create more generations of rabbits, and counted the number of generations between homogeneous generations, looking for a pattern compatible with the 'automatically skips a generation' process narratives and the descriptive frame of reference. He was caught between the disappearing coherence of the earlier process narratives, which resolved the interpretive contingencies the students had encountered, and the incoherence of the new information (the confounding pattern of inheritance in the screen images), which again introduced interpretive contingencies.

The evidence on the computer screen alone did not convince B21 to abandon the theory and develop an alternative interpretive frame of reference. The intrusion of new information from the screen (the appearance of four consecutive heterogeneous generations), the cultural context that gave weight to the teacher's rejection of the 'skips' theory, and the social organization of the classroom that emphasized grading all played a part in moving him away from the 'automatically skips a generation' theory. In the context of all three factors, B21 began to change his explanation of the screen information, but he did not change his descriptive interpretive frame of reference.

Process Narratives and Belief: Explaining Functional Fixedness and Oracular Reasoning

Reducing interpretive contingencies had helped the students to create the 'automatically skips a generation' process narratives. However, once those process narratives had been created and linked as an understanding, B21 displayed the difficulty of revisiting the previously discarded interpretive contingencies – such as attention to the rows of each generation's parents when noting a pattern – in order to change his belief in that understanding. The data show that the endurance of beliefs is a product of the difficulty of revisiting the social and individual interpretation activities, which led to the linking of information as the process narratives that had become expressions of coherence. It is the sublimation of complex interpretive contingencies by the use of process narratives and grey boxes that creates the difficulties in changing understandings or beliefs.

Functional Fixedness in the Production of Process Narratives

The difficulties that the students displayed in modifying frames of reference and process narratives show how closely their understandings of 'pattern' are linked to their interpretations of local resources. B21's enduring emphasis on the 'automatically skips' process narratives that resulted from such interpretation activity parallels the cognitive psychological concept of functional fixedness, in which individuals focus on certain functions and uses of an object or tool with respect to previous experience, the tool's most common function, or the manner in which the object or tool is categorized in regard to the task at hand (Frank and Ramscar, 2003; Glucksberg, 1962; Klein and D'Esposito, 2007: 174–178).[26]

The data show that the 'automatically skips' process narratives are interlocked with the descriptive frame of reference and the students' interpretation activities, which applied it when selecting, discarding, and linking information. The students reinforced a particular approach to forming coherent explanations, i.e.:

- A student noticed and interpreted specific visual information.
- Then, by expressing that interpretation as a process narrative to the other participants, he or she emphasized that both the interpretation (which is

also treated as information) and the frame of reference it conveyed were noteworthy and relevant to the task at hand.

B21's selective awareness of certain aspects of the screen images, which parallels functional fixedness, results from the interpretation activities that contend with and simplify the interpretive contingencies of finding missing information, mentally noting the absence of information needed to link available pieces of information, or developing placeholders for the missing information. The resulting process narratives and descriptive interpretive frame of reference constituted a belief that ear shape is an automatic result of producing a particular number of generations.

One example of the endurance of that belief occurred when B22 and B21 briefly mentioned genes inside the rabbits (Transcript Extract 3.9, lines B756-B757):

B756. B22: Once the genes get started they won't stop.
B757. B21: going. They're still inside.

Their comments about genes inside the rabbits influencing ear shape were prompted by the teacher's requests for the students to account for the pattern of ear shape displayed by the computer simulation, which seemed to differ from the pattern they had described when forming the 'skips each generation' explanation. As B21 attempts to create coherence in the context of the immediate information constraints and the teacher's comments, his explanation echoes G21's earlier visual and linguistic process narrative about the rabbits 'carrying' genes, when she gestured toward specific screen images while saying, 'It's inside you know like . look that one . and none of them got that gene. But each of them has has it in them (Transcript Extract 2.4, lines B55, B57, discussed in Chapter Two).

However, the reintroduction of the previously discarded linguistic information does not immediately induce B21 to abandon the 'skips' model or the descriptive frame of reference (Transcript Extract 3.9, lines B769-B773, B775). His frame of reference, which excludes certain aspects of the screen information from consideration, fixes or reifies the function of the images in regard to his interpretation of them. Consequently, he adjusts the expression of coherence among the visual information from homogeneous offspring automatically appearing in every other generation to homogeneous offspring appearing after every six generations. He continues to use the software to produce generations, while verbally predicting the generation in which the homogeneous offspring will appear by counting the generations displayed on the screen (Transcript Extract 3.9, lines B795, B803, B808). The previously developed process narratives and interpretive frame of reference contributed to a fixed interpretation and use of the screen images, which excluded attention to the ear shapes of each generation's parents when noting a pattern of inheritance.

The students' interpretation activities display the development of functional fixedness. It resulted from the students extending indexicality to non-verbal interpretation activities. The students covered gaps in linguistic information needed to complete process narratives by pointing at the visual information on the screen (Figures 2.6–2.8, 2.10, 2.11, 3.2, Transcript Extract 2.5). This linked the 'automatically skips' process narratives to a particular interpretation of the visual resources, which became the functioning concept of 'pattern' in regard to answering the task prompt question and demonstrating the computer simulation to the teacher. The fixedness of the interpretation of the screen images as the 'automatically skips' process narratives and the mistaken understanding of trait inheritance was not a result of the images produced by the computer simulation, but of the interpretation activities the students applied to them when creating process narratives.

Process Narratives and Oracular Reasoning

Contextual analysis of B21's perseverance in modifying the 'automatically skips' process narratives also provides an explanation of oracular reasoning. Oracular reasoning involves adjusting the logical components of a belief or understanding in response to evidence that undermines the validity or accuracy of those components – rather than abandoning the belief or understanding (cf. Evans-Pritchard, 1937; Mehan, 1990; Polanyi, 1952). The concept is often applied to account for acceptance of beliefs in the face of empirical evidence that contradicts them. However, in contrast to previous discussions of oracular reasoning, analysis of the interpretation activities that led to the 'skips a generation' explanation shows that B21's perseverance in applying the 'skips' explanation does not result directly from a logical postulation. Nor does it result from a resistant power struggle concerning the relevance of evidence or conflicting interpretations of evidence (cf. Mehan, 1990). Rather, it derives from the recalled process narratives and the social or individual interpretation activities that formed them by excluding contradictory or confounding information.

In the examples discussed here, the activities of interpreting and sorting information – not the information itself or the application of a formal logic by the students or patients – provided the framework for linking information in the context of the setting and task. Reconsidered from the context of process narratives as a basis for individual and shared understandings, oracular reasoning is not just a commitment to previously developed ideologies, explanations, or notions of self-interest. Instead, the activity of creating process narratives by accepting and rejecting various information and interpretations of information produces ideology, familiarity, or self-interest (cf. Saferstein, 1994).

Information Constraints in the Production of Belief

The creation of process narratives during interpretation activities explains how functional fixedness and oracular reasoning result from selecting and rejecting information during the application of interpretation activities in order to establish coherence. It explains how frames of reference and the culling of information reciprocally affect each other. Examining the creation of process narratives also shows how organizational constraints and cultural conventions affect participants' attention to certain visual and textual resources.

For instance, two factors that significantly affected the biology students' understandings of the computer simulation were the absence of information and the sorting out of information to form coherent process narratives. The absence of information about cellular genetic processes was a curricular convention of teaching trait inheritance, a component of the professional culture (discussed in Part Four). It presented students with interpretive contingencies that affected the culling of information and the emphasis on the descriptive frame of reference. For example, the students sorted out G21's expression of vague and ambiguous inferences about missing representations of recessive genes and cellular genetic processes. Furthermore, during the students' work with the computer simulation, their reiteration of process narratives not only focused their attention on particular information displayed by the computer screen, but it also focused attention on particular ways to use language and gestures to communicate about that visual information. The students' subsequent emphasis on the 'automatically skips' process narratives was a result of such interpretation activities.

The endurance of beliefs and ideologies is a product of the difficulty of revisiting the social and individual interpretation activities that led to the linking of information as the process narratives and grey boxes, which have become the mental and linguistic expressions of coherence. Both oracular reasoning and functional fixedness are expressions of the endurance of certain process narratives and the discourse framework for establishing coherence indexed by those process narratives. There is a relation between the recall of process narratives and belief (i.e., commitment to an understanding).

Process Narratives and Stories as Components of Understanding and Memory

As discussed briefly in the Introduction, some models of cognition have emphasized the role of stories in order to explain understanding and recall of information (e.g., Eggly, 2002; Pennington and Hastie, 1992; Polanyi, 1985; Schank and Abelson, 1995). Scholars of cognition have applied various abstract categories to explain the mental operations of recalling, reconstructing, and expressing stories (e.g., the *salience*, *availability*, *activation, reconstruction*, *translation*, *suppression*, *conjunction*, *elaboration*, *commentary*, *detail addition*, and *distillation* of memories [Schank and Abelson, 1995: 31–33, 71–72]). Such categorical distinctions treat memory and understanding in terms of detailed records of events that may be abridged during their expression.

The mental operations indexed by the abstract categories actually involve the recall of both process narratives and the interpretation activities that initially contributed to them. Rather than focusing on the artifacts, such as stories, which result from interpretation activities, the process narrative model of understanding emphasizes those activities, themselves, as fundamental to remembering and recalling information. The radiology patients showed this in their post-consultation telephone discussions when they recalled how they developed understandings at their consultations. The biology students showed it when they verbally reconstructed their prior use of the computer simulation as they wrote answers to a task prompt. These examples show how the mental salience and availability of memories depends on the prior creation of process narratives. The activation of memories depends not only on an immediate stimulus, but also on the previous interpretation activities of creating process narratives.

Process narratives do not function simply as artifacts of memory describing the outcomes of previous interpretation activities. As the data related to the radiology consultations and the genetics learning activities show, process narratives also trigger recall of the interpretation activities and information resources that produced them. Each process narrative indexes the interpretive frame of reference, which contributed to the coherent linking of the information in that process narrative. The confluence of the embedded frame of reference with the particular set of information linked in a process narrative establishes the suitability of the process narrative for combination with other process narratives as a story or extended explanation.

In contrast to the inferred neural processes emphasized by a story model of memory, the process narrative approach locates much of the complexity of processing information and forming recallable understandings in the interpretation activities related to particular information resources of a setting, the culture of the setting that affects access to information, and, often, to social interaction. The preceding analyses of the interpretation activities for creating and applying process narratives show how the linguistic, visual, and gestural information resources that shaped them become intertwined with them. Unlike approaches to memory and understanding that emphasize mental processes, the process narrative approach accounts for both the material and mental components of understandings. It explains more of the particulars of producing recallable understandings than a story model does.

Approaching understanding and memory by recognizing the interpretation activities that lead to process narratives contributes to understanding the mental operations that script theory and story-based memory emphasize as 'indexing'. However, process narratives remove any need to initially store full stories in memory. Process narratives subsume the categories, *mental paths* and *indexes*, and the inferred mental operations of *index extraction* (cf. Schank and Abelson, 1995: 17), resolving the problem of explaining how indexes relate to stories. In certain social contexts, a process narrative can function as a component of a story or as an index to other components of a story by emphasizing particular information resources in a setting. Such emphasis then prompts reconstruction of interpretation activities or prompts recall of related process narratives. For example, during the genetics inheritance learning activities analyzed in Chapters Two and Three, students reconstructed previous interpretation activities in order to revisit, recall, or revise process narratives when developing answers for the task prompt or when responding to the teacher's request for a revised answer. They expressed process narratives linking particular information that had been displayed on the computer screen and the earlier activities related to interpreting that information.

The interpretation activities that create process narratives are the basis of the subsequent retrieval, reconstruction, and expression of understandings as explanations or stories. An expressed story or explanation involves embellishing an initially recalled process narrative as that process narrative also triggers recall of the interpretation activities that formed it – including recall of the previously created process narratives that had contributed to it. Process narratives provide a less memory intensive and more flexible system of memory and recall than a story model of memory. Memory is not a collection of stories, but a collection of process narratives. We remember process narratives, not story indexes or skeletons (cf. Schank and Abelson, 1995).

The radiology consultations and the genetics learning activities show how the interpretation activities of organizing information into process narratives are central to understanding and recalling concepts and descriptions. Furthermore, analysis of the interpretation activities that produce and apply process narratives clarifies the processes and resources of understanding that previous categorical distinctions have treated as inferred mental operations.

5 Conclusion to Part One – Process Narratives and the Endurance of Understandings

The preceding examples show the role of process narratives in creating and recalling understandings. The activities of interpreting and organizing information to form process narratives contribute to the endurance of understandings – even in the presence of additional, contradictory information. The analysis of recorded interpretation activities shows how such emphasis on a particular set and organization of information develops and functions.

When the radiology patients' expressed understandings of the medical information days after their consultations, they expressed process narratives referring to particular images and interpretation activities they had experienced during the consultations. Patient P1 explained the physiological reasons why an embolizing agent would not disperse throughout the body. Patient P3 expressed an understanding of the size of the embolizing agent particles that would remain in her body, showing how she had applied information about their minute size to fill an information gap and produce a process narrative that dispelled her prior apprehensions. Each patient linked the interpretations she had developed during her consultation to the visual and verbal information. Analysis of the recorded consultations shows the interrelated verbal, gestural, and visual interpretation activities by which the patients created the process narratives and understandings they recalled later. The biology students also showed this when they used the 'automatically skips a generation' process narratives to recall details of their earlier use of the computer simulation in order to explain or revisit their written answers to prompt questions (Transcript Extract 3.7, B645-B666). As B21, G21, and B22 interacted with each other and the task resources, they also reinforced a particular interpretive frame of reference emphasizing description of the screen images. The interpretation activities that form process narratives become part of the resulting understandings.

Belief as the Endurance of Process Narratives

The classroom data show the endurance of the frames-of-reference and process narratives that the students developed to coherently organize their interpretation of the computer screen and the task prompt. For example, B21's response to evidence that undermined his previously developed 'automatically skipped' process narratives was not to abandon them, but to adapt them to the new evidence (Chapter Three, Transcript Extract 3.9).

The data show how the students contended with the contingencies of interpreting the images, the task prompt, and one another's comments and gestures. They reduced those contingencies by developing a linguistic and gestural format for discussing the task and a shared frame of reference about how to accomplish the task, both of which helped them to impute coherence by excluding certain information from consideration and discussion. Functionally, they had discarded the information about the sets of parents. This led to their belief in mistaken process narratives concerning the simulation's representation of trait inheritance.

Like the genetics learning activities, the radiology consultations also featured participants creating process narratives through patterns of interpretation activities that included gesturing and pointing at images displayed on a computer screen. However, the particulars and outcomes of such activities differed from those of the students due to the ways that the participants dealt with missing information. The radiology consultations supported interpretation activities and provided information resources, which patients used to complete process narratives without the contingencies related to missing information. When a patient made comments or asked questions that suggested that she was making inferences about missing information, the nurse and patient interacted to supply the missing information. They linked descriptions of the images with information that was not presented by the pictures and text on the computer screen. The orientation of both patient and clinician to the visual information contributed to a communication format in which clinicians provided explanations to patients, rather than proceeding to a different item in a previously developed diagnostic or explanatory agenda. The discussion of images during the radiology consultations functioned as a disruptive innovation that superseded the common communication patterns of many medical consultations, which limit opportunities for patients to express the extent of their understandings of medical terms and concepts (cf. Entwistle, Williams, Skea, MacLennan, and Bhattacharya, 2006; Fisher, 1986; Fisher and Groce, 1990; Price *et al.*, 2006; Skea *et al.*, 2004). The radiology consultations' patterns of communication provided patients with opportunities to link information as recallable process narratives about their symptoms and treatment options.

Both the interventional radiology consultations and the genetics learning activities feature people encountering new information that they try to understand for subsequent recall and application. The examples present two commonplace types of situations in which people try to develop understandings. The radiology consultation examples show people interpreting newly encountered information with the assistance of a clinician who already has expertise and understandings related to that information. Most of the preceding classroom examples have shown students interpreting newly encountered information without the direct participation of an expert – i.e., the teacher did not participate in the students' interpretation activities until they completed the 'automatically skips a generation' process narratives and understandings of the computer simulation. Despite that difference in the two research settings, analysis of both sets of examples displays the participants pursuing the activities of concurrently interpreting information, developing a relevant frame of reference, and linking certain pieces of information as process narratives. Analyzing the production of process narratives exposes the components of the interpretation activities that produce understandings – both accurate and mistaken understandings.

Developing understandings always involves interpretive contingencies, which include the concurrent activities of developing a relevant frame of reference, interpreting information and interaction, and contending with aspects of local culture and social organization such as time constraints and different degrees of familiarity or expertise with information resources. The examples discussed earlier show that a key contingency is seeking missing information that would link the available information in process narratives.

Coping with Interpretive Contingencies: Grey Boxes in Process Narratives

Comparison of the production of process narratives during the interventional radiology consultations and the genetics education activities presents the effects on understandings of access to or absence of information. Analysis of the radiology consultation data explicates how communication patterns that generate additional information reduce the interpretive complications of that contingency. During the consultations, gestures and movements related to the explanatory images produced communication patterns that supported patients' access to information and contributed to recallable process narratives. In contrast, during the genetics learning activities, the students' lack of access to information about genes and biology terms, such as *recessive*, added contingencies that complicated the students' creation of process narratives.

Part Two further examines the interpretation activities of coping with the contingencies encountered when relevant information is absent or searching for information is restricted – a situation which is common during the production of understandings in many settings. The genetics education data show that the absence of key information does not prevent the production of process narratives. However, it complicates the interpretation activities that lead to them. The students' interpretation activities involved applying grey boxes as placeholders in order to reduce the contingencies of dealing with restricted access to information about cellular processes. Part Two analyzes another set of genetics learning activities, explicating the creation of grey boxes, as well as their effects on process narratives and on the recall of resulting understandings.

PART TWO
GREY BOXES

Grey boxes are linguistic, gestural, or pictorial expressions, which function as placeholders for missing information. They operate syntactically, helping to cope with missing information and constraints on seeking information during the creation of process narratives. They move interpretation activity forward by linking available information. Part Two focuses on data from another educational setting. Certain grey boxes have become part of the traditional curriculum for teaching the Mendelian approach to trait inheritance. They are placeholders for missing information about the cellular processes by which genes affect the development of traits. However, all students do not automatically accept the standard grey boxes. Analysis of how students deal with the constraints on seeking missing information shows the interpretation processes of creating, accepting, and applying grey boxes.

Although the radiology consultation data contribute to explanations of the creation of process narratives, discourse frameworks (Part 3), and the effects of related interpretation activities on professional culture (Part 4), the communication patterns that the patients and clinicians developed as they discussed medical conditions and treatments satisfied the patients' pursuit of additional information. Consequently, the patients did not produce grey boxes as placeholders for missing information to the extent that the students did. Yet, Part Two is relevant to how patients develop understandings in many clinical settings. The communication patterns related to the professional culture of the biology teachers sometimes restrict students' pursuit of missing information, and introduce interpretive contingencies that affect the nature of students' understandings. Such restriction on seeking information is also apparent in many studies of medical consultations when the communication pattern is based on a form of diagnostic interview directed by the clinician (cf. Entwistle *et al.*, 2006; Fisher, 1986; 1993; Fisher and Groce, 1990; Frankel, 1990; Måseide, 1991; Price *et al.*, 2006; Skea *et al.*, 2004; West, 1984).

6 Cognitive Science of Grey Boxes

Grey boxes are part of a cognitive ecology of interpretation activities that lead to understandings. They result when interpretation activities confront emergent contingencies, such as ambiguity, absence of information, and lack of coherence among pieces of information. Student-teacher interaction provides an example of restrictions on information triggering the creation of a grey box. Comparison of the Mendelian genetics learning activities with research on people attempting to solve logic problems shows that difficulties in reasoning do not derive from the arbitrariness or specificity of available information, but from restrictions on information-seeking that lead to similar interpretive contingencies. Those contingencies contribute to an increased load on short-term memory until people grey-box the missing information.

Contingencies of Creating Grey Boxes

Grey boxes reduce the interpretive contingencies of searching for missing information. However, the activities of constructing and accepting grey boxes are also contingencies, which may increase the time and effort required to develop process narratives. A glimpse into a case examined fully in the next chapter provides an example of restrictions on information that trigger interpretive contingencies. Those contingencies are finally resolved by the creation of a grey box that contributes to a useful process narrative. This example began six minutes and sixteen seconds into a discussion by four students and a teacher of the same trait inheritance computer simulation featured in Chapters Two and Three. During prior discussion the teacher had deemphasized the students' attempts to apply information about genes or cellular processes to explain the computer screen's images. The computer screen first showed the straight-eared offspring resulting from mating a straight-eared and a floppy-eared rabbit. Then, when two of the first generation offspring were mated, it showed both floppy-eared and straight-eared offspring in the next generation. A student, G11, attempted to express a process narrative answering the teacher's question about the source of the factors that affected the reappearance of floppy ears in the second generation offspring, which had straight-eared parents:

> So okay okay they (gestures with pen as she refers to rabbits) okay the female and the male okay they-they got (jabs pen toward screen) together and they had babies (claps hands together as she says "babies") boy (giggles) and then okay (moves hand and points finger toward screen) the floppy ears, they came out. I don't know from where, but (Transcript Extract 7.9, lines A231, A233, A235, A237, A239).

The utterance, 'the floppy ears, they came out. I don't know from where' (Transcript Extract 7.9, lines A237 and A239) displays the student's difficulty in determining an interpretive frame of reference that simultaneously links the available information and is relevant to the information constraints. In the context of the students' preceding discussion with the teacher, 'where' can refer to the observable information on the screen, the reproductive cells of the rabbits, or the function of DNA within cells. This ambiguity reflects the increased cognitive load of recalling and considering multiple interpretive contingencies, which include:

- Limited information (the available visual and textual information only presented the physical traits, not the genes).
- The teacher's previous de-emphasis of the students' comments related to cell division or the functioning of genes within individuals.
- Finding, interpreting, and linking information pertaining to three frames of reference (i.e., observable traits in generations, transmission of genes across generations, and the functioning of genes within individuals).

Eventually, one of the students expresses a grey box, 'blueprints', which resolves the interpretive contingencies the students had encountered earlier (Transcript Extract 6.1, line A298). It functions as a placeholder for missing information about cellular processes, and provides a shared linguistic representation that avoids the digressions toward topics such as DNA, which were not elucidated by the information at hand.

Transcript Extract 6.1

A295. T1: /But what it went – they may/ not have those ears. Did they have the directions?
A296. B12: No, well yeah /they did/
A297. T1: /(???/??) what /(????)/
A298. B13: /they got the blue//prints/

The function and meaning of 'blueprints' did not depend on the students recalling experiences outside of the biology class, but on the word's relationship to the preceding activity of interpreting the screen images and the task prompt in order to explain the inheritance of traits across a sequence of generations. 'Blueprints' functioned as meta-information – as a marker and placeholder for the interpretation activities of seeking missing information about cellular processes and linking new information to the visual information on the computer screen.

Replacing both the unrewarded, confusing interpretation activities and the missing cellular process information with the term 'blueprints' led one of the students to develop a process narrative that answered the task prompt's request for an explanation of the inheritance of traits displayed by the computer simulation:

> *Floppy ears were hiding in the first generation blueprints. They came from hiding into the second generation and now they are visible.* (Expressed by B13 in Transcript Extract 7.14, lines A337, A339)

As a grey box, 'blueprints' operates syntactically, helping the students and the teacher to administer the linguistic and cognitive results of their work to develop understandings. It helps them communicate with each other in order to proceed with the interpretation activities of creating process narratives to answer a task prompt question. It functions as way of moving the interpretation activity forward by linking information to form an idiosyncratic process narrative – one that has coherence only in relation to the immediate activity and local resources. The data show that developing and applying grey boxes involves a process of eliminating the idiomatic meaning of linguistic terms or suspending the search for missing information that would replace them, while retaining their syntactical function.

Grey Boxes and Difficulties in Developing Understandings

Studies emphasizing mental models as a framework for cognition have noted representational devices that function like grey boxes. For example, experimental data concerning the effects of diagrams on solving reasoning problems also show that graphical devices are useful for developing correct answers (Bauer and Johnson-Laird, 1993: 373). Discussing the use of iconic diagrams and graphs, Bauer and Johnson-Laird emphasize the utility of diagrams in reducing the cognitive load of keeping in mind alternative models of a solution to a problem. In the trait inheritance learning example, the term, 'blueprints', functions like iconic diagrams by providing a recognizable locus of the contingencies encountered by the students and the teacher during their preceding discussion (cf. Johnson-Laird, 2002).

However, those contingencies extended beyond remembering alternative models of completed solutions or explanations. Analysis of the creation of process narratives shows that both restricted access to information and the activities of interpreting the expression of a problem also add contingencies that can tax short-term memory and complicate reasoning (as shown by the classroom examples in Part One). Those contingencies include the interpretation activities of developing, remembering, culling, and applying pieces of information as well as frames of reference. The mind-boggles that people encounter while trying to develop understandings when information is restricted result from juggling such a set of interpretation activities and task constraints.

Interpreting the Expression of Information: Specificity and Frame of Reference

The study of process narratives and grey boxes differs from studies emphasizing mental models in regard to recognition and analysis of the contingencies that affect reasoning and understanding. Examining the interpretation activities of developing grey boxes, shows that difficulties in reasoning do not derive directly from the arbitrariness or specificity of pieces of information (the expressed variables), but from the contingent interpretation activities triggered by the degree of specificity of the linguistic, graphical, or gestural representation of the variables in regard to qualities, states, and settings.

The genetics education data show that, in the conventional Mendelian genetics curricula, the form of expression of assigned problems (such as the questions in the task prompt discussed in Part One, e.g., Figure 2.1) and restrictions on seeking information are factors that affect interpreting problems and producing process narratives that demonstrate understanding. The

Mendelian genetics curriculum's avoidance of cellular genetics creates a 'not cellular processes' contingency. This contingency is also evident in modus tollens logic problems, which require a choice among candidate answers by applying the stipulation, if *p* then *q*; not *q*. Studies of reasoning and cognition that examine difficulties in solving modus tollens logic problems have emphasized the abstract or familiar content of the expressed problem, the context in which people consider the variables, and the complexity of the mental operations that increase the load on short-term memory (cf. D'Andrade, 1989; Johnson-Laird, 1983; Johnson-Laird and Byrne, 2002; Johnson-Laird, Legrenzi, and Legrenzi, 1972; Wason, 1968). However, examining the routine linguistic formats used to express the problems – forms of expression that are shaped by professional culture – provides another approach to understanding why abstractly expressed logic problems are more difficult to solve than problems expressed in terms of common experience. The difficulty in comprehending both modus tollens problems and the 'not cellular processes' formulations of Mendelian genetics derives from the particulars of expressing conditions and variables. Those forms of expression restrict interpretation activities.

D'Andrade (1989: 136, 138–140) presents an example of the relative clarity of a modus tollens problem expressed in terms of common experience in contrast to the abstract formulation (cf. Johnson-Laird *et al.*, 1972; Johnson-Laird, Byrne, and Schaeken, 1992): i.e., 'A garnet is a semiprecious stone, *q* is not a semiprecious stone', rather than 'if *p* then *q*, *not q*'. D'Andrade discusses the advantages of the commonplace wording over the abstract wording in terms of a dichotomy between contentful and contentless senses of contingency – with 'contingency' referring to the potential relationship among the expressed variables. He also mentions that the commonplace expression of the problem explicitly addresses cultural knowledge. His research featuring logic problems found higher rates of success in solving modus tollens problems when they were expressed in terms of commonplace situations than when they were expressed in terms of abstract nomenclature (D'Andrade, 1989).

Considering D'Andrade's garnet example in regard to the interpretation activities that produce process narratives and grey boxes shifts the explanation of the difference in understanding abstractly and colloquially expressed problems from the 'sense' of contingency to particular interpretation activities that connect with specific information resources and experiences. This also clarifies how cultural knowledge relates to both the expression of reasoning problems and the activities of interpreting them.

For example, even if one does not recognize the term 'garnet' or the term 'semiprecious stone', knowledge of one contributes to an inference about the other. A person interpreting the expression of a problem using those terms in order to solve it could apply information about jewelry or information about the use of 'stone' as a way of referring to attractive or valuable polished minerals rather than chunks of minerals found in a field (cf. D'Andrade, 1989: 139–140). Inferences or recall about garnets or semi-precious stones can involve information about specific objects with describable qualities – which can be organized as process narratives (e.g., 'a garnet is a red shiny stone used in jewelry, like the one in my sister's necklace' or 'At the jewelry store, garnet necklaces are not as expensive as diamond necklaces; so a garnet is a semi-precious stone'). Recall of direct or mediated experience with jewelry provides information that a turquoise would not be called a garnet, that a precious stone would not be called a semi-precious stone, and that a diamond is an example of a precious stone.

Such information supports inferences about the relationship between 'garnet' and 'semi-precious stone', which contribute to determining that an object is not a garnet when the restricting condition is 'not a semi-precious stone'. That conclusion can be made by an imagined comparative example (e.g., '*q* is a diamond' or '*q* is a garden pebble'); not only by a deduction restricted to the specific linguistic terms expressed in a problem or explanation.

In regard to such routine interpretation activities, an abstract, 'contentless' expression, such as the two dimensional computer simulation images lacking representation of cellular processes or the Mendelian nomenclature in biology teachers' trait inheritance explanations, presents the opportunity for people to seek many types of relevant information in order to clarify the variables and their relationship. In the genetics learning activities, the absence of information about cellular processes functions in that way. The interpretive contingencies include trial and error searching for relevant information and a useful frame of reference, as well as the culling of unproductive information and frames of reference. In contrast, the expression of a problem or explanation that indexes commonplace experiences, presents specific types of things and actions, which limit the kinds of information relevant to creating process narratives and answers. This also reduces the contingencies of searching for missing information. The presentation of patient-requested information at the radiology consultations functioned in this way.

Theories of mental models or schemata consider contingencies that affect reasoning in terms of the contingent relationship between variables in the expression of a problem or proposition (e.g., arbitrariness of nomenclature, such as: if *p*, then *q*; nested categories such as garnet and semi-precious stone [D'Andrade, 1989]; the effects of described settings on described actions, such as fog and the cancellation of a sports event [Johnson-Laird et al., 1992]). In contrast, examining the creation of process narratives and grey boxes emphasizes that the contingencies which affect reasoning include the activities of interpreting the variables – i.e., the contingent mental, physical, and social activities of interpreting, organizing, and seeking information in order to develop understandings.

The expression of negation provides an example. Johnson-Laird (2002) argues that, in regard to forming mental models, negation cannot be expressed by discrete representational devices; i.e., it must be expressed by meta-formulations or comparisons. Examining the production of process narratives shows that grey boxes serve as such meta-formulations or comparisons. However, they result not only from difficult mental maneuvers of abstract problem solving, but also from activities related to interpreting the particular information resources of a setting and from sociocultural constraints. The next chapter presents an example of genetics learning activities in which the linguistic expression of a problem and the other resources available for solving or making sense of it do not provide information adequate for developing coherent explanatory process narratives. Consequently, the students face the interpretive contingency of searching for missing information of a type suggested by the available information.

Similarly, modus tollens reasoning (if *p* then *q*; not *q*) features a form of expression of a variable (*not q*) that both denies the presence of another variable (*q*), and acknowledges its existence and relevance for understanding the problem. The form of expression, 'not q', lacks specificity, a condition that routinely triggers a search for relevant information. This is the same condition that affects the students learning Mendelian genetics and trying to answer assigned problems without applying information regarding cellular genetic processes. Patients in many conventional medical consultations also encounter it when they express information about symptoms, and the clinician then presents a diagnosis featuring medical terms, which the patient finds unfamiliar or ambiguous, and which do not clearly specify the relationship between the expressed symptoms and the prescribed treatments. The modus tollens problems, the Mendelian genetics curriculum, and conventional medical consultations present similar factors, which lead to the interpretive contingencies that complicate understanding:

- Their lack of specificity restricts available information for developing recallable process narratives.
- They feature a form of expression that suggests an information-seeking interpretive frame of reference.

Those contingencies contribute to an increased load on short-term memory until people grey-box the missing information. Analysis of the genetics education data shows that, in the context of restricted information, the interpretation activities that lead to process narratives include:

- Searching for information and frames of reference that would contribute to coherent process narratives,
- Recognizing the absence of relevant information,
- Developing grey boxes in order to mark the absence of information,
- Developing an interpretive frame of reference that substitutes grey boxes for information searching.

Students' and patients' difficulties in producing recallable understandings result from the contingencies of managing such interpretation activities. When the process of searching for missing information is confounded or discouraged, grey boxes serve as markers of absence, and as negations of unproductive approaches to seeking information. The next chapter examines how these aspects of grey boxes affect understandings.

7 Grey Boxes in the Production of Process Narratives – A Case of Creating A Grey Box

Chapter Seven examines grey boxes in regard to interpretive ambiguity, the effect of a critical mass of interpretive contingencies, forms of expression as resources for understanding, and localized aspects of grey boxes. As a consequence of the conventional Mendelian curriculum, students and teachers spend time and effort constructing a framework to cover the explanatory gap created by the absence of information about cellular biochemical processes. Students' awareness of contemporary genetic terms and concepts adds contingencies to their interpretation activities. When students repeatedly confront the information gap separating genes and traits during learning activities, they develop grey boxes that alleviate their disbelief or confusion. Grey boxes ease the cognitive load of interpreting and remembering multiple contingencies. Expanding on an example introduced earlier, this chapter examines four students and a teacher discussing a learning task featuring the use of a trait inheritance computer simulation. A result of the 10.5-minute discussion is the students' acceptance of the term, 'blueprints', as a placeholder for missing information about the cellular genetic processes. 'Blueprints' eliminates the interpretive contingencies related to finding and coherently linking missing information about the biochemical functioning of genes that affects the development of traits. The grey box helps the students develop a useful process narrative.

Grey Boxes and Missing Information

In the recorded genetics lessons, the curricula emphasize how the transmission of genes across generations affects the physical characteristics of people and other biological organisms. The learning activities generally include the following processes:

- Noting particular significant traits
- Mating of individuals with the noted traits
- Production of a resulting generation of offspring having certain traits
- Mating individuals with the noted traits from that generation
- Production of another generation of offspring having one or more of the noted traits.

However, as discussed in Part One, the lessons about trait inheritance do not explain the way that genes trigger the biochemical processes leading to an observable phenotype or trait. This missing information presents difficulties for students in regard to linking the information about patterns of traits within and across generations in order to explain trait inheritance. Expanding on the example introduced at the beginning of Chapter Six, the following analysis examines four students and a teacher during a 10.5 minute learning activity featuring the same trait inheritance computer simulation discussed in Chapters Two and Three. It involves the same teacher, but different students during a biology class at a different school during the prior academic year.

After using the simulation software to breed two generations of rabbits, the students' initial concern is how to answer the task prompt question, which the teacher reads as he begins to assist them, '[Assuming the variation (floppy ears)] wasn't actually lost, how might you explain the observation that this variation disappeared?' (Transcript Extract 7.1, line A1, quoting WINGS for Learning, 1991). The teacher encourages the students to find the answer by considering the simulation that he has run on the computer screen rather than searching for an answer in their textbook (Transcript Extract 7.1, lines A19-A20). He uses the computer mouse to clear the screen, reset the number of offspring produced, and create a generation of rabbits by mating a straight-eared rabbit and a floppy-eared rabbit.

Transcript Extract 7.1

A1. T1: (reading assignment question) '[Assuming the variation (floppy ears)] wasn't actually lost, how might you explain the observation that this variation disappeared?' Well? ..

A2. B13: We don't know. (T1 removes B13's hat and places it on table) Oh

Transcript Extract 7.1 (continued)

A3. G11: So, if it if it was /lost ../
A4. B13: /(referring to hat) I forgot about this/
A5. G11: Wait a minute. How did it get lost at first?
A6. T1: Well, it wasn't there, was it?
A7. G11: No
A8. B13: No
A9. T1: Is it lost?
A10. G11: No
A11. T1: How do you know?
A12. G11: 'cause it was there.
A13. B13: Was /it/
A14. T1: /Say/ I'm – I'm not
A15. G11: No it doesn't say
A16. T1: Huh?
A17. G11: if it was lost or not.
A18. T1: How do you know it's not lost?
A19. B13: It doesn't say (B13 moves head toward book or task prompt. T1 moves arm toward computer mouse or screen) in here /in the book/
A20. T1: /No but/ how does it say in here? (referring to the computer screen)
A21. B13: No it's supposed to be in /the book./
A22. T1: /No but/ how does – how does – how does? No it's not. That's
A23. B13: Se/e/
A24. T1: /(??)/ place you can look, but you have to be able to think here. (T1 uses computer mouse) . Right? Look at

The students respond to the teacher's question, 'Now what do we have? What kind of ears?' (Transcript Extract 7.2, line A57), by mentioning both quantity of genes and characteristics of the particular rabbits associated with different types of genes. Their interpretive frame of reference concerns the unseen causes of the physical characteristics of the screen images of rabbits. For example, B13 says, 'There wasn't as many female genes as there was male genes' (Transcript Extract 7.2, line A60). B13's use of the adjectives, 'female' and 'male' with 'genes', may represent a notion that each gender has a different type of genes, or it may refer to the specific rabbits on the screen, or it may do both. His concern with quantity may also take into account the configuration of the images on the screen, which presents more straight-eared rabbits than floppy-eared rabbits.

Transcript Extract 7.2

[Lines A25-A56 are omitted. During those lines G11 has an off-task conversation with another student, while T1 uses the computer mouse to clear the computer screen, resets the software to conform the number of offspring produced to the task prompt, and then uses the computer simulation software to mate a straight-eared and floppy-eared rabbit, producing a generation of straight-eared offspring.]

A57. T1: Now what do we have? What kind of ears?
A58. B13: We got straight /ears/
A59. G11: /We got/ straight ears, sticking-up ears
A60. B13: There wasn't as many female genes as there was male genes
A61. T1: Possibly. But now they have straight ears, right?
A62. G11: Yes
A63. T1: What happened to the droopy ears?
A64. G11: /The/
A65. B13: /They/ didn't /come out/
A66. G11: /the female/ – the – th' – the male's have – more – more power

The teacher simultaneously points out the specific characteristics of the screen images that apply to answering the question, and emphasizes the general point that the appearance, disappearance, and reappearance of ear shape is the relevant variation for the students to explore in regard to trait inheritance (Transcript Extract 7.2, lines A61-A63):

A61. T1: Possibly. But now they have straight ears, right?
A62. G11: Yes
A63. T1: What happened to the droopy ears?

Since, neither the computer simulation nor the teacher present information about how genes influence the cellular processes that produce traits, the students apply various linguistic terms as placeholders for the missing information that would complete explanatory process narratives. For example, when explaining why the offspring on the screen have the same ear shape as the male parent, G11's use of the phrase, 'Have more – more power', is a grey box in regard to explaining how genes affect traits ('the male's have – more – more power,' Transcript Extract 7.2, line A66). As a description of the screen images, the phrase indexes the quantity of straight ears. However, in regard to explaining how the rabbits' floppy ears appear, disappear, and reappear across generations, it simply serves as a placeholder marking the absence of information needed to link the pictorial and linguistic information provided by the screen, the teacher, and the task prompt. It covers this information gap, but does not explain such 'power' or how it operates.

The activity discussed in Transcript Extract 7.3, lines A67-A84, involves the teacher running a simulation which counters G11's comment that the male rabbits or the male rabbits' genes have more power to influence the ear shape of their offspring. The teacher mates a straight-eared female rabbit and a floppy-eared male rabbit in order to demonstrate that the gender of the parent does not affect the outcome of the simulation regarding the ear shapes of the offspring. The offspring have straight ears. The discussion, the new visual information on the computer screen, and the teacher's comments deemphasize 'power' linked to gender.

Attempting to respond to the new information, G11 stammers and pauses three times for one second or more as she expresses vague terms for the causes of the ear shape: 'So so the the whatta you call those things have more ... have more' (Transcript Extract 7.3, line A83). She does not complete the phrase beginning with 'more'. She does not find words to replace 'gene' and 'power'. G11's difficulty in finding words to express what she sees or infers shows that ruling out 'power' as a grey box creates a boggling difficulty in linking the available information in a way that helps her to explain the inheritance of ear shape across generations.

Transcript Extract 7.3

A67. T1: Oooh, /male's/
A68. B13: /As usual/
A69. T1: Ooh, okay, let's try, let's try /the other thing/
A70. B12: /Yep/
A71. T1: Let's see, let's try it the other way, /let's try the other way./
A72. B13: /Yep, the male's always got it/

A73. T1: Maybe [G11's first name]'s right, maybe the male's more powerful. Let's take . the female with straight ears, okay, [G11's first name], and we'll take the male with droopy ears. Whattya think, what's gonna happen?
A74. G11: /The female's gonna have/
A75. B13: /Uhhhhh/
A76. T1: Droopy ears now, huhn?
A77. G11: Yep
A78. T1: Okay, let's see (T1 runs the simulation)
A79. B12: (prior to the offspring appearing on the screen) No (straight-eared offspring appear)

Transcript Extract 7.3 (continued)

A80. T1: No
A81. G11: No
A82. B13: Haahaa, told you, haahaahaaha
A83. G11: So so .. the the whatta you call those things have more ... have more ..
A84. B13: There's more straight-ear genes than there is floppy-ear genes
A85. T1: Is it because they have more straight-eared genes?
A86. G11: /Yeah/
A87. T1: /Is that/ what you think is going on? Hmm .... Do you think there's any floppy-ear genes running around in this?
A88. B13: Ye/ah/
A89. B12: /Yeah/
A90. T1: What happened to the floppy ears?
A91. G11: Noo
A92. B13: There's not as many as there would be ...
A93. B12: As wu the um female genes ..

Responding to the teacher's comments and the screen information showing that the gender of the straight-eared rabbit does not affect the inheritance of straight ears, B13 says, 'There's more straight eared genes than there is floppy-ear genes' (Transcript Extract 7.3, line A84). He ascribes relevance to quantity. He also shifts from linking the influence of genes with gender to linking them to the specific traits. The ensuing discussion shows that the terms 'power' and 'genes' remain grey boxes for the students in regard to the task of linking the available information as coherent process narratives, which would explain the inheritance of traits.

Interpretive Ambiguity

In this example, the presence of the teacher during the entire discussion of the computer simulation constrains the students from developing an incorrect explanation – in contrast to the 'automatically skips a generation' example discussed in Part One. Yet, the interpretation activity reveals the same process of concurrently developing a communication format for discussing the information at hand, sorting and culling interpretations of information in order to establish coherent links among pieces of information, and finding ways to cope with missing information. The discussion follows a circuitous route in which the students present and recycle information about DNA and cell division, which the teacher does not accept. Ultimately, one of the students mentions the term 'blueprints', which the teacher accepts. The students use 'blueprints' as a grey box for missing information about cellular genetic processes, the biochemistry of DNA, and meiosis. Tracking the route to this solution reveals the role of grey boxes in the production of process narratives.

The interaction centers on finding terminology that addresses the visual information about the differences in the rabbits' ear shapes across generations, while implying an unseen cause of the pattern of appearance, disappearance, and reappearance of floppy ears across generations. As in the 'automatically skips a generation' data, the students devote much of their effort to figuring out a functional meaning of linguistic terms. In the 'automatically skips a generation' examples, much of the students' interpretation activity concerned the meanings of the terms 'pattern' and 'dominant' (discussed in Chapters Two and Three). In this case, much of the students' interpretation activity concerns the functional meanings of 'where' and 'come from', in regard to where the floppy ears come from when the screen images show that they reappear in a generation after being absent in the preceding generation (Transcript Extracts 7.4, 7.5, 7.6):

A97. B13: You gonna get floppy ears
A98. T1: I'm gonna get f – well where'd it come from?
A99. B13: Huh
A100. T1: Where did I get floppy ears from, if you think I'm going to get floppy ears. Why

A119. T1: Okay, now, where did the floppy ear – directions for making floppy ears come from? You've got a straight eared
A120. B12: mother
A121. T1: rabbit and there's another straight-eared rabbit. Where'd they get the directions for making floppy ears?

A143. T1: Where did the gene for floppy ears come from?

A176. T1: Where did – where did – where did-where did this rabbit get the directions for making it?

The interaction related to interpreting and applying terms, such as 'where' and 'come from', demonstrates how a missing information link creates contingencies that complicate the interpretation activities of the students and inhibit the development of useful understandings in the form of recallable process narratives. For example, uncertainty about the meaning of 'come from' challenges both the organizing of information as explanatory process narratives and the creation of a frame of reference for interpreting information about the inheritance of ear shape. The students' comments show that forms of 'come from' are used variously in relation to parents, many generations of a family, cell development, or the screen images. B13 focuses on information displayed by a prior operation of the simulation when he explains his correct prediction of the outcome of mating two straight-eared rabbits, whose parents were a straight-eared rabbit and a floppy-eared rabbit: 'Because I've already done this. You're going to get floppy' (Transcript Extract 7.4, line 101).

Transcript Extract 7.4

A94. T1: uh huh ... (to another group of students) Okay, /just give me a minute. (To G11, B11-3. T1 uses computer to demonstrate) Okay now what should I get if I take this straight-eared rabbit and this straight-eared rabbit/
A95. G11: /(writing or drawing with pen) The .. the girl (?started?) like this (????)/
A96. T1: and mate 'em?
A97. B13: You gonna get floppy ears
A98. T1: I'm gonna get f – well where'd it come from?
A99. B13: Huh
A100. T1: Where did I get floppy ears from, if you think I'm going to get floppy ears? Why
A101. B13: Because I've already done this. You're going to get floppy
A102. T1: /I am, huh?/
A103. B13: /Some some/ some were straight and some were floppy.
A104. T1: I am?
A105. B13: Yeah
A106. T1: Gonna bet your life on that?
A107. B13: Uh huh.
A108. T1: (Joking) So, if it isn't I own your soul now, right?
A109. B13: Yeah
A110. T1: You heard him right?
A111. G11: What happened ... I'm lookin' at-
A112. B13: Only if you're the devil ... (the simulation produces an F2 generation with floppy-eared and straight-eared offspring) told you there was floppy ears .
A113. T1: Got lucky this /time./
A114. B13: /Told you/
A115. T1: I'll coll/ect on you one of these days/
A116. B13: /I did it last time./
A117. B12: (loud yawning sound) Uuhhh
A118. B13: I did it last time.

Shortly after that discussion, the students jokingly apply information related to hypothetical promiscuity of the parent rabbits to explain where the floppy ears 'come from' (Transcript Extract 7.5, lines A119-A142). Then, the students mention ancestors and family resemblance (Transcript Extract 7.6, lines A147-A167). However, in regard to the students' attempts to explain the appearance of floppy-eared offspring resulting from mating straight-eared parents, 'come from' does not index any specific information about cellular processes that would clarify how genes influence the development of traits across generations.

The complexity of the interpretation activities involves the students concurrently making sense of linguistic and pictorial information, seeking additional information, developing a relevant frame of reference, as well as sorting and culling information to develop coherence. The path toward process narratives that are acceptable to the teacher involves students recycling notions of the power or strength of genes and the teacher repeatedly guiding the students away from the frame of reference concerning cellular genetic processes. A result of the 10.5-minute discussion is the students' acceptance of the terms 'directions' and 'blueprints' as placeholders for missing information about the cellular genetic processes.

The Route to Grey Boxes: Frustrated Information Searches

Grey boxes mark and suspend the interpretive contingencies of searching for missing information or keeping in short term memory the awareness that key information is missing. In that regard, they ultimately alleviate confusion or ambiguity related to developing a framework for a coherent explanation. A grey box does not index specific background or contextual information that would contribute to coherent process narratives. It only marks an effort to develop coherence between other pieces of more concrete information.

Creating and applying grey boxes involves interpretation activities that lead to their acceptance as part of the discourse framework for the work at hand. During the discussion of the computer simulation with the teacher, the students work to convince and train themselves that the linguistic terms they use to mark missing information about where genes or traits 'come from' can serve as links between the information presented by the computer simulation and by the teacher. Before accepting those terms as mere placeholders for missing information the students – guided by the teacher's responses and questions – purge interpretive frames of reference that emphasize cellular processes related to DNA and cell division.

During the discussion, the students present various frames of reference in order to find information that would link the information presented by the screen, the task prompt, and the information, and the teacher. These include:

- Power/strength of the genes
- Quantity of traits and genes
- Specificity of rabbits' traits in regard to gender
- Sexual activity
- Family resemblance
- Description of the simulation
- Description of human families

The students move the discussion across these different frames of reference as they search for ways to link information as process narratives that the teacher will accept. Their comments reflect the interpretive contingencies introduced by the ambiguity of the teacher's Socratic questions. For example, at one point the students link background information about animals reproducing to the candidate explanations expressed earlier, indicating that a male parent's ear shape influences the ear shape of the offspring. The students shift the frame of reference to commonplace experiences outside of the classroom and colloquial discourse. They joke about promiscuity of the rabbits (Transcript Extract 7.5, lines A122-A142). This frame of reference emphasizes the information that different traits among animals can result from the offspring having different fathers. It supports the students' expression of process narratives linking the screen information with such background knowledge – even if the information is incorrect.

Transcript Extract 7.5: Introducing a Colloquial Frame of Reference

A119. T1: Okay, now, where did the floppy ear – directions for making floppy ears come from? You've got a straight eared
A120. B12: mother
A121. T1: rabbit and there's another straight-eared rabbit. Where'd they get the directions for making floppy ears?
A122. B13: Because there was a – /there was a different/
A123. G11: /She did it with somebody else./
A124. B13: /father for/
A125. B11: /She was a player/
A126. B13: both of 'em ...
A127. B11: She /was a player/
A128. G11: /Mr. [T1's surname]/ she was a /player/
A129. B11: /heyy/

Transcript Extract 7.3 (continued)

A130. B13: She was a player
A131. B11: She /was here and there/
A132. G11: /She was screwing/ around
A133. T1: Is that why she
A134. B12: She a ho'
A135. G11: she was screwing around
A136. B13: She a ho' (laughs)
A137. B12: She a ho'
A138. G11: (pointing at rabbit on the computer screen) With the this right here right here
A139. T1: I didn't put her in the bedroom . .
A140. B13: She had gone before you put 'em in.
A141. B12: (laughs)
A142. B13: She was – she was a little row – uh . rowdy so she had to go get something.
A143. T1: Where did the gene for the /floppy ears come from?/
A144. B13?: /She (????)/
A145. T1: Huh?

G11 changes the subject from promiscuity, and provides an alternative to the sexual innuendos. She mentions that 'somebody' in the family background had the floppy ears, inferring that the factors affecting ear shape are inherited; not random or the result of other causes: 'Maybe maybe from from the – know like the background somebody had – maybe had floppy ears' (Transcript Extract 7.6, line A146). However, G11's utterance continues to emphasize the inheritance of family resemblance that was an underlying theme of the rude joking.

The interaction demonstrates the concurrent development of an interpretive frame of reference and explanatory process narratives. The students search for information that would contribute to process narratives relevant to the task prompt and acceptable to the teacher. An absence of such information moves them toward the use of grey boxes. For example, B11 adds 'ancestors' ('the ancestors or something') to 'background' as a way of indexing a perspective emphasizing the relevance of kinship (Transcript Extract 7.6, lines 146, 149).

As various students contribute to the discussion, 'ancestors' is replaced with 'first generation' (Transcript Extract 7.6, line A154). B13's use of the term *generation* shifts to conventional genetics discourse and a frame of reference that emphasizes describing the screen images. However, the emphasis on screen information does not persist as the discussion then moves from the rabbits' ears to human eye color and a personal example of human hairline inheritance within a family. B13's example of the inheritance of a widow's peak hairline (Transcript Extract 7.6, lines A162-A167) emphasizes family experience, e.g., ''cause, 'cause see no one else in my family has my grandfather's uh forehead except for me' (Transcript Extract 7.6, line A162).

Transcript Extract 7.6: Searching for a Frame of Reference

A146. G11: Maybe maybe from from the – know like the background somebody had – maybe had floppy ears
A147. T1: Oh, somebody in the background was watching? Oh, I –
A148. G11: Noo, no you know like you know how – you know the
A149. B11: the ancestors /or something/
A150. G11: /The an/cestors and everything
A151. T1: What do they have to do with it?
A152. B13: Yeah,
A153. B11: They probab/ly have the . floppy ears/
A154. B13: /sometimes the the /first generation will have 'em, but the second generation won't.
A155. T1: How can that be?
A156. B13: I don't know.
A157. B11: I don't know that's how it is with the eyes too
A158. T1: Is it with the eyes?
A159. B13: Yeah
A160. B11: Colored eyes
A161. T1: My folks have eyes like mine
A162. B13: 'cause, 'cause see no one else in my family has my grandfather's uh forehead except for me
A163. G11: /(laughs)/
A164. B12: /(laughs)/
A165. B13: I'm the second generation
A166. T1: You're the second gener – Really
A167. B13: I got the Mickey Mouse
A168. T1: Was he /also bald?/
A169. G11: /(laughing) He got the /Mickey Mouse.
A170. T1: (To B13) No?
A171. B13: No.
A172. T1: No
A173. B13: He had his hair. He had a lot of his hair before he died. . I don't know about now, he's been buried about . three years. He's lost his hair by now.
A174. B11?: (laughs)

The shared interpretive frame of reference in this part of the discussion results from the mention of commonplace experience – family resemblance concerning hairline. This information includes a process narrative about B13's family, which B13 finds analogous to the computer simulation's rabbits (Transcript Extract 7.6, lines A162-A167):

> 'cause, 'cause see no one else in my family has my grandfather's uh forehead except for me (line A162)
>
> I'm the second generation (line A165)
>
> I got the Mickey Mouse (line A167)

The exchange between B13 and the teacher not only presents information analogous to the screen images showing trait inheritance across generations, but also functions to emphasize the relevance of information about traits and generations (Transcript Extract 7.6, lines A154-A167). However, the 'family resemblance' frame of reference does not provide the students with the information that would answer the task prompt and the teacher's question about the source of inherited traits. The teacher does not indicate that B13's analogous example of hairline inheritance has provided the missing information that would explicate the teacher's earlier use of the terms, 'where' and 'come from'. In that context, B11 continues to seek the missing information. He asks, 'So where did it come from?' (Transcript Extract 7.7, line A175). The teacher responds by restating B11's question as 'where did this rabbit get the directions for making it?' (Transcript Extract 7.7, line A176).

Transcript Extract 7.7: T1 Shifts from Colloquial Frame of Reference

A175. B11: So where did it come from?
A176. T1: Where did – where did – where did-where did this rabbit get the directions for making it?
A177. B13: From his – from his – from his – from his
A178. B12: From the first couple, you know uh
A179. T1: Oh, they got in the bedroom with these guys?
A180. B13: (joking) yeah they were both doing it
A181. T1: They do what G11 said they were going to do?
A182. /(G11, B11, B12, B13 laugh)/
A183. B11: /(?) both got a train (?)/
A184. T1: I know who I put in that bedroom, and it wasn't the other ones.
A185. G11: (????)

Transcript Extract 7.7 (continued)

A186. B11: They must have a train /(??)/
A187. T1: /(???)/ put in the bedroom (using mouse to point to rabbits on computer screen) I put in
A188. G11: You put – you put bo .
A189. T1: these
A190. G11: yeah those two
A191. T1: Okay, so if-if-if-if all the directions we have for making things come from your parents, then where did they get this from
A192. B12: from their grandparents
A193. T1: From their grandparents who were in the bedroom with them?
A194. B12: No. I'm saying they get it from the genes from the grandparents. . They got it from the .
/Grandparents/
A195. G11 /May/
A196. T1: /Okay, so the/ genes they have
A197. B12: They had
A198. T1: the genes they had /came from who then?/

The teacher uses the term, 'directions', which refers to unseen factors that affect the inheritance of ear shape among the rabbits. B12's response, 'From the first couple' (Transcript Extract 7.7, line A178), leads to the teacher sardonically recycling the promiscuity frame of reference in order to prompt the students to consider the empirical evidence on the screen:

> 'Oh, they got in the bedroom with these guys?'[27] (Transcript Extract 7.7, line A179)
>
> 'I know who I put in that bedroom, and it wasn't the other ones.' (Transcript Extract 7.7, line A184).

The teacher's comments also reinforce the contingency of finding missing information, which complicates the students' attempts to answer the teacher's questions about where the directions for floppy ears come from.

In the context of the teacher's comments, B12 mentions kinship, expressing the source of the 'directions', saying, 'from their grandparents,' (Transcript Extract 7.7, line A192) which indexes at least three frames of reference and types of information:

- The colloquial sense of family resemblance
- Knowledge that DNA is inherited across many generations
- A reference to the sequence of boxes on the computer screen which represent generations

However, B12's answer does not satisfy the teacher, whose response suggests that it lacks empirical specificity ('From their grandparents who were in the bedroom with them?' Transcript Extract 7.7, line A193). The teacher's sarcastic expression of a counterfactual description emphasizes that an appropriate answer must note the direct generational link between inherited traits. B12 acknowledges this by clarifying his answer, saying, 'No. I'm saying they get it from the genes from the grandparents' (Transcript Extract 7.7, line A194). He deals with the teacher's teasing responses about direct parentage by inserting a mediating device, 'the genes', between the initial generation showing floppy ears and the third generation that also shows them.

This exchange displays the students' difficulty disengaging their knowledge of genes and DNA from the interpretation of the screen images and the task prompt question. The teacher proceeds to divert them from a frame of reference concerning the operation of genes to a frame of reference concerning the generational location of genes. He again focuses on the rabbits displayed on the screen when he asks, 'the genes they had came from who then?' (Transcript Extract 7.7, line A198). The difficulty that the students display in regard to finding terms to express a link between the observed sequence of traits across generations and a cause for the sequence results from the interpretive contingencies of dealing with the absence of information about cellular genetic processes.

In order to resolve their difficulties in recognizing and explaining the relationship between the images presented by the computer simulation and an explanation of trait inheritance, the students apply common expressions to cover the information gaps. For example, G11 uses 'weren't strong enough' in place of the missing information about cellular processes that would link genes and traits. G11 recycles her earlier concern with power and the workings of genes ('the male's have – more – more power', Transcript Extract 7.2, line A66) when she says, 'Maybe the genes weren't strong enough' (Transcript Extract 7.8, line A199). She returns to power as a frame of reference, although the teacher did not accept it earlier.

Transcript Extract 7.8: Recycling Genetic Processes

A199. G11: /Maybe Mr. [teacher's surname]/. Maybe w – maybe the-the-the genes weren't strong enough.
A200. T1: Maybe.
A201. G11: Their
A202. T1: But the genes must have come from what? That's the bottom line. Where did the genes come from?
A203. G11: The genes
A204. B13: From them (referring to rabbits on computer screen)
A205. T1: From these two
A206. G11: From the
A207. B12: Good
A208. G11: both of them
A209. T1: Now . /I don't/
A210. G11: /From the eggs/

Without elaboration, power is ambiguous as a guide to explaining the inheritance of ear shape displayed on the computer screen. It can direct attention to the cellular processes of genes in some unspecified way or it can again emphasize some commonplace use of the word, such as strength or size, which is also unspecified linguistically or pictorially. This is an example of how, in the absence of information about cellular processes, the various interpretive frames of reference expressed during the discussion complicate the process of discarding certain explanations and emphasizing others. The students' interpretation activities show how grey boxes develop and function.

Building the Grey Box

During the discussion of the screen images with the teacher, the students display a slow shift away from the interpretive contingencies of treating ambiguous terms as prompts for seeking additional information. As an alternative to those contingencies, the students eventually accept and apply certain linguistic terms as grey boxes for the missing information about how genes affect the development of physical traits. However, as the students seek additional information during their transition to using grey boxes, they express confusing mind boggles related to the information constraints presented by the teacher's comments and the screen images.

For example, after the students have mentioned gender, quantity or power of genes, and promiscuity to explain the ear shapes of the offspring rabbits, the teacher asks, 'But the genes must have come from what? That's the bottom line. Where did the genes come from?' (Transcript Extract 7.8, line A202).[28] He constrains the agenda for the discussion when he says, 'that's the bottom line'. In the context of his earlier utterances these comments emphasize that determining where the genes 'come from' relates to the rabbits' ear shapes and the sequence of generations displayed on the screen, while deemphasizing the students' prior comments about the power of genes and family resemblance. However, the students' uncertain responses show that his directive does not resolve their interpretive contingency of finding information to elucidate the meanings of 'where' and 'come from' (Transcript Extract 7.8, lines A202-A210, Transcript Extract 7.9). The information constraints of the screen images, task prompt, and the teacher's de-emphasis of cellular processes increase the students' interpretive contingencies. This leads to the eventual use of grey boxes by the students.

Yet, even as they begin that transition, they continue to seek and incorporate the type of information and frames of reference that the teacher has previously rejected. For example, B13 orients his comments to the immediate interaction with the teacher and the computer simulation. Answering the teacher's question, 'Where did the genes come from,' he refers to the images of generations of rabbits on the screen, saying, 'From them', which indexes both the screen images and the general concept of offspring inheriting genes from parents (Transcript Extract 7.8, lines A202, A204). G11 echoes this answer with her response, 'From the both of them' (Transcript Extract 7.8, lines A206, A208). Then, despite the teacher's emphasis on the screen images (e.g., 'From these two', Transcript Extract 7.8, line A205) and previous de-emphasis of cellular genetic processes as a way of explaining 'where traits come from', G11 offers the answer 'from the eggs' (Transcript Extract 7.8, line A210). She again suggests a frame of reference emphasizing that cell division and the cellular biology of reproduction are relevant for explaining the inheritance of traits across generations.

If the discussion were to emphasize the cellular processes related to G11's comments, a few more pieces of information would link them as a process narrative about where floppy ears come from, e.g., *The offspring rabbits inherit genes from their parents, because when the parents mate, the fertilized eggs contain their genes, and those genes are replicated within each of the offspring. Then the fertilized egg divides into various cells, and the genes trigger development of proteins to form the rabbit's physical characteristics, such as its ears.*

The transmission of genetic material across generations and its effect on the cellular biological components that led to different ear shapes was a potential answer to the question 'where do the floppy ears come from?' However, when the students presented answers or explanations that mentioned cellular processes, the teacher moved the discussion away from those topics. The conventional Mendelian curriculum, applied by T1 and the other teachers studied, does not explain trait inheritance by applying information about cellular genetic processes. Mendel's research occurred prior to the existence of such information. Consequently, the de-emphasis of cellular genetics as an explanation of trait inheritance is common in high school biology classes as well as educational exhibits (Saferstein and Sarangi, 2010).

The data show that the students have not developed a shared interpretive frame of reference with the teacher about the working meaning of 'where the floppy ear genes come from'. For example, B13 expresses surprise at G11's mention of eggs ('Eehggs?' Transcript Extract 7.9, line A212). His reaction to G11 de-emphasizes previously studied information about the cellular biology of reproduction as a perspective relevant to the task at hand (i.e., explaining 'where the genes for floppy ears come from'). G11 continues to emphasize a perspective based on the cellular biology of reproduction as she responds to B13's questioning of her mention of eggs.

She begins a narrative explanation of her viewpoint: 'You know when you have sex' (Transcript Extract 7.9, line A215). However, the teacher again directs the discussion away from the cellular perspective and toward the information presented by the computer simulation: 'I don't see the floppy eared . . they didn't use the floppy eared directions here' (Transcript Extract 7.9, lines A220, A222). The phrase, 'They didn't use the floppy eared directions,' presents two terms, 'use' and 'directions', which the students can apply as grey boxes for the missing information about cellular processes.

Transcript Extract 7.9: Dead Ends and Boggles

A211. T1: Okay s-but I don't see that
A212. B13: Eehggs?
A213. B12: Mm don't say /(?from the DNA?)/
A214. T1: /I don't – I don't s/
A215. G11: /You know when you have/ sex
A216. B11: (to G11, regarding the software interface on the screen) Wha-wha . what is that? The bank and the what?
A217. B12: I do have
A218. B13: They don't
A219. G11: (to one of the boys) Shut up.
A220. T1: I don't see the floppy /eared/
A221. B13: /They don't/ lay eggs.
A222. T1: They didn't use the floppy eared directions here.
A223. G11: They used the straight ears . .

Transcript Extract 7.9 (continued)

A224. T1: Yeah .. but then you're saying they got the floppy ear directions from this rabbit. Is that what you're saying?
A225. G11: No .
A226. T1: You're not?
A227. G11: No I'm not saying that
A228. B13: You're confusing us
A229. G11: Who's confusing you, I'm not.
A230. B13: No, she-he's confusing us
[Student from another group asks T1 a question. T1 responds]
A231. G11: So .. okay . okay they . (gestures with pen as she refers to rabbits) okay the female and the male
A232. T1: Yeah
A233. G11: okay they-they got (jabs pen toward screen) together
A234. T1: Yeah
A235. G11: and they had babies (claps hands together as she says 'babies').
A236. T1: Yeah ...
A237. G11: boy (giggles) . and then okay (moves hand and points finger toward screen) the floppy ears they came out.. /I don't know from/
A238. B13: /They did?/
A239. G11: where, but

G11's response ('They used the straight ears.' Transcript Extract 7.9, line A223) echoes both the emphasis on the screen images and the teacher's application of the word 'use' as a substitute for information about cellular processes. Both G11 and the teacher avoid specifying cellular processes by referring to the characteristics of the rabbits on the screen, as they respectively apply 'didn't use' and 'used' to descriptions of the screen images. While the teacher mentioned 'the floppy eared directions' (Transcript Extract 7.9, line A222), G11 omits the word 'directions' in her response (line A223). When the teacher then says, 'Yeah but then you're saying they got the floppy ear directions from this rabbit. Is that what you're saying?' he again presents G11 with 'directions' as a potential placeholder for the missing information about cellular processes (Transcript Extract 7.9, line A224). Applying 'directions' as a grey box would provide the students with a way of creating process narratives that explain the inheritance of floppy ears from parents having straight ears by describing the screen images and avoiding discussion of genes, DNA, or cellular process information.

However, G11 does not apply 'directions' as a grey box. Instead, she responds to the teacher by saying 'No' to his interpretation of her reasoning (Transcript Extract 7.9, line A225). When the teacher provides her with a chance to reconsider her answer with his question, 'you're not?' she answers, 'No I'm not saying that' (Transcript Extract 7.9, lines A226, A227). G11 denies that her preceding utterances led to the conclusion, which the teacher imputes to her reasoning, i.e., that the offspring rabbits' floppy ears were inherited from straight-eared parents. G11 does not yet accept 'directions' as a placeholder for the missing information about cellular processes.

A 'Critical Mass' of Interpretive Contingencies: The Turn Toward Grey Boxes

The interaction among the students and teacher presents confusing interpretive contingencies that the students cannot resolve due to restrictions on seeking cellular process information. This increase of students' interpretive contingencies was a result of the conventional curriculum for teaching about trait inheritance presented by teachers and textbooks. The curriculum featured students imitating a version of Mendel's research. T1 and the other teachers studied applied that conventional curriculum for teaching trait inheritance. In this case, the data show the teacher de-emphasizing information about reproductive cells and DNA, which the students may have encountered during the biology course or outside of school. Instead, he encourages the students to make the kinds of inferences that Mendel made. However, Mendel's inferences were based on understandings of biology that did not include information about the cellular processes and molecular biology of genes, DNA, RNA, proteins, hormones, and enzymes. The students' responses show that they have difficulty ignoring previously encountered information about genes that seems relevant for creating process narratives linking genes and traits to explain the appearance, disappearance, and reappearance of floppy ears across generations of rabbits.

The teacher's comments and questions presented the students with the interpretive contingency of finding an acceptable way to linguistically mark the missing information, without actually seeking the missing information, in order to complete explanatory process narratives that would refer to cellular genetic processes. For example, when the teacher said, 'They didn't use the floppy eared directions here', the word 'use' presents this interpretive contingency for the students, since 'using directions' implies that some agent, action, or process implements the directions (Transcript Extract 7.9, line A222). Yet, the screen images and task prompt do not present information about an agent, action, or process by which genes effect the development of cells. Such contingencies complicate the students' work of establishing a shared frame of reference for dealing with the key question, 'Where do the genes for floppy ears come from?' (Transcript Extract 7.8, line A202).

Eventually, repeated use of the word, 'directions', to mark the unseen and unspecified processes by which genes affect the development of physical traits would focus the students on applying the term as a placeholder in process narratives that describe the available information on the computer screen. However, prior to that, both the absence of information about genes or DNA in the screen images and the teacher's de-emphasis of the students' attempts to introduce it functioned to separate 'directions' from a search for cellular process information. Repeated encounters with such interpretive contingencies accustomed students to using grey boxes, and prepared them to apply the traditional grey boxes of nomenclature and computational tables featured in the conventional Mendelian genetics curriculum (e.g., alphanumeric symbols, Punnett squares, ratios).

The ensuing discussion of the computer simulation provides an example of this transition toward grey boxes. After indexing cellular processes without specifying them ('They didn't use the floppy eared directions here', Transcript Extract 7.9, line A222), the teacher shifts again to the descriptive frame of reference in the question he directs toward G11. He emphasizes the characteristics of the rabbits on the screen: 'but then you're saying they got the floppy ear directions from this rabbit. Is that what you're saying?' (Transcript Extract 7.9, line A224). This frame shifting boggles the students. G11's response 'No I'm not saying that' (line A227) backs away from her previous comments about genes coming from parents and eggs (Transcript Extract 7.8, lines 203, 205, 208, 210). B13, who began the learning interaction by expressing an understanding of when straight-eared and floppy-eared offspring would appear on the screen in relation to the traits of the parents, explicitly states that he is confused ('You're confusing us', 'he's confusing us', Transcript Extract 7.9, lines A228, A230).

The students must cope with the multiple contingencies related to making inferences about the nature of trait inheritance. These include the various interpretive frames of reference that have been introduced related to the transmission of traits across generations (e.g., strength of genes, gender, promiscuity, DNA).

G11 again tries to coherently link the information emphasized as being relevant during the discussion:

> So okay okay they (gestures with pen as she refers to rabbits) okay the female and the male, okay they-they got (jabs pen toward screen) together and they had babies (claps hands together as she says 'babies') boy

(giggles) and then okay (moves hand and points finger toward screen) the floppy ears, they came out. I don't know from (line A231) where, but (Transcript Extract 7.9, lines A231, A233, A235, A237, A239).

G11 tries to form a process narrative by organizing useful information and sorting out the confusing information the students had mentioned previously. This time she addresses the gap in cellular process information by applying a format for organizing available information that resembles the teacher's questioning of the students – including the use of the images on the computer screen. She combines talk and gesture to describe what the screen shows: i.e., the straight-eared female and the male mated and produced offspring; and some of the offspring had floppy ears. However, her descriptive narrative stalls at this point due to lack of information other than the appearance of the screen images:

and then okay the floppy ears, they came out I don't know from where, but. (Transcript Extract 7.9, lines A237, A239)

G11's incomplete process narrative describes the use of the computer simulation to produce certain screen images. She applies words that also refer to the social activities of individuals ('they got together and they had babies,' Transcript Extract 7.9, lines A233, A235). She also mentions the phenotype of the offspring that appear on the screen 'and then okay (moves hand and points finger toward screen) the floppy ears they came out' (Transcript Extract 7.9, lines A237). She begins to apply a grey box, 'came out', which functions as a placeholder for missing information about how genes affect the development of an individual's phenotype. However, G11 does not treat 'the floppy ears, they came out' as an adequate answer to the teacher's question. She adds, 'I don't know from where' (Transcript Extract 7.9, lines A237, A239). She notes the information gap, but she has not yet accepted the approach of reducing interpretive contingencies by simply marking the missing information with a grey box, rather than searching for missing information about cellular genetic processes.

G11's expressed confusion shows that she still has not identified a frame of reference for an appropriate answer to the teacher's questions about where the traits or genes for them 'come from'. In the terms of the interpretive perspective emphasized by the teacher, G11 does not know where the floppy ears *come from*. The earlier candidate answers mentioning genes, DNA, and eggs have been ruled out.

At this point in the students' interpretive work, 'came out', 'came from', etc. are not satisfactory as grey boxes, because they continue to add multiple contingencies that students must juggle in memory as they continue their interpretation activities. Those terms index aspects of the screen information (the appearance of a trait in one generation that did not appear in the preceding generation), but they can also index cellular process information that would link genes and traits. This indeterminacy presents an information gap when the students attempt to organize verbal and visual information as a process narrative.

Moreover, the teacher's questions both limited the interpretive frame of reference and made a fine distinction between relevant and irrelevant information, e.g.:

> But the genes must have come from what? That's the bottom line. Where did the genes come from? (Transcript Extract 7.8, line A202)
>
> but then you're saying they got the floppy ear directions from this rabbit. Is that what you're saying? (Transcript Extract 7.9, line A224)

Consequently, the questions add to the multiple contingencies of interpreting and organizing information that the students must keep in mind. On one hand, the students are being asked to find a biological process (i.e., inheritance of traits across generations), and on the other hand, they are asked to ignore related processes (e.g., meiosis and cellular chemistry related to genes). Those interpretive contingencies are not simply the result of this teacher's choice of words or pedagogy. They developed in all of the biology classes studied, taught by seven different teachers. The contingencies derived from the professional culture's emphasis on particular discourse frameworks that constitute the Mendelian curriculum (discussed in Parts Three and Four).

Dealing with Constraints on Information: Form of Expression as a Resource for Understanding

The teacher's comments and questions emphasize the available screen information. They also indicate that the students should not apply their understandings of DNA or cell division to an explanatory process narrative. The teacher's attempts to focus the students' interpretation activities limit both the information they can apply and the organization of information that counts as coherence – i.e., the teacher limits what information is worth considering and how the usable information can be linked as process narratives. These interpretive contingencies actually move the students toward accepting the use of certain terms as grey boxes and abandoning the frame of reference concerning the cellular processes of genes. Like Mendel, the students can resolve the absence of information by just assuming or accepting that hidden factors exist and that those factors affect ear shape – without considering how such factors function to affect ear shape.

Although G11's attempt to develop an explanatory process narrative stalled due to lack of information, it did provide an opportunity for the teacher to validate the linking of various screen images in order to explain the inheritance of traits (Transcript Extract 7.9, lines A231-A239). For example, the teacher said 'yeah' three times as G11 presented her incomplete process narrative, encouraging her to continue (lines A232, A234, A236). Although G11's process narrative was incomplete, it did link aspects of the screen images and operation of the software, e.g.:

- 'The female and the male' refers to the gender symbols next to the pictures of rabbits.
- 'The floppy ears, they came out' refers to the pictorial representations of rabbits with different shaped ears, the operation of the software to produce generations of rabbits, and the appearance, disappearance, and reappearance of floppy ears across three generations of rabbits presented on the screen.
- 'Got together' refers to use of the computer mouse to select images of specific rabbits, move them to the box in the upper right of the screen, and then mouse click the run icon to produce a new generation of offspring.
- 'Had babies' refers to the appearance of the new generations of offspring represented by boxed rows and columns of offspring rabbits and parent rabbits, which appear in a box above them.

Thus, despite the lack of an adequate answer to the teacher's questions, the discussion reinforced an interpretive frame of reference and a communication format that emphasized the computer screen images. This activity provides a foundation for accepting the absence of cellular process information, and using grey boxes in order to develop coherent process narratives that will function as acceptable explanations of trait inheritance answering the teacher's questions.

The teacher continues to use a Socratic approach to guide the students toward the explanation that he considers appropriate. He again models a way of using the term, 'directions', in place of information about cellular processes – by linking it to the information on the screen without explaining the particulars of 'directions' or how they function. He emphasizes the 'giving' and 'getting' of directions:

> So, who gave 'em the directions for making flop-who gave- (Transcript Extract 7.10, line A242)
>
> who gave [B13's first name] the directions (Transcript Extract 7.10, line A244)
>
> You get the directions from your parents not from your grandparents, right? (Transcript Extract 7.10, lines A253, A255, A257).

When the teacher asks, 'who gave [B13's first name] the directions?' he conveys the point that some aspect of the development of traits can be explained by considering source and location without considering cellular processes (Transcript Extract 7.10, line A244). By using the words, 'gave', 'making', and 'directions', he also conveys a frame of reference that emphasizes using grey boxes for missing information (Transcript Extract 7.10, lines A240, A242, A244). However, the students' responses show that the teacher's mention of 'gave', 'making', and 'directions', remains a source of confusion in regard to that frame of reference.

Tolerating Information Gaps

Transcript Extract 7.10

A240. T1: Hmm ..They must have the directions for making it, right?
A241. G11: Yes.
A242. T1: So, who gave 'em the directions for making flop-who gave-
A243. G11: the mo/ther/
A244. T1: /[B13's first name]/ who gave [B13's first name] the directions for /making his/
A245. G11: /the father ./ their parents. Their parents did.
A246. T1: Okay
A247. B12: Well their parents' parents . okay
A248. G11: Their parents . ya know . /got it out/
A249. B12: /Yo paren/ts' . parents
A250. B13: Your grandparents
A251. B12: Yeah grandparents ...
A252. G11: But no but-but how
A253. T1: You get the directions /from/
A254. G11: /but/
A255. T1: your parents not from your grand/parents,/
A256. B13: /See you/
A257. T1: /right?/

Transcript Extract 7.10 (continued)

A258. G11: /'cause/
A259. B13: (tapping his pen for emphasis) you-you get your genes from your parents, but your parents get the genes from their parents, /but they're your grandparents and then they/
A260. G11: /No, but [B13's first name] but/
A261. B13: get it from your great-/grandparents and your great-grandparents get it from your great-great grandparents/
A262. G11: /no see-ya see you're you're mixing yourself up/
A263. B12: /[rhythmically] da da da da da da da da da da/ da da da da
A264. G11: No, what he's trying to say-like say . like you know how your parents you know they got together and they had you . but how – say if you come out different, but how did you get – how did you come out different. See (pointing at rabbits on the screen) see these two here have straight ears but how did these two come – how did this one come out . different

When the students answer the teacher's questions, they revert to frames of reference related either to families or genetic processes. G11 mentions candidate answers to the teacher's question about who gave B13 the directions for his hairline: 'the mother . . the father . . their parents. Their parents did' (Transcript Extract 7.10, lines A243, A245). B12 adds, 'well their parents' parents' (Transcript Extract 7.10, line A247). G11 continues to mention parents (Transcript Extract 7.10, line A248). B13 then adds 'your grandparents' (Transcript Extract 7.10, line A250), which B12 echoes (line A251). B12 and B13 have returned to a family frame of reference by mentioning the chain of kinship. The teacher then seeks a more accurate explanation than that of family resemblance by asking, 'You get the directions from your parents not from your grandparents, right?' (Transcript Extract 7.10, lines A253, A255, A257). B13 responds by explaining what he meant when he said that each generation's parents 'get the genes from' their parents, mentioning a chain of kinship from parents to great-great grandparents:

> you get your genes from your parents, but your parents get the genes from their parents, but they're your grandparents and then they get it from your great-grandparents and they get it from your great-great grandparents. (Transcript Extract 7.10, lines A259, A261)

He reverts to applying the term 'genes' instead of the more general term 'directions'. G11 interrupts him, saying, 'no see-ya see you're you're mixing yourself up' (Transcript Extract 7.10, line A262).

The subsequent interaction shows that the students are in the process of recognizing and applying certain terms as grey boxes. Despite the students' expressed uncertainty about the content of such terms, the format of their answers begins to conform to the conventional task discourse emphasized by the teacher. The interpretation activities that develop a communication format for dealing with both available information and missing information contribute to the development of a shared frame of reference related to the ambiguous terms.

B12's use of 'parents' parents' instead of 'grandparents' (Transcript Extract 7.10, line A247) displays this adaptation to the Mendelian discourse. 'Parents' parents' is uncommon in everyday conversation, but describes both the arrangement of generations on the computer screen and the discussion's emphasis on parents as sources of 'directions'. This is an example of how the interpreting of information and the construction of coherence by formulating and eliminating candidate explanations produces a particular frame of reference linked to a localized set of information resources. The concurrent development of process narratives and interpretive frames of reference is evident in these exchanges. By saying 'parents' parents', B12 synchronizes a common term for a family relationship with its use in the genetics assignments and discourse – i.e., not in terms of personal experience or culturally shared notions of grandparents as they appear, interact, and play various roles in family life, but in terms of kinship over generations based on the production of generations of rabbits that serve as data for analysis in regard to the inheritance of ear shape.

This is an example of unpacking and reconfiguring indexicality – i.e., an example of recognizing and emphasizing one of the multiple meanings and associations based on personal and cultural experience of kinship, and attaching it to the task resources. In the latter capacity, 'parents' parents' also helps to acknowledge and to address the interpretive contingencies that the learning interaction displays to the students.

At this point, the students begin to construct the relevance of 'generation' not just in regard to the visible information on the screen, but also in regard to undisplayed factors that affect the inheritance of floppy ears. The frame of reference recognizing family relationships contributes to, but does not accomplish, the task of interpreting and organizing the information presented on the screen in order to form a coherent explanation of the appearance, disappearance, and reappearance of floppy ears in certain generations of rabbits. In order to develop a coherent explanation, the students must recognize and apply a different frame of reference, which emphasizes that completing the task involves linking an accurate description of the screen images to an explanation of unseen factors that cause the particular patterns of ear shape presented by those images.

As the discussion proceeds, the students begin to develop an interpretive frame of reference in which they accept certain linguistic terms as placeholders for missing information – as grey boxes – rather than continuing to search for information to fill the gaps related to cellular genetic processes. For example, in response to B13's description of the inheritance of 'directions' across distant generations of grandparents, G11 presents a narrative explanation that attempts to integrate reproduction with the information presented on the computer screen, which the teacher has emphasized. She frames her utterance as clarifying what the teacher is explaining, 'what he's trying to say' (Transcript Extract 7.10, line A264):

> *No, what he's trying to say-like say like you know how your parents you know they got together and they had you but how – say if you come out different, but how did you get – how did you come out different. See (pointing at rabbits on the screen) see these two here have straight ears but how did these two come – how did this one come out different.*

G11 expresses an incomplete process narrative that describes her interpretations of what the teacher is explaining. She links information presented by the screen and the teacher in order to show that she has developed a shared interpretive frame of reference with the teacher: 'No, what he's trying to say-like say like you know how your parents got together and they had you' She adds a conceptual question similar to T1's questions: 'but how – say if you come out different, but how did you get – how did you come out different.' She points to specific rabbits, and restates the question in terms of the immediate task resources, i.e., her frame of reference emphasizes the screen images and the generational pattern.

G11 does not present information or concepts that would link genes to the disappearance and reappearance of traits across generations of rabbits. Instead, she transmutes the teacher's series of questions about where the floppy ears, directions, or genes 'come from' (Transcript Extracts 7.4, 7.5, 7.7–7.9) into a question about *how* the floppy-eared rabbits 'come out' different: "See (pointing at rabbits on the screen) see these two here have straight ears but how did these two come – how did this one come out different' (Transcript Extract 7.10, line A264). Combined with her pointing toward the screen images, G11's utterance functions as a variation of a descriptive process narrative: i.e., *Mating two straight-eared rabbits triggers some unknown process that produces a mixture of straight-eared and floppy-eared offspring*. This formulation opens the door to substituting a grey-box term for the unseen cellular genetic process, and tolerating the absence of such process information.

Restating the teacher's question as 'how did you come out different?' G11 begins to reconcile the cellular process perspective (genes, DNA, eggs) with B13's descriptive perspective based on mapping of traits across generations (rabbits' ear shapes and human hairlines). While G11 does not actually answer the teacher's question, she does express a frame of reference for interpreting the information and dealing with the multiple contingencies. Her rephrasing of the ambiguous terms expressed by the teacher copes with two interpretive contingencies. 'How did you come out' matches the teacher's emphasis on the traits of parents and offspring, and it displays G11's cognizance of the teacher's rejection of answers emphasizing cellular processes (e.g., DNA, eggs). 'Come out different', in conjunction with G11's pointing at the screen, displays the drift away from a concern with cellular genetic processes and toward an emphasis on the visual information on the screen. She has discarded information that did not lead to coherence in the context of the teacher's comments.

The difficulty for the students remains that of explaining trait inheritance by interpreting 'how the floppy ears reappeared' in a way that does not involve information about cellular processes, but acknowledges that unseen factors link the varying ear shapes in the generations of rabbits displayed on the screen. The students' ensuing task interaction shows the process of developing a frame of reference that tolerates the absence of cellular process information by sorting out some information and emphasizing other information. Eventually, the students accept certain terms as grey boxes in order to cope with the emerging interpretive contingencies of restricted information. The students drift toward a frame of reference emphasizing the descriptive matching of traits across generations. This discursive and cognitive drift resulted from the intricate combination of digressions that recycled topics related to the constraints presented by the teacher's comments.

Recognizing and Accepting Grey Boxes

The students are moving toward recognizing and accepting a grey box as part of their frame of reference and communication format for completing the task (Transcript Extract 7.11, lines A265-A292). This interpretation activity includes tolerating the gap in cellular process information rather than searching for it or applying previously encountered information about DNA or cell division. For example, B13 shifts the discussion from biochemical process to location within generations by revisiting his earlier analogy between the reappearance of rabbits' floppy ears on the screen and the reappearance of a widow's peak hairline in his family:

> How come my mom and my my dad have the sa – have have . the straight forehead and I got the Mickey Mouse forehead I got the same forehead as my grandfather (Transcript Extract 7.11, line A265)

Responding, T1 and G11 reemphasize location in generations as a useful interpretive frame of reference (Transcript Extract 7.11):

A269. T1: No. Okay that means it must come from your mom and dad that's what it means.
A270. G11: From your parents

B13 agrees with their emphasis on parents, but explains that his preceding utterance had another point:

A271. B13: That's what we've been say/ing

A273. B13: so where did they get it from.

He acknowledges that the trait is transmitted ('comes from') from the parents, but then he emphasizes that the question at hand is 'where did they [the parents] get it from', i.e., where does the trait actually 'come from' – the frame of reference the teacher has emphasized throughout the discussion.

Transcript Extract 7.11: Searching for a Useful Frame of Reference

A265. B13: How come my mom and my my dad have the sa – have have . the straight forehead and I got the Mickey Mouse forehead? . I got the same forehead as /. my grandfather/
A266. T1: /(???)/ why you got the Mickey Mouse forehead (laughs).
A267. B12: Oooo (T1 grabs computer mouse and looks at screen) .
A268. B13: Hey now
A269. T1: No. Okay that means it must come from your mom and dad that's what it means.
A270. G11: From your parents
A271. B13: That's what we've been say/ing/
A272. T1: /Okay/ okay but now /see that means okay so/

Transcript Extract 7.11 (continued)

A273. B13: /so where did they get it from?/
A274. T1: so was the – was the direction for making floppy ears lost?
A275. B13: No
A276. T1: How do you know?
A277. B13: Because they made 'em right now
A278. T1: Which one made 'em? What generation?
A279. B13: The sec/ond/
A280. B12: /The/ first.
A281. B13: The first.
A282. T1: Oh the first one?
A283. B13: No, /the second one/
A284. B12: /Yeah/ look
A285. T1: They don't have any floppy ears
A286. B12: /Ohhh/
A287. B13: /No/ the first generation gave it to the second generation
A288. T1: (using mouse to point to rabbits on computer screen) Okay, so these guys didn't show it, but they must have what?
A289. B13: had it /had it/
A290. B12: /(points at 2nd generation on screen) had it/ (points at 3rd generation on screen)
/when they gave it to them/
A291. T1: /Okay it's because they/ – when you – yeah, because when you go to the next generation what do you see?
A292. B13: The first generation didn't have it, but the second generation did
A293. B12: yeah yeah
A294. B13: /because the because the first ge – it was having/

B13's utterance, 'so where did they get it from?' (Transcript Extract 7.11, line A273) shows the challenging interpretation activity by which the students shift frames of reference in order to deal with the de-emphasis of cellular process information. In regard to the immediately preceding utterances, B13's comment is redundant, simply repeating the teacher's earlier question. However, in the context of the students' previous mention of genes and eggs, B13's use of 'where' does not just index generations of a family or the arrangement of pictures of rabbits on the computer screen. It also serves as a placeholder for unseen and unspecified locations of genes within individuals. It functions as a grey box for the missing information about the processes by which genes influence the appearance of traits. By linking 'where' to parents rather than to the workings of genes, B13 begins to accept an interpretive frame of reference that emphasizes location in terms of individuals and kinship rather than cellular genetic processes. This eliminates an interpretive contingency, the restriction on searching for genetic process information, that the students encountered when the teacher deemphasized their previous attempts to link personal family experience and information about cell division with the information presented by the computer simulation.

As the teacher continues asking questions to elicit explanations of trait inheritance that fit his curriculum, he grey-boxes missing information about cellular processes by emphasizing a 'direction for making floppy ears' (Transcript Extract 7.11, line A274). 'Direction for making' reflects the grey boxes incorporated within the Mendelian curriculum (e.g., Punnett squares, ratios, nomenclature). The students' response to and appropriation of 'direction for making' moves them toward accepting and using the term, 'directions', and variations of it as grey boxes – i.e. as placeholders that do not prompt them to search for more information about cellular genetic processes.

For example, when the teacher asks B13 how he knows that the direction for making floppy ears was not lost when the F1 generation had only straight ears, B13 answers, 'because they made 'em right now', referring to the floppy-eared rabbits in the F2 generation, which the simulation had just displayed (Transcript Extract 7.11, lines A274, A277). The direction for floppy ears was not lost, because the simulation showed the floppy ears being made 'right now'. B13's use of the phrase, 'made 'em right now', both literally and figuratively locates the functioning of genes in the development of the last generation of rabbits displayed on the screen, yet it does not describe that functioning of genes or lead to such a description (Transcript Extract 7.11, line A277). Instead, 'made 'em' grey boxes cellular biochemical processes, and 'right now' links the appearance of floppy ears to the simulated breeding in which the offspring of two rabbits appear on the screen as new rows of rabbits placed beneath a row containing the parents. In the context of the preceding interaction, 'made 'em right now', substitutes the operation of the computer simulation for the biological processes of genetic inheritance. At this point in the discussion, the students have begun to apply a communication format that accepts the gap in process information without applying or searching for information about cellular processes.

Continuing that thread of the discussion, the teacher asks a question about generational location: 'Which one made 'em? What generation?' (Transcript Extract 7.11, line A278). While emphasizing generational location, his use of 'made 'em' also presents the students with the interpretive contingency of revisiting their earlier concern with cellular processes in regard to how the directions function within the rabbits. This produces some confusion among the students as B12 and B13 shift between expressing first or second generation as an answer (Transcript Extract 7.11, lines A279-A283). When the teacher questions their mention of the first generation, B13 changes his answer to 'the second one'. B12 then emphasizes the screen images, saying 'Yeah look' (lines 282–284).

In response, the teacher further emphasizes generational location by referring to the images on the screen:

> They don't have any floppy ears (Transcript Extract 7.11, line A285)
>
> Okay, so these guys didn't show it, but they must have what? (while using the computer mouse to point to rabbits on the screen, Transcript Extract 7.11, line A288)

In this exchange, the contingency of seeking information about cellular processes is displaced by reorienting the students to describing the location of traits in the generations displayed by the computer simulation.

The students have begun to replace the frame of reference emphasizing cellular processes with a descriptive frame of reference, emphasizing the characteristics of individual rabbits and generations on the computer screen. B13 links the visual information to create a process narrative about the location of the unseen genetic processes grey-boxed by the term 'directions': *'the first generation gave it to the second generation'* (Transcript Extract 7.11, line A287). He uses the pronoun, 'it', as a reference to a 'direction for making floppy ears' expressed by the teacher's earlier question, 'was the direction for making floppy ears lost?' (Transcript Extract 7.11, line A274).

At this point in the discussion, the students have begun using previously expressed terms as grey boxes ('directions', 'made it', 'had it') to link the pictorial information displayed on the screen in process narratives. For example, when the teacher uses the mouse pointer while mentioning the disappearance and reappearance of traits ('Okay, so these guys didn't show it, but they must have what?'), B12 repeats B13's responses, and points at the second and then the third generation of rabbits on the screen as he says, 'had it when they gave it to them' (Transcript Extract 7.11, lines A288-A290). The gestural emphasis on the screen information in combination with linguistic reference to 'it' increases the students' focus on the computer screen images as they describe the rabbits' physical characteristics and compare those characteristics across generations. This diminishes their concern with linking the screen images to information about cellular genetic processes. It also diminishes the interpretive contingency of replacing the grey boxes, 'made it', 'had it', and 'gave it', with information about cellular processes.

'Blueprints': A Grey Box that Eliminates Interpretive Contingencies

During the course of the discussion, the students have developed a frame of reference that does not involve seeking information about the workings of genes. As they have repeatedly encountered the information gap without filling it, they have become accustomed to using linguistic expressions to mark the missing information, rather than searching for it. Consequently, they organize the information they have encountered on the computer screen and in the discussion as process narratives that include grey boxes for missing information.

For example, referring to a straight-eared generation of rabbit offspring that precedes a generation having both floppy and straight-eared offspring, the teacher asks a question about 'directions' that prompts the students to answer without reverting to the cellular process frame of reference: 'they may not have those ears. Did they have the directions?' (Transcript Extract 7.12, line A295). This question reinforces the students' nascent acceptance of grey boxes and their emphasis on the screen images. B12 responds, 'well yeah they did' (Transcript Extract 7.12, line A296). B13 adds, 'they got the blueprints' (Transcript Extract 7.12, line A298), substituting 'blueprints' for 'directions'. After the teacher expresses approval by saying, 'Ahhh, good 'blueprints'. Okay we've got a fancy word there, 'blueprints'' (Transcript Extract 7.12, line A300), B13 reiterates, 'They got the blueprints of the babies' (line A301). In common usage, 'blueprints' indexes plans or directions for building something. In that sense, it is more specific than 'directions', which indexes any type of explanation of how to do something or get somewhere.

Transcript Extract 7.12: Blueprints

A295. T1: /But what it went – they may/ not have those ears. Did they have the directions?
A296. B12: No, well yeah /they did/
A297. T1: /(???/?? what/ /????)/
A298. B13: /they got the blue//prints/
A299. B12: /alright/
A300. T1: Ahhh, good 'blueprints'. Okay we've got a fancy word there, 'blueprints'.
A301. B13: They got the /blueprints of the babies./
A302. G11: /What blueprints? What's that?/
A303. B12: (Looks toward G11) DNA DNA

Transcript Extract 7.12 (continued)

A304. G11: What does that /mean?/
A305. T1: /Blue/prints for making what?
A306. B12: DNA
A307. T1: Making?
A308. B12: The genes
A309. T1: Floppy?
A310. B12: ears
A311. G11: (??) ..

'Blueprints' is a grey box in regard to the cellular genetic processes that the students had introduced earlier in the discussion. It provides the students with an alternative to mentioning or searching for missing information about DNA, zygotes, and cell division. As a substitute for information or inferences about cellular processes, 'blueprints' brings the students closer to the descriptive frame of reference and the curricular conventions for learning Mendelian genetics that the teacher has suggested during the discussion.

'Blueprints' counts as information, although it does not provide information. This is the function of a grey box. The term not only serves as a placeholder for missing information, but in that capacity it also eases the cognitive load of interpreting and remembering multiple contingencies, which have included searching for a way to link information about cellular processes to the information provided by the screen, the task prompt, and the discussion (particularly the teacher's comments). B13 has discovered a term that marks and covers the gap in cellular process information, and ultimately contributes to a process narrative that links the screen information, the prompt, and the preceding discussion.

While 'blueprints' receives a positive response from the teacher ('Ahhh, good', Transcript Extract 7.12, line A300), it does not immediately end the students' attempt to consider cellular processes. The students still do not show they can consistently apply a frame of reference emphasizing inherited traits displayed on the screen. For example, after B13 and G11 repeat 'blueprints' (Transcript Extract 7.12, lines A301, A302), B12 mentions DNA and making genes (lines A303, A306, A308). At this point, the teacher does not acknowledge B12's reintroduction of DNA (biochemical process). Instead, the teacher focuses on the visible traits displayed by the computer simulation. He asks the students how they would know that the blueprint for floppy ears was not lost (Transcript Extract 7.13, line A314),

Transcript Extract 7.13

A312. T1: Yeah /So the question is/
A313. B13: /Now how do we (?)/
A314. T1: how do you know that – how do you know that it wasn't lost? (??) the second generation would have it
A315. B13: Second that was
A316. T1: Second generation
A317. G11: It went-
A318. T1: You would have ended up seeing
A319. G11: Floppy ears
A320. T1: ears again
A321. G11: So

When the teacher does not immediately receive the response he wants, and prompts the students by hinting ('the second generation would have it', line A314; 'second generation', line A316), G11 begins to respond, 'It went' (Transcript Extract 7.13, line A317). The teacher interrupts G11 with another hint, 'You would have ended up seeing' (Transcript Extract 7.13, line A318), which reemphasizes observing phenotypic patterns as the appropriate frame of reference for completing the task. He again uses a leading question to emphasize an interpretive frame of reference consistent with the conventional Mendelian approach to trait inheritance. G11 responds, 'Floppy ears' (Transcript Extract 7.13, line A319). The teacher approves her response by echoing it, 'ears again' (Transcript Extract 7.13, line A320). The teacher's questions indicate his interest in having the students notice, as Mendel did, a causal relationship among phenotypic patterns in generations and then infer the presence of some factor passed on from the parents, without identifying it.

The teacher's participation in the discussion ends following line A321 (Transcript Extract 7.13), when a student from another group asks a question, which results in the teacher walking away. After the teacher leaves the group, G11 asks B13 to state the answer to the task prompt question (Transcript Extract 7.14, line A335).

Transcript Extract 7.14: Applying a Grey Box in a Process Narrative

A335. G11: So so what is it? . /(B13's first name)/
A336. B12: /(Still joking. Distorting his voice. (????)/
A337. B13: They was hidin' in the first (writing the answer) generation . blueprints (4 second pause)
A338. B12: Right there. They were hiding in the first generation blueprints

Transcript Extract 7.14 (continued)

A339. B13: (While writing answer to assignment) Theeeyyyy ..... came .. from .. hiding ..... into .. the ..... second ..... generation ... aand now . they .. are .. viissiiible
A340. B12: vissiii/ble/
A341. B13: /ble/
A342. B12: .. /visiiiiiiible/
A343. B13: /visiiiiiiible/

At the end of the discussion with the teacher, the answer developed by the students expresses no model of the biochemical functioning of genes that influences the development of traits such as ear shape. However, the term, blueprints, covers this information gap (Saferstein, 2007). Applied as a grey box that covers the gap in information about cellular genetic processes, 'blueprints' eliminates the interpretive contingencies related to finding such information and coherently linking it with the screen images. This shifts the students' attention to the other sources of information they can link as process narratives – i.e., the computer simulation, the task prompt, and the teacher's comments. As a grey box, 'blueprints' helps the students develop a process narrative that satisfies the task constraints. It emphasizes an organization of information that is specific to the task prompt and the computer simulation:

> *Floppy ears were hiding in the first generation blueprints. They came from hiding into the second generation and now they are visible.* (expressed by B13 in Transcript Extract 7.14, lines A337-A339)

'Blueprints' links the phenotypes of generations. By excluding the concern with cellular processes they had expressed earlier, the students have developed a coherent process narrative that explains the information presented by the computer simulation, the task prompt, the teacher, and each other.

In the process narrative that B13 verbally expresses after the discussion with the teacher, 'came from hiding' (Transcript Extract 7.14, line A339) serves as another grey box. It contributes to a process narrative indicating that unseen factors (i.e., genes for floppy ears) are present inside of parents, but may not be expressed in the observable characteristics of the offspring. It indicates that specific factors affecting specific traits exist within each rabbit. 'Came from hiding' reinforces the other grey box, 'blueprints'. Both function as markers for missing information concerning how recessive genes actually affect the development of traits.

The term, 'blueprints,' did not add new substantive information to the discussion. Prompted by the teacher's positive reaction to 'blueprints', the students applied it as a satisfactory placeholder for missing information. In the context of the preceding interaction, it related to the mention of genes, but it did not refer to specific aspects of genes and cellular processes that would explain why offspring of straight-eared rabbits have different ear shapes. The use of 'blueprints' as a grey box was influenced by the absence of cellular process information from the computer simulation and by the teacher deemphasizing or discouraging students' attempts to use DNA, egg cells, and cell division as information that would function as components of an answer to 'where do the floppy ears come from?' As a grey box, 'blueprints' removes the interpretive contingencies of finding such cellular process information or constantly being concerned about its absence.

Localized Aspects of Grey Boxes

During the genetics lessons in all of the biology classes studied, grey boxes, similar to 'blueprints' and 'came from hiding', served as placeholders that students would subsequently replace with standard Mendelian nomenclature, such as 'F1', 'F2', 'phenotype', 'genotype', and the computational devices, Punnett squares and ratios. The Mendelian nomenclature and computational devices are useful for completing assignments and passing tests about trait inheritance, but they do not address the role of cellular processes in trait inheritance. Like 'blueprints' and 'directions', they are grey boxes for that missing information.

The coherence of process narratives that include grey boxes is based on the particular interpretation activities, settings, and resources that led to those grey boxes. For example, during the biology class, the interpretation activity leading to B13's final written answer to the task prompt featured pointing and looking at the images on the computer screen, which showed floppy-eared rabbits in the second generation. Thus, when B13 said and wrote that the floppy ears 'came from hiding into the second generation aand now they are viissiiible' (Transcript Extract 7.14, line A339), he referred to the configuration of the computer screen images and to the prior operation of the computer simulation by the students and the teacher: i.e., floppy ears 'were hiding in the first generation blueprints', and were visible in the images depicting a second generation of rabbits. The grey boxes, 'blueprints' and 'came from hiding', contributed to a process narrative that functioned as a correct answer within the classroom's Mendelian discourse framework – rather than an understanding of how genes function within rabbits to produce inherited traits.

Acceptance of the Mendelian approach to inheritance often is not straightforward, because contemporary students have learned about genes, DNA, cell division, egg cells, and sperm cells in school and may have encountered genetics terms and concepts outside of the biology classroom. The data show that some students do not ignore such information when trying to develop process narratives explaining trait inheritance. Instead, those students often attempt to apply such information to the interpretation activities related to understanding inheritance (e.g., G11 mentions eggs in Transcript Extract 7.8, line A210; B12 mentions DNA and genes in Transcript Extract 7.12, lines A303, A306, A308).[29]

The students' awareness of contemporary genetic terms and concepts, however incomplete it may be, adds contingencies to their interpretation activities when they are constrained by the teacher, or by the limited amount of specified information, to produce process narratives that match Mendel's explanatory model. This presents an abrupt and seemingly arbitrary turn from applying previously learned understandings of DNA and cell division as evidence for visible phenomena. The students must keep in mind a 'not cellular processes' caution as they interpret and sort information to develop coherent explanatory process narratives. They must use information about traits, generations, dominant or recessive genes, but not seek new information or use previously encountered information about cellular genetic processes.

The students accomplish this shift in their approach to interpreting the information at hand by accepting conventional Mendelian grey boxes to serve as markers and placeholders for the missing information. The grey boxes consist of gestures, images, symbols, and linguistic terms, such as 'blueprints', associated with the nonlinguistic representations. Consequently, the students' linguistic descriptions of genetics concepts and processes are closely linked to the classroom discourse framework featuring particular information resources and interpretation activities.

8 Conclusion to Part Two – Grey Boxes, Context, and Content

Part Two has provided an introduction to grey boxes. Creating grey boxes is what people do to deal with restricted access to information, while trying to develop process narratives. Grey boxes mobilize resources in settings as components of process narratives. Analysis of interpretation activities related to the creation and use of grey boxes clarifies concepts of content and context applied to reasoning and cognition. Chapter Eight is a bridge to further explanation of grey boxes rather than a completion of such discussion. Important functions and applications of grey boxes can be explained only in the context of their function as components of discourse frameworks and professional cultures, which Parts Three and Four will examine.

The genetics learning activities show that developing grey boxes to reduce boggling contingencies is an interpretation activity of people solving problems or attempting to understand explanations when information is restricted. Grey boxes function as perceptible markers of missing information. The creation and application of grey boxes occurs when:

- Individuals have not previously developed relevant process narratives to recall;
- Routine communication patterns restrict the use of previously developed process narratives and discourage searching for new information;
- The setting does not contain information resources that would trigger recall of relevant process narratives or support interpretation activities linking new pieces of information as process narratives.

Part Two contains no examples from the radiology data, because the clinicians' extraordinary emphasis on informing patients through discussion of images provided substantive information to patients. This avoided the types of interpretation activities evident in the genetics education data that related to recognizing and creating grey boxes, i.e., the purely syntactical use of linguistic terms or gestures toward images. When the radiology patients expressed confusion or lack of understanding, verbally or through gestures and movements related to the computer images, the clinicians fostered discussion and gesturing that provided further explanation until the patient responded in a way that indicated substantive understanding of the medical information.[30] However, clinical consultations often lack such explanatory interpretation activities. Many studies of patient-clinician interaction have found that clinicians present patients with limited information and apply communication patterns that inhibit seeking information (cf. Entwistle et al., 2006; Price *et al.*, 2006; Skea *et al.*, 2004; Fisher, 1986; Fisher and Groce, 1990; Måseide, 1991). In such cases, patients often encounter briefly explained or unexplained medical terminology, test results, or medical images. Lacking the patient-prompted discussion displayed in the radiology consultation examples (analyzed in Chapters One, Nine, Thirteen, and Fourteen), those information resources may function as grey boxes that serve a syntactical role as placeholders in process narratives during consultation interaction yet inhibit the recall and transfer of those process narratives outside of the consultation.

Comparing the interpretation activities and process narratives developed in the genetics learning activities and those of the radiology consultations shows that the students develop process narratives incorporating grey boxes, whereas the patients develop process narratives that link substantive pieces of information, which explain aspects of a medical procedure or a physiological process. That functional distinction does not simply point out different objectives of the teachers and clinicians. Rather, it acknowledges findings that explain the interrelationship of information, interpretation and understanding – i.e.:

- Limited information leads to the use of abstract grey boxes that hinder subsequent recall outside of the setting in which they were developed;
- Substantive discussion of a process, which may include seemingly extraneous or complex information, diminishes or eliminates the use of grey boxes that impede the transfer of understandings.

Reconsidering Content and Context in Relation to Grey Boxes

Analysis of interpretation activities related to the creation of grey boxes and their effects on process narratives clarifies concepts of content and context that have been presented by explanations of reasoning based on mental models and cognitive schemata. The development of grey boxes applied to process narratives explains the relationship between representation and interpretation that leads to the recognition or attribution of 'content'. An absence of content (e.g., a 'contentless sense of contingency' [D'Andrade, 1989) is not just an absence of information, but also an absence of the opportunity to search for information. For example, the conventional Mendelian curriculum asks students to posit a causal relationship between genes and traits and not to consider how genes function within organisms to affect the development of physiology. The absence of relevant information and the restriction or constraint on obtaining the missing information creates the boggling interpretive contingencies of finding a way to solve a problem or produce an understanding without the information. The resulting disruption to the interpretation activities of producing process narratives is the contentless sense of contingency.

The examples in Chapter Seven show that, in order to use terms such as 'directions' or 'blueprints' as grey boxes to link available pieces of concrete information as process narratives, students worked at eliminating some of the meanings or frames of reference suggested by those commonplace words. During the interpretation activities of the assigned learning tasks, the students had accepted the 'not cellular processes' frame of reference; stopped seeking cellular process information; recognized the grey boxes, 'directions' and 'blueprints', as substitutes for cellular process information; and added them to process narratives. Consequently, the use of those grey boxes became a routine part of the activities of interpreting the available information resources.

In the conventional curriculum for teaching trait inheritance, the interpretation activities of recognizing and applying grey boxes become syntactically contentful when students accept and apply them in order to link substantive information as process narratives. However, the 'contentfulness' of the interpretive contingencies the students grapple with is linked to the specific interpretation activities and information resources of the classroom setting, which are embedded in the grey boxes.

A difference between analysis of process narratives and analysis of mental models involves recognizing and emphasizing such reciprocal effects of interpretation activities, setting, and culture on each component of an understanding. Examining the interpretation activities that produce and apply grey boxes shows that the contingencies affecting understanding are not full or empty of content, but that missing information or restrictions on searching for information guide people toward different types of content – i.e., toward creating either process narratives containing substantive information that transfer across settings, or process narratives featuring grey boxes that are only syntactically meaningful in regard to a particular setting (discussed in more detail in Parts Three and Four).

The interpretation activities of creating grey boxes and applying them to process narratives also clarifies 'context'. In explanations of reasoning based on mental models and cognitive schemata, the particulars indexed by 'context' often are unspecified or unexamined. For example, D'Andrade referred to a link between the representation of a problem and the content of that representation when he evaluated experiments showing that participants had more success answering logic problems stated in terms of familiar experiences than in terms of abstractions:

> content is not something which lies on the 'outside' (the *context*) of the representation of a problem. This just seems to be the case when one assumes that the *problem* is something made out of a particular logical form, rather than something made out of specific content. (D'Andrade, 1989: 141).

Context is presented as independent of content – as an unspecified external force or situation affecting reasoning.

Examining the interpretation activities related to producing and applying grey boxes presents a concrete explanation. 'Context' consists of the interpretation activities that mobilize and amplify resources in a setting, previously developed process narratives, and frames of reference related to cultural conventions – such as communication patterns. Analysis of the production and use of grey boxes in process narratives shows that when individuals create understandings, 'context' is not simply a situational link between material or mental artifacts (e.g., visual resources or recalled information) and a product (e.g., process narratives expressing an understanding), but it is also a component of understanding embedded in and retrievable through that product (discussed further in Part Three). In other words, process narratives trigger recall of the interpretation activities and information resources that constitute 'context'. Those activities and resources include linguistic expressions, gestures, and objects that contributed to linking information as process narratives. Thus, 'context' is not something that lies on the outside of the representation or interpretation of a problem or concept.

Grey Boxes and Discourse Frameworks

The relevance of grey boxes to understanding goes beyond their function of linking other pieces of information as process narratives. It amplifies as grey boxes become components of discourse frameworks and reinforce dependence on local information resources. The effects of grey boxes further multiply when professional culture reinforces the reliance on such discourse frameworks. In those cases, process narratives containing conventional setting-specific grey boxes become difficult to recall or lose functional meaning in settings lacking the information resources treated as grey boxes or during interactions in which some participants have not experienced the activities that created the grey boxes.

The interpretation activities that produce grey boxes reveal how communication patterns that restrict information function as components of professional cultures. The effects of grey boxes, communication patterns, and professional authority on understanding and the transfer of knowledge coalesce in discourse frameworks, which are discussed in Part Three.

PART THREE
DISCOURSE FRAMEWORKS

Parts One and Two have focused on how interpretation activities lead to recallable components of understanding. Part Three examines how information resources contribute to the creation of process narratives and grey boxes, and become embedded in the resulting understandings. Understandings involve not only the recall of process narratives, but also recall of components of the discourse frameworks that have contributed to them. I use the term, 'discourse' to indicate an expressed organization of representations. Discourse frameworks incorporate particular material information resources of a setting and the communication patterns people develop during interpretation activities. Discourse frameworks develop concurrently with process narratives and grey boxes, and reflect the same contingencies that shape them. As a result, a discourse framework may not automatically include all of the linguistic, visual, and technological resources available in a particular setting. Analysis of the radiology consultations and genetics learning activities shows that a discourse framework may reduce or reproduce constraints on understanding.

A discourse framework's form and operation derive from the concurrent interpreting and selecting of information resources that are relevant to producing coherent process narratives. For example, in the radiology consultations analyzed in Parts One, Three, and Four, the set of computer images related to fibroid tumors and treatment procedures existed prior to each patient's consultation, but the patterns of communication during the consultations determined how patients interpreted them and applied them to create recallable process narratives. During the genetics learning activities, a set of linguistic representations, nomenclature, and tabular computation devices relevant to the Mendelian explanation of trait inheritance also existed prior to a students' experience of classroom learning activities or a teacher's presentation of lessons about trait inheritance. However, as Parts One and Two of this book have shown, students and teachers engaged in complicated interpretation activities to develop process narratives and grey boxes relevant to the Mendelian model of trait inheritance. As the students began to develop process narratives and grey boxes, they concurrently produced or reproduced a discourse framework that supported the continuing production of process narratives.

Studies of clinical and classroom interaction have pointed out that the verbal, visual, and environmental resources that people routinely apply to interaction form a framework supporting routine activities. Armstrong (2002) discusses how physicians derive a repertoire of criteria for prescribing a medication from their history of treating particular patients and from consultation interaction with the patients – in addition to reading research reports about the medications' effectiveness. Studies of classroom learning activities have pointed out how the affects of learning resources, such as assigned readings, are integrated with patterns of interaction and the arrangement of the material components of a classroom environment (McDermott, Gospodinoff, and Aron, 1978). Studies of science education have noted that students learn science concepts by linking symbolic representations with everyday experiences (Goldenberg, 1995; Newman, 1990; Östman, 1998; Perkins, Crismond, Simmons, and Unger, 1995). Research examining the use of computers in science courses has found that students use a variety of graphical and textual representations (e.g., numbers, descriptions, pictures, models, data tables, formulas) to link new concepts with prior understandings (Arnseth and Säljö, 2007; Barowy and Laserna, 1997; Kaput, 1995). Barba (1993), Rosenthal (1996), and Säljö (1998) have discussed how science courses require students to develop a situated classroom discourse during learning activities. Analysis of genetics learning activities shows that students rely on certain visual resources at which they point and gesture (Saferstein, 2004, 2007). In conjunction with the genetics vocabulary, such resources become part of the discourse framework for interpretation activities.

The following data analysis will clarify the intertwined environmental, interactional, and cognitive components of discourse frameworks and the relationship of those components to understanding. Chapter Nine analyzes more interventional radiology consultation data in order to explain the components of a discourse framework. Chapter Ten analyzes a new set of classroom data in order to explain how the selection of such components occurs. Chapter Eleven discusses how discourse frameworks affect cognitive systems that support reasoning and understanding. Chapter Twelve considers the sociocultural variables relate to discourse frameworks and the production of understanding.

9 Components of a Clinical Discourse Framework

Chapter Nine examines the effects of verbal, visual, and gestural information on process narratives, the interrelationship of discourse frameworks and communication patterns, and the relation of discourse frameworks to patients' understandings of medical information. The data show how patterns of communication related to discussing images contribute to discourse frameworks that provide detailed information to patients. An example shows how the various components of the discourse framework contributed to a patient's process narratives related to a potential post-procedure complication, a sloughed necrotic fibroid. The process narratives that the patient recalls during a post-consultation telephone discussion correlate with specific interpretation activities related to particular visual information resources. Examining the components of the consultation discourse framework shows how the discussion of visual information resources contributes to a patient's participation and authority. The patient shapes the agenda of topics and forms of expression. The clinician applies the visual information to explanations that address the specific information gaps expressed by the patient. This contributes to a customized discourse framework, which suits the patient's concerns. The patient's understandings of symptoms and treatments of uterine fibroids result from the creation of that discourse framework.

Understanding Medical Information: Clinical Interaction and Visual Resources

Chapter One's analysis of interventional radiology consultations, which featured discussion of explanatory images, showed how visual resources contributed to patterns of interaction that helped patients to interpret medical information and develop recallable process narratives. The visual resources included pictures, diagrams, and text organized to inform patients about uterine fibroid tumor symptoms and treatments. The images fostered patients' questions, comments, and movements, which prompted the clinician to provide additional information. Such communication patterns precluded the grey box related interpretive contingencies that were so prevalent in the classroom data.

Further analysis of the radiology consultation data shows how patterns of communication related to discussing images during the radiology consultations contributed to a discourse framework that provided the type of detailed biological process information that was missing in the genetics learning activities. Discussing visual information contributes to recallable process narratives that link the internal biology of fibroid tumors, the mechanics of embolization, and the biological effects of the UFE procedure. The eliminated the need for localized grey boxes.

The video data show that the information displayed by the images does not directly produce patients' understandings of symptoms, the UFE procedure, and treatment options. Each patient's recallable process narratives result from creating a discourse framework, which includes extensive discussion, pointing, gesturing, and head movements related to the images. Following is a representative example of how patients' understandings of medical information relate to the discourse framework developed during a consultation.

Transcript Extract 9.1: P1 Telephone Post-consultation Discussion of Potential Medical Complications [R1 is the author]

1.40. P1: /Oh yeah/ I know um that's right, the . um some of the . things that I can . are uh they want me to be aware of
1.41. R1: Umm
1.42. P1: after the procedure.
1.43. R1: Okay.
1.44. P1: Right that-that I may need a D and C I mean there I forget what the percentage uh what'd she say? . Two or three percent I think or

Transcript Extract 9.1 (continued)

1.45. R1: /Uh-huh/
1.46. P1: /Oh oh/ okay I know what else I learned. I learned about that um there was another . side effect um I may get flu-like symptoms /either/
1.47. R1: /Ah ha/
1.48. P1: within 24 hours
1.49. R1: /Um hmm/
1.50. P1: /or/ within 3 to 5 days.
1.51. R1: Ye/ah/
1.52. P1: /And it/ . yeah okay so I really didn't understand that and I understand that better now. And then um . yeah then afterwards when the fibroids are you know if they die
1.53. R1: Uh /huh/
1.54. P1: /or/ whatever eh-eh uh I might have . there's a possibility of a . hu uterine infection.
1.55. R1: Uh huh
1.56. P1: I have to be aware of the um .. yeah of the symptoms of that
1.57. R1: Uh kay
1.58. P1: Okay yeah so I didn't know that. Actually yes I learned quite a bit. I forgot about all that (chuckles).
[Two utterances omitted in which R1 digresses to explain his minimal comments during the discussion]
1.60. P1: [partial] but yeah the flu-like symptoms are – you know – 'cause like my body's going to attack those foreign particles
1.61. R1: Uh huh
1.62. P1: Yeah my antibodies so I might feel like I have the flu. I didn't really – I never knew – I didn't know anything about that. So that's something I learned that was brand new.
1.63. R1: Uh huh
1.64. P1: And then also the um ... the uterine infection risk that I have to be aware of and know the symptoms of that.
1.65. R1: yeah.
1.66. P1: So uh th – yeah okay. I ha-and I had no idea of either one of those things.

2.17.[31] R1: You mentioned uh the possibility of infection afterwards as something that you hadn't uh you
2.18. P1: I hadn't yeah I didn't I I knew nothing about yeah.

Transcript Extract 9.1 (continued)

2.19 R1: Do you remember any of the um discussion or the the PowerPoint that related to . to that – that sticks in your mind?
2.20 P1: Um . okay. Yyeah . . the th-um there was a diagram of a uterus . annd fibroids um and I guess there was a picture of one right over the . at the cervix or something.

Various components of the discourse framework created during one of the radiology consultations contributed to patient, P1, developing process narratives related to a potential post-procedure complication, a sloughed necrotic fibroid (SNF). The clinicians wanted patients to understand and remember SNF and its symptoms in order to seek timely and appropriate treatment. During her post-consultation telephone discussion four days after her recorded consultation, P1 mentions that she did not know the information about SNF prior to the radiology consultation:

> the uterine infection risk that I have to be aware of and know the symptoms of that. So uh th – yeah okay. I ha-and I had no idea of either one of those things. (Transcript Extract 9.1, lines 1.64, 1.66)

The process narratives that P1 recalls and expresses during the telephone discussions link some of the information about sloughed necrotic fibroids and their treatment that she had observed and discussed at the radiology consultation:

> *Some of the things that they want me to be aware of after the procedure: that I may need a D and C. I forget what the percentage – what'd she say? Two or three percent I think* (Transcript Extract 9.1, lines 1.40, 1.42, 1.44)
>
> *And then afterwards when the fibroids, if they die or whatever, there's a possibility of a uterine infection. I have to be aware of the symptoms of that.* (Transcript Extract 9.1, lines 1.52, 1.54, 1.56)

P1 links a medical treatment (D and C, a dilation and curettage procedure) for a post-UFE complication to a cause (death of the fibroid tumors), an effect (a uterine infection), and response (awareness of the symptoms of a uterine infection, and getting medical attention that might result in the D and C). Examining the interpretation activities at P1's consultation details how communication patterns and information resources contribute to a discourse framework that supports recallable process narratives.

Components of Interpretive Interaction: The Effects of Verbal, Visual, and Gestural Information on Process Narratives

At the radiology consultation, verbal discussion of images was just one of the interpretation activities that led to the understandings of the UFE procedure and potential post-procedure complications, which P1 expressed four days later during the telephone discussion. The parenthetical descriptions in Transcript Extract 9.2 provide examples of the extensive gesturing toward the screen, nodding, and eye contact that occurred over a period of four minutes during the discussion of soughed necrotic fibroids (SNF) at the radiology consultation. While text listing post-UFE complications and their symptoms appeared on the computer screen, N1 had explained that a sloughed necrotic fibroid tumor, which is not expelled during menstruation, can lead to symptoms of a uterine infection weeks or months after the procedure (e.g., Transcript Extract 9.2, lines 509, 515, 517). She mentioned that a uterine infection is life threatening (Transcript Extract 9.2, line 517). She also explained that gynecologists and other physicians might not associate the symptoms with SNF, and might diagnose them instead as a uterine infection requiring hysterectomy (Transcript Extract 9.2, line 517). N1 emphasized that P1 should respond to certain symptoms by contacting the radiology practice and having an MRI before submitting to hysterectomy (line 517).

The transcript presents the many gestures and head movements of P1 and N1, which show their attention to each other and to the images displayed on the computer screen. The images presented information about the contingent topics, listed below, which a patient would need to interpret, organize as process narratives, and then recall months after having a UFE procedure in order to avoid the dangerous effects of a sloughed necrotic fibroid and to have control over treatment (from Transcript Extract 9.2, lines 505–522):

- The medical nomenclature, 'slough necrotic fibroid';
- The symptoms of a uterine infection, which might result from a sloughed necrotic fibroid tumor;
- The occurrence of symptoms weeks or months after the surgery indicating the presence of a sloughed necrotic fibroid tumor;
- The need for immediate treatment of such symptoms;
- The danger of a gynecologist mistakenly diagnosing the cause of the infection;
- The possibility that a mistaken diagnosis by a gynecologist would result in an unnecessary hysterectomy as treatment;
- When experiencing certain symptoms, contacting the interventional radiologist who performed the UFE procedure could result in a less invasive treatment, a D and C procedure.

Transcript Extract 9.2: SNF Discussion at the Radiology Consultation – Talk, Movements, and Images as Components of a Discourse Framework[32]

[Bold text pertains to P1's process narratives expressed during the post-consultation telephone discussion. The transcribed interaction occurred at the radiology consultation, eighteen minutes and fifteen seconds after the discussion of the embolizing agent analyzed in Chapter One.]

501. N1: Um the next (points right index finger toward list on screen) three I'm gonna (gestures with right hand toward screen) show you a ssslide that corresponds with those to explain those (leans toward computer, points at screen, and then leans back). Mortality one in 4000. Actually that number is um . decreased.*

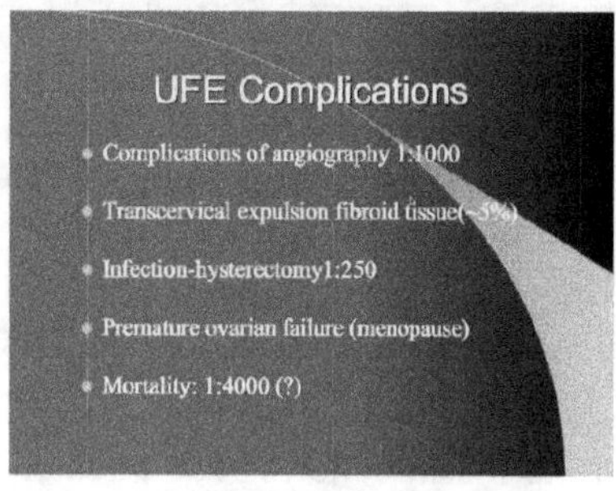

502. P1. Okay.

503. N1. **There have been four documented deaths with um after UFE**. One of 'em was a pulmonary embolism. The (reaches toward computer and advances to next image; then sits back) other three were um . . (advances image) **the other three were . . they** (P1 looks at N1) **developed an infection, refused to have a hysterectomy, and they died** (N1 looks at P1) **of the infection**.

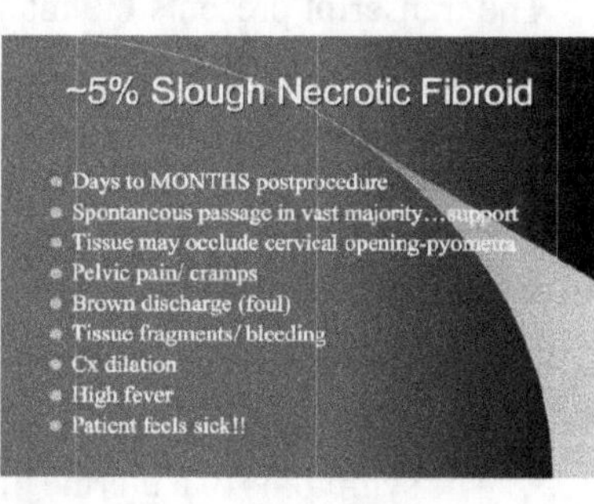

504. P1: (Turns head toward screen and nods) Okay.

505. N1: (Turns toward screen) So . (P1 looks toward N1) directly (N1 looks toward P1) related to the procedure itself, none, (P1 nods) but (N1 looks toward screen) those are the things that we know about. (P1 looks toward screen)

* The list Item, 'Mortality: 1:4000,' was a typo, corrected subsequently as 'Mortality: 1:40,000.'

Transcript Extract 9.2 (continued)

Okay, I (N1 points right hand toward screen) said I'd show (N1 looks at P1) you (P1 nods) those slides (N1 looks toward screen and stops pointing) that correlated with those – th **this is** (N1 moves right hand toward screen) **actually** (N1 looks at P1) **our main concern.** (N1 looks toward screen) **And it happens in** (N1 looks toward P1) **less than 5 percent of the patients** (P1 nods; N1 turns head toward screen) and **it's called sloughing a necrotic fibroid. In other words** (N1 lifts right arm and turns both hands palm up) **a** (P1 turns to look at N1) **fibroid is** (N1 turns both hands over) **closer to (N1 moves right hand back and forth) the lining** . (P1 nods. N1 moves left hand to meet right hand to form a spherical shape) **of the uterus and** (N1 moves right hand above left hand) **it actually** (N1 moves right fist down toward left palm) **falls** (N1 cups right fist with left hand) **into the lining** (P1 nods. N1 raises right fist from left hand) **of – or into the center cavity of the uterus.**

506. P1: and tries to come out through the cervix
507. N1: Well um eh . of (N1 points right hand at the screen) those (P1 turns head toward screen) five (N1 moves right hand back to left palm) percent, 95 percent (N1 looks at P1) of them (N1 moves hands away from each other; P1 looks at N1) just get passed in your cycle.
508. P1: Okay. (P1 nods and turns head toward screen)
509. N1: (N1 turns head toward screen and moves right hand in toward screen) **That five** (N1 looks at P1) **percent** (N1 moves right hand toward left hand) **that's** (N1 looks at screen) **left over if they get** (N1 looks at P1) **stuck** (P1 nods) **there and they** (N1 cups right fist with left hand; P1 looks at N1) **can't . go**

Transcript Extract 9.2 (continued)

	out, then it's (N1 separates hands) **gonna set you up for infection.** (P1 nods) **So what da we** (P1 smiles) **need to do? You need to** (N1 pokes right fingers into left palm, repeats for each of following points) **call us. We need to do an MRI right away – bring you in the hospital. I.V. antibiotics. Do an MRI. See what's** (P1 nods) **going on, and we may ask your** (N1 clasps hands) **gynecologist to do a D and C.**
510. P1:	(P1 Nods; turns toward screen) Okay. (P1 nods 4 times)
511. N1:	(N1 Turns head toward screen) Umm so (N1 unclasps hands and moves them toward screen) like I said this (N1 clasps hands on knee) is really our main concern. (N1 moves right hand toward screen) Th – our main concern is that you're (N1 moves right hand toward P1; looks at P1) educated to know .
512. P1:	what to look for
513. N1:	(N1 nods) what to look for, /and/
514. P1:	/(P1 nods) yeah/
515. N1:	to call us, (P1 nods) because (N1 turns head toward screen) we (N1 extends right arm toward computer) think a little bit differently. So, (N1 points right hand at screen) **what would you look for** (N1 moves right hand away from screen to left hand and looks downward) **is . generally it happens weeks to months after the** (P1 nods 3 times) **procedure . if it happens at all. And-so you've been** (N1 looks at P1) **feelin' pretty good** (P1 looks at N1). **and then all of a sudden you don't feel so good.** (P1 nods) **So, high** (P1 looks toward screen) **fever, foul smelling vaginal drainage,** (P1 nods twice and grimaces; N1 looks downward; then toward screen) . **and cramping. You just** (N1 looks at P1) **don't feel** (P1 nods five times) **good. Some'n's not right.** (N1 turns toward computer)
516. P1:	Okay.

Transcript Extract 9.2 (continued)

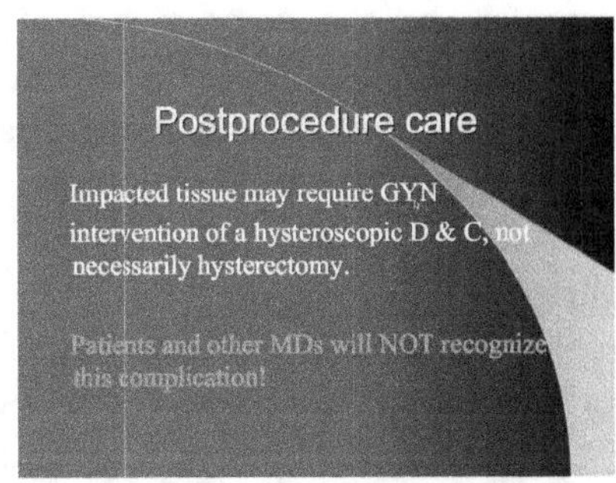

517. N1: (N1 moves right hand toward computer) So . um (N1 advances to next image) . (N1 clears throat) ... **A lot of** (N1 looks downward)... **gynecologists or any other medical doctors will think uterine infection** . (N1 looks at P1) if they (P1 looks at N1) see these symptoms (P1 nods) in you. (N1 looks upward) Um .. **uterine infection** (N1 looks at P1) **is life threatening** . (P1 looks toward screen) but .. we think a (P1 looks at N1) little bit differently. **They're thinking uterine infection, and we're thinkin' yeah you've got that fibroid (P1 nods 3 times) probably sittin' in there. If we get rid of that, then we're okay**. (P1 nods 5 times as N1 turns head toward screen) So . a gynecologist will tend to (N1 looks at P1) rush you into the operating room and do a hysterectomy (P1 grimaces and nods 4 times; N1 looks toward screen). Whereas, we're saying, "Well let's (N1 looks at P1) just take a look and make sure." We may still recommend a hysterectomy (P1 nods). but that's really . rare . (N1 looks toward screen; P1 looks toward screen) **and so if a D and C will take care of it, then most (N1 looks at P1) patients will opt . /to do that/**

518. P1: /(P1 nods toward N1. P1 looks back at screen.) **to do a D and C yeah/**

519. N1: We've actually had this happen (P1 looks at N1) to two patients (N1 turns head toward P1)

520. P1: (nods head) Okay

521. N1: and came out . **did a D and C and everything was fine**. (P1 nods and turns head toward screen) And they're (N1 looks away from P1) they're still glad. (P1 looks at N1) But at that point if you decide, "I'm done (N1 looks at P1) with this, y'know I want a hysterectomy," that's fine too. (P1 looks toward screen and nods head 3 times) That's your decision .. (N1 turns head toward screen) So it's just so that you're aware and know what to look for. (N1 advances to next image)

522. P1: Alright.

Comparing P1's post-consultation process narratives, concerning SNF and its treatment, with the patterns of communication involving talk, images, gestures, and head movements during her radiology consultation reveals how P1 interpreted and organized information. She developed a discourse framework that supported recallable process narratives, which functioned as an understanding of post-procedure precautions that could help her to interpret symptoms she might experience after UFE in order to take effective action to treat them.

During the telephone discussion, P1 expressed information that formed process narratives related to what she should do if she recognized symptoms of a uterine infection, which could indicate a sloughed necrotic fibroid – although she did not mention the term (Transcript Extract 9.1):

> *some of the things that I can are uh they want me to be aware of after the procedure. I may need a D and C* (from lines 1.40, 1.42, 1.44)
>
> *afterwards when the fibroids are you know if they die there's a possibility of a hu uterine infection. I have to be aware of the um yeah of the symptoms of that* (from lines 1.52, 1.54, 1.56)
>
> *there was a diagram of a uterus annd fibroids and I guess there was a picture of one right over the at the cervix or something.* (from line 2.20)

P1 presented an overview of N1's explanation, which had linked the term, sloughed necrotic fibroid, to causes, symptoms, and concerns, including potential for a uterine infection. At the radiology consultation, the nurse had explained SNF, its symptoms, and patient response to those symptoms as she elaborated on text that was displayed on the computer screen concerning potential complications of UFE (Transcript Extract 9.2, lines 503–521). During the post-consultation telephone discussion, P1's SNF-related process narratives link and condense information expressed by the verbal, textual, and pictorial information she encountered at the consultation. P1 recalls and expresses certain information concerning post-procedure concerns and care, but does not mention all of the information that the nurse verbally presented at the consultation. P1 does not organize the information exactly as the nurse did. The process narratives that P1 recalls during the telephone discussion correlate with the moments at the consultation when she completed N1's utterances, voiced comprehension or participation, and turned her head toward images and gestures that related to the nurse's verbal explanation. The following sections examine the talk, gestures, head movements, eye contact, and images at the radiology consultation, which constituted a discourse framework linked to the process narratives that P1 recalled four days later during the telephone discussion.

Verbal Information

Some of the process narratives that P1 expresses during the post-consultation telephone discussion emphasize information discussed at the radiology consultation at points when she had completed or acknowledged the nurse's comments. Such interaction constituted and displayed P1's attention to the nurse, P1's use of the information that the nurse had presented, and their shared frames of reference. During the telephone discussion P1 recalls information that had been presented at the radiology consultation concerning the possibility of uterine infection resulting from fibroids dying. She expresses the process narrative:

> *then afterwards [after UFE] when the fibroids are you know if they die or whatever eh-eh uh I might have there's a possibility of a hu uterine infection.* (Transcript Extract 9.1, lines 1.52, 1.54)

During the telephone discussion, P1's mention of fibroids dying ('then afterwards when the fibroids are you know if they die', Transcript Extract 9.1, line 1.52) correlates with a point in the radiology consultation discussion when P1 had completed the nurse's utterance, 'it actually falls into the lining of – or into the center cavity of the uterus', by saying, 'and tries to come out through the cervix' (Transcript Extract 9.2, lines 505, 506).

Similarly, during the telephone discussion P1 recalled information she had encountered at the consultation, which concerned the probability of SNF occurring and its relationship to the treatment (a D and C procedure):

> *I may need a D and C – I mean there – I forget what the percentage . uh what'd she say? Two or three percent I think.* (Transcript Extract 9.1, line 1.44)

This process narrative correlates with two exchanges during the radiology consultation. During the telephone discussion, P1's mention of the percentage of UFE patients who have a D and C to treat SNF, 'Two or three percent I think' (Transcript Extract 9.1, line 1.44), correlates with a part of the consultation when the nurse had said, 'it happens in less than 5 percent of the patients', while explaining text on the computer screen that began with the heading, *~5% Slough Necrotic Fibroid* (Transcript Extract 9.2, lines 505–507):

505 (partial). N1: this is actually our main concern. And it happens in less than 5 percent of the patients and it's called sloughing a necrotic fibroid. In other words a fibroid is closer to the lining . of the uterus and it actually falls into the lining of – or into the center cavity of the uterus.
506. P1: and tries to come out through the cervix
507. N1: Well um eh . of those five percent, 95 percent just get passed in your cycle.

The nurse mentioned percentages twice during this explanation. The second mention, 'of those five percent, 95 percent just get passed in your cycle', reduced the percentage of patients who would need a D and C below 5%. In between the nurse's mentions of percentages, P1 had marked her engagement with the nurse's explanation by saying 'and tries to come out through the cervix' to complete the nurse's utterance, 'it actually falls into the lining of – or into the center cavity of the uterus' (Transcript Extract 9.2, lines 505, 506). A few seconds later, P1 again expressed an overlapping comment that completed the nurse's utterance (Transcript Extract 9.2, lines 517, 518):

517 (partial). N1: so if a D and C will take care of it, then most patients will opt . /to do that/
518. P1: /to do a D and C yeah/.

By completing the nurse's recapitulation of previously presented information about the etiology and treatment of uterine fibroids, P1 displayed that she understood and recalled the information that the nurse had explained (Transcript Extract 9.2, lines 509–517).

During the subsequent telephone follow-up discussion, P1 showed that she had coherently linked the SNF information as a process narrative. Her mention of 'Two or three percent I think', is consistent with the nurse's comments and the textual information, which P1 had encountered and acknowledged at the radiology consultation.

The information about uterine infection that P1 recalls (e.g., 'I might have there's a possibility of a hu uterine infection,' Transcript Extract 9.1, line 1.54) also correlates with the nurse's consultation explanation that SNF involves a fibroid close to the lining of the uterus falling into the uterine cavity (e.g., 'if they get stuck there and they can't go out, then it's gonna set you up for infection,' Transcript Extract 9.2, line 509).

During the radiology consultations, the interpretation activities related to the images produced patterns of verbal communication in which other patients also displayed engagement in the discussion by completing or overlapping the nurse's explanations. These patterns were components of the discourse framework that supported the patient's linking of verbal and visual information to create recallable process narratives concerning her medical condition and its treatment. The discourse framework also provided the nurse with an opportunity to evaluate the patients' understandings, and provide more information or continue to another topic.

Head Movements and Eye Contact

The discussion of images changed the conventional positioning of participants during consultations so that both the clinician and the patient often faced the computer screen rather than each other. The recorded data show that, when both participants were positioned to observe the computer screen, the patient made conspicuous movements (e.g., turning her head, pointing), which non-verbally indicated a response to the screen images or the nurse's explanations. This provided the opportunity for noticeable but nonverbal, expression of understanding or confusion. When the nurse noticed a patient's head and body movements related to visual or verbal information, she often made comments that elicited questions or provided additional information about the screen images.

The process narratives that P1 expressed during the post-consultation telephone discussion contain information that correlates with her head movements and nodding when the same information was discussed during the radiology consultation. P1 looked at the nurse for a total of 88.7 seconds during the two minutes and forty-six seconds that she and the nurse discussed the computer screen text concerning SNF (see Appendix B for the detailed timings of P1's head movements toward the nurse or the images). P1 nodded her head after the nurse provided certain information (e.g., Transcript Extract 9.2, lines 504, 508, 509, 514, 515). P1 also turned her head toward the screen as the nurse pointed at or looked at the text there in conjunction with her verbal explanations (Transcript Extract 9.2, lines 505, 507).

P1's head movements marked her attention to particular information, such as the nurse's mention of potential for a uterine infection. The nurse said the words 'uterine infection' three times as she explained that a patient experiencing the symptoms listed on the computer screen should contact the radiologist, because a gynecologist might misinterpret the symptoms and treat them with a hysterectomy rather than a D and C (Transcript Extract 9.2, line 517). P1 turned her head or nodded after each mention of uterine infection by the nurse. For example, the nurse explained that infection could result if sloughed necrotic fibroids did not get passed during menstruation:

> That five percent that's left over [not passed during menstruation], if they get stuck there and they can't go out, then it's gonna set you up for infection. (Transcript Extract 9.2, line 509)

P1 nodded after the nurse said 'gonna set you up for infection'.

The nurse continued to explain how a patient should respond to symptoms of SNF, saying, 'A lot of gynecologists or any other medical doctors will think uterine infection if they' (Transcript Extract 9.2, line 517). At that point, P1 looked at the nurse for 20 seconds, while the nurse explained that the radiologist would diagnose the symptoms as SNF and recommend a D and C – instead of a hysterectomy, which gynecologists would often schedule. A second later, the nurse said, 'uterine infection is life threatening' (Transcript Extract 9.2, line 517), and P1 turned her head toward the screen, which showed text reiterating the nurse's comments. Then, while the nurse said, 'They're thinking uterine infection, and we're thinkin' yeah you've got that fibroid probably sittin' in there,' P1 nodded three times (Transcript Extract 9.2, line 517).

Although P1 did not speak the words, 'uterine infection', during the radiology consultation, she applied them four days later as part of a process narrative that was consistent with the nurse's use of them during the consultation. During the post-consultation telephone discussion, P1 emphasized potential infection as information she obtained at the consultation. She responded to my inquiry about information she recalled from the consultation by saying,

> *then afterwards when the fibroids are you know if they die or whatever eh-eh uh I might have there's a possibility of a hu uterine infection. I have to be aware of the um yeah of the symptoms of that.* (Transcript Extract 9.1, lines 1.52, 1.54, 1.56)

Both the recorded data and discussions with the nurse indicated that she monitored the nonlinguistic responses of patients, and adapted the presentation and discussion of the medical images to her interpretation of the patients' responses. Opportunities to respond non-verbally to images – and for the clinician and patient to notice each other's non-verbal responses to images – became a component of the discourse framework that supported the patient's recallable understanding of potential complications of UFE.

Information from Text in the Images

During the post-consultation telephone discussion, P1 recalled process narratives and medical terms, which had been presented by text in the screen images discussed at her radiology consultation. The nurse had expressed information related to a D and C procedure while elaborating on the list of potential complications displayed on the computer screen (Figure 9.1 Images B and C).

During the telephone follow-up discussion, P1 recalled the possibility of needing a D and C procedure related to fibroids dying and creating the risk of a uterine infection. The images concerning SNF that could be treated with a D and C contributed to a process narrative expressed by P1:

> *some of the things that I can are uh they want me to be aware of after the procedure. Right that-that I may need a D and C – I mean there – I forget what the percentage uh what'd she say? Two or three percent I think.* (Figure 9.1, Rows A and C, lines 1.40, 1.42, 1.44)

A few seconds later, P1 expressed a related process narrative:

> *afterwards when the fibroids are you know if they die or whatever eh-eh uh I might have there's a possibility of a hu uterine infection. I have to be aware of the um yeah of the symptoms of that.* (Figure 9.1, Rows A and B, lines 1.52, 1.54, 1.56)

These process narratives express information that correlates with the following bullet-pointed text, which the computer screen had displayed during the radiology consultation:

- Transcervical Expulsion fibroid tissue (–5%) (Figure 9.1, Row A)
- Tissue may occlude cervical opening (Figure 9.1, Row B)
- Impacted tissue may require GYN intervention of a hysteroscopic D and C, not necessarily hysterectomy. (Figure 9.1, Row C)

During the radiology consultation, images containing textual information that correlated with P1's post-consultation process narratives concerning post-procedure infection and D and C had appeared on the computer screen for 3 minutes and 58 seconds (Figure 9.1). Lists of information directly referring to SNF (Figure 9.1, Rows B, C) appeared on the screen for 3 minutes and 3 seconds. When the computer screen displayed the lists, the nurse's explanation linked pieces of information they contained, culminating in a suggested action by the patient, 'you need to call us', and a treatment involving an MRI and a D and C procedure (Transcript Extract 9.2, lines 505, 507, 509):

> this is actually our main concern. And it happens in less than 5 percent of the patients and it's called sloughing a necrotic fibroid. In other words a fibroid is closer to the lining of the uterus and it actually falls into the lining of – or into the center cavity of the uterus.

> Well um eh of those five percent, 95 percent of them [sloughed necrotic fibroids] just get passed in your cycle.
>
> That five percent that's left over if they get stuck there and they can't go out, then it's gonna set you up for infection. So what da we need to do? You need to call us. We need to do an MRI right away – bring you in the hospital. I.V. antibiotics. Do an MRI. See what's going on, and we may ask your gynecologist to do a D and C.

The nurse reiterated the description of symptoms, emphasizing information about specific symptoms contained in the screen lists. (Transcript Extract 9.2, line 515):

> So, what would you look for is generally it happens weeks to months after the procedure if it happens at all. And-so you've been feelin' pretty good and then all of a sudden you don't feel so good. So, high fever, foul smelling vaginal drainage, and cramping. You just don't feel good. Some'n's not right.

The nurse's explanation provides a reason for a patient to call the radiology practice instead of a gynecologist or other MD (Transcript Extract 9.2, lines 517, 519, 521): i.e., calling a gynecologist could lead to a hysterectomy, while calling the radiologist would probably lead to a D and C procedure.

While the images that emphasized SNF appeared on the screen, the nurse and P1 discussed SNF and its treatment for 2 minutes and 46 seconds. P1 looked at the image titled, '~5% Slough Necrotic Fibroid', (Figure 9.1, Row B) for 46.4 seconds as the nurse explained it (Transcript Extract 9.2, lines 503–516). P1 also was looking at the screen when the nurse mentioned the D and C procedure as a treatment for SNF. The image on the screen included the text, 'Impacted tissue may require GYN intervention of a hysteroscopic D and C, not necessarily hysterectomy' (Figure 9.1, image C). When the nurse said, 'if a D and C will take care of it, then most patients will opt,' P1 nodded, briefly, looked at P1, and then looked at the screen as she completed N1's utterance by saying 'to do a D and C yeah' (Transcript Extract 9.2, lines 517, 518).

A preceding screen image, displayed for 55.3 seconds, also contained two bullet points presenting information relevant to SNF (Figure 9.1, Row A):

- Transcervical expulsion fibroid tissue (−5%)
- Infection-hysterectomy 1:250.

Figure 9.1: Correlation of Consultation Visual Information with P1's Understandings

	Consultation Images	**P1 Post-consultation Telephone Discussion** (From Transcript Extract 9.1)
A	UFE Complications • Complications of angiography 1:1000 • Transcervical expulsion fibroid tissue(~5%) • Infection-hysterectomy1:250 • Premature ovarian failure (menopause) • Mortality: 1:4000 (?) Image 39: "Infection-hysterectomy 1:250" (3rd bullet point)	1.40. P1: Oh yeah I know um that's right, the . um some of the . things that I can . are uh they want me to be aware of 1.41. I1: Umm 1.42. P1: after the procedure. 1.54 (partial). there's a possibility of a . hu uterine infection.
B	~5% Slough Necrotic Fibroid • Days to MONTHS postprocedure • Spontaneous passage in vast majority…support • Tissue may occlude cervical opening-pyometra • Pelvic pain/ cramps • Brown discharge (foul) • Tissue fragments/ bleeding • Cx dilation • High fever • Patient feels sick!! Image 40: "Tissue may occlude cervical opening"	1.52 (partial). P1: And then um . yeah then afterwards when the fibroids are . you know if they die 1.56. P1: I have to be aware of the um . . yeah of the symptoms of that 2.20 (partial). P1: there was a diagram of a uterus . annd fibroids and I guess there was a picture of one right over the . at the cervix or something.
C	Postprocedure care Impacted tissue may require GYN intervention of a hysteroscopic D & C, not necessarily hysterectomy. Patients and other MDs will NOT recognize this complication! Image 41:"Impacted tissue may require GYN intervention of a hysteroscopic D & C, not necessarily hysterectomy."	1.44 (partial). P1: I may need a D&C 1.56. P1: I have to be aware of the um . . yeah of the symptoms of that

This set of information presented by the nurse and the screen images correlated with a comment P1 expressed four days later during the post-consultation telephone discussion: 'there's a possibility of a hu uterine infection. I have to be aware of the um yeah of the symptoms of that" (Figure 9.1, Rows A, C, lines 1.54, 1.56). P1's recall of the textual information as a component of process narratives did not result simply from the contiguous flow of information in the set of medical images or the nurse's explanation presented during the consultation. Rather, the textual information combined with verbal comments, gestures, and head movements to form a discourse framework that supported the production and recall of those process narratives.

The Multimodal Discourse Framework: Effects of Gestures, Images, Head Movements, and Eye Contact

During the radiology consultation, P1's interpretation of the nurse's verbal explanations occurred in the context of pointing and looking at the images on the computer screen as well as nonverbal displays of attention to the nurse's utterances and gestures (Figure 9.2, A, B, C). For example, in addition to the nurse's verbal explanation, the information about a fibroid falling from the lining of the uterus into the uterine cavity also included gestures by the nurse as she explained the screen text concerning SNF (Figure 9.2, C). As she said, 'a fibroid is closer to the lining of the uterus and it actually falls … into the center cavity of the uterus,' the nurse made a fist with her right hand, illustrating the fibroid tumor, and moved it down to her left cupped left hand, illustrating the tumor falling into the uterine cavity (Figure 9.2, C).

As discussed above, during the post-consultation telephone discussion, P1 also mentioned that a picture viewed at the consultation had provided information relevant to her process narrative concerning the possibility of uterine infection following UFE. When I asked her if she could elaborate on any information in the set of images that related to her earlier mention of the possibility of uterine infection, she responded by recalling the picture that had been presented 7 minutes and 50 seconds prior to the nurse's explanation of SNF (Figure 9.2, A):

2.17. R1: You mentioned uh the possibility of infection afterwards as something that you hadn't uh you

2.18. P1: I hadn't yeah I didn't I I knew nothing about yeah.

2.19. RI: Do you remember any of the um discussion or the the PowerPoint that related to . to that – that sticks in your mind?

2.20. P1: Um . okay. Yyeah . . the th-um there was a diagram of a uterus . annd fibroids um and I guess there was a picture of one right over the . at the cervix or something.

The picture provided visual information about the type of fibroid that might fall into the uterine cavity when embolization deprives the tumor of blood, i.e., the sloughing of a necrotic fibroid. The picture showed a large fibroid tumor within the uterine cavity, which blocked the cervix. This visual information was consistent with N1's later gesture of her fist falling into her cupped hand as she says, 'a fibroid is closer to the lining of the uterus and it actually falls into the lining of – or into the center cavity of the uterus,' which prompted P1's completion, 'and tries to come out through the cervix' (Figure 9.2, C).

Figure 9.2: Modes of Representation for Sloughed Necrotic Fibroid

A *

B

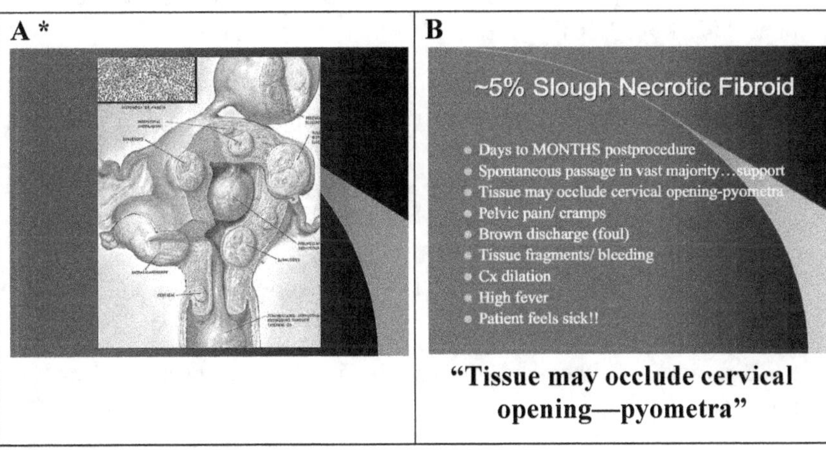

"Tissue may occlude cervical opening—pyometra"

C

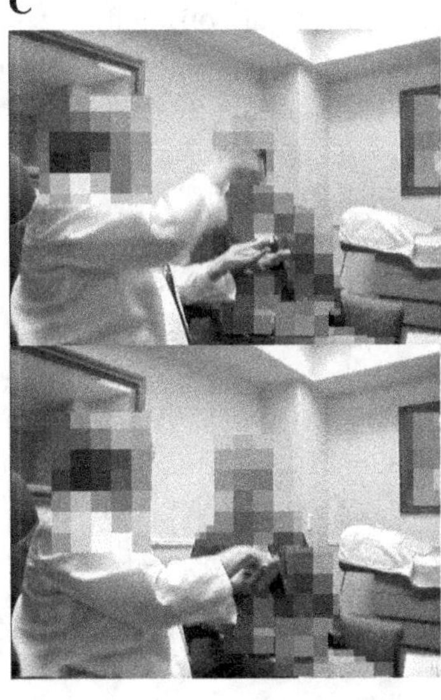

505. N1: this is actually our main concern. And it happens in less than 5 percent of the patients and it's called sloughing a necrotic fibroid. In other words a fibroid is closer to the lining . of the uterus and it actually falls into the lining of—or into the center cavity of the uterus.

506. P1: and tries to come out through the cervix

[Transcript Extract 9.2]

The discourse framework at the radiology consultation, which supported the understanding that P1 developed, featured P1 and N1 responding to each other and the computer images verbally and gesturally in order to clarify particular pieces of information concerning SNF. Their utterances, gestures, and head movements in relation to verbal and visual information concerning SNF resulted in P1 linking pieces of that information as the process narratives describing potential UFE complications, which she expressed twice four days later during the telephone discussion:

> *afterwards when the fibroids are you know if they die or whatever eh-eh uh I might have there's a possibility of a hu uterine infection. I have to be aware of the um yeah of the symptoms of that.* (from Transcript Extract 9.1, lines 1.52, 1.54, 1.56)
>
> *the uterine infection risk that I have to be aware of and know the symptoms of that.* (from Transcript Extract 9.1, line 1.64)

After both of these comments P1 also stated that she had not encountered this information prior to the radiology consultation:

> I didn't know that. Actually yes I learned quite a bit. (from Transcript Extract 9.1, line 1.58).
>
> I had no idea of either one of those things. (from Transcript Extract 9.1, line 1.66)[33]

The understandings that P1 expressed during the post-consultation telephone discussion resulted from the discourse framework featuring patterns of gestural as well as verbal interaction related to the multiple modes of information presented at the radiology consultation.

The Interrelationship of Discourse Frameworks and Communication Patterns

The images and the clinician's prepared explanations were only part of the discourse framework during the radiology consultations. The patient's comments, questions, and movements also affected the sequence in which a clinician displayed the images, the extent of each explanation, and the discussion of information that was not included in the images or standard explanations. For example, a patient, P6, responded to an image showing a drawing of a uterus with various types of fibroid tumors by pointing at one of the tumors and asking a question:

> What is that (pointing at the screen) right at the bottom?" (Figure 9.3, Row B and Row C, line 4).

This prompted the nurse to provide a more detailed explanation:

> These that are on a stalk like a mushroom stem are called 'pedunculated. The this one is so bad that it's actually protruding through the cervix into the vagina. You'd know if you had this one. Your doctor would have done a hysteroscopic removal (Figure 9.3, Row C, lines 5, 7, 9).

Fifteen seconds later, the patient asked another question about types of fibroids, related to the picture. The nurse's verbal and gestural explanation of a pedunculated fibroid in the computer image provided an opportunity for the patient to inquire about the treatment for such a fibroid in regard to information she had previously encountered:

> So when they say that fibroids are on the uterine wall externally do you have one in here or no? (Figure 9.3, Row D, lines 18, 20)
>
> Ohhh and you just and you can scrape that one off right? (Figure 9.3, Row F, lines 22, 24)

Verbally and by pointing at the screen image, the nurse's responses provided more information about the treatment of such a tumor and the chances of a tumor regrowing after surgical removal:

> The problem being with a lot of fibroids is that they can't always get every cell. They can't tell, and so then the chances of them growing is about 45 percent but also that's dependent on your age. (Figure 9.3, Row E, and Row F, lines 27, 29)

Figure 9.3: A Patient Responding to Images and Explanations
[From Transcript 13.2, Chapter Thirteen]

A	1. N1: (moves right arm toward screen) This is just kind of a nasty picture depicting all the different places /where you could have a/ 2. P6: /Wowwwwwwww/ 3. N1: fibroid
B	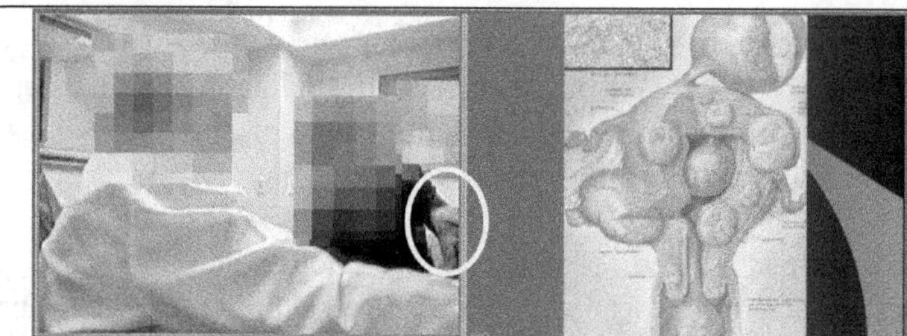 **P6 points at fibroid in screen image** *
C	4. P6: What is that (pointing at the screen) right at the bottom? 5. N1: (clearing throat) anh hammm (moves arm toward screen) These that are on a stalk . 6. P6: Ss 7. N1: like a mushroom stem 8. P6: /Right/ 9. N1: /are called/ 'pedunculated. The this one is so bad that it's actually protruding through the cervix into the vagina. You'd know if you had this one. Your doctor would have done a hysteroscopic re/moval/ [For N1's extended explanation, see Chapter Thirteen, Transcript Extract 13.2, lines 10-17.]

Figure 9.3 (continued)

<table>
<tr><td>D</td><td>18. P6: /So when they say/ that fibroids . are . on the . uterine wall externally
19. N1: Exter/nally (nodding)/
20. P6: /do you/ have one in here or no?</td></tr>
<tr><td></td><td>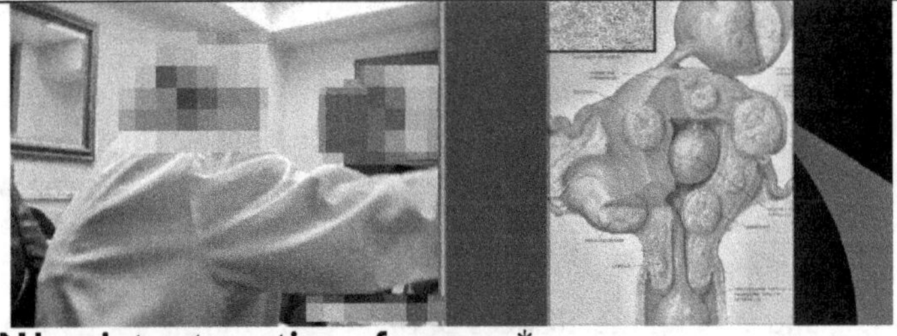
N1 points at portion of screen *</td></tr>
<tr><td>F</td><td>21. N1: (leans forward and points at a portion of the screen) That's what this is. This is
22. P6: Oh/hh and you just . and you can scrape that/
23. N1: /external. This's called a . This is internal/
24. P6: one off right?
25. N1: This? (moves arm to point at another area of the screen)
26. P6: Yeah.
27. N1: (leaning back in chair) Well . if your gynecologist went in . laparoscopically, (moves arm toward screen) she could cut into the muscle and take that out (P6 nods). The problem being with a lot of fibroids is they can't always get every cell. They can't tell
28. P6: mmhmm
29. N1: and so then the chances of them regrowing is about 45 percent but also that's dependent on your age. So, (clearing throat) hm hhmmmm, so no /they don't/</td></tr>
</table>

* Fibroids drawing in Rows B, E Copyright Paul Indman, M.D. Used with his permission.

The nurse's explanation of each image sustained the emphasis on particular information that the clinicians had selected when they created the sequence of images. However, patients often would speak, gesture, or move toward the screen. The nurse would treat such actions as indicating interest in different information contained in the image (e.g., Figure 9.3, Row F):

21. N1: (leans forward and points at a portion of the screen) That's what this is. This is
22. P6: Oh/hh and you just . and you can scrape that/
23. N1: /external. This's called a . This is internal/
24. P6: one off right?
25. N1: This? (moves arm to point at another area of the screen)
26. P6: Yeah.
27. N1: (leaning back in chair) Well . if your gynecologist went in . laparoscopically, (moves arm toward screen) she could cut into the muscle and take that out (P6 nods). The problem being with a lot of fibroids is they can't always get every cell. They can't tell
28. P6: mmhmm
29. N1: and so then the chances of them regrowing is about 45 percent but also that's dependent on your age. So, (clearing throat) hm hhmmmm, so no /they don't/

In this example, the image showing various types of fibroids prompted the patient's movements and questions, which led to detailed explanations from the nurse. Those explanations, in conjunction with the screen image, provided opportunities for the patient to ask other questions related to types of fibroids and their treatment. The nurse's answers sometimes diverged from the preselected sequence of topics

The nurse's responses and use of visual resources were oriented toward providing information that satisfied or expanded on the patient's inquiries. Often this involved referring to the relevant parts of an image or moving to another image in order to provide visual support for the verbal explanation. For example, when P6 introduced the topic, degree of tumor shrinkage after a UFE procedure, by mentioning a percentage she had recently read, the nurse corrected her (Figure 9.4, Row A, lines 40–43), and began an extended explanation. The nurse pointed at the computer screen, saying, 'I'm gonna show you a picture too,' and then advanced to a drawing of the abdominal cavity and uterus before and after a successful UFE procedure (Figure 9.4, Row A, lines 45, 47).

While the nurse was speaking, the patient looked at the screen and nodded as the nurse pointed at parts of the drawing that contributed to her explanation of how uterine fibroid tumors can compress organs surrounding the uterus (Figure 9.4, Rows A, B, C, lines 47–55). The patient also commented verbally, expressing understanding and agreement in regard to the nurse's comments (Figure 9.4, Row C, lines 48, 50).

Figure 9.4: Adapting to the Patient's Concerns*
[Bold indicates gestures mentioned in text]

<table>
<tr><td>A</td><td>40. P6: /And/ what . after the procedure what's. I read somethinn . this weekend that said they only impact their size by 20 percent. Is that accurate?
41. N1: (Shaking her head) No.
42. P6: Okay
43. N1: Not /really/
44. P6: /So what/ what is the extent o/f the/
45. N1: /Generally/ we're seeing . (points right index finger toward screen and moves are toward computer) I'm gonna show y/ou/
46. P6: /Okay/
47. N1: a picture too (P6 looks at the screen and leans toward it. N1 clicks the mouse twice. Image goes past the one N1 wants, advancing to an image of an MRI of the abdomen with fibroids) Hhho (N1 clicks on mouse once to go back to an image showing two drawings of a uterus with fibroids before and after UFE) (N1 moves arm toward screen) This (leans forward moves arm around screen) . is . let's say this is what the size /of your uterus is now/</td></tr>
<tr><td>B</td><td>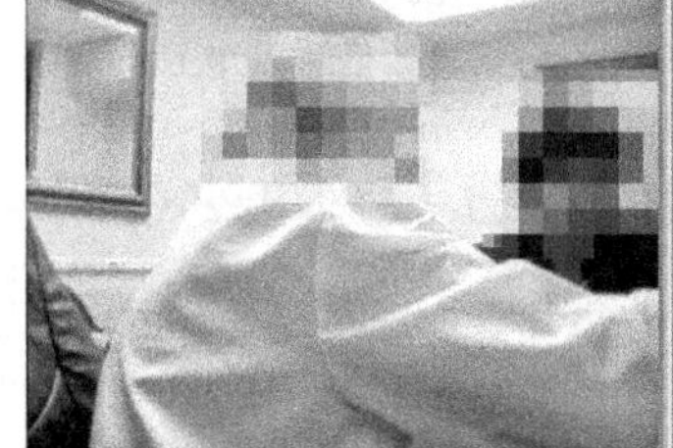 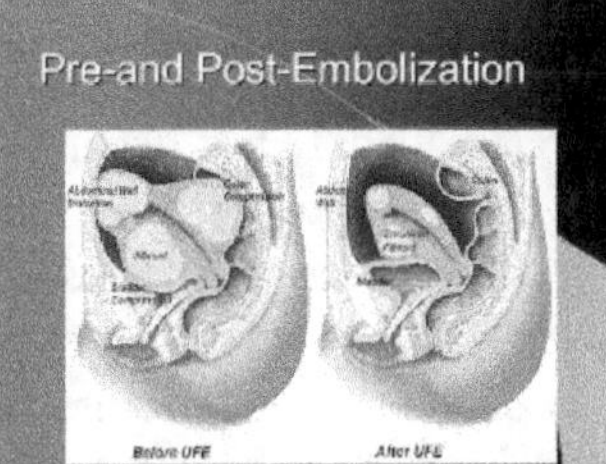
</td></tr>
<tr><td>C</td><td>48. P6: /Oh wow look at your bladder/ (leaning forward to look at screen).
49. N1: (pointing at image on screen) and so you can see how it impacts the tail/bone here/
50. P6: /mmhmm/
51. N1: (pointing at image on screen) and your bowel r/uns/
52. P6: /mmm/
53. N1: between here and here so you can see /why/
54. P6: /(nods and smiles; looks at N1) pff/
55. N1: um there would be that feeling of fullness or having (P6 nods head) constipation actually having constipation. Pelvic floor pressure. Look at that poor bladder.
56. P6: (exhales) Phhhh</td></tr>
</table>

Figure 9.4: (continued)

D	57. N1 (clears throat) Excuse me. 58. P6: (P6 turns toward husband behind N1) (????) /(P6 laughs)/ 59. N1: /So (turns toward P6's husband) Frequent urination (N1 turns toward screen)/ (P6 turns toward screen) urgency (P6 smiles, turns toward husband, then back toward screen) There are reasons for that. 60. P6: (chuckles) 61. N1: So we we
E	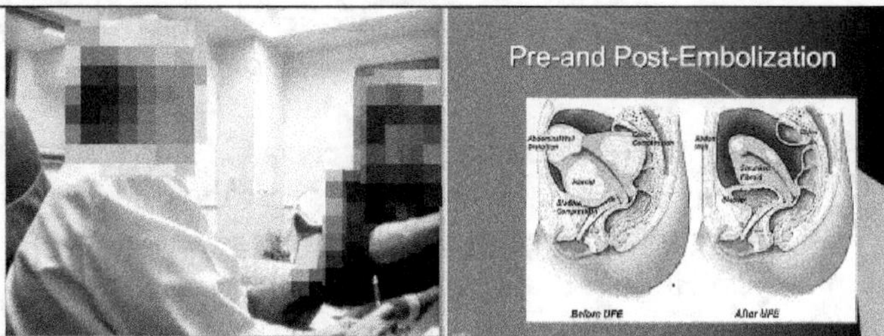
F	62. P6: **(moves right hand toward screen, pointing index finger and moving it around the drawing)** Woo/oww. Look at the difference!/ 63. N1: /talk about (looks at P6) 50%. (P6 looks at N1)/ Basically 50% shrinkage. Most women get more than that (P6 nods) . but usually with 50% shrinkage, 90% of the--90% of the patients have relief of 90% of their symptoms. 64. P6: /(??) (Nods and looks toward screen)/ 65. N1: /That's a lot of s . /percentages there, but . does that make sense to you? (points at screen) So it allows your bladder to expand again, and it—look at how much room it gives back to the belly. 66. P6: Wooow. /(looks toward husband)/ 67. N1: /So that's that's what we're (N1 moves right hand toward computer) looking at./ (moves hand away from computer) Did that answer that question? (P6 Nods) (N1 moves right hand toward computer) Okay. (N1 advances image)

* Diagram in Rows B, E Copyright Mark Cockerill, M.D., Used with his permission.

By pointing and referring to relevant parts of the image on the screen, the nurse then explained the relationship between the shrinkage of tumors and the relief of pressure on the organs surrounding the uterus (Figure 9.4, Rows A, B, C, lines 47–55). This provided information relevant to her subsequent mention of the percentage by which the tumors shrink and the relation of the amount of shrinkage to symptom relief (Figure 9.4, Rows D, F, lines 61, 63, 65):

> So we we talk about 50%. Basically 50% shrinkage. Most women get more than that. but usually with 50% shrinkage, 90% of the – 90% of the patients have relief of 90% of their symptoms. That's a lot of s percentages there, but does that make sense to you? (points at drawing) So it allows your bladder to expand again, and it – look at how much room it gives back to the belly.

The patient displayed her attention to the nurse by pointing at parts of the before and after UFE images (Figure 9.4, Row E), while commenting on the amount of compression of the organs and the nurse's explanation of how such compression relates to common symptoms of constipation and frequent urination: 'Woooww. Look at the difference!' (Figure 9.4, Row F, line 62).

In this example, components of the discourse framework contributing to the nurse's explanation included:

- The patient's question,
- Advancing the presentation in order to provide relevant visual information, verbal and visual information about the physiological consequences of fibroids,
- Pointing by both the nurse and the patient at specific parts of the screen image
- Relating the screen image and verbal description to common symptoms that the patient may have experienced,
- Presenting percentages expressing the probable amount of shrinkage and the amount of symptom relief that could be anticipated, based on outcomes of the UFE procedure among the practice's patient population.

The effectiveness of the discussion of the images in developing patients' understandings of the uterine fibroid tumors and the embolization procedure results from the ways that their use affects the consultation discourse framework for both the patient and the clinician. The images prompt the patient's questions, comments, or movements, and the clinician responds by providing more information. Such discussion often introduces useful ancillary information that is not included in the images and standard explanations. Each patient's verbal and gestural responses to the images prompt the clinician to provide additional information pertinent to that patient's particular concerns. The components of the discourse framework creates opportunities for both the patient and clinician to apply interpretation activities that contribute to their understandings of each other's concerns related to the treatment of the patient's uterine fibroid tumors.

The Relation of a Discourse Framework to Process Narratives

Post-consultation telephone discussions with patients showed that the visual resources, pointing, gesturing, and verbal discussion, which constituted the discourse framework of their consultations, had provided the information that the patients used to create recallable process narratives. Revisiting P3's consultation, discussed in Chapter One, provides another example. The nurse presented explanations combining verbal description and gestures directed at a diagram showing a uterus, fibroid tumors, and a catheter depositing spheres representing the embolizing agent (called 'beads' by the nurse) in the uterine artery. The image and the nurse's comments indicated how the embolization process blocks arteries supplying blood to the fibroid tumors and causes the fibroids to shrink:

> (N1 moves right hand toward screen, pointing index finger) And you can see these are called end (N1 moves hand around screen) blood vessels. They just go (N1 moves right arm to her side) to the fibroid. They don't (N1 moves left hand in front of her face and then away from her body; looks at P3) connect to any other (N1 moves left arm to her side) blood vessels. (N1 moves right arm toward screen) So they just stop (N1 moves right arm to her side) there. (Transcript Extract 9.3, line C67)
>
> So as the fibroid (N1 moves hands together in front of her chest, clenches right hand and cups it with left hand) shrinks down (N1 make shaking motion with clasped hands), those beads stay right with it. (Transcript Extract 9.3, line C69)

Transcript Extract 9.3: Visual Resources in the Radiology Consultation [Bold text pertains to P1's process narratives expressed during her post-consultation telephone discussion.]

C67. N1: (N1 moves right hand toward screen, pointing index finger) And you can see these are called end (N1 moves hand around screen) blood vessels.

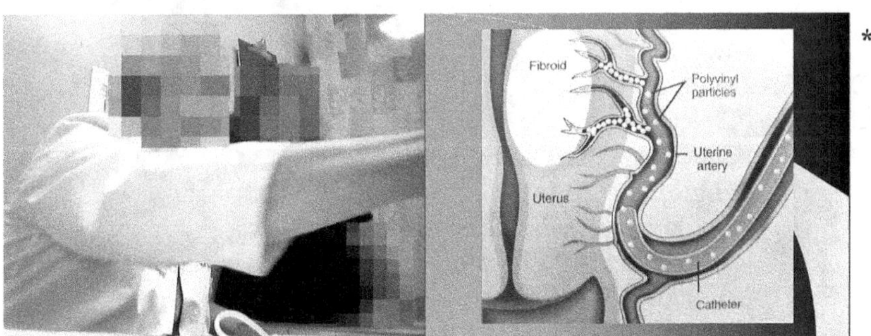

*

They just go (N1 moves right arm to her side) to the fibroid. They don't (N1 moves left hand in front of her face and then away from her body; looks at P3) connect to any other blood vessels. (N1 moves right arm toward screen) So they just stop there.

C68. P3: Got it. Okay.

C69. N1: So as the fibroid (N1 moves hands together in front of her chest, clenches right hand and cups it with left hand) shrinks down (N1 makes shaking motion with clasped hands), those beads stay right with it. **And these (N1 moves right hand in front of her face with thumb and index finger slightly apart. N1 looks at P3.) are microscopic /size. (N1 looks at screen; moves hand toward computer) They d (N1 points at the screen) they're not** (N1 moves right hand away from screen) **that big/**

C70. P3: /Umhmm. **Is it the size of (P3 looks at N1) a sand/ (P3 looks at screen) particle or something like that?**

Transcript Extract 9.3 (continued)

C71. N1: Yyeah yeah. **Actually (reaches down to get sample vials of the beads and gives one to P3. P3 holds it in front of her face with left hand) hold that up to the light. (P3 holds vial up toward light) See 'em?**

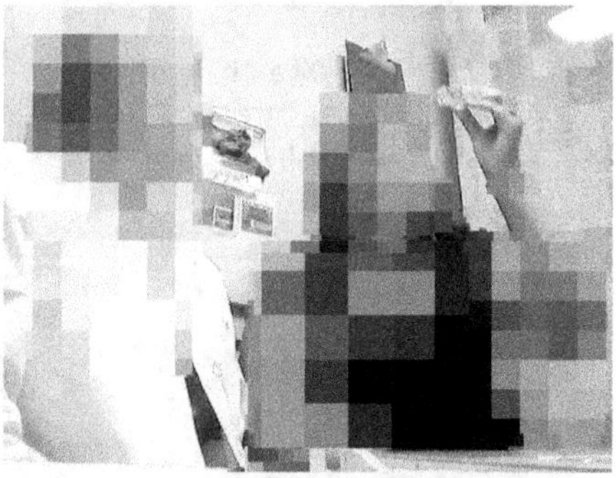

C72. P3: **Oh yeah. Wow.**
C73. N1: (Chuckles)
C74. P3: (Chuckles) Ha ha okay. (P3 gives vial to N1. N1 takes the vial and hands her another vial. P3 holds second vial up to the light. N1 looks toward P3) These are them dry?
C75. N1: Um hmm . .
C76. P3: Wow. (P3 gives vial to N1. Both look toward it) That's not (?) Okay.

---

* Line C67 diagram Copyright David Klemm and Society of Interventional Radiology. Reprinted with their permission. All rights reserved.

For explanatory purposes, the components of the diagram were not drawn to the actual scale of the arteries and the particles of embolizing agent. In the context of explaining the mechanics and effects of the embolization procedure, the nurse addressed the fact that the components of the diagram did not represent the actual size of the embolizing agent particles. While pointing at parts of the image displayed on the computer screen, she emphasized that the particles were not as large in relation to the arteries, uterus, and fibroid tumors as depicted in the heuristic diagram:

> **And these** (N1 moves right hand in front of her face with thumb and index finger slightly apart. N1 looks at P3.) **are microscopic size.** (N1 looks at screen; moves hand toward computer) They d (N1 points at the screen) **they're not** (N1 moves right hand away from screen) **that big.** (Transcript Figure 9.5, line C69, image B)

P3 immediately inquired further about the actual size of the embolizing agent's particles by asking an analogical question, 'Is it the size of a sand particle or something like that?' (Figure 9.5, line C70). P3's question digressed from the topic of the nurse's explanation of the diagram, i.e., the use of the catheter during the embolization procedure and the resulting shrinkage of the fibroid tumors due to blockage of blood to them. At that point, the sequence of images on the computer screen had not emphasized the nature of the embolizing agent injected into the uterine arteries during the embolization procedure.

However, the nurse responded by departing from her immediate topic and from the presentation's predetermined sequence of images and topics in order to clarify the size of the embolizing agent. Rather than deferring an answer until later in the sequence of images, when a photo of the embolizing agent would appear, the nurse reached into her purse and handed P3 vials containing the embolizing agent, which P3 then inspected (Transcript Extract 9.3, line C71). P3's question had resulted in the nurse diverging from the prepared set of images by presenting the vials. However, the question and the nurse's action both occurred in the context of prior images, gestures, and verbal comments that constituted the discourse framework.

The patient-initiated digression from the predetermined sequence of medical images prompted the interpretation activities that contributed to the process narratives that P3 later expressed during the post-consultation telephone discussion (Chapter One, Figure 1.4, Row C, lines T68, T70):

> *In in viewing the-the the material used, it was um it helped me realize that you know it w-it wasn't like these little black plastic balls that they were sticking in this to embolize the (?) the arteries.*
>
> *It was truly just it-it it as much as it wasn't a natural substance that's gonna go into the body, it's it's as tiny and minute minute as possible y'know anything that's smaller than that wasn't gonna do anything.*
>
> *So It made me realize that okay this really isn't such a bad procedure and these things going into my body don't look harmful at all whatsoever.*

The patient-initiated digression to discuss the nature of the embolizing agent triggered interpretation activities, which helped P3 to create recallable process narratives that resolved her concerns about a key aspect of the embolization procedure, the nature of the embolizing agent, and related risks. The discourse framework related to P3's understanding of the nature of the embolizing agent and her decision to undergo the UFE procedure included the following information:

- The image showing a diagram of the arteries containing the embolizing agent particles,
- N1's verbal and gestural explanation of the mechanics and effects of the embolization procedure,

- The patient's utterances and movements, which expressed interest in additional information related to the images and explanations,
- The vials containing the embolizing agent,
- The gestures and pointing by the nurse related to the medical images.

The recorded data of all patients in the study indicate that the consultation discourse frameworks developed by the participants featured both the visual information and a communication pattern in which a patient would address her concerns by eliciting information that digressed from the clinician's explanation of an image. Then the clinician would provide additional verbal and visual information to which the patient would respond verbally and gesturally. This communication pattern produced ancillary information that contributed to the understandings that the patient was able to recall outside of the clinical setting. The patient's creation of recallable process narratives was not based only on the visual information displayed on the computer or the nurse's preconceived explanation of those images. Rather, each patient's long-term understanding of her medical condition and treatment options resulted from interpretation activities that featured the patient shaping the agenda of topics and forms of expression. Guided by that agenda, the clinician applied the visual information resources to explanations that addressed the specific information gaps expressed by the patient. This contributed to a customized discourse framework that suited the concerns of each patient.

Clinical Discourse Frameworks: Overcoming Barriers to Expressing, Understanding, and Recalling Medical Information

The variety of visual and gestural resources is more limited in many clinical consultations than in the interventional radiology consultations analyzed here. Many medical consultations lack the discussion of visual information resources (e.g., pictures and diagrams), which would provide patients with an opportunity to produce questions, comments, or gestures in order to elicit medical information that contributes to recallable process narratives. Visual test results or medical records are available primarily to clinicians, and function as resources that help them generate questions directed to the patient or that remind the clinician of a sequence of diagnostic activities (cf. Cicourel, 1988; Måseide, 1991). Patients' opportunities to explain their health and medical conditions, to ask questions, and to receive answers to follow-up questions often are limited by the ways that clinicians respond to them and shape clinical interaction (cf. Anspach, 1993; Cicourel, 1982, 1988; Fisher, 1993, 1995; Fisher and Groce, 1990; Frankel, 1990; Måseide, 1991, 2007; Street,

1992; Street *et al.*, 2005; West, 1984). Clinicians often consider their exercise of control over topics and discussions during consultations as an effective and rational practice for coping with time constraints (Måseide, 1991).

Constraints on patients' access to medical information are particularly relevant to the treatment of uterine fibroid tumors, the subject of the interventional radiology consultations analyzed here. The conventional format of clinical consultations restricts women's opportunities to introduce or extend topics of discussion with clinicians (Entwistle *et al.*, 2006; Price *et al.*, 2006; Skea *et al.*, 2004; Fisher, 1986; Fisher and Groce, 1990). This often leads to a lack of response by the physician and patient to each other's comments. Such communication patterns contribute to a discourse framework that limits women's opportunities to obtain information needed to develop recallable process narratives relevant to treatment decisions.

Studies have documented various recurring communication patterns during consultations that limit women's opportunities to express their concerns, ask questions, and obtain explanations of surgical variants or alternatives to hysterectomy (Entwistle *et al.*, 2006; Price *et al.*, 2006; Skea *et al.*, 2004). For example, Entwistle *et al.*'s interview data (2006) confirmed that most of the women studied were not told of the different types of hysterectomies and the reasons why their physicians recommended a particular type. A significant number of women interviewed felt they had not received enough information about the nature and extent of the surgical procedure, such as whether or not their cervix would be removed. They also felt that their concerns were minimized and questions not adequately answered by their doctors. Skea *et al.* (2004) found that a significant minority of women scheduled for hysterectomy to treat menstrual problems were not satisfied with the information provided during consultations, and that the communication with clinicians during consultations led to indecision about selecting treatment. The researchers noted that it was common, after a consultation had ended, for women to think of questions, which did not occur to them during the consultation. Price *et al.* (2006) found that women with chronic pelvic pain felt their clinicians' comments during consultations were very general and did not personalize the information expressed in regard to their particular symptoms and history. The patients indicated that the clinicians did not understand the concerns they expressed, and that clinicians did not believe or listen to their comments. Some women felt that the doctors actually discouraged them from asking questions by packing up notes, standing up, or avoiding eye contact while inviting questions from the patient.

Such communication patterns often reduce opportunities for patients to produce process narratives that would support recall of medical information in the other settings where they make decisions about adhering to treatments or undergoing medical procedures. In addition, during consultations, restricted discourse frameworks may inhibit patients from expressing the extent to which they understand the medical information presented to them. This can result in the situation many of us have experienced after leaving a clinical consultation – difficulty recalling, explaining, and applying the information encountered during interactions with clinicians.

Those outcomes can result when a consultation discourse framework does not support the type of communication patterns in which a clinician responds to the patient's questions, comments, and movements. Influence over communication patterns is a key component of a patient's opportunity to affect a consultation discourse framework in ways that support the creation of process narratives. Consultations that do not support the type of discourse framework evident in the radiology consultations provide fewer opportunities for patients to influence the interpretation activities and resulting communication patterns.

Examining the components of the discourse frameworks of the radiology consultations shows how a patient's participation and authority during a consultation are supported by the presence of information resources that she responds to and discusses with the clinician. Comparison of the consultation interpretation activities with the process narratives that patients expressed days later during telephone discussions shows that understandings related to the UFE procedure did not result directly from the information presented on the computer screen, but from the creation of a discourse framework that both reduced the interpretive contingencies encountered by the patient and increased those encountered by the clinician (the effects of a shift in the balance of interpretive contingencies are analyzed in Chapter Thirteen).

The interventional radiology consultations offer a model for improving patient education – presenting examples of how a discourse framework that supports the creation of transferrable understandings can develop when experts interact with clients to provide explanations in organizational settings. The consultations also provide points of comparison with more common restrictive types of explanatory interaction between professionals and clients. The next chapter explicates the production of a restrictive discourse framework and the resulting interpretive contingencies by examining another education setting.

10 A Restrictive Discourse Framework

Chapter Ten examines a discourse framework based on interpretation activities that restrict information and searching for information. This is a common occurrence. Restrictive discourse frameworks can occur in any situation in which an expert provides explanations to individuals or groups who do not have detailed knowledge about the topics being discussed. As demonstrated in Part Two, the understandings developed in such circumstances often incorporate grey boxes. The creation or acceptance of grey boxes involves a discourse framework that features particular types of communication patterns related to particular information resources. Both the learning activities in Part Two and the learning activities in this chapter involve grey boxes related to visual information resources. In Part Two, the analysis emphasized the interpretation activities that led to the creation and use of those grey boxes. This chapter emphasizes the information resources that contribute to a discourse framework supporting grey-boxed process narratives. The data analysis explains why understandings developed in a particular setting can be difficult to recall in a different setting, which lacks the communication resources that shaped the initial discourse framework.

The example analyzed in this chapter took place in the biology course of another teacher, T2, taught eight and nine years after the two examples from T1's classes. T2's classes occurred at a different high school (see Chapter Twelve for more detail about the schools and classrooms). In contrast to T1's courses featuring students using a computer simulation, T2's courses featured lectures, pen on paper classroom activities, and students' whiteboard presentations of answers to assigned trait inheritance questions. Despite different interpretive resources, learning activities, and pedagogical approaches, students in both teachers' courses arrived at the same understandings of trait inheritance, which emphasized a descriptive frame of reference and a reliance on classroom resources as grey boxes.

In T2's courses, the development of a discourse framework for interpreting information about trait inheritance and developing recallable understandings involved an initial lecture explaining:

- The location on parents' chromosomes of genes that affect development of a particular trait;
- The transmission of the genes from each parent to their children through the fertilization of egg cells;
- The relation of the dominant or recessive qualities of the inherited genes to the children's traits;
- The use of tables and nomenclature to document traits across generations, and to predict the probability of particular traits appearing in a generation of offspring.

Figure 10.1: Development of the Visual Map

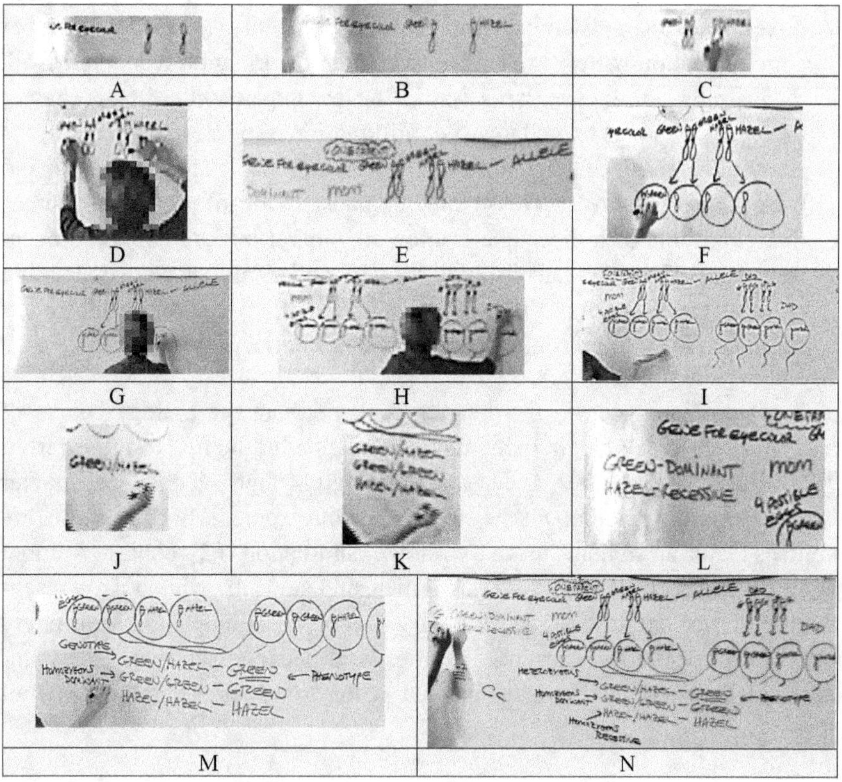

A	B	C
D	E	F
G	H	I
J	K	L
M	N	

Throughout the introductory lecture, T2 wrote vocabulary terms and drew diagrams on the whiteboard, elicited responses from students, and answered students' questions. The information on the whiteboard became progressively more intricate and interrelated as the teacher proceeded (Figure 10.1). The teacher linked her explanations of trait inheritance to the diagrams and terms on the whiteboard, pointing at them and drawing lines between them in order to clarify verbal information. The images included drawings that stood for reproductive cells, symbols that represented chromosomes, and lines linking the various images in order to show both the sequence of cell division processes (meiosis) and the relationship between parents' cells and offspring (Figure 10.1, A-N). Textual labels further clarified the phases of cell division and the biological and genetic processes represented by the drawings.

Transcript Extract 10.1

1. (Many students talking to each other)
2. T2: Okay. And let's start with um I'm going to draw a pair of homologous chromosomes on the board. Sooo (starts to draw and stops) I'm gonna try to at least do decent ones (erases drawing)
3. G?: Should we write this down?
4. T2: Uhh, no you don't have to (7.5 second pause while she draws two chromosomes represented by figure 8's with a dark area near the intersection representing an allele) Okay. What can you tell me about homologous chromosomes? . . . (Speaks G31's first name)
5. G31: there's four of 'em . .
6. T2: Okay. You're thinking of when each . . (points at the drawings of chromosomes with both hands) each one of the homologous chromosomes makes an exact copy of itself and they come together and (taps the drawings) there's four and we call that a tetrad. /Right./
7. G31: /Right./
8. T2: Okay. What can you tell me about information . on a pair of homologous chromosomes that are in you know your cells right now? (B2's first name)
9. B32: They have the same like traits . as each other.
10. T2: Okay. They have the same traits as each other, but are theyyy necessarily exactly identical?
11. A few students: No
12. T2: No. Okay. What-what is meant by that? Who can explain what I mean by that? (G37's first name)
13. G37: Like those are the genes that would be for like eye color, but one would be like blue and one brown.

Transcript Extract 10.1 (continued)

14. T2: Okay. Good . . . Both of the genes could be for eye color, but one might be . brown eyes and one might be blue eyes or it could be green eyes. We have alternate forms sometimes of that gene. So let's look at a gene (writes 'eye color' on whiteboard to left of drawing of chromosomes with genes). Let's use eye color since it was brought up . . . Keeping in mind that we're . oversimplifying here because as you know eye color involves you know many genes not just um one. (G32's first name).

At the beginning of the lecture the teacher introduced a frame of reference about cellular processes by presenting the information, linguistic terms, and drawings related to chromosomes, cell division, and genes – e.g., she drew a whiteboard diagram of processes by which chromosomes and the genes on them replicate within cells and become features of new cells. The teacher's questions, drawings, and explanations as well as the students' answers and comments presented previously studied information about biological processes that occur inside human cells (Transcript Extract 10.1, lines 4–14).

However, as the rest of the lecture shows, the teacher diagrammed those processes of cell division only to emphasize the locations of alleles for particular traits. At the point in the process of genetic inheritance where the inherited genes affect traits, she changed the explanatory mode of expression from the pictorial diagram of cellular processes (i.e., components of cell division, Figure 10.1, A-F) to the matching of pairs of words that represent a relationship between the location of alleles and a particular type of physical characteristic (Figure 10.1, J-N, Transcript Extract 10.3, line 34). This presented students with a discourse framework that featured the use of words, such as 'allele', and tables containing nomenclature, as grey boxes that covered gaps in information about the actual cellular processes by which genes affect traits.

The teacher's explanation of trait inheritance shifted from an emphasis on the relevance of cellular processes to an emphasis on predicting outcomes without regard to those processes. Referring to a student's question about the reasons for the dominance of some genes over others, she mentioned that the ensuing discussion would 'get into that in detail' (Transcript extract 10.2, lines 17, 18). The detail she eventually provided was the Mendelian approach to trait inheritance, which emphasizes locating and tabulating alleles and traits rather than explaining cellular processes. Ultimately, such de-emphasis of cellular processes guided students' interpretation activities toward a Mendelian discourse framework that focused on the locations of genes and the use of particular grey boxes to bridge gaps in cellular information: e.g., forms of the expressions, 'hidden', 'dominated', and 'masked' (Transcript Extract 10.2, line 18).

Transcript Extract 10.2

15. G32: Are homologous pairs like after they've done like the crossing over? Is that what they're called after it?

16. T2: No, homologous pairs is what you have right now in your cells. You have 23 homologous pairs of chromosomes. Meaning that you have all of your chromosomes set up in pairs . so that they're containing similar information, but it's not necessarily exactly identical. And you got those homologous pairs. (Gesturing to show separate sources coming together, [Rows A, B]) You got one set from your mom and one set from your dad and they come together and they . they form those homologous pairs, which we're gonna see what happens when they kind of come together. /(Speaks G33's first name)./

17. G33: /So, would/ in our . um . chromosomes in our homologous pairs like . I could have a gene for blue eyes, but it's just not activated or whatever

18. T2: Exaaactly. We all have many genes that are hidden, because they're being dominated by the dominant gene. So when you have a homologous pair of chromosomes and you have two um genes, alternate forms of those genes, very often one is being masked or hidden by another. And we're gonna get into that in detail um today. Yes, so very likely you know many of us have hidden alleles or forms of genes in our chromosomes (speaks another girl's first name).

19. G2: Then how do we have like different colored eyes from our parents if like one should be /like more dominant?/

20. T2: /Yeah/ the truth is because . eye color is involves many many genes. It's not like the ear lobe trait or the widow's peak trait which we're still gonna look at which is just it's there or it's not there. Eye color is probably not the best example to use because it's much more involved. There're several genes that control that. So that's why you can have . . aa and you're gonna see also even if it was very straightforward, offspring can have traits that neither one of their parents have. And we'll we'll see why as we go through the problems today that'll make a little more sense to you. Okay ? Alright. So let's go back to our homologous pair here. Um, we're gonna deal with the gene for eye color. So let's just choose two different eye colors here. Let's choose um . . .

Shifting the Discourse Framework from Diagramming Process to Tabulating Text

The teacher did not present an explicit statement that the initial concern with cellular processes ended with the diagram of the allocation of chromosomes and genes to reproductive cells. Rather, a shift from pictorial modeling to text matching and tabulation expressed a change in the explanatory frame of reference. The students' acceptance of that change was key to their production of a discourse framework that would support an understanding of trait inheritance useful for successful completion of course work.

However, as their ensuing questions showed, some of the students did not automatically accept and apply the Mendelian discourse framework and its grey boxes. Instead, they continued to seek information about cellular processes. During the lecture, five students asked six questions related to the cellular processes by which genes affect the development of traits (Transcript Extract 10.2, line 17, 19; Transcript Extract 10.6. lines 54, 56, 58; Transcript Extract 10.8 lines 95, 97). Students' questions and digressions show that some of them perceived and were interested in filling a gap in information concerning a significant aspect of trait inheritance, the processes by which the dominant or recessive quality of genes affect the development and expression of traits, such as eye color.

The students' questions digressed from the teacher's attempt to shift to the Mendelian tabulation frame of reference. The teacher replied to the questions by emphasizing the conventional Mendelian approach, by briefly mentioning cellular processes and indicating that those concerns were not relevant to the immediate task, or by saying that the rest of the lecture and subsequent work on the assigned problems would clarify the questions.

Such communication patterns were common in all of the classes studied, taught by seven biology teachers during the two educational research projects considered in this book. The absence of information that would resolve students' questions about cellular processes contributed to the multiple interpretive contingencies related to creating process narratives within the restricted discourse framework. Students eventually found that they could cope with or reduce such contingencies by applying, as grey boxes, the visual and linguistic resources provided by the teachers.

Figure 10.2: Visual Grey Boxes for Cellular Processes

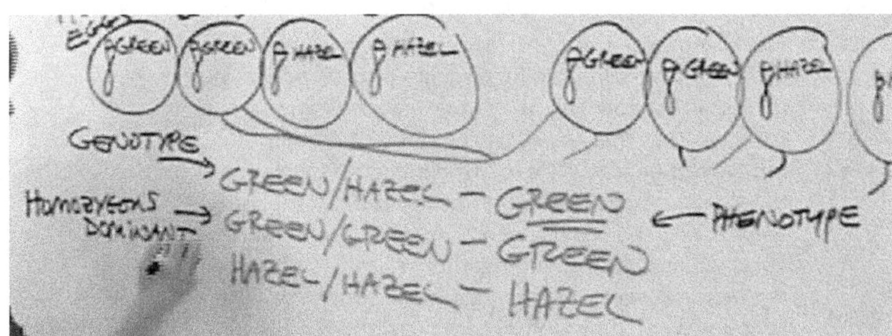

For example, the interaction related to interpreting the textual, verbal, gestural, and pictorial information presented by T2 contributed to a discourse framework and frame of reference that featured particular Mendelian grey boxes, such as the tabular arrangement of words representing eye colors and the use of lines or arrows to connect diagrams or text to express change of location (Figure 10.2). These served as placeholders for missing cellular process information. The following analysis of the videotaped lecture considers how the teacher's presentation of information and the related interaction contributed to a discourse framework featuring grey boxes.

Developing the Linguistic, Gestural, and Pictorial Components of the Discourse Framework

At the lecture, 30 students sat at tables facing the teacher, who stood at the front of the classroom near a whiteboard that covered most of the front wall. T2 began by presenting aspects of reproductive cell division (meiosis) that pertained to trait inheritance. She drew two chromosomes on the board, represented by vertical infinity symbols (Figure 10.1, A; Transcript Extract 10.1, line 4). She represented genes as a darkened area on each of the chromosomes. One of the chromosomes comes from the mother and one from the father. In addition to the drawings, the teacher used hand gestures to illustrate separate sources of the genes contained in a pair of homologous chromosomes. For example, she raised her right hand to represent the mother and her left hand to represent the father (Figure 10.3).

Figure 10.3: Gestures as Components of a Discourse Framework

16. T2: No, homologous pairs is what you have right now in your cells. You have 23 homologous pairs of chromosomes. Meaning that you have all of your chromosomes set up in pairs . so that they're containing similar information, but it's not necessarily exactly identical. And you got those homologous pairs. (gesturing to show separate sources) You got one set from your mom and one set from your dad and they come together and they . they form those homologous pairs, which we're gonna see what happens when they kind of come together.

"one set from your mom"

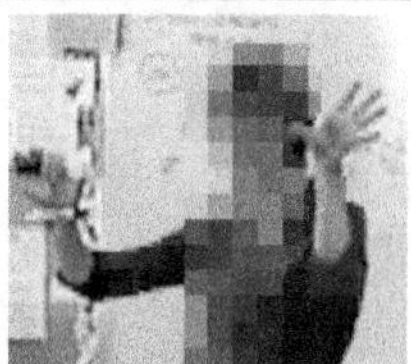

"one set from your dad"

As the teacher drew each component of the diagram, she asked the students questions pertaining to their prior study of reproduction and cell division (meiosis) during the course (Transcript Extract 10.3, lines 30, 32). When students responded to the teacher's questions, they linked verbal explanations, including information learned in prior lesson units, to the diagrams and to the teacher's gestures, which related to the information on the whiteboard (Transcript Extract 10.3, lines 31, 33).

Transcript Extract 10.3

30. T2: We could use hazel .. even though green and hazel are pretty close but that's okay. Okay. These are a homologous pair of chromosomes in the cells, and what's gonna happen before they go through cell division, before they go through meiosis? What what happens to all chromosomes and all genes just before the cell divides? (speaks G36's first name)

31. G36: Don't they double?

32. T2: They double. Exactly. They're gonna make a copy of themselves. So what you're gonna end up with is (draws another chromosome with a darkened area representing a gene next to each of the original two on the board) a pair of sister chromatids .. that are exactly identical to each other. (writes 'hazel' above pair of chromosomes on right) So this one's gonna have information or

Transcript Extract 10.3 (continued)

the geel – (sardonically marks and corrects slip of the tongue) the geel – the gene or the allele for hazel eyes and this one's gonna have information for (writes green above the pair of chromosomes on left) . . green eyes. Okay. These . two (simultaneously taps each pair of chromosomes with one hand) alternative forms of the same gene for eye color, that's what's known as alleles. So when you wrote down your definition, actually maybe somebody could read it. (G31's first name), what's your definition for allele?

33. G31: Genes that exist on alternate forms.

34. T2: Okay genes that exist in alternate forms. It's the same gene. It's the gene for eye color, but it could be an alternate form of that gene. (A digression to focus a student's attention is omitted.) Okay so we have green eyes and hazel eyes. Those are the two alleles for eye color. (writes a dash and 'allele' to the right of 'hazel'). That's an allele.

The teacher incorporated into the lecture a student's mention of different eye colors as examples of information on a pair of homologous chromosomes (Transcript Extract 10.1, line 14):

> Let's use eye color since it was brought up. Keeping in mind that we're oversimplifying here because as you know eye color involves you know many genes not just um one.

The teacher wrote 'genes for eye color' on the whiteboard next to her drawing of chromosomes with genes. She invited the students to participate in selecting the eye colors of the parents, which she wrote on the board as labels for the drawings representing genes on chromosomes (Figure 10.4, Rows A, B; Figure 10.1: B). She then drew another chromosome next to each of the original two. The teacher reviewed meiosis by drawing and explaining the duplication of each chromosome to form a homologous pair (Figure 10.4, Rows A, B; Figure 10.1: C). She explained alleles by pointing at the drawing and eliciting a student's definition of the term, which the student read from the vocabulary homework (Figure 10.4, Row C, lines 32–34; Figure 10.1: D). The teacher diagrammed how, for each parent, the two pairs of chromosomes within a reproductive cell divide, leading to four new cells (represented by a drawn arrow), each containing one of the four chromosomes from the cell that has divided (represented by a drawing of a chromosome, labeled either green or hazel) (Figure 10.4, Row B; Figure 10.1: F).

By pointing at the images and text on the whiteboard, the teacher reinforced gesturing toward visual materials in the classroom as part of the discourse framework for linking verbal and graphical information as process narratives (Figures 10.1, 10.4). In the early part of the lecture, this linked linguistic and pictorial descriptions of certain genetic processes and some of their cellular components as resources constituting a discourse framework for explaining trait inheritance. However, it did not present information about what the genes actually do within cells to affect the development of a trait. Thus, in contrast to the use of gestures toward images in the radiology consultations, the teacher's gestures and drawings would ultimately contribute to a restrictive discourse framework in which particular pictorial and linguistic information resources functioned as grey boxes.

Developing the Linguistic, Gestural, and Pictorial Components of a Discourse Framework

At the point in the process of genetic inheritance where the inherited genes affect traits, the teacher shifts the explanatory mode of expression from the pictorial diagram of cellular processes (i.e., components of cell division, Figure 10.1, A-F) to the matching of pairs of words that represent a relationship between the location of alleles and a type of physical characteristic (Figure 10.1, N, Transcript Extract 10.3, line 34):

> Okay so we have green eyes and hazel eyes. Those are the two alleles for eye color. (writes a dash and 'allele' to the right of 'hazel'). That's an allele. Okay. Now that the chromosomes have doubled and they're gonna go through the stages of meiosis. If we actually watched the chromosomes go through every stage of meiosis I mean we could do that, but what we would see at the end is how many cells are produced at the very end of meiosis. What's the end result of meiosis? (B1's first name)

Rather than presenting a pictorial and directional representation of the biochemical cellular processes of genetic inheritance, like her initial drawing of cell division (Figure 10.1, A-F), the subsequent diagram and the teacher's explanation merely match words within the drawings of reproductive cells to words used as labels (Figure 10.1, N). The position of the words in the diagram implies a nesting in which the category, 'Gene for eye color', contains the term, 'allele', which is linked by a line to drawn pairs of chromosomes (two for each parent). Each pair of chromosomes is labeled either 'green' or 'hazel', and arrows point to the circular reproductive cells, which, in turn, have either 'hazel' or 'green' written within them (Figure 10.1, H, I; also Figure 10.5, rows A-B, lines 40, 41, 45). This approach presents students with a model for using words such as 'allele' and for using graphics such as tables or diagrams as grey boxes that cover gaps in information about the actual cellular processes by which genes affect traits. The explanation of trait inheritance shifts from an emphasis on the relevance of process to an emphasis on predicting outcomes without regard to process details.

However, for some students the words and images that the teacher has written on the whiteboard do not reduce the interpretive contingencies of dealing with the absence of cellular process information. Rather than simply accepting the Mendelian grey boxes, those students express further questions and comments related to cellular processes. They apply a frame of reference concerning how dominant or recessive genes function to produce particular trait variations.

The discourse framework featuring T2's whiteboard diagram, like that of T1's computer simulation lessons, provides an example of how teachers creatively cope with the amalgamation of historical and recent scientific discoveries that is fostered by curricular standards and the pedagogical expertise incorporated in the professional culture. Restrictive discourse frameworks function in a way that focuses students' interpretation activities on particular elements of standard curriculum. Those frameworks help to deflect digressive questions and comments that could diminish or replace the historical science by emphasizing recent discoveries.

Figure 10.4: Visual and Verbal Information about Cellular Processes

A	20. T2: So let's go back to our homologous pair here. Um, we're gonna deal with the gene for eye color. So let's just choose two different eye colors here. 
B	32 (partial). T2: They double. Exactly. They're gonna make a copy of themselves. So what you're gonna end up with is (draws another chromosome next to each of the original two on the board) a pair of sister chromatids . . that are exactly identical to each other. 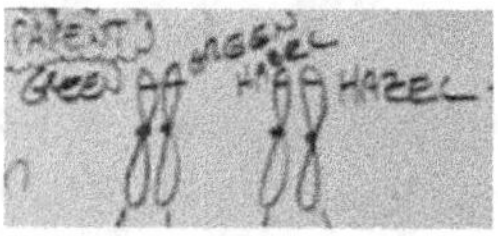 (writes 'hazel' above pair of chromosomes on right)
C	32 (continued). T2: So this one's gonna have information or the geel—(sardonically marks and corrects slip of the tongue) the geel--the gene or the allele for hazel eyes and this one's gonna have information for (writes green above the pair of chromosomes on left) . . green eyes. Okay. These . two (simultaneously taps each pair of chromosomes with one hand) alternative forms of the same gene for eye color, that's what's known as alleles. So when you wrote down your definition, 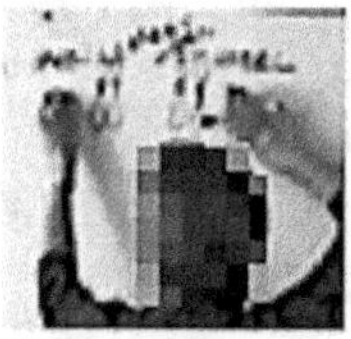 actually maybe somebody could read it. (G31's first name), what's your definition for allele? 33. G31: Genes that exist on alternate forms. 34. T2: Okay genes that exist in alternate forms. It's the same gene. It's the gene for eye color, but it could be an alternate form of that gene. . (A digression to focus a student's attention.) Don't worry about doing that now. I'd much prefer that you pay attention. Okay so we have green eyes and hazel eyes. Those are the two alleles for eye color. (writes a dash and 'allele' to the right of 'hazel'). 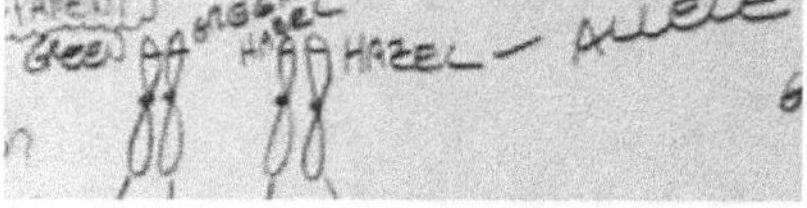 That's an allele. Okay. Now that the chromosomes have doubled . and they're gonna go through the stages of meiosis. If we actually watched the chromosomes go through every stage of meiosis I mean we could do that, but what we would see at the end is how many cells are produced at the very end of meiosis. What's the end result of meiosis? (B1's first name)

Figure 10.4 (continued)

	35. B31: Four. 36. T2: Okay four. What kind of cells diploid or haploid? 37. B31: Haploid. 38. T2: Okay four haploid cells. (draws arrows beneath each of the chromosomes) What actually happens is each one of these chromosomes containing the genes ends up in (draws a circle at the end of each arrow to represent sex cells) . . a different sex cell . . . Okay? So (draws a chromosome in each of the circles) I could kinda draw the chromosome again and . . . so we have a chromosome with (points at the word 'green' next to the left set of homologous chromosomes) information here for what color eyes?

For example, at this point in T2's lecture, the whiteboard diagram, verbal comments, and gestures combine to express a set of process narratives concerning genetic inheritance (summarized in brackets):

- *(points at the drawings of chromosomes with both hands) each one of the homologous chromosomes (taps the drawings) makes an exact copy of itself and they come together and there's four and we call that a tetrad.*

  What can you tell me about information on a pair of homologous chromosomes that are in you know your cells right now?

  They have the same traits as each other, but are theyyy necessarily exactly identical?

  Both of the genes could be for eye color, but one might be brown eyes and one might be blue eyes or it could be green eyes. We have alternate forms sometimes of that gene
  (Transcript Extract 3.1, lines 6, 8, 10 14).

  [Each chromosome of a homologous pair of chromosomes contains one of two alternative forms of a gene for a particular trait. Each of these alternative forms is called an 'allele'.]

- *(draws two chromosomes represented by figure 8's with a dark area near the intersection representing an allele)*

  (points at the drawings of chromosomes with both hands) each one of the homologous chromosomes (taps the drawings) makes an exact copy of itself

Okay. What can you tell me about information on a pair of homologous chromosomes

let's look at a gene (writes 'eye color' on whiteboard). Let's use eye color since it was brought up.
(Transcript Extract 10.1, lines 4, 6, 8, 14).

[In this example, the dark section of the chromosomes in the homologous pairs and the duplicate chromosomes formed during meiosis represent an allele for eye color.]

- *So what you're gonna end up with is (draws another chromosome with a darkened area representing a gene next to each of the original two on the board) a pair of sister chromatids that are exactly identical to each other. (writes 'hazel' above pair of chromosomes on right) So this one's gonna have information [misspoken words omitted] the gene or the allele for hazel eyes and this one's gonna have information for (writes green above the pair of chromosomes on left) green eyes. Okay. These two (simultaneously taps each pair of chromosomes with one hand) alternative forms of the same gene for eye color, that's what's known as alleles.*
(Transcript Extract 10.3, line 32).

[An allele is a genic segment of a chromosome that affects the development of a particular trait.]

- *Okay genes that exist in alternate forms. It's the same gene. It's the gene for eye color, but it could be an alternate form of that gene. Okay so we have green eyes and hazel eyes. Those are the two alleles for eye color. (writes a dash and 'allele' to the right of 'hazel'). That's an allele.*
(Transcript Extract 10.3, line 34).

[The alleles carry information that leads to a child having either green or hazel eyes.]

Students' questions show that this explanation can support an interpretive frame of reference emphasizing the cellular processes of reproduction and genetic inheritance. However, as the teacher continues the lecture she modifies the discourse framework, showing how they can also support an interpretive frame of reference that emphasizes tabulating the location of nomenclature representing alleles and traits in particular parents and offspring.

Complicating and Contesting the Discourse Framework: Introducing A Shift from Diagramming to Tabulation

When the teacher explains the second row of cells in the diagram, she begins to linguistically express a shift from diagramming cellular processes to the customary curricular emphasis on tabulating the location of traits and genes. Applying the emphasis on location, she draws arrows and circular cells to show the next phase of cell division:

> (draws arrows beneath each of the chromosomes) What actually happens is each one of these chromosomes containing the genes ends up in (draws a circle at the end of each arrow to represent sex cells) a different sex cell Okay? So (draws a chromosome in each of the circles) I could kinda draw the chromosome again and so we have a chromosome with (points at the word 'green' above next to the left set of homologous chromosomes) information here for what color eyes? (Figure 10.5, Row A, line 38)

The teacher explains that the circles represent the reproductive cells that develop during meiosis by saying, 'What actually happens is each one of these chromosomes containing the genes ends up in a different sex cell' (Figure 10.5, Row A, line 38). Then she draws a chromosome in each of the circles representing reproductive cells – the same figure-eight symbol used in the preceding part of the diagram, but lacking the darkened area indicating a gene for eye color. She points at one of the chromosomes, then at the word 'green' written next to the one of diagrammed sets of homologous chromosomes, and again at the chromosome in the reproductive cell as she asks, 'information here for what color eyes?' (Figure 10.5, Row A, line 38). When a student answers, 'green', the teacher writes 'green' within the circle next to the chromosome. She points at another of the circles representing reproductive cells and elicits another answer from the students, which she writes in that circle. After answering a digressive question from a student, the teacher finishes the diagramming of genes in reproductive cells by writing 'hazel' in the remaining two circles (Figure 10.5, Row B, line 45).

As the teacher adds more information to the diagram, the mode of representing cellular genetic processes begins to shift from pictorial and verbal representations of cells, chromosomes, and genes to a tabular organization of textual representations of genes and their effects on physical traits. Until this point in the lecture, the diagram and verbal explanations had depicted cellular processes of reproduction: i.e.:

- A chromosome that contains the gene affecting development of a particular eye color doubles, forming an identical pair of chromosomes.
- The two chromosomes in each pair then separate, and each of them moves into one of two reproductive cells.
- This results in each of those reproductive cells containing one of the identical chromosomes and its gene affecting development of a particular eye color.

In contrast, the new section of the diagram does not express how genes or alleles affect the development of traits by presenting images representing biological components of cellular reproduction processes. Such details of cellular and molecular processes by which genes affect the development of traits are omitted when the teacher begins writing colors in the reproductive cells. When the teacher begins writing words in the circles respectively representing reproductive cells from the female or male parent, 'green' and 'hazel' mark the place of missing genetic process information (Images in Figure 10.5, Rows B, C). Those words do not just express a quality of eye color associated with a gene on a chromosome. They also function as grey boxes for the cellular genetic processes by which the gene affects the production of that eye color.

The evolving discourse framework begins to feature grey boxes as placeholders for missing cellular process information. As the teacher proceeds, she identifies the diagram as representing the cell division that produces the reproductive cells of one parent, specified as the mother (Figure 10.5, Row B, lines 45, 46). Next to the existing diagram, the teacher draws a duplicate representing the father's reproductive cells, chromosomes, and genes in order to emphasize a functional equivalence with the existing diagram of the mother's reproductive cells, chromosomes, and genes related to eye color (Figure 10.5, Row B, line 49). After eliciting an answer from the students, which identifies the father's reproductive cells as sperm, the teacher further marks the new set of circles by drawing flagella at the bottom of them and saying, 'we can easily make them look like sperm cells' (Figure 10.5, Row B, line 51).

At this point the teacher's explanation and the diagram have added a process narrative that begins to shift from an emphasis on cellular processes to an emphasis on tabulating the locations of alleles for particular traits:

> *The alleles move from the parents to their children, as each of the four chromosomes resulting from the duplication of a homologous pair of chromosomes becomes part of one of the four sex cells (eggs or sperm) that develop during meiosis.* [Based on Figure 10.5, lines 38, 40, 45, 47, 49, 51]

Figure 10.5: Linking Pictorial and Linguistic Information

A	38. T2: Okay four haploid cells. (draws arrows beneath each of the chromosomes) What actually happens is each one of these chromosomes containing the genes ends up in (draws a circle at the end of each arrow to represent sex cells) . . a different sex cell . . . Okay? So (draws a chromosome in each of the circles) I could kinda draw the chromosome again and . . . so we have a chromosome with (points at the word 'green' next to the left set of homologous chromosomes) information here for what color eyes? 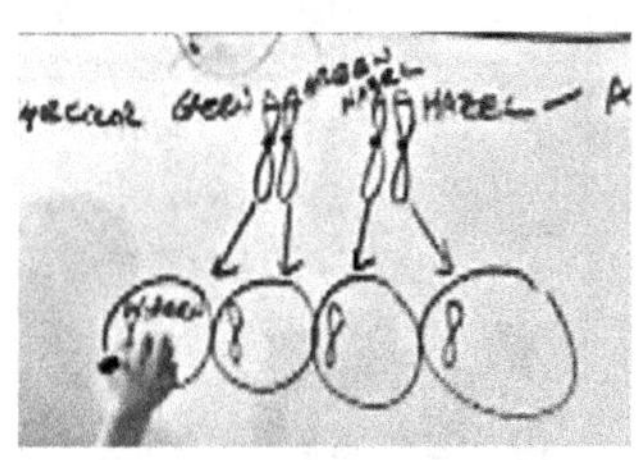 39. Students: Green 40. T2: Green (writes 'green' on board in circle representing egg cell; then points at next circle) and here (points at next circle) for what color eyes? 41. Students: Green (T2 writes 'green' on board in second circle)
B	45. (Partial[34]) T2: Alright, so here we have (writes 'hazel' in the third circle from the left) umm . . . gene for hazel eyes, (writes 'hazel' in the 4th circle) or the allele for hazel eyes, I should say, and also (points at the chromosome in the rightmost circle) on this chromosome here. These are our four sex cells. . Okay? . Alright. Let's say this is . one parent (writes 'One Parent' above the diagram). So we have one parent here, who produced these sex cells. Do you want to make this parent the father or the mother?  46. B?: The mom. 47. T2: The mom? Okay. So we have four (writes '4 possible eggs' to the left of the four circles) . possible . eggs. Okay, four possible egg cells. Let's say you have um . a father with the same exact gene possibilities. Okay? He has um also (points at the darkened area of the top left chromosome labeled 'green') one allele for green eyes and (points at the darkened area of the top right chromosome labeled hazel)

Figure 10.5 (continued)

B

one allele for hazel eyes. Alright? So let's say dad (writes 'Dad' at the top right of the initial diagram; unclear utterance while briefly moving left hand toward the previous diagram) the same thing (while drawing a copy of the existing diagram under 'Dad'). And we know that meiosis occurs . um very in a very similar way for both males and females. So here we're gonna have green (writes 'G's and 'H's next to respective drawings of the father's chromosomes, mirroring the diagram of the mother's chromosomes), green, hazel and hazel . and (draws an arrow from each of the dad's homologous chromosomes and then circles representing his sex cells at the end of each arrow) these are gonna end up in four different sex cells in this case they're going to be .

48. G?: Sperm

49. T2: sperm cells (draws flagella at bottom of circles) . . so we can easily make them look like sperm cells. So we have (writes g's and h's in each circle to represent the inherited allele) green, green, hazel, and hazel. Are you following that? Same thing that happened here with with mom (points at diagram at left side of board, then at the new diagram on its right side) just happened here with dad. Okay? They both produced sex cells through meiosis. And the end results from mom would be (points at the drawing of each of the mother's sex cells) por four possible egg cells with these genes in them and maybe I shouldn't have abbreviated (erases g's and h's in the father's sperm cells). maybe that's . maybe it's too soon to do abbreviations (erases the father's sperm cells and redraws the circles) ... Maybe I should write 'em out . just like I did the mom (drawing on board) . which is like this (draws a chromosome and writes the word green in each of the left two circles prior to speaking it) . .
Green . . . green, hazel and hazel (draws a chromosome and writes 'hazel' in each of the right two circles) . . . .

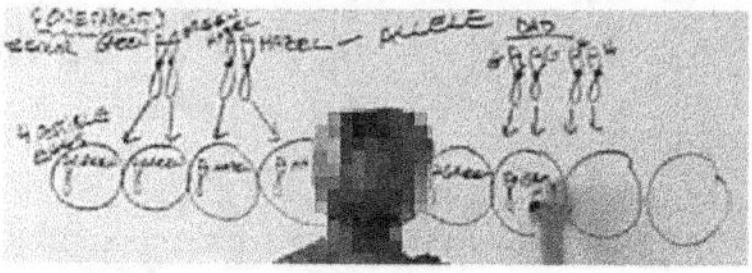

50. G32: So in each sex cell there's really 23 chromosomes?

Figure 10.5 (continued)

51. T2: Exaaactly. Good point. In each sex cell there's gonna be 23 chromosomes and not only that there's gonna be hundreds of genes on a single chromosome. So we're looking at one gene on one chromosome here. And that's it we're o we're oversimplifying this. Okay? So, again, this is dad (draws flagella on circles representing dad's sex cells), this is mom (points to the 'mom' diagram while she draws on the 'dad' diagram), this is dad. These are the possible sperm cells (points at the 'dad' diagram) that could be produced and (points at the 'mom' diagram) these are the possible egg cells that could be produced. This is the stuff that we've kind of gone over already, this is meiosis. What we're gonna look at today. (A digression to focus some students' attention) And those of you trying to finish your vocab, I really want you to pay attention to this. Otherwise you're going to find yourself um really behind. Um what we're gonna look at today is what happens if mom (tapping the board near the chromosome and 'hazel' in one of the mother's egg cells) has information for hazel eyes and dad is donating information for (tapping the board near the chromosome and 'green in one of the father's sperm cells) green eyes and it comes together (touches hands together) to produce um uh uh to fertilize it to produce an offspring that now has information for hazel eyes and green eyes. What's going to be the physical appearance of that offspring. And also what are the chances of all (gestures toward the diagram) the different possible combinations um occurring. Okay? Are we gonna end up with um . (taps inside drawing of sperm cell with 'green') one allele for green eyes and one (taps inside drawing of egg cell with 'hazel') allele for hazel or two alleles for green or two alleles for hazel. And that's what today's gonna be all about. Trying to predict what would be the outcomes of offspring reprodu of two parents producing. What would their offspring look like? (G33's first name)

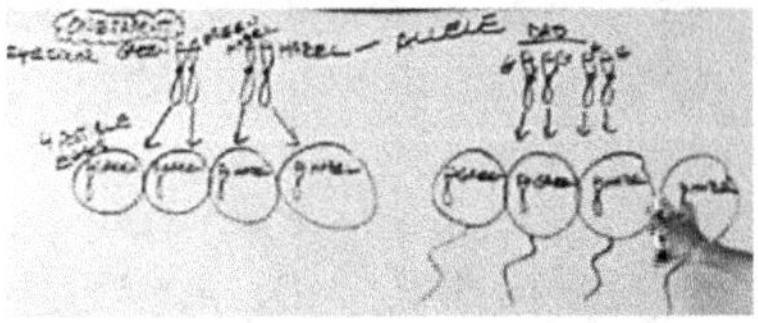

Key components of this process narrative include:

> 'Okay four haploid cells. (draws arrows beneath each of the chromosomes) What actually happens is each one of these chromosomes containing the genes ends up in (draws a circle at the end of each arrow to represent sex cells) a different sex cell.' (Figure 10.5, Row A, line 38)
>
> 'so here we have (writes "hazel" in the third circle from the left) umm gene for hazel eyes, (writes "hazel" in the 4th circle) or the allele for hazel eyes, I should say, and also (points at the chromosome in the rightmost circle) on this chromosome here. These are our four sex cells. Okay? Alright. Let's say this is one parent (writes "One Parent" above the diagram). So we have one parent here, who produced these sex cells.' (Figure 10.5, Row B, line 45)
>
> 'So we have four (writes "4 possible eggs" to the left of the four circles) possible eggs.' (Figure 10.5, Row B, line 47)

The teacher also mentions that the objective of the learning activity is to predict the eye colors that would appear in offspring of the mother and the father represented by the reproductive cells and alleles in the diagram. The teacher uses the diagram by gesturing toward and mentioning the words 'green' and 'hazel' within the circles representing egg cells or sperm cells (Figure 10.5, Row B, second half of line 51):

> what we're gonna look at today is what happens if mom (tapping the board near the chromosome and 'hazel' in one of the mother's egg cells) has information for hazel eyes and dad is donating information for (tapping the board near the chromosome and 'green in one of the father's sperm cells) green eyes and it comes together (touches hands together) to produce um uh uh to fertilize it to produce an offspring that now has information for hazel eyes and green eyes. What's going to be the physical appearance of that offspring. And also what are the chances of all (gestures toward the diagram) the different possible combinations um occurring. Okay? Are we gonna end up with um . (taps inside drawing of sperm cell with 'green') one allele for green eyes and one (taps inside drawing of egg cell with 'hazel') allele for hazel or two alleles for green or two alleles for hazel. And that's what today's gonna be all about. Trying to predict what would be the outcomes of offspring reprodu of two parents producing. What would their offspring look like?

The responses to the components of the diagram by the students and the teacher display multiple interpretations. The details of the drawings of cells (e.g., the dark area on the infinity sign representing an allele, the flagella representing sperm cells) prompted an emphasis on the qualities and developmental processes of cells, which were displayed in the questions asked by some of the students. In contrast, as the lecture progresses, the teacher uses the section of the diagram representing cell division only as a way of tracking the location of genes as they move from parents to offspring. The pictorial representation of cells, chromosomes, and genes representing the mother and the father are maps showing where the alleles for different eye colors are located during various phases of reproduction. They are not intended to explain how the alleles operate within cells to affect eye color.

However, some of the students do not accept the dearth of cellular process information. For example, G32 refers to the topic of a question she had expressed earlier (Transcript Extract 10.2, lines 15, 16). She again asks about 'crossing over' as the teacher completes the part of the diagram representing the mother, and begins to set up the shift toward tabulating nomenclature with location of alleles by writing the word 'green' in the circles representing reproductive cells:

> When does the crossing over occur then? What happens in that? (Transcript Extract 10.4, line 42)

G32 seeks information missing from the developing discourse framework by referring to the lessons about DNA and other cellular genetic processes earlier in the semester. Such questions support a frame of reference concerning genetic processes within cells and the effects of molecular biochemical processes on traits (i.e., a cellular and molecular process of genes crossing over pairs of chromosomes).

Transcript Extract 10.4

42. G32: When does the crossing over occur then? What happens in that?
43. T2: Okay. Crossing over occurs during prophase one of meiosis, but you can really only see the results of crossing over when um . when you have multiple genes on a chromosome. And we're gonna study that. We're just not going to do that right now, but we'll see how crossing over allows for um the different genic combinations that I was telling you /about./
44. G32: /So/crossing over didn't change the two greens?
45. T2: (Turns to board and gestures toward diagrams of chromosomes, pointing each hand at a different chromosome) What crossing over could do is (crossing hands over each three times to point at one and then the other of the 2 chromosomes) switch

Transcript Extract 10.4 (continued)

> these two so that (points with left hand at a darkened part of a chromosome, representing a gene and labeled, 'hazel') the hazel gene ended (points at a gene on the other chromosome, labeled 'green') up here and the green gene (moves hand back to the 'hazel' gene) ended up there, (turns to face students) but, since we're only looking at one trait this time, it's not gonna affect our sex cells in any way. So for now we're just gonna not deal with crossing over, but it actually wouldn't affect anything at this point. Okay. We'll get to it when we get to looking at two traits at one time . . . Alright, so here we have (writes 'hazel' in the third circle from the left) umm ... gene for hazel eyes, (writes 'hazel' in the 4th circle) or the allele for hazel eyes, I should say, and also (points at the chromosome in the rightmost circle) on this chromosome here. These are our four sex cells. . Okay? . Alright. Let's say this is . one parent (writes 'One Parent' above the diagram). So we have one parent here, who produced these sex cells. Do you want to make this parent the father or the mother?

The teacher uses the diagram both to acknowledge G32's interest in previously studied concepts and to return the topic of discussion to the traditional Mendelian discourse framework. First, she attempts to defer discussion of the topic (Transcript Extract 10.4, line 43):

- She presents a one-sentence description of crossing over and its relationship to the molecular biology of genes and chromosomes.
- She also mentions meiosis, which the diagram depicts.
- Then, she attempts to close the topic by saying, 'And we're gonna study that. We're just not going to do that right now, but we'll see how crossing over allows for um the different genic combinations that I was telling you about' (Transcript Extract 10.4, line 43).

However, G32 continues to seek more information that would link the cellular process of 'crossing over' to the diagram and explanation of trait inheritance. Overlapping the teacher's utterance, G32 asks, 'So crossing over didn't change the two greens?' (Transcript Extract 10.4, line 44).

The teacher provides a slightly longer explanation. She uses the diagram by gesturing at the images of genes on chromosomes, labeled, 'hazel' and 'green', in order to make the point that any crossing over of the two genes would still result in one hazel and one green allele, and have no effect. She begins to close the topic, saying:

> So for now we're just gonna not deal with crossing over, but it actually wouldn't affect anything at this point. Okay. We'll get to it when we get to looking at two traits at one time (Transcript Extract 10.4, middle of line 45)

Then the teacher continues to develop the diagram and the shift from depicting cell division toward tabulating nomenclature:

> Alright, so here we have (writes 'hazel' in the third circle from the left) umm gene for hazel eyes, (writes 'hazel' in the 4th circle) or the allele for hazel eyes, I should say. (Transcript Extract 10.4, end of line 45)

However, as the lecture continues, other students continue to digress from the teacher's emphasis on tabulating the locations of genes by asking questions related to cellular genetic processes. The teacher's responses to the students' questions and the information she puts on the whiteboard continue to emphasize information about the location of genes related to the inheritance of eye color and to deemphasize the cellular processes by which genes affect the development of traits. The diversions and delays in regard to providing information that would answer the students' questions about cellular processes create interpretive contingencies for the students. The ensuing questions and comments by students show how those contingencies contribute to the students' production of a discourse framework that supports the creation of process narratives containing particular Mendelian grey boxes.

Interpretive Contingencies of the Developing Discourse Framework

The developing whiteboard diagram provides an example of such interpretive contingencies. The words 'green' or 'hazel', written by the teacher within each circle representing a reproductive cell (Transcript Extract 10.5, Picture B), relate to the darkened area on a chromosome used to represent an allele in the preceding diagram of cell division (Transcript Extract 10.5, Picture A). However, unlike the preceding section of the drawing, the written words do not express a model of cellular components and processes. This collapses the aspects of cellular processes represented pictorially in the first part of the diagram (location, movement, development) into a functional equivalency between the allele and the trait in regard to 'green' and 'hazel'. It conflates the alleles and the traits, since the words index both. Thus, the shift from pictorial to textual representation does not contribute to a discourse framework that supports creation of a process narrative explaining how alleles affect the traits, which are the result of cellular development – unless students shift their interpretive frame of reference from one emphasizing cellular processes to one that emphasizes simply matching origins with outcomes and inferring a causal relationship.

Transcript Extract 10.5: Beginning a Shift from Pictorial to Tabular Representation

45. [partial] T2: Alright, so here we have (writes 'hazel' in the third circle from the left) umm . . . gene for hazel eyes, (writes 'hazel' in the 4th circle) or the allele for hazel eyes, I should say, and also (points at the chromosome in the rightmost circle) on this chromosome here. These are our four sex cells. . Okay? . Alright. Let's say this is . one parent (writes 'One Parent' above the diagram). So we have one parent here, who produced these sex cells. Do you want to make this parent the father or the mother?
46. B?: The mom.
47. T2: The mom? Okay. So we have four (writes '4 possible eggs' to the left of the four circles) . possible . eggs. Okay, four possible egg cells. Let's say you have um . a father with the same exact gene possibilities. Okay? He has um also (points at the darkened area of the top left chromosome labeled 'green') one allele for green eyes and (points at the darkened area of the top right chromosome labeled hazel) one allele for hazel eyes. Alright? So let's say dad (writes 'Dad' at the top right of the diagram) (?) the (draws a copy of the existing diagram under 'Dad') same thing. And we know that meiosis occurs . um very in a very similar way for both males and females. So here we're gonna have green (writes 'G's and 'H's next to respective drawings of the father's chromosomes, mirroring the diagram of the mother's chromosomes), green, hazel and hazel . and (draws an arrow from each of the dad's homologous chromosomes and then circles representing his sex cells at the end of each arrow) these are gonna end up in four different sex cells in this case they're going to be .

While drawing and explaining the diagram of the father's cell division and allocation of alleles, the teacher deftly shifted her use of the diagram from explaining cellular genetic processes to mapping the locations of alleles, expressed as words or nomenclature. The teacher began an explanatory transition from modeling cellular processes to tabulating textual labels. This also shifted the developing discourse framework away from using pictorial representations and toward using textual and tabular representations. Figure 10.6 shows the endpoint of that shift.

Figure 10.6: Completed Diagram of Trait Inheritance

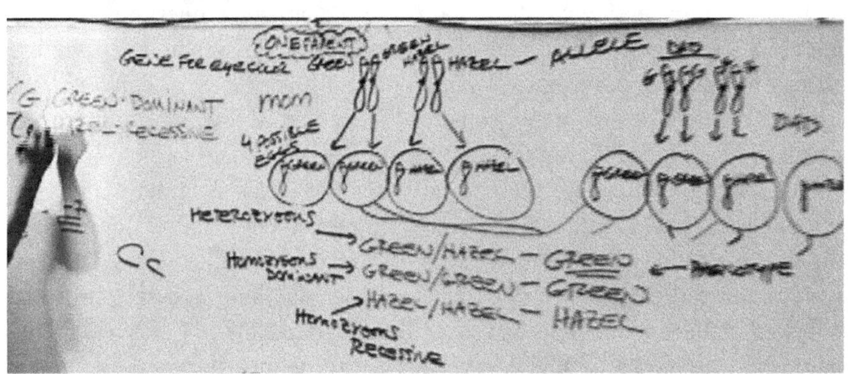

The development of the final diagram accompanies a series of activities that move the interpretive frame of reference away from cellular processes and toward location mapping featuring standard Mendelian grey boxes. Shortly after the point in the lecture when the teacher finishes diagramming the father's cell division she no longer verbally or gesturally emphasizes the parts of the diagram that pictorially represent cellular components and processes (i.e., images depicting chromosomes, genes, and changes to them). She begins to focus on the diagram as a map of the locations of alleles, rather than an explanation of cellular genetic processes.

In the short term, this shift from diagramming cellular processes to tabulating nomenclature increases the interpretive contingencies that students face as they try to compose a discourse framework that supports linking the available information as coherent process narratives. Some students express the interpretive contingencies of this shift by continuing to ask the teacher questions emphasizing cellular processes. The teacher's responses de-emphasize the cellular process frame of reference by providing minimal information or postponing answers. These exchanges display the interpretation activities and visual information resources that eventually guide the students toward accepting the conventional Mendelian discourse framework featuring particular grey boxes.

The teacher's approach to explaining trait inheritance during the lecture presents the cellular biology of reproduction only as a component of a discourse framework, which supports generating the Mendelian nomenclature that contributes to the Punnett squares used to compute the probability of specific traits appearing. However, the students' questions express an interpretive frame of reference that emphasizes the cellular processes of genes – an approach they encountered in their study of DNA earlier in the biology course. The teacher's de-emphasis of the previously studied information and frames of reference as she responds to the students' questions presents additional interpretive contingencies. As the students develop a discourse framework that supports an explanation of trait inheritance acceptable to the teacher, they are able to apply some of the frames of reference and process narratives developed during their earlier studies, but not all of them.

For example, after the teacher duplicates the initial diagram (Transcript Extract 10.5, line 47) in order to show the movement of alleles during cell division for both parents, a student, G32, who had asked about 'crossing over' six minutes earlier, seeks clarification about the diagram's accuracy in regard to actual cellular processes (Transcript Extract 10.6, lines 54, 56). G32 compares the teacher's diagram and explanation of the inheritance of alleles and traits to a previous topic of study concerning the redistribution of chromosomes during cell division. She mentions that during the earlier study of mitosis the students and teacher focused on the replication of one chromosome, although they learned that each reproductive (sex) cell actually contains 23 chromosomes. She asks for reassurance that the board diagram is also a simplified version of what actually happens in the body:

> in our human body actually making like the sex cell, there'd be 23 chromosomes that would be being like divided and everything? (Transcript Extract 10.6, line 56)

Transcript Extract 10.6: Heuristic

54. G32: So okay like when we were learning about mitosis, we only used like fo we only used like ff one chromosome for like each cell . or for each sex sex cell, but there's really in 23.
55. T2: Right and /w/
56. G32: /It's/ it's just like kinda . like . So like when you're doing this up here, like if it was in uh it's like it was in our human body actually making like the sex cell, there'd be 23 chromosomes that would be being like divided and everything?

Transcript Extract 10.6 (continued)

57. T2: Yeah. 23 and like I said on each of those 23, hundreds of genes. If you want to get just an idea of what kinda information is really on the human chromosomes, that poster that's starting to fall down back there . says human genome landmarks, and on there on the different 23 chromosomes, they kind of identify certain traits on them. So we're just trying to see (points toward the whiteboard diagram) the patterns of inheritance. We kno now know how (points toward the diagram) sex cells are produced. Now we're gonna see what . how does this determine what kinda offspring is going to be produced, what the genes will be like of the offspring, what the physical appearance will be like of the offspring. So we oversimplify it just to make it easier to learn. But you're right. It's very complicated. (Male student's first name)
58. B31: Um do genes account for like your like if you're double jointed or like you can touch your tongue to your nose and stuff like that?
59. T2: Yeah. Your genes account for everything that you are. Mmm-hh. In one way or another. In combination with your surrounding environment also. Meaning not even just you know the air around you but also the hormones in your body and other uh chemicals in your body can have an impact on your genes as well.

G32's question prompts the teacher to acknowledge the student's reference to the complexity of cellular processes, and then shift emphasis away from that complexity and toward the Mendelian emphasis on specific traits:

> If you want to get just an idea of what kinda information is really on the human chromosomes, that poster that's starting to fall down back there . says human genome landmarks, and on there on the different 23 chromosomes, they kind of identify certain traits on them. So we're just trying to see (points toward the whiteboard diagram) the patterns of inheritance. We kno now know how (points toward the diagram) sex cells are produced. Now we're gonna see what . how does this determine what kinda offspring is going to be produced, what the genes will be like of the offspring, what the physical appearance will be like of the offspring, what the physical appearance will be like of the offspring. So we oversimplify it just to make it easier to learn. But you're right. It's very complicated. (Transcript Extract 10.6, line 57)

Rather than digressing from the Mendelian explanation of trait inheritance, the teacher defers discussion of the complex biological relationship of chromosomes, alleles, and traits by mentioning that a poster on the wall provides more detail about the various traits affected by specific alleles on the 23 different chromosomes. The poster presented text and images in the form of a list of the traits affected by specific alleles. The mention of the poster does not actually incorporate it in the discourse framework, unless students independently apply it to their work on the assignments.

After referring to the poster, the teacher shifts the topic of discussion back to the whiteboard diagram and Mendelian frame of reference by saying,

> So we're just trying to see the patterns of inheritance. We kno now know how sex cells are produced. Now we're gonna see what how does this determine what kinda offspring is going to be produced, what the genes will be like of the offspring, what the physical appearance will be like of the offspring. (Transcript Extract 10.6, line 57)

She indicates that students do not need to consider the details of how genes affect traits ('So we're just trying to see the patterns of inheritance'). By saying, 'Now what we're gonna see,' she emphasizes the developing diagram on the whiteboard. Then she tells the students that it will correlate the physical traits of offspring with their genes by showing how the allocation of alleles and reproductive cells will determine the genes and traits of offspring ('Now what we're gonna see how does this determine what kinda offspring is going to be produced, what the genes will be like of the offspring, what the physical appearance will be like of the offspring'). In her comment, 'determine' functions as a grey box for the missing cellular process information. The teacher emphasizes that the whiteboard diagram's information about the location of alleles will show how the parents' genotypes affect the phenotypes of their children – without using information about how genes actually affect the cellular development within the bodies of the children that results in traits such green or hazel eye color.

The teacher has attempted to shift from a discourse framework incorporating the student's mention of cellular processes in the human body back to one emphasizing patterns of inheritance and the location of particular alleles and traits in parents and offspring. However, the teacher's acknowledgment that the actual cellular processes are very complicated and, therefore, have been oversimplified to make the lesson easier to learn, does not resolve the contingencies that some students encounter as they interpret information and formulate a discourse framework, which support the creation of process narratives that constitute an understanding of the teacher's explanation of trait inheritance.

The students' questions display a process of gradually adopting some components of the discourse framework that the teacher has expressed through talk, images, and gestures. For example, B31 immediately asks: 'Um do genes account for like your like if you're double jointed or like you can touch your tongue to your nose and stuff like that?' (Transcript Extract 10.6, line 58). The wording of the question provides an example of how students develop a discourse framework that includes grey boxes in order to manage the interpretive contingencies presented by the conventional curriculum for trait inheritance. B31's question is formatted in a way that elicits an answer of yes or no. He does not ask how genes affect physical characteristics. Although B31 inquires about a causal connection between genes and specific traits, he uses an ambiguous term, 'account for', as a grey box that covers the absence of cellular process information. The teacher answers, 'Yeah. Your genes account for everything that you are', but then elaborates by saying, 'the hormones in your body and other uh chemicals in your body can have an impact on your genes as well' (Transcript Extract 10.6, line 59).

While the substance of the teacher's answer does not preclude considering the effects of cellular processes in order to explain the inheritance of traits, her form of expression reinforces the shift away from such details. She applies 'account for' and 'have an impact' as grey boxes for missing biochemical details about the relationship of genes, hormones, and chemicals. This reinforces the transition away from a discourse framework that includes details of cellular genetic processes, and toward a discourse framework that grey-boxes those details. The teacher and student have begun the interpretation activities that routinize the use of grey boxes. The interpretive contingency the students must deal with becomes finding grey boxes that the teacher recognizes as appropriate, rather than searching for information about DNA and cellular processes. When the teacher continues the lecture, and presents the traditional Mendelian grey boxes of nomenclature and tabulation formats, the students use those resources to resolve that contingency.

From Map to Table: Mendelian Grey Boxes Enter the Discourse Framework

After responding to the students' questions, the teacher says, 'So what we're looking at today' (Transcript Extract 10.7, Row B, line 65), emphasizing that her agenda for the immediate lesson differs from the topics of the preceding student questions about information they had studied previously or encountered outside of school. Then she returns to the whiteboard diagram, labeling sections of it with the words 'mom' and 'dad'. Next, she asks a question, which limits the students' response options, focusing them on the diagram and its use as a map of the locations and quantities of alleles and traits:

> What are all the possible combinations if any one of these sperm cells (points at images of sperm cells) were to fertilize any one of these egg cells (points at images of egg cells)? (Transcript Extract 10.7, Row A, line 65)

A student answers 'Green and hazel' (Transcript Extract 10.7, line 66). After accepting that answer, the teacher asks another restrictive question, 'Okay, that's one possible combination. (G32's first name) what's another?' which prompts the following exchange (Transcript Extract 10.7):

68. G32: Green
69. T2: Okay. (writes 'green' on board) Green and what?
70. G32: Just green.
71. T2: (writes 'green' again) Green and green.

The teacher writes the students' answers on the board, beginning to arrange them as a table (Figure 10.7, line 71, 2nd image). Such emphasis on the diagram's labels and their function as components of lists and tables contributes to a discourse framework supporting an interpretive frame of reference that is an alternative to the concern with cellular processes and DNA expressed by students' preceding questions. The table is a formatted list of combinations, which functions as a grey box for the biochemical qualities and operations of alleles (Transcript Extract 10.7, line 71, 3rd image).

At this point in the lecture, the students begin the tabular representation of alleles and traits. The teacher's use of words provided by the students to visually represent the alleles within reproductive cells functions as a transition from the earlier pictorial representation of location, sequence, and directional movement, which indicated a process. She names the significant cellular components, and shows their relationship by means of the tabular arrangement of textual labels (Transcript Extract 10.7, line 71, 2nd and 3rd images). This arrangement is a grey box for missing cellular process information about how alleles affect the development of traits. Without detailing the cellular processes, it links the location of the alleles in egg cells, sperm cells, and fertilized egg cells with particular eye colors. It organizes linguistic terms in an arrangement that indicates correlations between the location of certain alleles in the eggs or sperm of parents and the possible combinations of alleles in offspring.

Transcript Extract 10.7: From Diagram to Text

65. T2: So what we're looking at today is let's say that we have mom producing these 4 egg cells (writes 'mom' on board next to representations of egg cells) and we had dad producing these um four sperm cells (writes 'dad' next to representations of sperm cells). Maybe we can do this right here (gestures toward blank section of board). What are all the possible combinations if any one of these sperm cells (points at images of sperm cells) were to fertilize any one of these egg cells (points at images of egg cells)? What are the possible gene combinations that could occur? (G31's first name), give me one.

66. G31: Green and hazel

67. T2: Okay, you could have (writes 'green/hazel' on board) um the allele for the green eyes and the allele for the hazel eyes. Okay, that's one possible combination. (G32's first name) what's another?

68. G32: Green

69. T2: Okay. (writes 'green' on board) Green and what?

70. G32: Just green.

71. (partial) T2: (writes 'green' again) Green and green. Okay . yeah . and that might happen like this one might happen if you if this (points to one of images of egg cells labeled 'green') egg was fertilized (draws line from the egg to one of the images of sperm cells labeled hazel) by this sperm. (Points at the text 'green/green') This one might happen if this egg (draws another line from the egg labeled 'green' to a sperm labeled 'green') was fertilized by this sperm. So we're looking at all the possible combinations here.

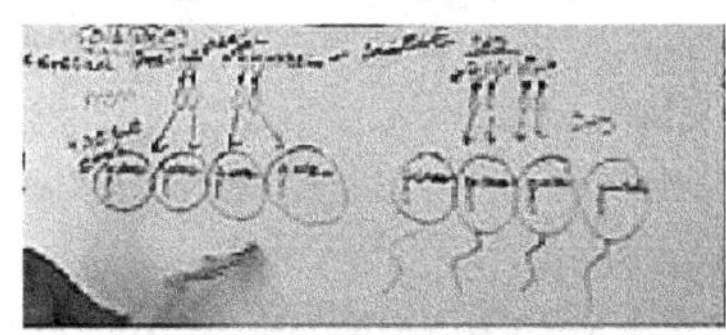

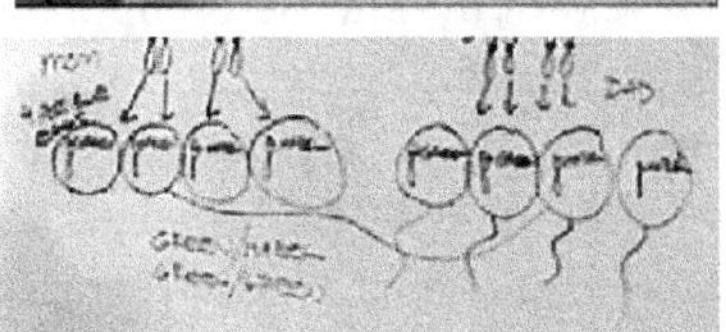

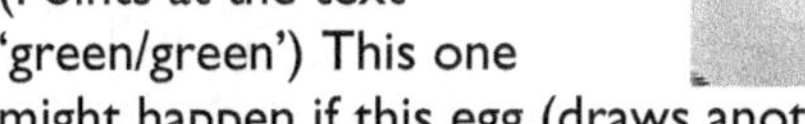

For example, the teacher expresses a representational equivalency between the text, 'Green/Hazel', and the pictorial diagram, which maps the movement of each parent's alleles into the child's cells through fertilization (Transcript Extract 10.7, lines 68–71). By pointing at the diagram of the *mom*'s and *dad*'s reproductive cells, and then drawing a line linking an egg cell containing an allele for a particular eye color with a specific sperm cell containing an allele for a particular eye color, the teacher emphasizes that the pairs of words (green/hazel and green/green) can replace the diagramming of cells in order to represent the possible outcomes of the cells merging when parents mate. Like Mendel, the students must infer a causal connection from the correlations presented by the discourse framework, rather than describing a causal cellular process.

Continuing the Shift from Diagramming to Tabulating

The teacher encourages this shift to tabulation and correlation by providing textual labels for parts of the diagram and arranging words as a table. Next to the diagram, she writes 'green-dominant' and 'hazel-recessive' (Figure 10.7, Row A). However, she does not draw a pictorial representation of the cellular processes related to 'dominant' and 'recessive'. Instead, the teacher erases part of the pictorial representation, the flagella denoting the father's sperm cells and the lines linking possible pairings of mother's and father's alleles in their offspring. She replaces them with the tabular list of paired colors which represent both the individual genes inherited from each parent and, in the context of the attribution of dominance and recessiveness, the eye color of an offspring (Figure 10.7, Row B). This emphasizes the tabulation of linguistic terms featuring various combinations of words representing green or hazel alleles inherited from parents as well as a relationship between each allele combination and a word representing the eye color inherited by the offspring ('green' or 'hazel').

As she proceeds, the teacher points to the tabular list on the whiteboard, rather than the pictorial diagram above it (Figure 10.7, Row B). She provides detailed explanation regarding how to tabulate the vocabulary terms and nomenclature (Figure 10.7, Row C, lines 140, 142). This continues the shift of the interpretive frame of reference and the discourse framework toward nomenclature and tabulation, and away from the cellular biology. It also shows the students that tables correlating vocabulary and nomenclature can function as grey boxes for the missing information about cellular processes (Figure 10.7, Row C).

Figure 10.7: Components of Tabulation

A	79. T2:	Okay so I'm going to tell you that green eyes-she's right- (finishes writing 'dominant' on board) are dominant and the allele for (writes 'hazel - recessive') hazel eyes is recessive. Actually, let's go ahead and read a 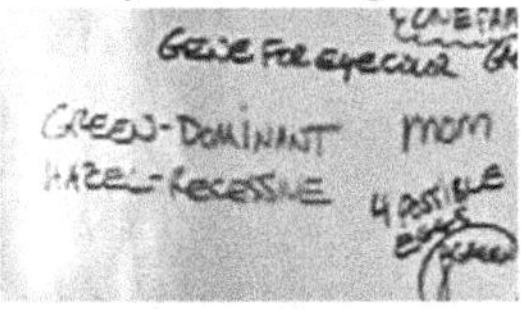 definition that you wrote down for each of these and then we'll try to make sense of it. (B3's first name) do you have one of the definitions?
B	130. T2:	Okay so (points at column of allele pairs in table on white board) which one of these would be homozygous dominant genotype?
	131. G38:	Um, green green.
	132. T2:	Good! Green green. (Points at 'green-dominant' on white board) Green is dominant so here (points at 'green/green' in table) you're gonna have (Writes 'homozygous dominant' with arrow pointing at 'green/green' row of 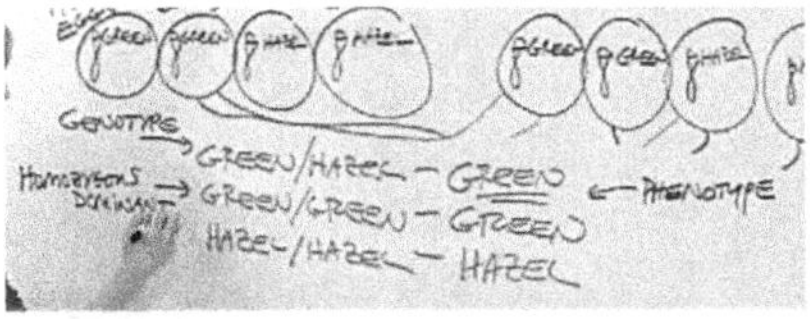 the table on white board) . this is . the homozygous . . dominant . Okay? Two copies of the dominant allele.
C	140. T2:	We're getting ready to learn how to actually solve these problems, but one more thing we need to do before we are we will be totally ready. And that is, when we're going through genetic problems and you know I say that okay, we have a parent with uh who's heterozygous for green eyes and we have a parent who's homozygous recessive for hazel eyes, what kind of um offspring can we . can we predict? You don't want to have to keep writing green and green or hazel and hazel we like to assign symbols to what's represent what's gonna be our dominant allele and what's gonna represent our recessive allele. So hopefully from your reading you might have picked up on what those symbols are. How do we represent what's the dominant allele and what is the recessive allele? (Girl's first name).

Figure 10.7: Components of Tabulation (continued)

C

141. G?: When something is dominant, it's capitalized and it's just something like for hazel it'd be capital 'H' if that's dominant. Or if it's recessive it would be lower case 'h'.

142. T2: Okay. Yeah, usually we use a capital letter to represent the dominant allele and a lower case letter to represent the recessive allele. Think of things that are really important. We capitalize them. So, the dominant allele is gonna be . y'know it's the one we're gonna capitalize. So, in this case we usually try to pick a letter that makes sense with the traits that were looking at and also . that looks very different in its capital form compared to its lower case form. If you choose a letter like umm the letter 'c' (writes 'Cc' on board), . . . it's really hard to tell the difference between the capital 'C' and the lower case 'c'. So, a good example, if this is our problem, would be to use (writes '(G)' on the board in front of 'green-dominant') capital 'G' for the green eyes, and then a (writes '(g)' in front of 'hazel-recessive'. . lower case

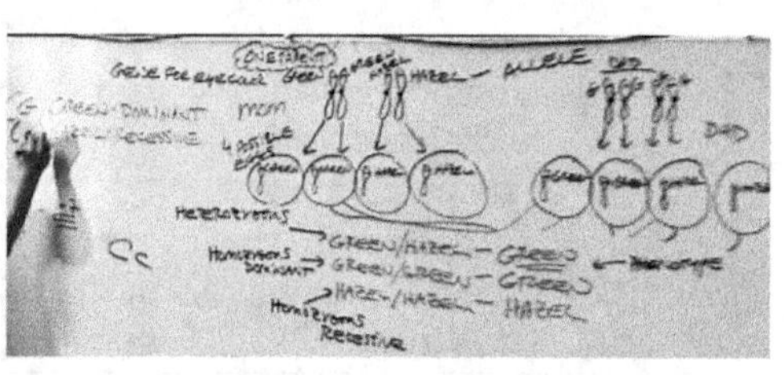

'g' for the hazel eyes. Now some students want to use a capital 'G', but a lower case 'h'. We don't do that because we're looking at the same gene. So we use the same letter to represent that gene, but these (points at '(G) green-domninant' and '(g) hazel-recessive') are just are two different forms of the gene for eye color. /So we use/

143. G33?: /How do/

144. T2: the same letter, but just a upper case and a lower case form of that letter.

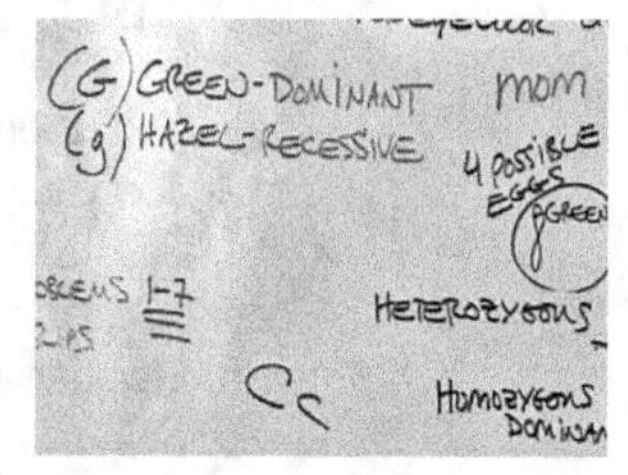

The tabular arrangement of words on the whiteboard describes only the particular physiological outcomes (green or hazel eyes) that correlate with the presence of particular combinations of alleles. It does not express the cellular processes by which specific combinations of alleles affect the appearance of specific traits. In this regard, the visual resources on the whiteboard reflect the verbal discussion. The tabulation of the words 'green' and 'hazel' simply asserts that there is a causal relationship between alleles and traits. The arrangement of the text, 'green/hazel' (representing a set of two alleles that influence the development of green or hazel eye color) next to the word, 'green', correlates a particular combination of alleles with a particular eye color of a child (images in Figure 10.7, lines 132, 142). Similarly, the word 'green' written next to the word 'dominant' expresses the linguistic and visual recognition of another relationship, i.e., another correlation with the use of 'green' in the tabular list below it on the whiteboard (Image in Figure 10.7, Line 142).

The shift from a discourse framework featuring diagrams of components and processes to one featuring tabulation of nomenclature was reinforced as the teacher positioned the textual labels and added additional text to support the concepts of dominant and recessive alleles and traits (Figure 10.7, Rows A-C). For example, she wrote the words, 'homozygous dominant', followed by an arrow pointing at the previously written 'green/green – Green', which became a row in the table of possible pairings of alleles for green and hazel eyes when eggs and sperm merge (Image in Figure 10.7, Row B). Above the column containing 'homozygous dominant' was the label, 'Genotype', and above the row containing 'Green' was the label, 'Phenotype'. Subsequently, the teacher added the Mendelian alphabetical nomenclature, an upper case 'G' and a lower case 'g', in parentheses before 'Green-Dominant' and 'Hazel-Recessive' respectively (Figure 10.7, Row C, line 142, 2nd image). The arrangement of words combined with dashes, arrows, and lines linking them expressed a categorical relationship among the vocabulary words that the students had defined in their homework assignment. The dashes, arrows, and lines present nested relationships among linguistic terms by functioning as grey boxes for missing cellular process information. As the students accept such grey boxes as part of the discourse framework, they also begin to accept the shift from diagramming cellular processes to tabulating linguistic terms as the basis for developing process narratives that count as understandings of trait inheritance in the classroom setting.

Using the Discourse Framework to Deal with Missing Information

The teacher uses the tabular arrangement and categorical labeling of textual representations of alleles and traits to present the relationships between particular combinations of alleles and particular traits (Figure 10.7, Rows B, C). This indicates that two alleles affect the presence of a trait. This visual information contributes to a discourse framework that supports subsequent discussion of dominant and recessive alleles and traits. It prompts students to develop an interpretive frame of reference like that expressed by the teacher in order to coherently link the new information as process narratives. However, despite the teacher's verbal and graphical emphasis on tabulating combinations of genes with particular traits, some students do not easily shift from a cellular process frame of reference to the tabulation perspective.

For example, after the teacher introduced a discussion of the meaning of 'recessive' in regard to alleles and traits, a student, B33, digressed from the teacher's emphasis on the dichotomous mapping of green/hazel eye color to dominant/recessive alleles. He asked if the cause of various shades of a particular eye color related to combinations of alleles: 'When the green hazel or the green green would they have like a different shade er?' (Transcript Extract 10.8, line 95). In response, the teacher again acknowledged the incompleteness of the model she was explaining and the complexity of actual processes of trait inheritance: 'In this case, we're just gonna say it's either green or it's hazel. I mean in-in reality there could be a blending of of diff of the different genes that make the actual eye color, but now we'll just say it's green or hazel' (line 96). Such answers by the teacher emphasize a frame of reference based on Mendelian tabulation, but do not end every student's application of a frame of reference concerning the link between cellular processes and human traits.

Transcript Extract 10.8: Blending, Changing

90. T2: Okay it is the term that is used to describe the allele that is masked or hidden or dominated by the dominant allele. So, let's go back to this (pointing at the words 'green – dominant' on the board). If green eye color is our dominant allele and (pointing at the words 'hazel – recessive') hazel eye color is the recessive allele, let's now look at the combinations that we listed here. (erases flagella under images of sperm cells. Then points at the list of allele combinations.) These are the . the genes or the alleles that were donated by the parents. So now we're gonna look at what's gonna be the actual um physical make-up of the child – is it gonna have green eyes or is it gonna have hazel eyes. (Pointing at 'green/hazel') So if we have one green allele and one hazel allele, what's gonna be the actual eye color of that offspring?

91. Students: Green

92. T2: Green. Um (G35's first name) why don't you tell me why.

93. G35: Because green uh . is the dominant.

94. T2: Okay. Green is (points with left hand at 'green' in list of eye color combinations on the board) the dominant and it's going to (moves

Transcript Extract 10.8 (continued)

hand to 'hazel') hide or (taps 'hazel') mask or prevent the (moves hand back and forth under 'hazel') expression of this (taps 'hazel' 3 times) hazel eh (turns toward the board) allele. So the um (writes 'green' on the board following 'green/hazel') . eye color here is going to be . green. (turns toward students) (B33's first name).

95. B33: When the green hazel or the green green would they have like a different shade er?

96. T2: In this case, we're just gonna say it's either green or it's hazel. I mean in-in reality there could be a blending of of diff of the different genes that would make the actual eye color, but now we'll just say it's green or hazel. (B31's first name)

97. B31: Um can genes become like um uh like can they become dominant? Like because I had blue um like really really blue eyes when I was . born and now I have hazel eyes. Does that mean like uh my hazels were like recessive and now they're dominant?

98. T2: Um the expression of the genes can um change in that either the chemicals in your body could change the expression. Or um at certain points of your life certain genes are turned off and certain genes are turned on. I'm not exactly sure what causes the babies' eye color, because that's pretty common that hair color and eye color change as a baby gets older, or even as we go from being you know five years old to – I'm sure many of you had different hair color then than you do now. So I don't know if that's um chemicals in your body, your hormones, that are causing that or if it's a change in the turning off or on of genes as as you grow older. I would have to look into that, but I think that's a great question. (says G33's first name).

As the introductory lecture continues, the communication patterns provide an example of how the teacher's use of Mendelian terminology in her comments and whiteboard diagram begin to affect a student's creation of a discourse framework that fits the teacher's objectives. Following the teacher's emphasis on the descriptive tabulation of genes and traits, a different student, B31, immediately asks another question that pertains to cellular processes:

> Um can genes become like um uh like can they become dominant? Like because I had blue um like really really blue eyes when I was born and now I have hazel eyes. Does that mean like uh my hazels were like recessive and now they're dominant? (Transcript Extract 10.8, line 97)

The student's question expresses the beginning of a shift of interpretive frame of reference from process modeling to tabulation. He integrates the conventional Mendelian grey boxes, 'dominant' and 'recessive', into his discourse framework, linking those terms to descriptions of eye color: 'really really blue eyes' and 'hazels'. However, he expresses a concern with genes *becoming* dominant, presenting a frame of reference oriented toward the ways that cellular, biochemical processes involving genes can affect traits. At this point in the study of trait inheritance, he is just beginning to integrate grey boxes into a discourse framework that will support linking the information presented by the teacher as coherent process narratives.

The student's question presents an opportunity to consider the actual developmental processes triggered or affected by genes. However, the teacher emphasizes genes as entities that operate separately from other biochemical processes, which affect the development of the body.

> So I don't know if that's um chemicals in your body, your hormones, that are causing that or if it's a change in the turning off or on of genes as as you grow older. I would have to look into that, but I think that's a great question. (Transcript Extract 10.8, line 98)

The teacher's mention of 'chemicals in your body, your hormones' and 'a change in the turning off or on of genes' (Transcript Extract 10.8, line 98) briefly suggests the relevance to trait inheritance of cellular processes other than those presented by the diagramming and discussion of cell division. However, her next comment, 'I would have to look into that, but I think that's a great question,' defers more detailed discussion, and closes that topic. This functions to deemphasize the relevance of cellular processes to the developing discourse framework.

The teacher's de-emphasis of cellular processes as a topic of discussion does not resolve every student's concern with obtaining information related to the functioning of genes in the body. Students continue to display interpretive contingencies related to conforming their frames of reference to a discourse framework based on the conventional Mendelian explanation of trait inheritance. Another student, G33, follows B31's digression about changing eye color with another personal anecdote about her eye color changing after she was a baby (Transcript Extract 10.9, line 99).

Transcript Extract 10.9

99. G33: For the for my genes like went uh went uh umm like a year ago. Ya know that's not when I was a baby.
100. T2: No. That's what I'm saying I mean and it can change throughout your your lifetime too. Some women experience changes in hair color or texture and stuff when they're pregnant, which is all about hormones in the body. So I mean there like I said your genes are not just it's not like you're definitely gonna have what your . what your gee – it's like your genes determine exactly what . the way things will be. It's an interaction between your genes and your surrounding environment, hormones in your body being a surrounding environment. Okay. Alright. So this is an easy one (returns to the gene combination list and points at 'green/green'). If you have a copy for the green allele and another copy for the green allele, what's gonna be the eye color?
101. G33 and other students: Green.
102. T2: Okay green (writes 'Green' to the right of 'Green/Green – ') .. Now what if you have a copy for the (points at 'Hazel/Hazel – ') hazel allele and the hazel allele? What's going to be the eye color?
103. Students: Hazel
104. T2: Hazel . (writes 'Hazel' to the right of 'Hazel/Hazel – ') But keep in mind if you look here .. this is the only way to get hazel eyes. If we're saying that hazel eyes is recessive – and again we're just using this as an example – if we're saying that hazel (points at 'recessive' in 'Hazel-Recessive' at the left side of the diagram) eyes is the recessive allele, the only way for an individual to have hazel eyes is to be (points at 'Hazel/Hazel – Hazel') what we call homozygous recessive. 'Homozygous recessive' is one of those vocab words that you were to define and (points at 'Hazel/Hazel – Hazel') it means that you have two copies of the recessive allele. . It's the only way. If you have (points at 'Green' in 'Green/Green – Green') even one copy of the dominant al allele like here (points at 'Green/Hazel – Green') . you're gonna have the dom you're gonna display or express the dominant trait. (G36's first name).

The teacher responds by mentioning that genes alone do not influence traits. The teacher's comment, 'It's an interaction between your genes and your surrounding environment, hormones in your body being a surrounding environment,' acknowledges G33's interest in cellular processes (Transcript Extract 10.9, line 100). However, the teacher again shifts away from that frame of reference, and focuses on the table of allele combinations on the whiteboard. Pointing at the words 'green/green', she asks a known answer question, 'If you have a copy for the green allele and another copy for the green allele, what's gonna be the eye color?' (Transcript Extract 10.9, line 100). A few of the students answer, 'Green' (line 101). This use of the common classroom discourse pattern of interrogation, response, and evaluation (Heath, 1982; Mehan, 1979; Poole, 1994) begins to shift the grounds for setting the discussion agenda back to the teacher's emphasis on listing and tabulating alleles and traits, rather than exploring and modeling cellular processes (cf. Molotch and Boden, 1985).

Despite the teacher's attempt to move forward with her planned lesson, a student's question about the processes that create the qualities of genes and traits displays interpretation activities that continue to negotiate this creation of a discourse framework relevant to the customary Mendelian curriculum. Rather than simply accepting the use of grey boxes in place of missing cellular process information, G36 asks, 'how do the genes like get like determined if they're dominant or recessive?' (Transcript Extract 10.10, line 105). The teacher's response addresses the issue of how genes affect traits by acknowledging that cellular biochemical processes play a part (Transcript Extract 10.10, lines 108, 110). She attempts to diminish the immediate relevance of information about cellular biochemical process by emphasizing that the consistency of those processes within a species reduces the need to know what they are.

Although G36 does not get information about cellular processes to fill the gap she expresses, she does get information that links genes and traits: i.e., the chemistry related to the genes affects whether they are dominant or recessive, and the chemistry is the same throughout a species (Transcript Extract 10.10, lines 108, 110). The teacher's explanation seems to support the inference suggested by G36's question, i.e., that unspecified cellular processes are relevant to the dominant or recessive characteristic of a gene. However, the teacher immediately shifts the interpretive frame of reference to location, 'the whole species', and categorization, 'because they're recessive'. This is consistent with the conventional Mendelian curriculum. The restrictions on seeking cellular process information guide students toward incorporating Mendelian grey boxes in the discourse framework for understanding trait inheritance.

Transcript Extract 10.10: Recessive

105. G36: How does it like how do the genes like get like determined if they're dominant or recessive?
106. T2: . . (deep sigh)
107. G36: It just kind of happened.
108. T2: It happened I it's a it's a chemistry thing. Um it tends to be the same in the whole species though. So, it's not like in your body

Transcript Extract 10.10 (continued)

brown's gonna be dominant and in (boy's first name)'s body blue's gonna be dominant. It tends to be a species thing.
109. G36: Oh
110. T2: So it duh it is carried from um speesh you know all the indi individuals in that species.
111. G36: Is that why like some traits are really rare?
112. T2: Because they're recessive. Yes. Right.

As the teacher continues her response to G36, the phrase, 'it is carried', serves as a grey box for missing information about how inherited alleles affect eye color (Transcript Extract 10.10, line 110). In that capacity, 'it is carried' reinforces the teacher's de-emphasis of cellular processes by conflating them with the transmission and location of alleles. Since it marks both cellular processes and location, it eliminates the interpretive contingency of seeking the missing cellular process information when the students subsequently develop process narratives that link the information about location and tabulation presented by the teacher.

Completing the Shift to Tabulation and Computation

The teacher completes the shift in the discourse framework by discussing the nomenclature that students will need to use when solving assigned problems. She uses vocabulary terms that had been assigned as homework for the students ('heterozygous', 'homozygous', 'recessive'), and mentions characteristics (green eyes), discussed earlier in the lecture to categorize various sets of alleles:

> when we're going through genetic problems and you know I say that okay, we have a parent who's heterozygous for green eyes and we have a parent who's homozygous recessive for hazel eyes, what kind of um offspring can we can we predict? (Transcript Extract 10.11, line 140)

The teacher proceeds with the completion of the diagram on the whiteboard. She writes upper and lower case letters that represent dominant and recessive alleles and maps them to a tabular list of the combinations of alleles in the offspring of the parents, which were presented by the initial diagram of cell division (Figure 10.7, Row C). This provides a tabular list in the form:

(G) GREEN – DOMINANT
(g) GREEN – RECESSIVE

The list provides explanatory information for linking the letters to their conventional usage as nomenclature. It also provides specific information about the procedures for tabulating genes and traits.

In contrast to the first part of the diagram, the textual representations are not part of a pictorial representation of genetic processes (e.g., the word, 'green', inside a circle representing a reproductive cell). Instead, they are presented as a separate device for completing an upcoming assignment. T2 explicitly shifts the diagram from an explanation of actual organisms to the expression and arrangement of symbols and procedures for answering assigned tasks, 'genetic problems' (Transcript Extract 10.11, lines 140–146). She applies the diagram when answering questions students might have about those assignments. Both the information and the frame of reference emphasizing pragmatic application affect the students' ensuing interpretation activities.

Transcript Extract 10.11: Shift from Cellular Process to Conventional Nomenclature

140. T2: We're getting ready to learn how to actually solve these problems, but one more thing we need to do before we are we will be totally ready. And that is, when we're going through genetic problems and you know I say that okay, we have a parent with uh who's heterozygous for green eyes and we have a parent who's homozygous recessive for hazel eyes, what kind of um offspring can we . can we predict? You don't want to have to keep writing green and green or hazel and hazel we like to assign symbols to what's represent what's gonna be our dominant allele and what's gonna represent our recessive allele. So hopefully from your reading you might have picked up on what those symbols are. How do we represent what's the dominant allele and what is the recessive allele? (Girl's first name).

141. G39: When something is dominant, it's capitalized and it's just something like for hazel it'd be capital 'H' if that's dominant. Or if it's recessive it would be lower case 'h'.

142. T2: Okay. Yeah, usually we use a capital letter to represent the dominant allele and a lower case letter to represent the recessive allele. Think of things that are really important. We capitalize them. So, the dominant allele is gonna be . y'know it's the one we're gonna capitalize. So, in this case we usually try to pick a letter that makes sense with the traits that were looking at and also . that looks very different in its capital form compared to its lower case form. If you choose a letter like umm the letter 'c' (writes 'Cc' on board), . . . it's really hard to tell the difference

Transcript Extract 10.11 (continued)

between the capital 'C' and the lower case 'c'. So, a good example, if this is our problem, would be to use (writes '(G)' on the board in front of 'green-dominant') capital 'G' for the green eyes, and then a (writes '(g)' in front of 'hazel-recessive'.. lower case 'g' for the hazel eyes. Now some students want to use a capital 'G', but a lower case 'h'. We don't do that because we're looking at the same gene. So we use the same letter to represent that gene, but these (points at '(G) green-domninant' and '(g) hazel-recessive') are just are two different forms of the gene for eye color. /So we use/

143. G33: /How do/

144. T2: the same letter, but just a upper case and a lower case form of that letter. (says G33's first name).

145. G33: How do you know what color it is then? Like what the 'g' stands for?

146. T2: It will tell you. Your genetic problems will tell you: this is the dominant gene, um the parents have this genotype and it will be a little word problem and it'll give you all the information you need to know. Okay? Alright

Students contribute to and assimilate this shift in frame of reference by asking questions about the appropriate use of the genetics nomenclature, rather than the operation of genes within the body. For example, a student, G33, earlier had asked for confirmation that recessive genes were present in cells, but were not activated (Transcript Extract 10.2, line 17). However, at this point in the lecture, she asks a question emphasizing the mechanics of solving a problem: 'How do you know which color they stand for? I mean what the "g" stands for?' (Transcript Extract 10.11, line 145). She has shifted her frame of reference and discourse framework from modeling the operation of genes to tabulating representations of alleles and traits. The teacher further reinforces both the frame of reference and discourse framework by emphasizing the procedures for solving the assigned problems: 'Your genetic problems will tell you: this is the dominant gene, the parents have this genotype and it will be a little word problem and it'll give you all the information you need to know' (Transcript Extract 10.11, line 146).

The addition of a pragmatic context for the use of nomenclature supports its function as a component of the discourse framework – i.e., as a grey box for the missing cellular process information. The students' focus on the pragmatics of applying the information about tabulating location and nomenclature to an assignment deemphasizes prior concerns about cellular processes. The missing information about cellular processes will remain missing, marked by vocabulary terms and nomenclature that students can use to complete the assigned tasks without having to understand those cellular processes. The result is a discourse framework that includes nomenclature organized in another tabular format, the Punnett square, and the computation of ratios for the probability of different traits appearing when crossing parents with particular traits.

This discourse framework is both restricted and restrictive. The focus on Mendelian grey boxes limits the available information resources and deemphasizes consideration of a cellular process frame of reference. This discourse framework reduced the immediate interpretive contingencies related to the missing cellular process information by showing the students that they had been presented with or would have access to enough information about trait inheritance to complete their course work. The discourse framework that the students displayed when they applied those traditional grey boxes in process narratives involved various modes of communication, such as pointing at tables featuring genetics nomenclature, which the teacher had demonstrated as she pointed and gestured at the drawing on the whiteboard during her lecture. In the classroom, the Mendelian grey boxes became displays of a particular way of understanding trait inheritance. This discourse framework also contributed to process narratives and understandings that relied on the particular linguistic, gestural, and pictorial grey boxes introduced during the lecture, which were linked to classroom resources and activities.

The Effects of Discourse Frameworks on Understanding and Recall

This section discusses the consequences of the conventional Mendelian discourse framework for understanding trait inheritance. It examines how one of the students mentioned above, G33, applies the tabular frame of reference and Mendelian grey boxes in a subsequent class. Then it examines her attempts to recall what she learned in the classes during a discussion a few weeks later. The classroom activities and the follow-up discussion show how the classroom discourse framework affects the recall of process narratives related to trait inheritance.

During a class three weeks after the introductory lecture (including 12 days of winter holiday), the teacher answers G33's question about an assigned genetics problem. The interaction displays how gesturing at classroom resources contributes to and reinforces the Mendelian discourse framework. The gesturing, pointing, and visual resources do not merely add emphasis to verbal interaction, they are also components of the social and individual interpretation activities through which the students store and recall information by creating process narratives. For example, when the student discusses her question with the teacher, the components of the discourse framework include the task prompt, the vocabulary terms and nomenclature discussed during the introductory lecture, written answers to assigned learning tasks, and the Punnett square encountered in prior classes.[35] Like the teacher during the introductory lecture, the student applies gesturing at images and text as a resource for creating process narratives that relate to organizing and understanding information about trait inheritance.

As G33 works during the class to create a Punnett square, she asks T2 a question about the assignment. The substance of G33's question deals with the use of the Punnett square to organize information about parent rabbits' alleles in order to predict the probable traits of their offspring. One of the parents is described as heterozygous for both fur color and tail length. The other parent is described as homozygous recessive for both traits. This would result in repetition of the same nomenclature to represent the same combinations of alleles in all of the columns of the Punnett square. G33 asks the teacher if she can abbreviate her Punnett square by showing only one column.[36]

G33 does not mention the cellular processes of gene activation she had referred to in a question she asked early in the introductory lecture ('So, would in our . um . chromosomes in our homologous pairs like . I could have a gene for blue eyes, but it's just not activated?' Transcript Extract 10.2, line 17). The Punnett square, genetics vocabulary, and genetics nomenclature have become grey boxes for the missing information that had been of interest to her and other students during the lecture when they asked questions about cellular processes.

Both G33 and the teacher pointed at the worksheet and the text of the question as they discussed the answer (Transcript Extract 10.12, lines 1–3). During this brief 25-second interaction, the student and the teacher gestured, pointed, and looked at each other's gestures a total of 16 times. In one instance, the student pointed at the paper in concert with her comments while neither she nor the teacher looked at it (Transcript Extract 10.12, lines 6, 7). G33's use of pointing and gesturing toward text and images on her work sheet is consistent with the communication format of using images as part of explanations, which the teacher presented during her introductory lecture. Pointing at images has become part of the classroom discourse framework for the trait inheritance learning activities. Pointing at visual information helps the students to develop process narratives without having to think about or mention the cellular biochemical processes that actually link alleles to traits. This reduces the interpretive contingencies displayed by students' digressive questions during the introductory lecture.

Transcription Extract 10.12: Verbal, Gestural, and Textual Components of the Allele Discourse Framework in the Classroom

1. G33: Wait Miss (T2's surname) . . . because this is (G33 points with pen to text, while looking at paper. T2 looks at and leans toward paper where G33 points.) only one . can I just put this up there and then like . (G33 points to paper with right and left hands. T2 moves away from paper. G33 shifts gaze away from paper toward T2) multiply with these? Or do I still have to do the whole like Punnett square four times?

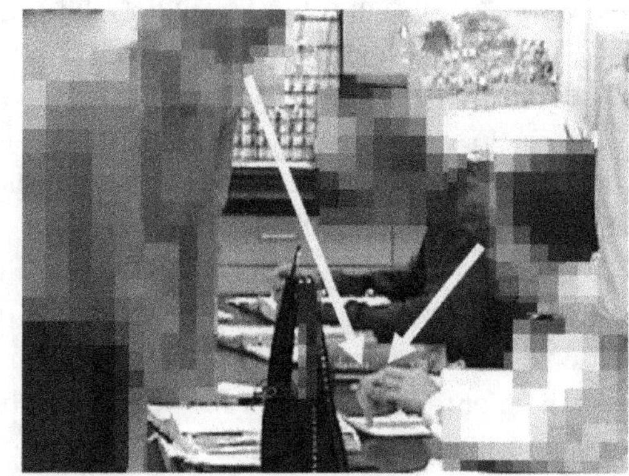

2. T2: You just do like (T2 covers part of worksheet with left hand. G33 looks at T2's hand and worksheet.) one column (T2 looks toward G33 and her answer sheet).
3. G33: (G33 looks at paper on which she has written) Yeah okay. So I can do like—(T2 turns to face G33) I can put 'em all (G33 moves right hand to point at spot on paper) like all—all these (G33 moves hand down paper) down here and (G33 points at top of sheet of paper; then looks up at T) just that one up there?
4. T2: Right.
5. G33: and then—but then when I multiply that by 4's?
6. T2: You don't have to because what you're going to see is . you would see (T2 gestures with left hand; then with right hand. G33 moves left had, pointing toward T2's hand gesture. G33 begins pointing toward her paper while looking at T2.) four /without the (???)/
7. G33: /(G33 moves pointing finger up and down sheet of paper) Oh is that just like a sim/plified (T2 begins to move her hands downward) ratio.

8. T2: Right.
9. G33: (while looking at and writing on her paper)/Great./
10. T2: /uh/--exactly.

G33's pointing is part of an inquiry that displays and reproduces the frame of reference emphasizing tabulation and computation. She had exhibited her shift to this frame of reference in her question near the end of the introductory lecture about the use of genetics nomenclature: 'How do you know what color it is then? Like what the "g" stands for?" (Transcript Extract 10.11, line 145). Her pointing while working on the assigned learning activity reinforces the use of nomenclature and tables as components of the Mendelian discourse framework. It also reinforces the shift in the interpretive frame of reference from cellular genetic processes to the process of completing the assigned learning activity.

Acceptance of the Mendelian Discourse Framework

G33's explanation of her answer to the assignment question later in the class session, after she has written it on the whiteboard, displays in more detail her use of the Mendelian discourse framework and its grey boxes (Saferstein, 2007: 435–437). After G33 had written the genetics nomenclature, a Punnett square, and ratios on the whiteboard, she explained them from her seat while the teacher pointed at them.

G33's presentation includes the following representational devices that are part of the trait inheritance discourse framework in the classroom (Saferstein, 2007: 435–436):

- Relational table (Punnett Square)
- Nomenclature (F1 generation, upper/lower case letters representing alleles and traits)
- Genetics vocabulary (trait, alleles, dominant/recessive, heterozygous/homozygous, genotype/phenotype)
- Linkage displays (arrows, proximity of symbols, gestures pointing out links between symbols)
- Commonplace language contextualized to relate to the curricular model of genetics (parent, fur color, tail length, brown, yellow, long, short, length, mouse, generation)
- Mathematical representation and syntax (converting sample cases to quantities in order to calculate and display ratios) – e.g., the use of colons to separate elements of a ratio that may be applied to words as well as numbers (e.g., *brown, long: brown, short: yellow, long: yellow, short*; or *1:1:1:1*)
- Task-specific identifiers (parent one, parent two)
- Graphical/pictorial symbols (flowers, rabbits, people, genes, chromosomes)

Figure 10.8: Shifting Frames of Reference: Applying the Mendelian Discourse Framework

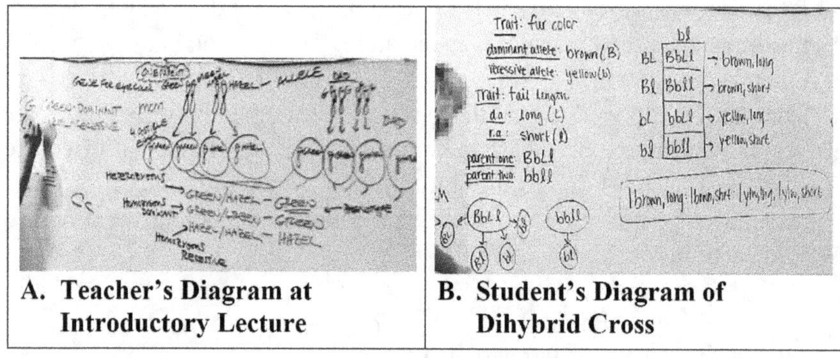

A. Teacher's Diagram at Introductory Lecture

B. Student's Diagram of Dihybrid Cross

The student's modes of expression (Figure 10.8, B) replicate those presented by the teacher during the introductory lecture (Figure 10.8, A). However, the student's diagram reverses the relative positions and area occupied by the drawing of cell division and the table correlating alleles with traits. In G33's diagram, the Punnett square and nomenclature occupy most of the space, while the smaller drawing of cell division is placed at the bottom of the illustration, off to the left side (Figure 10.8, B). This reflects the shift in the student's frame of reference from the concern with cellular processes she had expressed in comments during the introductory lecture (Transcript Extract 10.2, line 17; Transcript Extract 10.9, line 99).

G33 diagrams processes of cell division by adopting the teacher's tabular organization of allele combinations and traits, in which the Punnett square features a short-form nomenclature of single letters to represent alleles (Figure 10.8, B). G33's explanation of the diagram expresses process narratives that describe how to apply Punnett squares and ratios to predict the inheritance of traits. Those process narratives contain grey boxes comprised of the visual resources, nomenclature, and genetics vocabulary of the biology classroom and genetics lessons. G33's interpretation activities during the introductory lecture and the assigned learning activity led to her reliance on this conventional Mendelian discourse framework featuring the linguistic and pictorial information resources of the classroom as a way of explaining trait inheritance.

The whiteboard diagram and verbal explanation link the general category, 'trait', to the categories, fur color and tail length (Transcript Extract 10.13, lines 2, 4, 6). Each of the subcategories is further delimited as containing two possibilities, brown/yellow and long/short. Each set of possible traits is then linked to genetics nomenclature for brown or yellow fur as 'B' or 'b', and a long or short tail as 'L' or 'l'. In regard to the production of process narratives, this not only delimits general categories in terms of specific instances within those categories, but it also shifts the categorical distinctions from a frame of reference based on commonplace experience (e.g., families and physical appearance) to a frame of reference that emphasizes the tabulation of symbols and the computation which converts those symbols to a ratio.

The student's explanatory process narratives shift from a description of biological processes to the processes of tabulating and computing abstract symbols:

> *... trait one is or fur color and the dominant allele is brown ... and the recessive allele is yellow* (Transcript Extract 10.13, lines 2, 4).
>
> *... trait two is for tail length and the dominant allele is long and ... the recessive allele is short* (Transcript Extract 10.13, line 6).
>
> *... the heterozygous mouse has brown fur and is heterozygous for long tail. So that means it's ... big B little b, big L little l* (Transcript Extract 10.13, line 6).
>
> *... it's mated with the yellow mouse with the short tail. So it has to be homozygous recessive for ... fur color and for length* (Transcript Extract 10.13 , line 8).

The process narratives expressed by G33 explain the use of the components of the classroom genetics framework rather than the biological functioning of genes. Moreover, even the tabular representation, a Punnett square, extends the computational frame of reference. Incorporating the information acquired during her earlier interaction with the teacher when developing the solution to the dihybrid cross problem, G33 simplifies the Punnet square by showing only one reproductive cell resulting from the division of the homozygous recessive parent cell, rather than four identical cells. This reflects the 'simplified ratio' that G33 mentioned at the end of her earlier interaction with the teacher ('Oh is that just like a simplified ratio?' Transcript Extract 10.12, line 7). (Explained in Note 36.)

Transcript Extract 10.13: A Student's Use of the Tabulation Discourse Framework

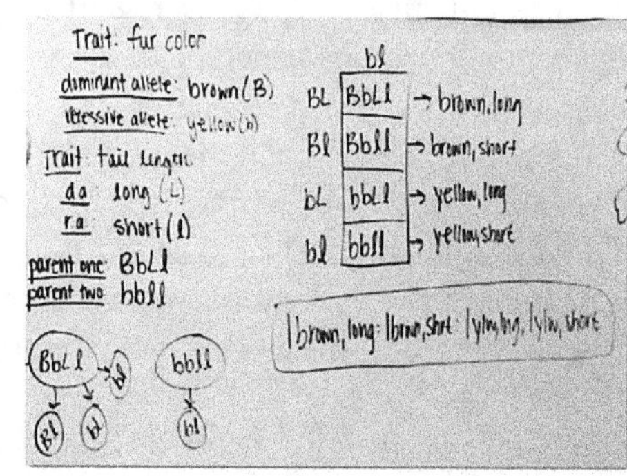

1. T2: Tell us what you did (student's name).
2. G33: Umm alright trait one is for fur color (refers to text on board, 'Trait: fur color') and the dominant allele is brown (refers to text on white board, 'dominant allele: brown (B)')
3. T2: yep
4. G33: and the recessive allele is yellow (refers to text on white board, 'recessive allele: (b)')
5. T2: uh huh
6. G33: and trait two is for tail length (refers to text on white board, 'Trait: tail length') and the dominant allele is long and short (refers to text, 'd.a.: long (L)'). I mean the recessive allele is short (refers to text on white board, 'r.a.: short (l)') uh and it says that um the heterozygous mouse has brown fur and is heterozygous for long tail. So that means it's uh (T2 points at 'BbLl') big B little b, big L little l.
7. T2: Yep 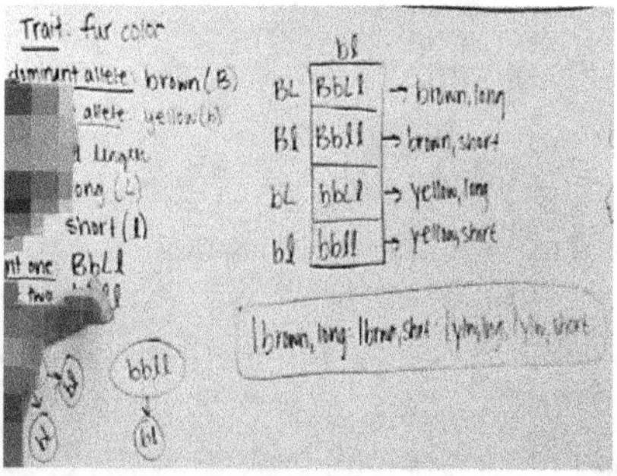
8. G33: and then uh it's mated with the yellow mouse with the short tail. (T2 points at 'bbll') So it has to be homozygous recessive for uh fur color and length.
9. T2: Right.
10. G33: So then your sex cells uh (T2 points at small circles containing 2 letters) that's how it splits off
11. T2: Yep.
12. G33: and then that one is just other, it's just simplified.
13. T2: (Points at drawing) Right.

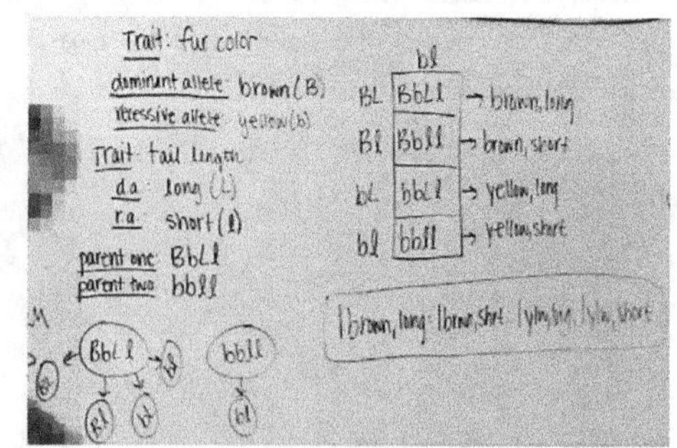

Following G33's explanation, the teacher makes a point of showing the class why the Punnett square is abbreviated, further emphasizing the computational and tabular frames or reference. G33's expression of the relationship of linguistic, pictorial, and tabular representations of the relationship between alleles and traits presents the conflation of process and outcome that is central to the conventional Mendelian discourse for explaining trait inheritance. For example, the following formulations feature 'is' as a grey box for cellular processes by which alleles affect the development of physical characteristics:

the dominant allele is brown (Transcript Extract 10.13, line 2)
the recessive allele is yellow (line 4)
the dominant allele is long (line 6)
the recessive allele is short. (line 6)

In regard to the conventional Mendelian discourse framework used to explain trait inheritance, G33's utterance, 'the recessive allele is short', expresses an accurate description of a physical trait, short tail length (symbolized by 'l'), as a variable in the computation of a ratio by using a Punnett square (Transcript Extract 10.13, line 6). However, the student's statements do not accurately describe alleles. The actual alleles are not yellow or brown, long or short. Rather, they are segments of chromosomes consisting of chemicals that affect the development of proteins or enzymes, which, in turn, contribute to the development of cells constituting a particular fur color and tail length. The terms, 'is', 'dominant', and 'recessive', function as grey boxes, marking such missing information.

G33's utterances show that she has learned to convert commonplace physical characteristics to genetics terms and nomenclature, and to express a relationship among the latter as process narratives:

the heterozygous mouse has brown fur and is heterozygous for long tail. So that means it's uh (T2 points at 'BbLl') big B little b, big L little l. (Transcript Extract 10.13, line 6)

and then it's mated with the yellow mouse with the short tail. (T2 points at 'bbll') So it has to be homozygous recessive for uh fur color and length. (Transcript Extract 10.13, line 8)

The collaborative explanation of the Punnett square and diagram featuring the student speaking and the teacher gesturing further reinforces pointing at visual resources as a form of grey box that is a component of the discourse framework for dealing with trait inheritance in the classroom.

Figure 10.9: Verbal and Visual Expressions of 'Allele' in the Classroom Discourse Framework

<table>
<tr>
<td>trait one is for fur color and the dominant allele is brown and the recessive allele is yellow (from Transcript Extract 10.13, lines 2, 4)

trait two is for tail length and the dominant allele is long and the recessive allele is short (from Transcript Extract 10.13, line 6)</td>
<td>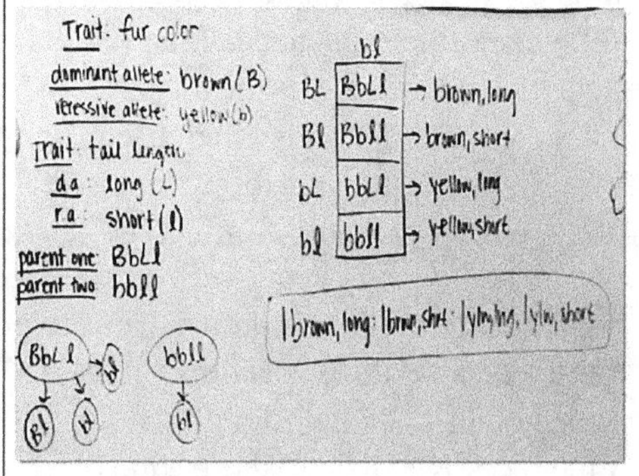
</td>
</tr>
</table>

When the resources of the classroom discourse framework were at hand, G33 was able to express process narratives that linked information such as Mendelian terminology, nomenclature, and computational devices. However, during a follow-up discussion with researchers four weeks later in a different room, lacking those resources, G33 had difficulty recalling and expressing the process narratives she had presented in the classroom (Saferstein, 2007: 437–439). In particular, she could not recall the word, 'allele', a term that was a component of the process narratives she had expressed when explaining her whiteboard diagram in the classroom (Figure 10.9). At the follow-up discussion, G33 and another student, G34, could not recall 'allele' when trying to explain genetics concepts they had learned. Their attempt to reconstruct the classroom interpretation activities as they tried to remember 'allele', shows the extent to which the process narratives they had developed to explain trait inheritance were based on using the resources in the classroom discourse framework as components of grey boxes. It also shows how grey boxes based on resources specific to a particular discourse framework inhibit recall in a setting that lacks those resources.

The Limitations of Discourse Frameworks that Emphasize Grey Boxes: Transitory Recall of Vocabulary and Concepts

G33's utterances as she attempts to remember and explain *allele* show that the contexts for recalling and expressing process narratives not only involve the immediate activities of the follow-up discussion, but also include recalling and referring to aspects of classroom activities, which occurred six and four weeks earlier during the introductory lecture and G33's explanation of her whiteboard diagram. These included:

- G33's explanation of the diagram she had drawn on the whiteboard during the classroom assignment (Figure 10.9);
- Her work on the classroom assignment, when she and the teacher reinforced pointing at text and images as part of the discourse framework for coping with missing information about cellular processes (Transcript Extract 10.12);
- The introductory lecture, where she and other students asked the teacher questions concerning alleles and traits (e.g., Transcript Extracts 10.2, 10.9).

At the follow-up discussion, G33's utterances show her attempting to reconstruct the discourse framework that had supported a coherent linkage of information as process narratives. In the classroom, the whiteboard images had functioned as a set of grey boxes, which reduced interpretive contingencies – such as those students had displayed in questions related to cellular processes during the introductory lecture. The follow-up discussion took place in the teacher's workroom, where there were no visual resources to function as grey boxes and no opportunities to gesture and point at such visual resources in order to incorporate them in process narratives. The absence of the classroom-based grey boxes resulted in a lack of coherence among the pieces of information that G33 recalls.

G33's attempt to jog her memory and reconnect information as process narratives begins with her mention of the subject of the classroom assignment she had presented: 'Umm . dihybrid cross' (Transcript Extract 10.14, line B2). When she does not immediately recall other information, G33 asks the other student, G34, 'What else?'. G34 adds, 'Just like the Punnett square that I remember mostly, how to do it and stuff" (Transcript Extract 10.14, line B7). As G33 tries to recall a particular concept she learned, she produces the incomplete formulation 'And what was that called the ... on the gene that a part of it is . remember that?' (Figure 10.10, Row A, line B8).

As G34 and G33 collaborate to recall the word, allele, they try to verbally reconstruct the discourse framework of the genetics lessons (Figure 10.10, Row A). They attempt to link pieces of information from the classroom learning activities that had introduced them to the use of 'allele'. At the introductory lecture, the teacher had presented a diagram of a parent's chromosome, featuring a darkened area representing a gene for green eyes (Figure 10.10, Row B). As she expanded the diagram, she duplicated the chromosome to show cell division, and then she drew the chromosome, pairing it with a chromosome from the other parent, which contained a gene for hazel eyes. The teacher then explained that the paired genes, which related to the alternative eye colors, labeled green and hazel, were called alleles (Figure 10.10, Row B, lines 32–34).

Figure 10.10: Trying to Reconstruct the Classroom Discourse Framework

A. Follow-up Discussion (from Transcript Extract 10.14)

B8. G33: And what was that called the . . . **on the gene** that **a part of it** is . remember that?
B9. G34: No (laughs, others laugh) no
B10. G33: **they're exactly the same**, except like **one is on the chroma**--never mind

B14. G33: It's like--**it's where it's--a gene is**--uh uh . . **they're the same, but they're slightly different**.
B15. G34: Remember that? uh it's like a vocabulary word. It was like a major thing . . uhh

B17. G33: **It's the trait**, the trait that
B18. I1: the trait.
B19. G33: **for blue eyes and green eyes**. **They're the /same trait/**,

B21. G33: **but they're coded for different things**

B. Classroom: Introductory Lecture (from Transcript Extract 10.3)

32 (partial). T2: (**writes 'hazel' above pair of chromosomes on right**) So this one's gonna have information or the geel—(sardonically marks and corrects slip of the tongue) the geel--**the gene or the allele for hazel eyes and this one's gonna have information for (writes green above the pair of chromosomes on left) . . green eyes**. Okay. **These . two (simultaneously taps each pair of chromosomes with one hand) alternative forms of the same gene for eye color, that's what's known as alleles.** So when you wrote down your definition, actually maybe somebody could read it. (G38's first name), what's your definition for allele?
33. G38: Genes that exist on alternate forms.
34. T2: Okay **genes that exist in alternate forms**. **It's the same gene**. **It's the gene for eye color, but it could be an alternate form of that gene**. . (A digression to focus a student's attention.) Those are the two alleles for eye color. (writes 'allele' to the right of 'hazel'). That's an allele.

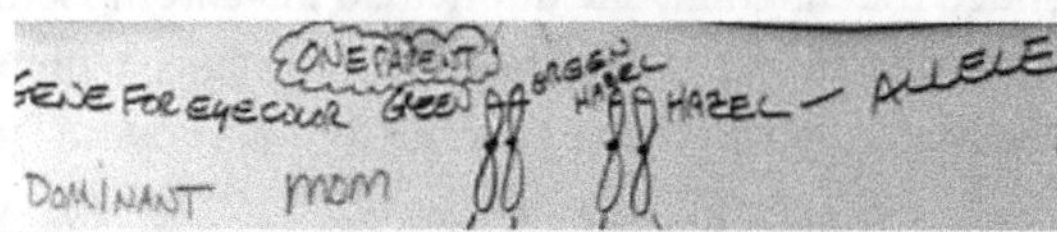

At the follow-up discussion, the students' attempts to recall the word, 'allele', are complicated by the earlier use of such visual and gestural grey boxes, which had become part of the absent discourse framework that had supported the process narratives developed and applied in the classroom. For example, G33's comments during the follow-up discussion attempt to associate chromosomes with genes, in the same way that the introductory lecture began:

> on the gene that a part of it is remember that? They're exactly the same, except like one is on the chroma – never mind. (Figure 10.10, Row A, lines B8, B10)

G33's first attempt to explain the elusive word without the classroom's visual resources contains the utterance 'on the gene that a part of it is' (Figure 10.10, Row A, line B8). In the context of her following comments, this begins to reconstruct the teacher's lecture diagram and explanation. G33 indexes something that is a component of, 'part of', trait inheritance. However, rather than placing the component on the chromosome, as the teacher diagrammed it, G33 locates it 'on the gene'.

When G33 elicits help from G34 by asking, 'remember that?' G34 answers, 'No', and laughs (Figure 10.10, Row A, lines B8, B9). However, a few seconds later, after G33 has mentioned that it relates to 'a gene' and that 'they're the same, but they're slightly different', G34 recalls some of the classroom activities related to 'allele', although she does not recall the word (Figure 10.10, Row A, lines B14, B15). She says, 'Remember that? uh it's like a vocabulary word', emphasizing aspects of the introductory lecture and a related vocabulary assignment. G33 elaborates on G34's recollection that the missing genetics term was a vocabulary word by saying, 'It was like a major thing' (Figure 10.10, Row A, line B15). This characterization of the term and concept correlates with their importance in regard to the lecture, subsequent classroom activities, and an explanation of trait inheritance.

At the introductory lecture, the teacher had asked a student to read a definition of 'allele' that was part of an assigned learning activity (Figure 10.10, Row B, lines 32–34). During the early part of the lecture, the teacher and students had used the word, 'allele', in the context of the whiteboard diagram of the cellular processes related to division of reproductive cells, which included the drawings showing genes on chromosomes (Figure 10.10, Row B). G33 had used 'allele' during subsequent classroom learning activities, such as explaining her whiteboard diagram, which answered an assigned trait inheritance problem (Figure 10.9):

> trait one is for fur color and the dominant <u>allele</u> is brown
> and the recessive <u>allele</u> is yellow

> trait two is for tail length and the dominant <u>allele</u> is long and short. I mean the recessive <u>allele</u> is short

However, at the follow-up discussion, G33 has difficulty expressing the process narratives that coherently link the information fragments she recalls (Transcript Extract 10.14, line B10). She abruptly stops trying to link information by saying 'never mind' in the middle of a word beginning with 'chroma' (chromosomes and chromatids were mentioned early in the introductory lecture).

At this point in the discussion, I encourage G33 to try to remember and express the term and concept (Transcript Extract 10.14, line B11). She then recapitulates the sequence of information presented at the introductory lecture:

> It's like – it's where it's – a gene is – uh uh they're the same, but they're slightly different. It's the trait, the trait that for blue eyes and green eyes. They're the same trait, but they're coded for different things. (Transcript Extract 10.14, lines B14, B17, B19, B21)

In this set of utterances, G33 tries out various expressions, which index types of information that would be relevant to recovering a process narrative containing the word, 'allele'. The utterances, 'it's where', 'they're the same, but they're slightly different', 'It's the trait for blue eyes and green eyes', and 'they're coded for different things', function as attempts to reconstruct the classroom grey boxes for missing information about the cellular processes by which alleles affect traits.

Transcript Extract 10.14: Follow-up Discussion of Learning Activities

[R1=Researcher (Author); G33=Student discussed above; G34=Another Student; R2=Second Researcher. Bold text indicates terms indexing grey boxes related to biochemical processes.]

B1. R1: In terms of this particular topic, umm .. what – are there things that you remember that stand out?
B2. G33: Umm . dihybrid cross
B3. G34: Yeah
B4. G33: and uh ...
B5. R1: Um hmm
B6. G33: What else?
B7. G34: Just like the Punnett square that I remember mostly, how to do it and stuff
B8. G33: And what was that called the ... **on the gene** that **a part of it** is . remember that?
B9. G34: No (laughs, others laugh) no
B10. G33: **they're exactly the same**, except like **one is on the chroma** – never mind

Transcript Extract 10.14 (continued)

B11. R1: No, go ahead.
B12. G34?: It's when umm
B13. R1: I'm not grading you – we're not grading you on all this. I mean – I – I'm just curious
B14. G33: It's like – **it's where it's – a gene is** – uh uh .. **they're the same, but they're slightly different** .
B15. G34: Remember that? uh it's like a vocabulary word. It was like a major thing .. uhh
B16. R1: wh-yuh
B17. G33: It's **the trait, the trait that**
B18. R1: the trait.
B19. G33: for blue eyes and green eyes. They're **the /same trait/**,
B20. R1: /Uh-huh uh-huh/
B21. G33: but they're **coded for different things**
B22. R1: Okay
B23. G34: Oh, I know what you're talking about but I for/get the word/
[A few repetitive utterances are omitted]
B32. R1: Yeah I know what the word is .... 'Allele'?
B33. Students: 'Allele'
B34. R2: 'Allele'
B35. R1: Yeah
B36. (laughter)
B37. G34: Oh yeah, 'Allele'
B38. G33: duh, it's so easy

The teacher's emphasis on tabulation and nomenclature during the introductory lecture (including her de-emphasis of students' concerns with cellular processes), and G33's use of visual resources during her classroom learning activities (at her desk and in her whiteboard diagram and explanation) had grey-boxed the missing linguistic information about cellular processes related to alleles. Consequently, at the follow-up discussion, G33's attempts to reconstruct the discourse framework and process narratives she had applied in the classroom show that she recalls no process narrative to describe the composition and function of genes that would differentiate 'chromosomes', 'genes' and 'alleles' – e.g., 'It's like – it's where it's – a gene is – uh uh .. they're the same, but they're slightly different' (Transcript Extract 10.14, line B14).

During the lecture and subsequent classroom learning activities, diagrams and tables had functioned as grey boxes for that missing information. The importance of those classroom information resources to understanding and recall was emphasized at the follow-up discussion when G33 expressed an ambiguous description of the functioning of alleles, 'they're the same, but they're slightly different'. While this distinction is fuzzy when expressed verbally at the follow-up discussion, it was clearer in the classroom setting, where 'same' and 'different' were linked to nomenclature, such as 'g' and 'G' (at the lecture) or 'b', 'B', 'l', 'L' (in G33's whiteboard diagram and explanation, Figure 10.11: 3), and also were linked to written labels, such as 'green eyes', 'hazel eyes', 'dominant allele', and 'recessive allele'. Furthermore, during the lecture introducing trait inheritance, the teacher linked the 'same, but different' distinction to a diagram of two homozygous pairs of chromosomes in which each pair contained genes for eye color labeled either green or hazel (Figure 10.11: 2).

Figure 10.11: Correlating Information, Understandings, and Discourse Frameworks

1. Follow-up Discussion

G33: It's like--it's where it's--a gene is--uh uh . . they're the same, but they're slightly different (Transcript Extract 10.14, line B14)

G33: It's the trait, the trait that for blue eyes and green eyes. They're the same trait but they're coded for different things (Transcript Extract 10.14, lines B17, B19, B21)

2. Introductory Lecture and Diagram

G37: Like those are the genes that would be for like eye color, but one would be like blue and one brown.

T2: Okay. Good. . . Both of the genes could be for eye color, but one might be brown eyes and one might be blue eyes or it could be green eyes. We have alternate forms sometimes of that gene. So let's look at a gene (writes 'gene for eye color' on board). Let's use eye color since it was brought up. (Transcript Extract 10.1, lines 13, 14)

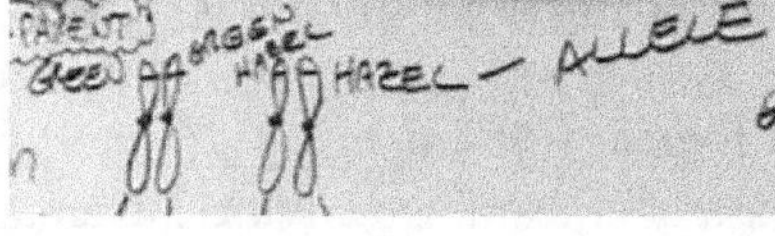

3. G33 Explains Her Whiteboard Diagram as Teacher Points

Umm alright trait one is for fur color and the dominant <u>allele</u> is brown and the recessive <u>allele</u> is yellow and trait two is for tail length and the dominant <u>allele</u> is long and short. I mean the recessive <u>allele</u> is short (l)') uh and it says that um the heterozygous mouse has brown fur and is heterozygous for long tail. So that means it's uh (T2 points at 'BbLl') big B little b, big L little l. (Transcript Extract 10.13, lines 2, 4, 6)

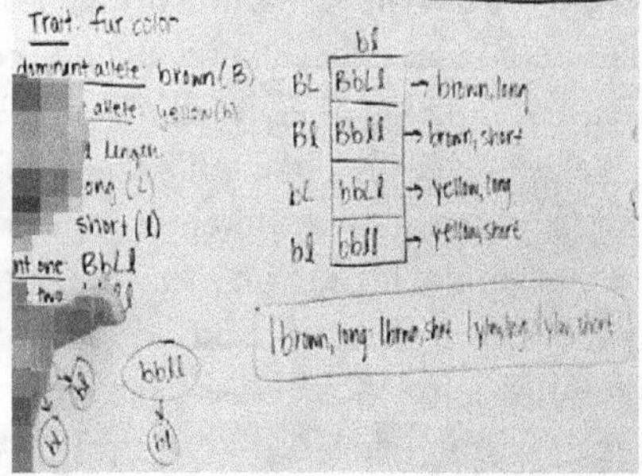

At the follow-up discussion, when the 'same, but different' distinction does not lead to recall of the word, 'allele', G33 continues to express information that correlates with the classroom activities and resources that had represented 'same, but different'. She links traits with specific eye colors:

It's the trait, the trait that for blue eyes and green eyes. (Figure 10.11: 1)

Her utterance correlates with the activities and discussion during the teacher's introductory lecture. Early in the lecture, the teacher had introduced a 'same, but different' distinction when she asked the students, 'What can you tell me about information on a pair of homologous chromosomes' in human cells (Transcript Extract 10.1, line 8). When a student answered, 'They have the same traits as each other', the teacher responded, 'They have the same traits as each other, but are they necessarily identical?' (Transcript Extract 10.1, line 10). In order to explain the 'same, but different' distinction, the teacher and another student then mentioned pairs of eye colors as examples, including the colors blue, brown, and green. That interaction led to the teacher's explanation of alleles (Figure 10.11: 2, lines 13–14):

13. G37: Like those are the genes that would be for like eye color, but one would be like blue and one brown.
14. T2: Okay. Good ... Both of the genes could be for eye color, but one might be . brown eyes and one might be blue eyes or it could be green eyes. We have alternate forms sometimes of that gene. So let's look at a gene (writes 'gene for eye color' on board). Let's use eye color since it was brought up

As G33 and G34 attempted to recall the word, 'allele', at the follow-up discussion, they reconstructed both the sequence of topics of the lecture and the 'same, but different' distinction. During the lecture, when the teacher explained her drawing of genes on chromosomes, she wrote 'gene for eye color' on the whiteboard next to the drawing, while saying, 'So let's look at a gene. Let's use eye color since it was brought up' (Figure 10.11: 2, line 14). Then, shortly after discussing eye color, the teacher asked the students for the definition of 'allele', which had been presented in a vocabulary assignment. The definition read by a student (copied from a textbook) and the teacher's response expressed the 'same, but different' distinction with the term 'alternate forms' (Figure 10.10, Row 2):

33. G38: Genes that exist on alternate forms.
34. T2: Okay genes that exist in alternate forms. It's the same gene. It's the gene for eye color, but it could be an alternate form of that gene. . (A digression to focus a student's attention.) Okay so we have green eyes and hazel eyes. Those are the two alleles for eye color. (writes a dash and 'allele' to the right of 'hazel') That's an allele . .

At the follow-up discussion, G33 and G34 reconstructed this sequence of mentioning eye color and then a genetic source of the trait. G33 shifts from describing the traits, blue and green eyes, to correlating those traits with a vague mechanism for producing them: 'They're the /same trait/, but they're coded for different things' (Figure 10.11: 1). Her utterance, 'coded for' correlates with the classroom activities of substituting nomenclature for both the diagrams of cellular processes and the words describing the resulting traits.

When applied during the introductory lecture and the subsequent classroom learning activities, 'allele', had been linked to diagrams, textual labels, and tables correlating genes and traits that functioned as grey boxes for missing information about the cellular processes by which alleles affect traits (Figure 10.11: 2, 3). As discussed earlier in this chapter, the teacher used various forms of visual representation to emphasize the location of genes and to tabulate correlations between genes and traits. However, neither her drawings, nor her verbal explanations described the cellular processes by which genes affect traits.

Subsequently, G33's classroom activities showed that she was able to use the visual representations that supported the teacher's pointing. As explained in the preceding section of this chapter, during the classroom learning activities G33 had applied such resources to the process narratives and grey boxes that she had expressed. She used the term, *allele*, when she completed a classroom learning activity by drawing a diagram and Punnett square on the whiteboard and explaining her answer to the assigned question while the teacher pointed at the visual resources on the board (Figure 10.11: 3). G33's presentation of her solution had linked the verbal explanation of 'allele' to written labels and diagrams on the whiteboard.

However, during the follow-up discussion, the visual resources in the classroom discourse framework that had functioned as grey boxes in the process narratives applying 'allele' are absent, and G33's attempts to recall the word, 'allele', reflect those missing elements of the classroom discourse framework:

> It's like – it's where it's – a gene is – uh uh they're the same, but they're slightly different. (Figure 10.11: line B14)

> It's the trait, the trait that for blue eyes and green eyes. They're the same trait, but they're coded for different things. (Figure 10.11: lines B17, B19, B21)

G33's utterance mentioning eye colors and coding is vague in regard to the biological particulars of 'same trait', 'coded', and 'different things'. 'Same trait' is linked to eye color, while 'coded for' expresses an unspecified biological process that produces 'different things', i.e., the respective blue or green eye color of particular individuals. Her use of 'they're' suggests multiple factors related to the inheritance of eye color, and displays the conflation of traits and genes that had been managed during the classroom activities by the use of diagrams, nomenclature, and Punnett squares as grey boxes. This conflation correlates with the textual expression of alleles during the classroom activities. For example, the nomenclature for hazel and green eyes, 'G' and 'g', which the teacher had presented, also conflated causes (genetic material) and effects (traits, such as green and blue eyes).

In that context, during the follow-up discussion G33's use of the plural 'they're' with both the singular 'same trait' and the plural 'different things' (Figure 10.11, Section 1) makes sense descriptively if not grammatically. However, despite being rooted in the representations applied in the classroom (Figure 10.12), the verbal expression of the conflation of traits and genes hinders G33's and G34's attempts to recover the key word, 'allele', during the follow-up discussion. This is due to the absence of the visual resources that functioned as grey boxes in the classroom and contributed to the coherence of the process narratives containing 'allele' that were expressed there.

At the follow-up discussion, the students tried to verbally reconstruct the activities and describe the information resources settings that had contributed to their understandings of the term, 'allele'. Their difficulty in recalling 'allele' shows the tight coupling of the trait inheritance process narratives with the classroom discourse framework they had developed (Figure 10.12). The grey boxes that linked information as process narratives depended on the presence of the discourse framework developed in the classroom.

Figure 10.12: Activities and Grey Boxes Constituting the Allele Discourse Framework in the Classroom

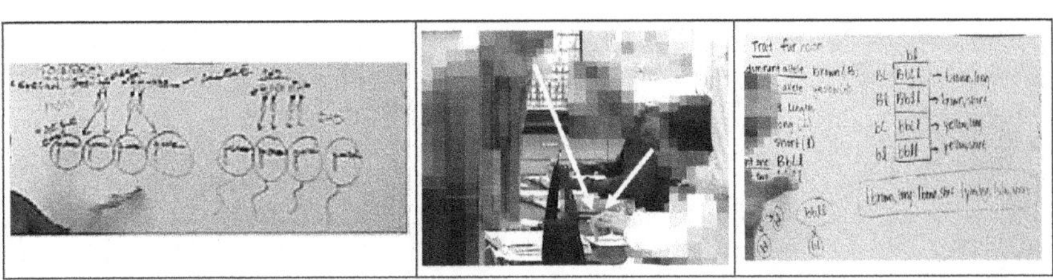

The students' understandings of 'allele' and other information about trait inheritance derived from the classroom discourse framework in which they had cognitively overlaid verbal, textual, and pictorial resources with the interpretation activities of organizing that information as process narratives. This example shows how understandings depend on recalling the interrelationship of interpretation activities with a particular discourse framework. Examining the ways that discourse frameworks reflect particular interpretation activities and affect the creation of process narratives further explicates the interrelationship of environment and cognition in the production of understandings.

11 Cognitive Science of Discourse Frameworks

Chapter Eleven discusses how discourse frameworks affect cognitive systems that support reasoning and understanding. It examines the relation of discourse frameworks to content and context, diagrams and memory, and tacit knowledge. Analysis of the creation and application of discourse frameworks provides a way of integrating the findings of studies based on mental models and coherence based reasoning, as well as filling their gaps. It replaces logic problems and experiments with empirical examples of how cognition occurs in commonplace settings and relates to the interpretation activities, information resources, and cultures of those settings. The radiology consultation and genetics education data show the cognitive function of resources in a setting in regard to the creation of recallable understandings.

Discourse Frameworks as Material and Behavioral Components of Cognitive Systems

Analysis of how people create and use discourse frameworks expands on the discussion of cognitive systems begun in the Introduction, elucidating the concept that cognitive systems *impose* coherence on decision tasks (Simon, 2004: 517). The discourse frameworks of the clinical and classroom data show that cognitive systems do not only involve individual or collective perception, interpretation, and storage of information. Rather, they include individual and social interpretation activities combined with particular resources in a setting and the conventions (including constraints) affecting the use of those resources (cf. Cicourel, 1973; Knorr-Cetina, 1999; Saferstein, 1992; Suchman, 1987).

Examining the creation and recall of process narratives reveals that the understandings are not just coherently organized mental models expressing a state and condition. The radiology consultation and genetics education data show how the resources in a setting function as external components of memory that help resolve the interpretive contingencies of creating and organizing process narratives. The use of those resource becomes integrated with the process narratives. Consequently, understanding is not a matter of mentally organizing information as logical constructs. Rather, it involves developing and reconstructing a discourse framework that has supported the creation and recall of process narratives. This presents a different approach to understanding and recall than that of explanations based on mental models. Revisiting the earlier discussion (Chapters Four and Six) of modus tollens-like information restrictions and contentless contingencies in regard to discourse frameworks clarifies this difference.

Discourse Frameworks and the Modus Tollens 'Not q' Contingency

Considering the interpretation activities related to discourse frameworks shows how the differential understanding of abstract and commonplace expressions of modus tollens problems relates to discourse frameworks. Modus tollens problems involve the conditions:

if p then q
not q
therefore not p

When applied as a condition of a reasoning problem, modus tollens transforms 'if p then q' into 'if not p then not q' (D'Andrade, 1989: 136). In the basic expression of the objects and conditions that constitute a modus tollens problem using arbitrary nomenclature rather than commonplace experiences, the interpretive transformation of the conditions to 'if not q then not p' involves reorganizing the linguistic terms ('if' and 'then') that indicate an operation of the variables, as well as the linguistic term ('not') that indicates a state of the variables. Making that interpretive transformation in order to solve the problem when it is expressed with such abstract nomenclature is straightforward if one approaches the problem with the frame of reference that it is a puzzle, which involves manipulating the stated variables without recalling process narratives about commonly experienced things and activities (e.g., 'this is just a logic problem, accept the premises without linking them to prior experience'). Thus, an interpretive contingency introduced by an abstractly expressed logic problem is that of applying an interpretive frame of reference that disregards commonplace experience.

The form of the linguistic expression of modus tollens problems complicates the acceptance of the 'not q' frame of reference. If an individual interprets the expression of a modus tollens problem without applying a puzzle-solving frame of reference, negation expressed by the position of the state modifier, 'not', is problematic in the 'not q' expression of a variable. In colloquial English, a phrase in the form 'not q is true' is unusual. A more common form of expression involves reorganizing the words as 'q is not true'. Interpreting the uncommon construction invokes a comparison with the more common construction, which involves considering information that is not expressed by the problem as stated. That comparison contributes to a frame of reference, which supports searching for relevant information, rather than one that emphasizes literal use of the stated variables. When applying commonplace interpretive frames of reference and communication formats other than those of formal logic, 'not q' must be something other than q. If people know about or have experience with a pertinent setting, object, or behavior, they often apply that experiential information as the 'not q'.

In that regard, the recorded genetics learning activities show that when the biology students initially encountered the teachers' de-emphasis of questions about cellular processes and emphasis on the abstract grey boxes of standard Mendelian vocabulary and nomenclature, some of them mentioned commonplace topics such as families, breeding of animals, and previously studied information about DNA and RNA, in attempts to form explanatory process narratives. However, as shown in Chapters Seven and Ten, teachers discourage and eliminate such information from acceptable explanations of trait inheritance.

In the biology classes, the discourse framework emphasizing Mendelian grey boxes had the unintended consequence of reproducing a 'not q' interpretive contingency. Students encountered it when they tried to find additional information to link incomplete sets of available information as process narratives that explained the relationship between genes and traits. The form and content of the teachers' questions and comments emphasized an interpretive perspective and interpretive vocabulary that conjoined the production and transmission of traits without considering information about cellular genetics. This contingency was a consequence of patterns of interaction through which teachers withheld information and shifted the interpretive frame of reference toward abstract Mendelian grey boxes, and not toward students' previously encountered information about cellular processes or kinship. This presents the 'not q' contingency like that of modus tollens logic problems.

Formal logic problems also exclude use of information that is not specified by the wording of the problem. In that context, like the constraints on seeking and applying cellular process information in Mendelian genetics learning activities, the abstract variables lead to contingencies related to interpreting the available information. That is why abstract modus tollens logic problems are more difficult to solve than versions of the problems that include representations of familiar experiences.

Experiments that examined the difficulties of understanding and solving modus tollens logic problems have found that, when the problems were expressed in terms of commonplace examples, rather than abstract alphabetical and mathematical nomenclature, respondent's mistakes often resulted from adding information that was not specified in the wording of the problem (D'Andrade, 1989: 140). One example featured a problem stipulating:

GIVEN: If it is raining then the roof is wet.
SUPPOSE: The roof **is not** wet.
THEN:
(a) It must be the case that it is raining.
(b) Maybe it is raining and maybe it isn't.
(c) It must be the case that it is not raining.

D'Andrade discusses a student who made a mistake when he explained that it might be raining even if the roof were not wet, because there might be a tree over the roof shielding it from the rain (1989: 140). However, the wording of the problem did not mention a tree or other circumstances that would shield the roof from rain. The student immediately acknowledged his error when this was pointed out. Such acknowledgment in the case of logic problems that were expressed in commonplace terms differed from the responses of people who made similar mistakes when attempting to solve abstract modus tollens problems. The latter group usually insisted their answers were correct and could not recognize their errors. Comparing these outcomes, D'Andrade concluded that the 'tree over the roof' student's immediate recognition of his mistake related to the ease of noticing that some erroneous pragmatic information (the imagined tree) had been added, in contrast to the difficulty of noticing that a logical inference based on an abstract problem's wording was missing (D'Andrade, 1989: 140).

The analysis of discourse frameworks and grey boxes presents another explanation. The effects on reasoning and understanding resulting from the creation of grey boxes during the genetics learning activities show that recognizing a mistaken process narrative is not just a result of noticing erroneous information or noticing an absence of information (Saferstein, 2014). Rather, the genetics lessons show that noting erroneous information requires finding that it does not contribute to a coherent process narrative, and then reengaging the interpretation activities that had linked certain information to form the inaccurate or invalid process narrative – i.e., seeking, organizing, and culling information. Recall Chapter Two's example of the student, B21, revising the 'automatically skips a generation' process narrative when the computer simulation produced a different pattern of images than previously noted. He revised 'a generation' to 'every sixth or seventh generation', ignoring the parents of each generation in his model of a pattern as he tried to maintain the 'automatically skips' aspect of the process narrative. The discourse framework's restrictions on access to cellular process information complicated B21's revision of the interpretive frame of reference that had contributed to a flawed process narrative. Such restrictions present the contingencies of coping with constraints on the trial and error interpretation activities of searching for information or applying prior experiences.

In the case D'Andrade described, the student mistakenly considered prior experiences to find information (the tree over the roof), which would link the available pieces of information already provided by the expressed problem ('If it is raining, then the roof is wet', 'the roof is not wet') (D'Andrade, 1989: 140). In order to develop the 'tree over the roof' process narrative, the student had shifted his frame of reference away from emphasis on the linguistic representation of the logic problem, and instead oriented it toward commonplace experiences and situations that were consistent with one of the provided pieces of information. Consequently, he ignored the stated premises of the problem, which indicated that, since the roof would get wet when it is raining, nothing sheltered the roof from the rain. D'Andrade's example shows the mobilizing of previously developed process narratives in order to provide missing information gained through prior experiences. T1's and T2's students responded in the same way when faced with restrictions on applying or searching for absent information about cellular processes of trait inheritance. For example, T1's student, B13, inserted information about family resemblance in the discussion leading to the 'blueprints' grey box, and T2's students', G32 and B31, asked digressive questions about crossing over and changing eye color (Transcript Extracts 7.6, A157-A173; 10.2, line 15; 10.4, lines 42–44; 10.8, lines 97–98).

Such activity of searching for and comparing information that counts as 'not q' is a way of filling information gaps in order to produce coherent process narratives (e.g., mentioning family resemblance or cellular process information in the classroom examples). The expression of a modus tollens problem in terms of familiar experiences provides the problem-solver with an opportunity for trial and error production of process narratives and for comparison of candidate process narratives.

In contrast, the limited information expressed linguistically in an abstractly expressed modus tollens problem restricts the respondents' interpretation activities – like the restriction on seeking or applying cellular process information during Mendelian genetics lessons. When logic problems were expressed abstractly, D'Andrade's respondents were guided toward an interpretive frame of reference that involved accepting and applying grey boxes, such as 'not q', rather than seeking more information – similar to the genetics students guided toward applying Mendelian grey boxes. This produced the contingency of reconstructing a discourse framework in order to develop a useful interpretive frame of reference – one that did not involve applying experiential information or seeking new information. Thus, revising a mistake required revisiting previous interpretation activities and applying different interpretation activities related to the restrictive abstract expression of a problem.

At the radiology consultations the discussion of images produced a discourse framework that supported revising mistakes by applying prior knowledge and seeking information. This did away with any 'not q' constraints on interpretation that patients may have briefly encountered. Consider the example of P1 obtaining information about the fixed placement of embolizing agent particles near fibroid tumors (Chapter 1, Figures 1.1, 1.3). P1 developed an understanding of that aspect of UFE by asking a question based on the pragmatic notion that particles suspended in a liquid can flow in various directions and the static computer screen image illustrating the nurse's initial explanation did not indicate direction of blood flow. P1's question implied the addition of unspecified information – the possibility of the particles flowing in any direction ('Now what keeps those little particles there instead of coming back into my – and giving me a blood clot' [Figure 1.1, Row B, Column 1, line 2]). However, the consultation discourse framework incorporated communication patterns that supported seeking information and applying previously encountered information. This provided P1 with the opportunity to create a process narrative explaining the direction of blood flow. She linked the nurse's verbal explanation with the computer screen diagram of the abdominal cavity and with the nurse's hand gesture simulating the direction of blood flowing in the artery depicted in the diagram ("they don't come back out because you know the blood flow in the arteries is one-way" [Figure 1.1, Row C, Column 2, line 1.4.5]).

Two components of the radiology consultation combined to produce the patient's understanding:

- Her interpretation of information beyond that presented by the initial verbal and visual explanatory resources – i.e., the type of inferential reasoning exhibited by D'Andrade's 'tree over the roof' student (D'Andrade, 1989: 140);
- A discourse framework that incorporated the opportunity for the patient to obtain the additional information that she could link with the initial information as recallable process narratives.

Considering D'Andrade's examples of contentless and contentful contingencies in this regard emphasizes that restating modus tollens logic problems in terms of commonplace experiences provides respondents with a path toward recalling process narratives that might apply to interpreting the variables and conditions expressed in the wording of the problem. Such reconfiguring of interpretation activities and frames of reference provides the opportunity to avoid or replace grey boxes either presented in the problem or resulting from constraints on searching for information missing from the linguistic expression of the problem. Thus, the reasoning problem's 'content' is a product of both the interpretation activity and the resulting process narratives; not just the information presented in the initial expression of the problem.

Content and Context in Discourse Frameworks

The interpretation activities related to the Mendelian genetics discourse framework further explicate the components of reasoning that have been considered as contentful and contentless contingencies (cf. D'Andrade, 1989). Contentless contingencies actually involve a lack of access to a previously developed discourse framework that incorporates grey boxes based on local information resources – such as T2's whiteboard diagram featuring a nested arrangement of linguistic terms and lines or arrows, which indicated relationships between alleles and traits without providing cellular process information to explain them (Figure 11.1). As discussed in Chapter Ten, when G33 explained a similar diagram she had drawn on the whiteboard, like T2 she presented a nested arrangement of genetics terms including conventional Mendelian grey boxes, such as the terms, 'dominant' and 'recessive', the nomenclature for alleles (e.g., BbLl) (Figures 10.8, 10.10, 11.1). She applied the discourse framework that the teacher had developed during the introductory lecture. Her verbal explanation of the diagram featured descriptive process narratives that also incorporated the grey boxes, which the teacher's diagram had presented during the introductory lecture. However, when G33 attempted to discuss what she had learned about trait inheritance during a follow-up discussion away from the classroom, visual components of the classroom discourse framework, such as written nomenclature and nested genetics terms were absent. As she encountered difficulty in recalling the word 'allele' that she had presented in the classroom, G33 attempted to verbally reconstruct the missing components of the classroom discourse framework (examined in Chapter Ten).

In regard to the production and effects of discourse frameworks, the significant aspect of G33's confounded explanation is not her difficulty recalling the word, 'allele', but her attempt to verbally reconstruct the classroom's Mendelian genetics discourse framework in the absence of its visual grey boxes. G33's recall of information she encountered during the introductory lecture – in the sequence it had been presented – displayed the intertwining of interpretation activities, discourse frameworks, and resulting process narratives.

The visual components of the classroom discourse framework matched portions of G33's comments during the follow-up discussion when she tried to recall the word, 'allele'. In the context of G33's memory of the classroom discourse framework, her vague utterance, 'They're the same trait, but they're coded for different things', made sense as a description of her classroom interpretation activities. In the absence of visual components of the classroom discourse framework, the utterance expressed her recall of some components of the process narratives she had produced in the classroom. As a participant in the follow-up discussion, the utterance also made sense to me, because I had observed and recorded G33's interpretation activities in the classroom discourse framework a few weeks earlier. However, in order to explicate G33's utterance in this book, I had to review the recordings of the classroom interpretation activities and the actual discourse framework, which G33 had only indexed during the follow-up discussion. In most commonplace situations, people do not have the option of reviewing recordings. The problem of reconstructing grey-boxed process narratives is what the phrase, 'you had to be there', means in regard to the difficulty of expressing certain experiences and understandings when the discourse framework that supported their creation is absent. Context and content are intertwined in discourse frameworks.

Diagrams and Memory

The preceding chapters' examples of people incorporating environmental information resources in discourse frameworks show how an approach to understanding based on the creation of process narratives differs from and elaborates on the experimental research approaches based on mental models and coherence based reasoning. Experimental studies of reasoning have concluded that visual resources, such as diagrams, semantic graphs, and trial evidence, simplify the conceptualization of complexities presented by certain types of logic problems. Studies based on mental models have found certain uses and formats of diagrams to be beneficial for lessening the cognitive load on short-term memory needed to recall or remember multiple contingent concepts and interpretations of information while solving reasoning problems (Bauer and Johnson-Laird, 1993; Johnson-Laird, 2002).

The different uses of diagrams in the radiology consultations and the biology classes – in regard to providing information or functioning as grey boxes for missing information – show that diagrams do not always provide information or simplify organizing complicated sets of information. In the radiology consultations the medical images, which include diagrams, contributed to patients' understandings of symptoms and treatments for uterine fibroid tumors. However, the effects of the images on patients' understandings often were a function of the communication patterns, including talk, movements, and gestures, by which the patients interpreted the images and obtained information that was missing from the images. In the biology classes, the diagrammatic images on computer screens or whiteboards affected students' understandings in a different way. They contributed to a discourse framework featuring grey boxes that substituted for missing information. In such situations, the diagrams served a syntactical function enabling individuals to set aside certain interpretive contingencies of restricted information access. However, the diagrams did not contribute to complete substantive understandings that resolved those interpretive contingencies.

Analyzing the interpretation activities of T2's genetics lecture explicates the development of a discourse framework featuring diagrams. In T2's lecture, one type of contingency that diagrams collapse and simplify is the interpretation activity needed to make sense of the form and content of the linguistically expressed variables of a reasoning problem. Before the tabular diagramming of nomenclature could lessen the interpretive contingencies expressed by some students' digressive questions, those students had to adjust their interpretive frames of reference from the use of a diagram that modeled cellular processes to a diagram that featured grey boxes, which correlated nomenclature representing trait variations with symbolically implied unexamined relationships between alleles and traits.

Early in the introductory lecture, the teacher began nesting categories of information about the biology of trait inheritance when she wrote 'allele' and linked it by a dash to the pictorial and textual diagram representing part of the process of cell division (e.g., Figure 10.1, Picture E; Transcript Extract 10.3, lines 32, 34). As the teacher expanded the diagram during the lecture, the visual linkage of linguistically expressed categories suggested hierarchical or sequential relationships without expressing the particular processes or functions that constitute those relationships (Figure 11.1). Consequently, when students faced restrictions on searching for the missing information about cellular processes, the forms of representation used to express nested categories, such as positioning, dashes, and arrows, functioned as grey boxes for the missing information. When the students began to accept the shift from diagramming cellular processes to tabulating linguistic terms, they also accepted the grey boxes as part of the discourse framework for developing and applying process narratives that counted as understandings of trait inheritance in the classroom setting.

Figure 11.1: Nested Terms: Components of the Trait inheritance Process Represented in T2's Diagram and Tables

<table>
<tr><td>A</td><td>
Genotype
<ul>
<li>Parents' cells
<ul>
<li>Chromosomes
<ul>
<li>Genes (parts of chromosomes)</li>
<li>Alleles (alternative forms of a gene for a particular trait)</li>
</ul></li>
</ul></li>
<li>Parents' reproductive cells (gametes) formed during meiosis
<ul>
<li>Chromosomes
<ul>
<li>Alleles (information leading to green or hazel eyes)</li>
</ul></li>
</ul></li>
</ul>
Phenotype
<ul>
<li>Green eyes</li>
<li>Hazel eyes</li>
</ul>
Movement of alleles (genes) into parents' reproductive cells and then into children's cells
<ul>
<li>Parents' cells contain homologous pairs of chromosomes, each containing a particular allele</li>
<li>The allele is duplicated with its chromosome resulting in four chromosomes, each with the same allele</li>
<li>Each of the four chromosomes containing the particular allele becomes part of one of four reproductive cells (eggs or sperm)</li>
</ul>
</td></tr>
<tr><td>B</td><td>
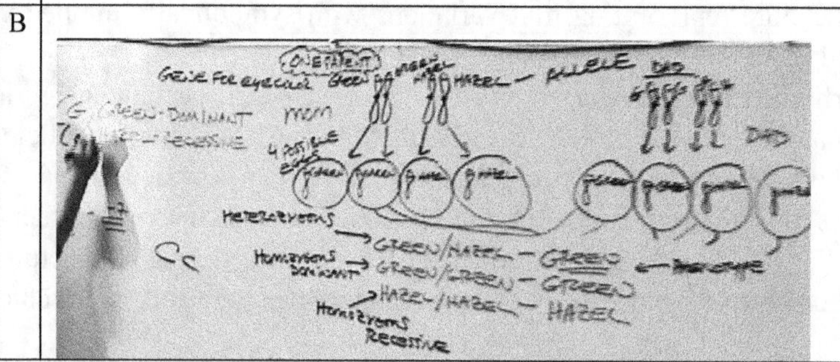

</td></tr>
</table>

T1's student, B21, presented an example of using a discourse framework including Mendelian grey boxes. B21 had participated in creating the mistaken 'automatically skips a generation' explanation of the reappearance of the recessive trait, floppy ears (discussed in Chapters Two and Three). In that example, despite encountering new visual information that contradicted the 'automatically skips' process narratives, he persisted in attempting to apply them. Rather than revisiting the inferential frame of reference related to the term 'recessive', which he and his two collaborators had eliminated during their previous interpretation activity, B21 attempted to deal with the contradictory information by redefining 'skips' to mean appearing every six or seven generations (Chapter Three, Figure 3.6).

However, during subsequent classes the 'and not' restriction on using information concerning cellular genetic processes presented B21 with the interpretive contingencies that led him to adopt a conventional Mendelian visual grey box – the Punnett square. During a class five weeks later (including a week of Spring holiday), B21 displayed fluency with the Mendelian discourse framework as he explained an assigned problem to another student who had been unable to provide the teacher with a satisfactory answer (Saferstein, 2014). He expressed process narratives consistent with the Mendelian curriculum. B21 had resolved his difficulty of discarding the 'automatically skips' process narratives. He elegantly drew and explained a whiteboard diagram featuring a complex Punnett square and a calculation of three types of probable traits.

In this example, B21 shows that he has developed an operational understanding of using a Punnett square and nomenclature to represent the inheritance of parents' alleles by offspring and the resulting traits. He has learned to interpret the computer screen's visual information (Figure 11.2) in terms of the Mendelian alphabetical nomenclature, and to represent the link between alleles and traits by organizing the nomenclature in the cells of a Punnett square (Figure 11.3). The administrative activity of correctly placing nomenclature in the Punnett square cells leads to conversion of the nomenclature to computable numbers by counting groupings of similar traits (discussed in Note 35).

The codominance explanation that B21 presented involves a combined expression of two alleles on the nature of a trait, rather than a dominant allele canceling out the effects of a recessive allele on the expression of a trait. Information about cellular processes is still missing. The discourse framework of B21's preceding learning activities included use of a computer simulation to mate a brown-furred rabbit and a white-furred rabbit, producing a generation of offspring in which all the individuals had beige fur. Mating rabbits from the offspring generation produced a generation in which individuals respectively had brown fur, white fur, or beige fur (Figure 11.2).

Figure 11.2: Computer simulation's representation of codominance

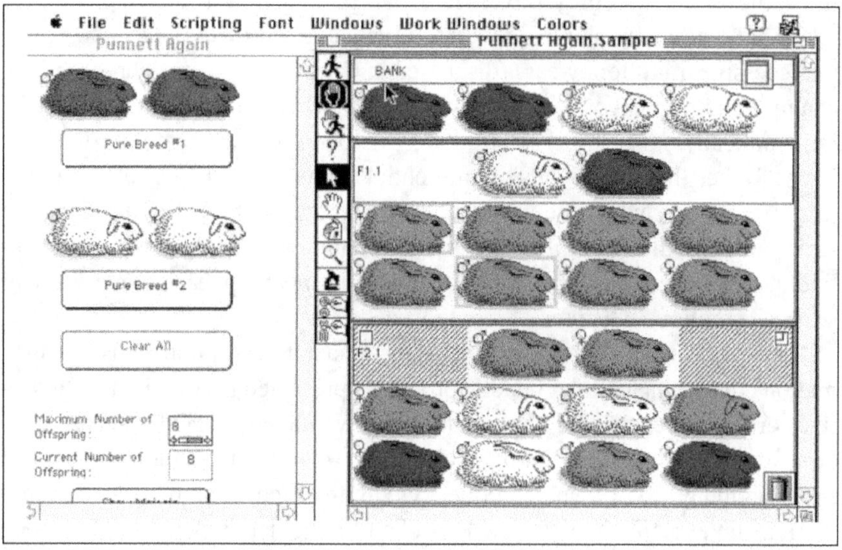

(WINGS for Learning 1991)

When B21 explains codominance to the other student, he incorporates use of the whiteboard into the discourse framework by transforming the computer simulation's pictorial information to a Punnett square, which also becomes part of the explanatory discourse framework. The nomenclature used by B21 to explain the appearance of three fur colors correlated with the images presented by the computer simulation (W stands for an allele associated with white fur, B stands for an allele associated with brown fur).

B21's use of Punnett squares and nomenclature directs attention to the visible differences between individual offspring, and substitutes the location of symbols within the square for the unseen and unexplained cellular processes. For example, B21 grouped the combinations of alleles in three color categories: brown (BB), beige (BW or WB), and white (WW) (Figure 11.3, Rows E, F, G). His organizing of nomenclature in the cells of Punnett squares and grouping of the results substitute for a substantive explanation of genetic processes.

Figure 11.3: Co-dominance explanation: the shift to grey boxes
[grey highlighting = grey boxes, **bold** = use of Mendelian nomenclature, symbols, and indexical expressions counting as understanding of trait inheritance by mapping across phenotype and genotype, *italics* = emphasis on location]

A		(B21 **starts drawing a Punnett Square** to show E. how to answer the question. **Writes a B over each of the two columns**) Because *in the first line* you had two **pure breeding** rabbits (????) (**writes a W at the left of each of the two rows**) **two whites**, right?
B		**These two genes** . (**writes W and B in each of the four cells of the Punnett square**) you **cross bred** . them both. All of them became beige . alright . . alright.
C		And then *in the second one* there's **two genes**. (**writes a B and a W to the right of the Punnett square**) That means the **two genes** they have in them **are brown and white**. Right? (**draws a Punnett square beneath the B and W**) (????)
D		Then when you **cross *(points marking pen at the first Punnett square) like this one*** you have (**writes BB in top left cell of second Punnett square**) **two browns**, (**writes BW in the top right cell**) **a brown and white**, (**writes WB in the bottom left cell**) **white and brown**, and a (**writes WW in the bottom right cell**) **white and white**.
E		This is the reason that we came up with three different colors. (*points at BW in the top right cell*) (??) ***these two made a beige*** . and that's one (writes a vertical mark at the right of the Punnett squares). (***points pen at BB in top left cell***) and ***we had a darker color***. (writes a second vertical mark next to the first mark) That's two. (*points pen at WW in bottom right cell*) ***Then we had a white*** .
F		(B21 writes a third vertical mark next to the others) three.
G	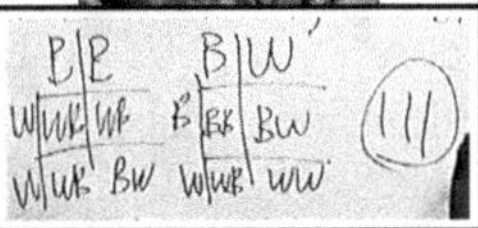	(B21 draws a circle around the three vertical marks) That's why we got the three colors.

Punnett squares conflate computation with biological processes. Thus, when B21 says, 'you cross bred . them both. All of them became beige' (Figure 11.3, Row B), 'cross bred' is a reference to parents' traits and alleles. It notes a relationship between traits and alleles, but does not explain it. The biochemical functioning of the alleles is grey-boxed by 'became beige', which notes outcomes in terms of offspring traits. Furthermore, B21's use of the term, 'pure breeding' (Figure 11.3, Row A) indexes aspects of the visual resources, such as the rows of rabbits, which were displayed by the computer simulation (Figure 11.2) and then represented as tabular and computational grey boxes by the Punnett square and ratio on the whiteboard, which B21 described:

> This is the reason that we came up with three different colors. (points at BW in the top right cell) (??) these two made a beige and that's one (writes a vertical mark at the right of the Punnett squares) (points pen at BB in top left cell) and we had a darker color. (writes a second vertical mark next to the first mark) That's two. (points pen at WW in bottom right cell) Then we had a white (writes a third vertical mark next to the others) three. (Figure 11.3, Rows E, F)

These grey boxes present the biological role of kinship in trait inheritance in terms of location in the Punnett square rather than as processes of cell division, transmission of DNA, or the relationship of alleles to hormones and proteins in the development of tangible traits. For example, B21 explains fur color related to the inheritance of co-dominant alleles as he places letters in the cells of a Punnett square and points at them (Figure 11.3, Rows A, B):

> Because in the first line you had two pure breeding rabbits (????) (writes a W at the left of each of the two rows) two whites, right? These two genes (writes WB in each of the four cells of the Punnett square) you cross bred them both. All of them became beige.

The process narratives that B21 expresses as he explains codominance depend on the presence of the graphical devices of Punnett squares and Mendelian nomenclature.

The discourse framework supported a computational manipulation of Mendelian genetics nomenclature, which did not require the missing biological information that would have contributed to substantive process narratives explaining the cellular processes by which genes affect the development of traits. Instead it emphasized familiarity with the administrative aspects of organizing nomenclature. In situations where components of professional culture, such as the standard Mendelian curriculum, emphasize patterns of interaction that restrict clients' information seeking, grey boxes function as triggers for recall of the administrative aspects of creating process narratives to complete tasks. This administrative function of grey boxes is shown by B21's use of Punnett squares (Figure 11.3).

Ultimately, the Mendelian curriculum's explanation of the relationship between alleles and traits depends on students tabulating certain words and nomenclature rather than mapping those words to pictures or diagrams. The Punnett squares applied in the classroom were tables organizing nomenclature (Figures 10.9, 11.3). Such tabular matching of nomenclature operates like a magic trick in which the audience's attention is misdirected by sleight of hand, resulting in the conclusion that particular activities create particular outcomes. However, the actual causal activities behind the 'magic' are unknown to the audience. In the case of alleles and traits, a discourse framework featuring grey boxes (e.g., the table of matching terms or the Punnett square) functions to divert attention from the missing information about the processes by which alleles actually affect traits. The discourse framework's diagrammatic resources provide a functional, though not substantive, solution to the problem of restricted information by supporting the production of process narratives incorporating grey boxes. The understanding and recall of grey-boxed content (e.g., the diagrammatic Punnett squares) are cognitively combined with a context consisting of the interpretation activities that produced a particular discourse framework and related process narratives.

Discourse Frameworks and Tacit Knowledge

Identifying the components of discourse frameworks explicates the cognition glossed as tacit or procedural knowledge – i.e., individual's understandings related to routine activities and environments, which are developed through repeated practice or observing others. The creation and use of a discourse framework featuring certain images and words as grey boxes, in conjunction with the experience and recall of the interpretation activities that led to the discourse framework, constitute tacit or procedural knowledge (Saferstein and Sarangi, 2010). The process narratives produced in a discourse framework incorporate its non-linguistic grey boxes. Consequently, in the absence of the material information resources that were components of the discourse framework, those process narratives cannot be expressed linguistically with the coherence that had informed their linking of pieces of information when those material resources were present – the understandings created and applied still exist, but cannot be communicated (cf. Polanyi, 1958, 1967).

For example, in G33's classroom explanations related to 'alleles', the visual expression on the whiteboard of Mendelian nomenclature in a Punnett square depicted an analogical relationship between the arrangement of letters and G33's verbal explanation of the combinations of alleles for fur color and tail length (Chapter 10, Figure 10.9). During the earlier interpretation activities of the introductory lecture and other course work, G33 had incorporated the Punnett square grey box into her trait inheritance discourse framework. However, at the follow-up discussion outside of the classroom, G33's access to the trait inheritance discourse framework was limited to her memories of classroom activities and her verbal description of those memories. The process narratives G33 had developed in the classroom incorporated visual grey boxes, such as the introductory lecture's analogical table and her Punnett square. When those were unavailable in the setting of the follow-up discussion, she could not verbally complete the process narratives that would explain alleles in the way that her diagramming and pointing at the visual grey boxes did during the biology class. The cognition glossed by the terms tacit knowledge or procedural knowledge is not a mental model or a combination of a mental model and aspects of a physical environment, but a visual and linguistic discourse framework – a set of interpretation activities and resulting process narratives, which feature grey boxes based on particular environmental resources.[37]

Discourse Frameworks and Mental Models

In contrast to the preceding analyses of the production of understandings, research intended to explain mental models and cognitive schemata has featured reasoning problems and experimental situations. That approach focuses on the artifacts of interpretation, rather than the interpretation activities that are fundamental to explaining how people form understandings. It lacks attention to the relationship between discourse frameworks and the reasoning that produces understandings (Saferstein, 2014). For example, experimental studies of reasoning have concluded that visual resources, such as diagrams, and semantic graphs, reduce the contingency of keeping in mind alternative models of solutions or explanations (Bauer and Johnson-Laird, 1993; Johnson-Laird, 2002). However, those studies do not include, as part of the reasoning, the contingencies of creating, finding, and organizing those alternative models while producing a discourse framework. Johnson-Laird compares the use of visual representations of variables and conditions developed by Peirce with mental models in order to explain fundamental operations of reasoning:

> The fundamental operations of reasoning based on mental models are insertion (the addition of entities, properties, or relations to models), and deletion (the elimination of models when they are combined with other, inconsistent, models). In the case of reasoning based on quantifiers, the theory also proposes that individuals search for alternative models. (Johnson-Laird, 2002: 91)

Such explanations emphasize how the mental organization of previously interpreted information affects reasoning, rather than emphasizing the interrelation of information resources, settings, interaction, and culture that contribute to interpreting the information (cf. Johnson-Laird, 2002). They do not consider the placeholder function of grey boxes, which can preclude deletion yet do not always eliminate inconsistencies (e.g., the lack of coherence or clear relationship between pieces of information). Nor do they consider the processual effects on interpretation of searching for information and restrictions on information searches. In such circumstances reasoning may involve the creation and application of grey-boxed process narratives.

Examining the development of discourse frameworks and process narratives shows that the insertion and deletion of interpreted information are not just mental operations, but also involve a complex of interrelated activities, information resources, and sociocultural constraints of settings that constitute the discourse frameworks. The preceding analysis of interpretation activities demonstrates that such interrelation affects the searching – not only the searching for fully formed alternative models, but also for pieces of information to link as process narratives that contribute to understandings. For example, some of the interpretation activities in the recorded radiology consultations and genetics lessons show people inserting and deleting pieces of information as they develop discourse frameworks and process narratives. Furthermore, the data also show people interpreting pieces of information prior to or while inserting and deleting it. The data show that the production of accurate understandings is not based on mental operations, which either include or exclude the artifacts of interpretation during reasoning, but on the interpretation activities that develop discourse frameworks – including particular communication patterns and uses of information resources.

Discourse Frameworks and Cognition

Analyzing understanding in regard to discourse frameworks, process narratives, and grey boxes amplifies certain concepts of understanding and reasoning that have begun to explain how cognition operates in relation to social interactions and culture. Studies of cognition applying theories of mental models and schemata have also noted contingencies that complicate reasoning. For example, studies of reasoning, which feature participants solving logic problems, have emphasized that deduction often involves considering alternative mental models as solutions, and that the difficulty of remembering those alternative models while developing a solution can lead to errors (cf. Bauer and Johnson-Laird, 1993: 372–373; D'Andrade, 1989). However, the mental model approach limits the type of contingencies considered, emphasizing the expression of contingent relationships among variables.

Some coherence based reasoning studies are more process oriented than mental model research due to a focus on the logic of jury verdicts (e.g., Pennington and Hastie, 1992; Simon, 2004; Simon, Snow, and Read, 2004; Simon, Stenstrom, and Read, 2015). However, they emphasize artifacts in the form of the pieces of information that jurors apply or omit, rather than the interpretation activities that lead to applying or eliminating information or arguments. The allied constraint satisfaction theory emphasizes satisfying the constraints of neural and mental operations of constructing understandings, rather than the effects of culture, social organization, and setting (e.g., Holyoak and Simon, 1999; Simon and Holyoak, 2002; Lee and Holyoak, 2008). That approach also places emphasis on the results of interpretation activity instead of the activity itself.

In contrast, the process narrative approach finds that the contingencies of the interpretation activities through which people mobilize information resources are central to explaining how people develop understandings. A set of process narratives can contribute to the creation and expression of mental models as well as the construction of coherence, but each process narrative in the set also can function separately as an index of certain interpretation activities related to a particular discourse framework. Analysis of the creation and application of discourse frameworks clarifies the different emphases of mental models and process narratives in regard to the effects of resources in settings and the effects of interaction, professional culture, and organizational arrangements on interpretation activities.

12 Sociocultural Complexities of Interpretation Activities and Discourse Frameworks

Chapter Twelve discusses the complex sociocultural variables related to discourse frameworks and the production of understanding. It describes the diversity of the research participants and settings in the context of earlier chapters' discussion of their interpretation activities. Topics include: socioeconomic categories, gender and interpretation activities, and recognizing agency by analyzing processes of understanding. The chapter considers how analysis of process narratives, discourse frameworks, and grey boxes can contribute to changing restrictive discourse frameworks to benefit all participants.

Discourse frameworks can incorporate components reflecting the cultural and social systems affecting participants. These components may include expressed or unexpressed aspects of social location and personal history, which affect background knowledge and interaction. The diversity of the participants in the clinical and educational settings discussed in preceding chapters reflects social and political changes in the US over the decades preceding the research. It reflects the effects of those changes on access to education, medical care, and opportunities for clinical and educational careers. Such diversity confounds the separation of the interactional, mental, and environmental components of interpretation activities and their outcomes into ecologically valid variables based on categories related to gender, race, or ethnicity. Therefore, in order to emphasize how participants affect the social organization of clinical and educational settings through their interpretation activities, I have chosen to present categorical demographic description after readers have considered the detailed analysis of the actual interpretation activities. The following paragraphs describe the diversity of the participants and settings presented here, which entail commonplace complexities related to the current social and cultural realities of many clinical and educational settings.

Socioeconomic Categories

The patients in the recorded radiology consultations are all female due to their medical concern, uterine fibroid tumors. In order to protect the privacy of all participants, the discussion of the data here does not identify the races and ethnicities of the specific participants whose talk and actions have been transcribed. In the data that had been collected when I selected the examples presented in this book, four of the patients are African American, one is Asian or Asian American, and seven are white. The nurse and radiologist involved in the recorded consultations and discussions are white. The radiology practice had ethnic, racial, and gender diversity in its group of clinicians. The consultations were held at clinical suites or hospitals situated in communities that were diverse in regard to household incomes, with many upper middle or high-income households. However, the radiology practice also drew patients from other areas of the county.

During the radiology consultations, the discussion of images affected the balance of interpretive contingencies between each patient and the clinician, shaping the patterns of consultation interaction and the discourse frameworks. This increased the agency of all patients to influence the agenda of topics and forms of expression in ways that contributed to their understandings of medical information. It also changed the professional culture of the clinicians in regard to the routine patterns of interaction that they applied to consultations. The resulting understandings of medical information contributed to patients' authority over their treatment decisions.

In the examples from T1's biology classes discussed in this book, the students self-selected to form work groups. In regard to ethnicity, race, gender, and language community, some of the student task groups were diverse, while others were homogeneous. The task group in the examples from T1's class analyzed in detail in Chapters Two, Three, and Eleven, includes two Asian American students, one African American student, and one white student who spoke infrequently during the learning activities involving the computer simulation. In the examples from T1's class discussed in detail in Chapter Seven, the task group includes three Chicano or Latino students and one African-American student. Each of the two groups consists of one female student and three male students. In the 'automatically skips a generation' group, one of the boys rarely participated in the recorded learning activities and seldom appears in the transcripts. The gender composition of the other task groups in T1's classes varied.

In the class during which T2 presented the lecture and whiteboard diagram introducing trait inheritance, 30 students are present (Chapters Ten and Thirteen). Two of those students are Chicano or Latino; two are Asian or Asian American. In the examples from T2's class discussed in detail in Chapters Ten and Thirteen, the five students who ask digressive questions during the introductory lecture are white. Three are female. The two female students participating in the follow-up discussion analyzed in Chapter Ten are white.

One of the teachers is Asian American. That teacher is a member of a different Asian American community than the Asian American students in the task group in one of his classes discussed in previous chapters. The other teacher who participated in the data discussed here is white.

The data include learning activities in two schools in which T1 taught biology. One of those schools was an established urban school. The other was a newly built suburban school. T2 taught at a different suburban school. The schools varied in regard to the family income levels of the student populations: i.e., one of T1's schools included many students from lower middle income to middle income families. T1's other school included many students from middle income and upper-middle income families. T2's school included many students from upper-middle and upper income families.

The age of the three schools' buildings ranged from new to five years old to twenty years old. However, the age of classroom facilities and relative prosperity of a schools' neighborhood, did not directly correlate with each biology classroom's technology resources. The school with oldest buildings was the location of a classroom containing computers used during the genetics lessons, while a more recently built school in a more prosperous neighborhood was the location of the biology course that did not have computers in the classroom, even though that course took place nine years later than the course in the older school.

T1's two classes discussed in previous chapters occurred in different schools in which some of the environmental and curricular factors differed. Yet, in both settings the patterns of interpretive interaction related to using the computer simulation and task prompt to investigate and explain the inheritance of traits were consistent. In both the 'blueprints' and the 'automatically skips' groups, the students engaged in the trial-and-error interpretation activities of developing process narratives. Those activities related to the standard Mendelian grey boxes that were part of the professional culture of biology instruction. The emphasis on Mendelian grey boxes also was consistent with the emphasis of T2's classes, years later, which did not use computers.

All of the participants in the data examples discussed throughout this book spoke fluent English during the recorded activities. One radiology patient, P9, who spoke with an accent, presented brief responses during her radiology consultation (discussed in Chapters Nine and Thirteen). In that context, the nurse repeated explanations in a manner suggesting that she was unsure of P9's English fluency as they interacted during the consultation. When analyzing the video recordings of P9's radiology consultation, I also was uncertain about her fluency in regard to her understanding of the nurse's verbal explanations. However, P9 spoke fluent English during her telephone post-consultation discussion with me and indicated no difficulty in understanding or responding to my utterances.

Recognizing Agency by Analyzing Processes of Understanding

In the context of such varied and multiple components of social and cultural diversity, which now apply within many clinics and classrooms, accurately locating one of those categories as a causal factor affecting understanding is unfeasible, unless participants explicitly refer to gender, race, ethnicity, religion, or sexual preference in a way that produces a response such as a change in the interaction or the learning activity. For example, there was one oblique reference to race during the recorded learning activities of the classes discussed in the preceding chapters. It occurred in one of T1's classes. The group of students is not one of those discussed in the examples analyzed elsewhere in this book. It includes four students, two of whom, G22 and B24, are African American. The brief comment occurred after the group had completed a computer simulation learning activity concerning the inheritance of straight or floppy ears by rabbits presented on the screen as having white fur color. When G22 used the computer mouse to open the software file for the next assigned task, the screen showed two sets of parent rabbits, one of which had brown fur. After the brown rabbits appeared, G22, commented, 'Ooh they're brown'. Then, the other African American student in the group, B24, called out, 'All, I got some Black bunnies, yaaayyyy'.

B24's comment suggests that, when interpreting certain visual information, he applied or considered applying frames of reference related to historical structured inequalities. However, those were not the only frames of reference he applied to the visual information. Along with the other students in the group, B24 participated in the routine activities of using the computer simulation to answer the task prompt questions and engaging in gossip about peers.

Conventional curricula for Mendelian genetics have included terms that can have uncomfortable colloquial uses when applied to people: e.g., all of the courses studied included the terms 'purebred' or 'pure breeding'. One teacher (not one of the teachers in the data presented here) used the term 'half breed' at one point, when discussing heterozygous offspring of homozygous dominant and homozygous recessive parents, such as the offspring of the floppy-eared and straight-eared rabbits displayed by the computer simulation. However, aside from B24's comment about the brown rabbits, issues related to race and ethnicity did not surface during the students' interpretation activities.

Unexpressed awareness of such issues can be an additional burden for students, sometimes leading to disengagement (Ogbu, 1991, 2003). On the other hand, although commonplace, those issues may not always inhibit the interpretation activities that constitute engagement in learning activities (cf. MacLeod, 1987). If students of color in the recorded groups had interpreted the presentation of white rabbits in the earlier computer simulation task as an expression of white privilege or as a lack of consideration for the diversity of student populations, the recordings show that the rabbit images also functioned as a part of the course work to which those students committed their attention and action. The design of the software could have initially featured rabbits with brown fur and later added rabbits with white fur for the codominance learning task. Perhaps that would have affected students who were disengaged. However, even if such a change were to engage more students with the assignment, the missing cellular process information and emphasis on Mendelian grey boxes – resulting from curricular conventions and patterns of interaction related to professional culture – would present those students with the same interpretive contingences that led to the complicated trial-and-error interpretation activities discussed in previous chapters.

Analysis of the creation of discourse frameworks, process narratives, and grey boxes presents the construction of the particular social identities pertinent to the activities of participating with others in order to complete the pragmatic work of medical consultations and learning activities. Manifest status differences *are* the consistent patterns of interaction that result from participants mobilizing resources as they interpret each other's linguistic expressions. Rather than emphasizing behavioral or status differences that precede interaction as determinants of understandings, analysis of process narratives, discourse frameworks, and grey boxes explains the role of interpretation activities in developing understandings – and in producing and reproducing professional culture and professional authority, including the restriction of information by professionals that occurs in particular settings.

Gender and Interpretation Activities

The purpose of emphasizing interpretation activities prior to noting races and ethnicities of the participants in the data also applies to gender – i.e., sustaining attention on the interpretation activities of forming understandings.[38] Elinor Ochs, discussing her research on the social construction of patterns of gendered interaction across cultures, has provided a pertinent explanation of the relationship among discourse, interaction, and gender roles in regard to family and community settings (Ochs, 1992). Such analysis also explicates the 'constitutive routes' of language and interaction in clinical and educational settings. Ochs emphasizes the constitutive role of language in regard to gender roles:

> ... the relation between particular features of language and gender is typically non-exclusive.... Hence, strictly speaking we cannot say that these features pragmatically presuppose male or female. (Ochs, 1992: 340)
>
> ... Knowledge of how language relates to gender is not a catalogue of correlations between particular linguistic forms and sex of speakers, referents, addressees and the like. (Ochs, 1992: 342)

The analysis of discourse frameworks, process narratives, and grey boxes in clinical and educational settings shows how the female and male participants develop the patterns of interaction that constitute their roles, identities, and relationships during clinical consultations and classroom learning activities. The data analysis confirms and expands on Ochs's findings about language use, showing that broader components of interaction, including the use of material resources to create meaning, are non-exclusive in regard to gender. It shows how Ochs's findings also apply to professions and organizational settings, revealing that the interpretation activities pertaining to students' collaborative use of computers or to patients and clinicians' discussion of images consist of components that can apply to both genders.

Gender and Professional Status in the Radiology Consultations

For example, the discussion of images during the radiology consultations, analyzed here, was originated and promoted by male physicians, but came to be delivered most often by a female nurse or later by female and male physician assistants. When a male radiologist conducted one of the consultations, analysis of the recorded data did not show systematic differences from the nurse's consultations in regard either to the interaction with the patient when discussing images or in regard to the understandings that the patient expressed during her post-consultation telephone discussion – with the exception that, when the visual information concerned the actual UFE procedure, the radiologist specified more technical details related to performing the actual embolization procedure than the nurse did (cf. Siouta, Broström, and Hedberg, 2012 for similar findings regarding explanations of a therapeutic medication by nurses and physicians).

The interpretation activities of creating process narratives and discourse frameworks affected the patients' understandings of medical information, rather than the gender of the clinician or the differences in professional status ascribed to a physician or nurse. The effects of categorical distinctions such as affect, personality, professional status, gender, race, and ethnicity are the result of materially manifested patterns of interaction and forms of expression. The events that are often categorized and dichotomized as 'physician consultation'/'nurse consultation' or 'male clinician consultation'/'female clinician consultation' directly result from particular tangible patterns of interaction, not the gender of the clinician. When those patterns are beneficial to patients' understandings of medical information, it is possible for female or male physicians to apply patterns of interaction routinely applied by particular female or male nurses. Explaining the creation and effects of discourse frameworks reveals the components of pragmatic organizational identities and roles.

Gender and Interpretation Activities in the Genetics Lessons

I designed the second genetics education study, which included T2's classes, to consider gender, race, and ethnicity in regard to differential educational opportunities (Saferstein and Oiye, 1999). However, early data analysis showed the complex set of factors that confound clear-cut characterization of activities and their components in terms of those categorical distinctions. An ecologically valid explanation of the classroom educational activities first required examining the holistic set of complex components of interpretation activities that led to students' understandings of learning tasks and trait inheritance concepts. The discussion and comparison of the clinical and classroom data presented in this book are a result of that analysis.

In the high school genetics classes, due to restrictions on cellular process information, students sought other sources of information. In the context of the topics, sex and mating, which are components of trait inheritance curricula, students sometimes turned to their pragmatic understandings of the world developed apart from formal educational activities and resources. Applying such colloquial understandings may also import the residue of historical structured inequalities in the form of prejudiced or insensitive characterizations of people, roles, activities, or settings. This creates the potential for students to express and consider their social experiences outside of the classroom, which may include stereotypical models of gender roles. The mention of male power or dominance to account for the inheritance of traits was a common early response among students working with the computer simulation. However, the interpretation activities through which the participants expressed, interpreted, and responded to those characterizations created the effects of such references, not a particular utterance or action.

For instance, in one of T1's classes featuring the trait inheritance computer simulation, a video recording of two girls and one boy, working as a group without the teacher, shows the boy making a joking analogy between the dominance of the male rabbit's straight-ear genes and the power of human males (this group does not appear in the data analyzed in other chapters). When one of the girls reads a worksheet question asking for a prediction about the shape of the next generation of rabbits' ears, the boy states in a facetious tone, 'I think that, uh, they will all be the same, because the male is the dominant force in this society.' All three students giggle. One of the girls responds sarcastically, 'You wanna write that?' affirming that the quip about male dominance is inappropriate. The boy acknowledges this by agreeing that it would not be a good answer.

A similar case occurred early in T1's interaction with the 'blueprints' group of students, after they had run the computer simulation with the result that the offspring of a male straight-eared rabbit and a female floppy-eared rabbit all had straight ears. Both T1 and the task prompt asked students to use the computer simulation in order to test and disprove the possibility that, when strait-eared and floppy-eared rabbits are mated, the sex of a parent rabbit might be related to the appearance of a homogeneous straight-eared offspring generation. When the teacher requested an explanation of the computer simulation images, a male student, B13, first presented an answer based on quantity of genes acquired from the respective parents, saying, 'There wasn't as many female genes as there was male genes' (Transcript Extract 7.2, line A60). He answered descriptively, indexing the genes for floppy and straight ears in terms of the specifics of the screen images, i.e., the female parent's floppy ears and the male parent's straight ears. When the teacher then asked for an explanation of the presence of only straight ears in the offspring, B13 responded, 'They didn't come out' (Transcript Extract 7.2, line A65), while the only female student in the group, G11, initiated an overlap of his utterance, offering the explanation that 'the male's have – more – more power' (Transcript Extract 7.2, line A66). As the teacher begins to respond to her, B13 interjects, 'as usual' (Transcript Extract 7.3, line A68). B13 introduces gender politics that reflect social experiences, such as discussions and debates. He also begins a teasing, wisecracking form of interaction, which the other students and the teacher adopt as they construct a discourse framework for the interaction. Another boy, B12 interjects, 'yep' (Transcript Extract 7.3, line A70), in agreement with B13's 'as usual', and then, B13 adds, 'Yep, the male's always got it' (Transcript Extract 7.3, line A72).

Rather than telling the students that their explanations are wrong or challenging the boys' comments as sexist, T1 applies his Socratic pedagogical approach, challenging the students to test the accuracy of their answers by predicting the outcome of a second running of the computer simulation, which would mate a straight-eared female parent with a floppy-eared male. When the students do not immediately volunteer a relevant prediction, T1 suggests one based on their earlier linking of the offspring's ear shape to that of the male parent. He says, 'Droopy ears now' (Transcript Extract 7.3, line A76). He applies G11's use of the term 'droopy' to describe the rabbits' floppy-ears, and predicts that the outcome of the computer simulation would be a generation of floppy-eared rabbits resembling the father. G11 responds, 'Yep' (Transcript Extract 7.3, line A77), in agreement. The teacher then runs the simulation, which shows that the offspring all have the female parent's trait of straight ears. G11 responds by revising her answer to 'no', acknowledging that the prediction of floppy or droopy ears was wrong (Transcript Extract 7.3, lines A79-A81). B13 then stops his wisecracking about male power and reverts to his initial explanation that the respective quantity of inherited straight or floppy ear genes affected the characteristics of the offspring, rather than the gender of the straight-eared parent (Transcript Extract 7.3, line A84). By expressing their interpretations of the visual resources, the students shifted the focus of the discussion away from sexist social stereotypes.

Although the students' comments in both examples acknowledged stereotypical gender roles in society, the outcomes of the interactions – what 'got done' by means of the talk and gesturing – did not reproduce unequal power structures within the task groups or produce a division of interpretation activities according to gender. The female students often participated in the joking or teasing surrounding such comments, and through their participation exerted their own power to influence the interpretation activities and completion of learning tasks. The insertion of social experience resulted from the interpretation activities of creating process narratives by seeking information due to the restriction of cellular process information.

Another example occurred later in the classroom discussion of the 'blueprints' group of students, after T1 asked the students to explain why the generation produced by mating two of the straight-eared offspring rabbits contained both straight-eared and floppy-eared rabbits. Lacking information about cellular genetic processes, the students turned to colloquial discourse and began risqué joking about the female parent mating with more than one of the male rabbits. The female student in the group, G11, participated in the risqué joking, and then stopped it by re-emphasizing the teacher's question about trait inheritance.

The students facetiously accounted for the heterogeneous ear shapes of the offspring by indicating that the female rabbit mated with more than one male (Transcript Extract 7.5, lines A122-A130). They knew this was not the case, since they had seen the teacher operate the computer mouse to place the male and female parents in the mating box. Responding to the teacher's question, 'Where'd they get the directions for making floppy ears?', B13, a male student, says, 'Because there was a – there was a different father for both of 'em'. However, before he can complete his utterance, G11, a female student, initiates an overlap of 'there was a different', by saying, 'She did it with somebody else'. B11, another male student joins in the explanation, by adding the colloquial expression, 'She was a player', which he repeats. As he repeats it, G11, also repeats it, prefacing her repetition by saying the teacher's name, a common form of expression by students, which draws attention to their own contributions during learning activities.

The students then build on their use of non-academic topics and forms of expression, by uttering colloquial expressions for promiscuity (Transcript Extract 7.5, lines A131-A138). B11 says, 'She was here and there'. G11 again initiates an overlap saying, 'She was screwing around'. Before the teacher can complete a Socratic question, B12 and B13 each say, 'She a ho'', and G11 repeats her earlier characterization of the mother rabbit, 'she was screwing around'. G11 then adds to the fictional scenario of the female rabbit's promiscuity, by pointing at a male rabbit on the screen while saying, 'With the this right here right here'. The female student joins the male students in applying and escalating the colloquial sexist characterizations.

The teacher begins to respond to G11's scenario of a particular male rabbit being the second father of the heterogeneous offspring by treating it as a literal explanation of the operation of the computer simulation: 'I didn't put her in the bedroom [the software interface's mating box]' (Transcript Extract 7.5, line A139). B13 continues the risqué colloquial scenario by saying, 'She had gone before you put 'em in' (Transcript Extract 7.5, line A140), and B11 recycles the promiscuity theme, 'She was – she was a little row – uh . rowdy so she had to go get something' (Transcript Extract 7.5, line 142).

The teacher reemphasizes the Socratic frame of reference by returning to his initial query and again asking, 'Where did the gene for the floppy ears come from?' G11 then cooperates with the shift back to the appropriate explanatory frame of reference by saying 'Maybe maybe from from the – know like the background somebody had – maybe had floppy ears.' The teacher, treating G11's mention of 'somebody from the background' as a continuation of her earlier risqué comments about a second male mating with the mother rabbit, responds by sarcastically referring to his operation of the computer simulation, 'Oh, somebody in the background was watching?' G11 attempts to clarify, indicating that the teacher had misinterpreted her answer, 'Noo, no you know like you know how – you know the.' B11 then expresses words that clarify G11's comment about 'somebody in the background', by saying 'the ancestors or something', and G11 verifies that interpretation by adding, "The ancestors and everything" (Transcript Extracts 7.5 and 7.6, lines A143, A146-A150). The subsequent interaction clarifies that the teacher's pedagogical objective was for the students to link the trait, ear shape, to the dominant or recessive aspect of the genes inherited by the offspring. The students and teacher shift back to the emphasis on explaining and understanding the relationship between trait inheritance and genetic inheritance.

The recorded data show how participants in any interaction develop multiple purposes for their linguistic and gestural expressions and interpretations. In this case, the students got a number of things done through their risqué joking. They engaged in 'locker room talk', but while doing that, they also had fun during a science class, avoided answering a difficult question, challenged the teacher to depart from his Socratic approach, pushed the limit of acceptable classroom discourse, and confronted the contexts of sex and mating contained in explanations of Mendelian genetics. However, those aspects of the joking did not have enduring effects on the ensuing interpretation activities, which eventually led to the process narratives that explained the inheritance of ear shape in the computer simulation's images.

G11 contributed to and escalated the risqué joking about promiscuity and infidelity, but she also collaborated in the teacher's attempt to end it and focus on the learning task. As discussed in Chapter Seven, her efforts to interpret the teacher's questions and formulate process narratives contributed interpretation activities that led to the task prompt answer, which featured the use of 'blueprints' as a Mendelian grey box. G11 was an active agent in creating and expressing ways to recognize the social and cultural options and constraints that related to others' comments and actions (cf. Saferstein, 1994). These included using linguistic and gestural components of interaction, which contribute to the shifting of topics and forms of expression in order to meet organizational and personal objectives.

Authority and Agency

Various studies have confronted the complexities of reconciling the opportunities for patients and students to exercise their agency with the persistence of structural influences on routine activities in organization settings (cf. Anspach, 1992; Fisher and Groce, 1990; MacLeod, 1987; Måseide, 1991, 2007; Ogbu, 1991; Swinglehurst, Greenhalgh, and Roberts, 2012; Willis, 1979). In this book, I chose to consider how people make their way through the environment they have inherited as they construct their day-to-day routines by using the available interactional and material resources of a discourse framework to express themselves and produce results that shape those environments.

During the turn of a phrase or a comment on an image, any interaction presents opportunities for misunderstanding, hostility, insult, or domination. Individuals whose communities have endured historical structured inequalities bear the additional burden of working through patterns of interaction that have also been affected by those structured inequalities. However, people often cope with those burdens in order to do all sorts of things. The data analyzed throughout this book show the relationship between routine interpretation activities and the iron cages of bureaucratic and institutional structures. The data analysis also explains how the agency of patients and students, when exercised in particular ways supported by relevant information resources, can change or reproduce the routines and cultures that form those structures.

For example, the historical changes in the social organization of clinical practice, from medical practitioners' homes to neighborhood offices to large institutional settings (Armstrong, 1995), increase a patient's contact with unfamiliar discourse frameworks and confusing grey boxes derived from restrictions on information. Bureaucratized medical treatment presents patients with variations in discourse frameworks that are specific to different medical specializations. Each specialist consulted by a patient expresses a different set of unfamiliar medical terms and descriptions of physiology. This increases patients' difficulty in knowing what questions to ask in order to produce recallable understandings of treatment options. Removing such negative effects of organizational environments and professional cultures on patients' understandings of their medical conditions and treatment options requires recognizing the components of interpretation activities, some of which may enlist structured social inequalities into the routine arrangements of clinical consultations. As shown by the radiology consultation data discussed here, changes to traditional organizational routines and professional cultures can occur that enhance all patients' understandings of medical information relevant to treatment decisions.

In the final lines of *An Essay on Liberation*, Herbert Marcuse, a foundational figure in the development of critical social and political theory, confronts a key concern related to asking questions and developing beneficial understandings. He addresses skeptics, who objected to the vagueness of social activists in regard to conceptualizing the results of changes that would liberate people from constraining social and economic systems. In response, he emphasizes that such liberation will provide people with the opportunity to think about *what* they are going to do to expand and reinforce justice and equality (Marcuse, 1969: 91). However, identifying the components of interpretation activities – and the ways that professional cultures and organizational systems are implicated in those activities – is central to liberation from the frames of reference and patterns of interaction that constrain *how* we think about *what* we are going to do – i.e., how we understand our options to act.

The data analysis presented and discussed here shows how the relationship among interpretation activities, environmental resources, and cultural conventions affects routine activities, which limit or expand understandings of options to make decisions and act on them. Empowering understandings need not be deferred until the completion of transformative changes in social structure. Rather, as changes to routine activities and settings promote understandings, they contribute to changes in social organization, and ultimately to changes in social structures. In that regard, Part Four examines the function and consequences of discourse frameworks, process narratives, and grey boxes in regard to the (re)production of professional culture and its effects on understanding.

PART FOUR
EFFECTS OF PROFESSIONAL CULTURE ON UNDERSTANDING

Part Four shows how examining process narratives, grey boxes, and discourse framework reveals specific interpretation activities that shape the effects of professional cultures on the production of understandings. Comparison of the clinical and educational data reveals paradoxes of intentions and outcomes in explanatory interaction. The effects of professional authority on the production of understanding are constituted by the balance of interpretive contingencies between professionals and their clients. Understanding the components of that balance is key to changing professional culture in ways that improve patients' and students' creation of understandings that they can recall and apply outside of clinics and classrooms. Part Four also considers systemic approaches to improving patients and students' useful understandings of medical and biological information.

13 Culture, Authority, and Understanding – A Balance of Interpretive Contingencies

Chapter Thirteen examines the interactional production of professional culture and its effects on patients' and students' understandings. Biology classroom and radiology consultation examples show a relationship between participants' respective interpretive contingencies and changes to the interactional routines of a professional culture. In the classrooms, the teachers applied standard communication patterns of the professional culture, which limited the interpretive contingencies presented to them by students' digressive questions and comments. In the consultations, the ways that patients' expressed interest in the visual medical information overrode the standard consultation communication patterns, and increased the clinician's interpretive contingencies. This expanded the patient's influence over the content and form of the communication patterns. The resulting changes in consultation communication correlated with the patients' subsequent recall of medical information. The effect of communication patterns on the balance of interpretive contingencies among participants is a key factor in reproducing or changing professional culture, and in the creation of understandings.

Culture, Cognition, and the Organization of Work: Managing Administrative and Creative Contingencies

The discourse frameworks and communication patterns that constitute professional cultures affect how professionals and their clients deal with interpretive contingencies, such as the absence of information, as they attempt to create process narratives. The particular orderliness of interpretation activities, as people routinely repeat them in specific settings for specific purposes, is an aspect of the recognizable and categorizable culture. I approach culture as shared knowledge about sets of practices and social networks that help people to survive and flourish in a particular setting. The interpretation activities applied to interaction and settings create, reproduce, and change culture. The tangible aspects of a culture are not just the mental, linguistic, or material artifacts that result from the interpretation activities that constitute reasoning or creativity. Rather, they include the routine patterns of interpretation activity (e.g., linguistic expression, use of visual or material resources) that result in those artifacts, which are the recallable and expressible process narratives.

Examining the details of interpretation activities is important, because it is during the process of interpreting information that people contend with social, cultural, and environmental resources and constraints to develop the understandings, which underlay the decisions and actions that create or reproduce forms of social organization. The power of clinicians and teachers to expand or restrict patients' and students' understandings stems from their influence on patterns of interaction that produce or resolve interpretive contingencies.

As in other occupations, clinicians and teachers engage in activities that have creative and administrative capacities (cf. Saferstein, 1992, 1994). The creative capacity involves interpretations and inferences that relate newly encountered information with previously encountered information about substantive concerns. The administrative capacity generally involves dealing with the time and coordination constraints of organizational settings in order to arrange a sequence of activities. It also involves organizing and coordinating the expressive architecture that people develop to communicate and interpret information while pursuing a task.

Both the administrative and the creative capacities present participants with interpretive contingencies. For clinicians, creative contingencies include interpreting a patient's symptoms, test results, and comments in order to apply knowledge of medical treatments that would help the patient. Clinicians' administrative contingencies include concern with time constraints and concerns about privacy and liability (cf. Anspach, 1993; Cicourel, 1987; Sarangi & Clarke, 2002). In many medical consultations, the endurance of the clinicians' culture and its effects on patients stem from the routine patterns of interaction that deal with such contingencies – presenting the unintended consequence of limiting patients' access to information that would support recallable understandings of medical information (cf. Entwistle *et al.*, 2006; Fisher, 1986, 1993; Fisher & Groce, 1990; Frankel, 1990; Måseide, 1991; Price *et al.*, 2006; Skea *et al.*, 2004; West, 1984).

In contrast, at the interventional radiology consultations examined in this and earlier chapters, the patient's verbal and gestural expressions of interest in the series of medical images increase the clinician's interpretive contingencies. Those contingencies include explaining the images, interpreting the patient's utterances and movements regarding the images, and providing ancillary information to the patient, while managing the administrative constraints of completing the UFE explanation. This turns the tables in regard to authority over the interpretation activities. As the clinician responds to increased interpretive contingencies, the participants develop communication patterns that incorporate the patient's comments and questions. That communication format becomes a component of both the clinician's and the patient's discourse frameworks. It results in the patient obtaining information relevant to creating recallable process narratives and understanding medical information.

During classroom learning activities, teachers' administrative capacities include formal and informal assessment of students' relative degrees of understanding, as well as managing classroom activities in regard to time constraints and institutional standards. Fitting certain learning activities into blocks of time adequate for completing them involves the teachers and students managing their interpretation activities in particular ways. Teachers' creative capacities involve interpreting students' difficulties and addressing them suitably. However, through their training and classroom experiences, teachers develop routine interpretive frames of reference and explanations to fit common student responses to learning tasks. The forms of expression that biology teachers use to de-emphasize and restrict students' digressive questions are examples of such routine interpretation activities (discussed in Chapters Seven and Ten). The data analyzed in this book show that the standard communication formats developed by teachers during genetic inheritance learning activities treat certain types of questions and comments by students as digressions by restricting or de-emphasizing them. This diminishes the contingencies that students' digressive questions and comments present to teachers. Those forms of expression lead to communication patterns, which efficiently manage creative contingencies in a way that does not increase administrative contingencies. Those patterns help teachers cope with the contingencies of administering the classroom activities in order to complete a lesson plan.

Examining the interpretation activities that express and (re)produce professional culture shows why visual resources contribute to understandings in certain situations, and why, in other situations, they do not. The following section explains how teachers apply particular aspects of professional culture to diminish the interpretive contingencies they encounter.

Reproducing Professional Culture and Its Effects

In regard to the biology teachers' professional culture, the dead hand of Mendel operates through patterns of interaction between teachers and students, which de-emphasize cellular process information and emphasize the conventional grey boxes of nomenclature and tables. As the teachers contend with the contingencies they face when interpreting and formulating responses to students' digressive questions, those patterns of interaction incorporate the conventional Mendelian visual resources.

The students' questions related to cellular processes created interpretive contingencies for T2, including:

- Searching for information that is not part of the conventional set of explanatory resources for teaching Mendelian genetic inheritance,
- Providing a response that addresses the students' concerns without losing the narrative thread begun during the preceding discussion
- Completing the introductory lecture within the available time.

Figure 13.1: Grey Boxes that Reduce the Teacher's Interpretive Contingencies

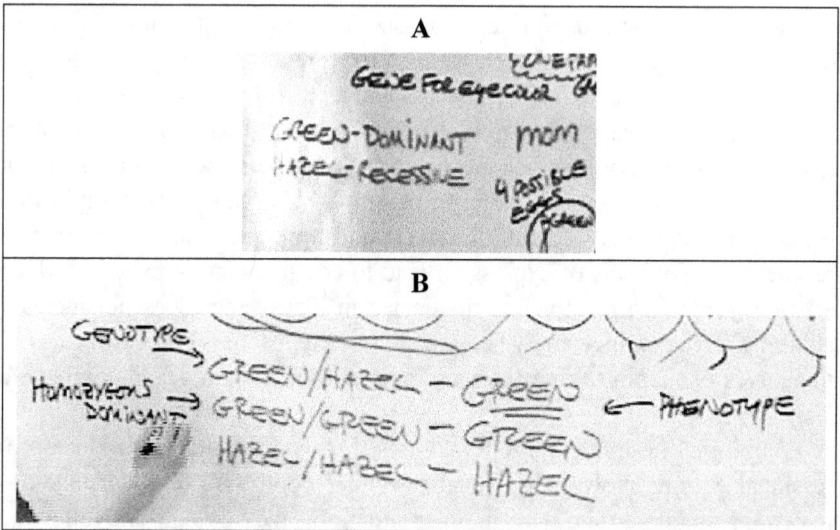

Teachers routinely reduce such contingencies by turning to the conventions of the professional culture. Their patterns of communication reorient students to visual resources, vocabulary, and completing assignments. T2 expresses these conventions through her explanation of the set of visual resources she presents during the lecture introducing trait inheritance. Her verbal explanation and her pointing at the developing table on the whiteboard emphasize the use of Mendelian nomenclature and vocabulary (i.e., types of grey boxes) to link alleles to traits – omitting information about the cellular processes by which alleles operate to produce differences in eye color (Figure 13.1). The writing of the table functions in various ways:

- It provides students with a graphic device that reduces the interpretive contingencies of seeking or recalling cellular process information;
- It clarifies the terms and relationships the teacher wants the students to learn;
- It provides the teacher with a visual resource at which she can point in order to emphasize the descriptive/location frame of reference of the Mendelian explanation of genetic inheritance.

Such interpretation activities and information resources are commonplace in the professional culture of teachers. They contribute to discourse frameworks that present certain information resources and interpretive frames of reference in lieu of others. They also provide students with a model of how those classroom resources and frames of reference apply to the production of process narratives. By emphasizing the conventional visual and linguistic grey boxes, a biology teacher can resolve the contingencies presented to her by students' digressive questions about cellular processes. T2's introductory lecture provides an example. The presence of the tabular arrangement of nomenclature on the whiteboard (Figure 13.1) functioned as an anchor that helped the teacher to resolve the interpretive contingencies presented to her by the students' digressive questions related to cellular genetic processes.

When a student continued a series of digressive questions concerning the nature of recessive genes, the teacher first emphasized the conventional Mendelian visual resources (nomenclature and tables) by pointing at them and adding vocabulary terms (Transcript Extract 13.1, beginning of line 118). This reinforced the restriction of information about cellular genetics, while providing an alternative frame of reference to that of searching for missing information: i.e., applying specific graphical and linguistic grey boxes which function as syntactical placeholders in process narratives concerning genetic inheritance.

Transcript Extract 13.1

113. B31: Ok can someone with hazel eyes give like . . the gene of green eyes whatever? Does it have to have /(?)/

114. T2: /Yes./ And we're gonna look at that because what if right now you're carrying recessive genes recessive alleles that you're not showing because they're recessive /they're being hidden/

115. B31: /Ohh yeah yeah/

116. T2: yeah, they're being hidden by your dominant allele but that allele could end up in a sex cell that would go on to be reproducing. To produce a new offspring. So you could pass on traits to offspring that aren't actually shown or visible in the parent generation and we're /gon/

117. B31: /Could/ that allele be dominant? . If it was recessive in real

118. T2: . It stays recessive but (points to 'hazel/hazel – hazel' on board) just because it's recessive it doesn't mean you'll never see it. It just means the only way you can see it (again points to 'hazel/hazel – hazel' on board) is when you have two copies of it. So if you if if somebody an if two people both donate a recessive allele that they're not showing in their own physical makeup, if those two recessive alleles come together for their child then their child could have a trait that they don't have. And we are gonna come back and look at some of your family traits like the (points to her hair with both hands) widow's peak and (points to her ears with both hands) the earlobes and the (points to her mouth with both hands) tongue rolling that I had you examine. Probably not gonna do it today, but we'll definitely come back to it and you'll be able to see: "Whoa, this trait appeared here but it wasn't in any of my parents. How did that happen?" And you'll be able to understand that that your parents must have been carrying a copy of that allele even though they didn't show it themselves . So we'll get to all that. Alright let's go back to do a little more vocabulary. I'm trying to work in this all this vocabulary that you defined because you have to know what it means to do these problems. What we just listed here guys . (picks up marker and gestures with it toward list of allele pairs and corresponding eye colors) the eye color that's gonna result in the offspring. Is that the genotype or is that the phenotype? . Okay so this is the time when you should look at your definitions an' . when I say that oh that the individual will have hazel eyes or the individual will have green eyes, is that a genotype or a phenotype?

T2 completed her response by deferring further discussion of cellular genetic processes, and emphasizing earlier learning activities (Transcript Extract 13.1, line 118). She elegantly linked the administrative process narratives about completing an assignment with the use of nomenclature and tabulation as grey boxes for the missing cellular process information:

> Alright let's go back to do a little more vocabulary. I'm trying to work in this all this vocabulary that you defined because you have to know what it means to do these problems. What we just listed here guys (picks up marker and gestures with it toward list of allele pairs and corresponding eye colors) the eye color that's gonna result in the offspring. Is that the genotype or is that the phenotype? Okay so this is the time when you should look at your definitions an' when I say that oh that the individual will have hazel eyes or the individual will have green eyes, is that a genotype or a phenotype?

During T2's introductory lecture, the matching of visually expressed nomenclature across generations led to a discourse framework that supported the same interpretive frame of reference that was displayed in T1's classes when students worked with a computer simulation of genetic inheritance – i.e., the matching (and ultimately the tabulation) of traits and locations of traits without concern for the cellular processes affecting development of those traits (Chapters Two, Three, Seven). The biology classroom data show that particular pedagogical approaches do not change the complexity of the students' interpretation activities as they deal with the contingencies related to the omission of cellular process information. T1's approach used a computer simulation in conjunction with a Socratic, discovery pedagogy, while T2's students experienced more traditional transmission based pedagogy, featuring a lecture, pen-on-paper classroom activities, and whiteboard presentations. The data from both teachers' classes show that the constraints of professional and organizational cultures, which emphasized replication of an idealized version of Mendel's foundational research on genetic inheritance, overrode the differences in pedagogy and technology, and resulted in similar interpretation activities by T1's and T2's students. The teachers' professional culture was reproduced as the available explanatory resources and conventional forms of expression constrained students to apply a standard set of interpretation activities in order to cope with the contingencies related to the missing cellular process information.

Turning the Table of Interpretive Contingencies: Reducing Professional Control over a Discourse Framework

Aspects of the communication patterns in the genetics education classroom activities resemble many common situations in which one participant has sought the benefit of another participant's accredited expertise – i.e., experts often focus discussion on agendas constituted by topics and forms of expression that are conventions of their professional culture (cf. Cicourel, 1988; Saferstein, 1994). The biology teachers demonstrated this by persistently presenting limited information and redirecting topics in response to students' questions that digressed from those agendas. Similarly, in many clinical consultations clinicians apply conventions of professional culture in the form of communication patterns that shape the interpretive agenda by de-emphasizing or ignoring patients' follow-up questions (Entwistle *et al.*, 2006; Fisher, 1986, 1993; Fisher and Groce, 1990; Frankel, 1990; Måseide, 1991; Price *et al.*, 2006; Skea *et al.*, 2004; West, 1984). Such patterns of interaction reproduce the professional culture and its effects on patients' understandings of medical information.

The clinical professional culture is very robust, yet the nurse at the radiology consultations avoided its constraints by routinely participating in differing patterns of interaction. Although the radiology clinicians' professional agenda concerning the relevance of particular information was incorporated in the selection and arrangement of the explanatory images, the opportunity for a patient to gesture and orient her gaze and body position to particular features of the screen images affected the topics and detail of clinician's responses (Chapters 1, 9). The resulting discourse framework included the opportunity for a patient to interpret the visual resources in ways that digressed from the clinician's preconceived sequence of images and topics – e.g., by eliciting more information and commenting on the screen images.

How did the radiology patients' digressions produce different results than the students' digressions in the genetics learning activities and the findings of studies of clinical consultations in which patients did not get adequate responses to their questions? During the radiology consultations, the patients' questions, comments, gestures, and movements in relation to the images on the computer screen reduced the clinician's authority over communication patterns and topics. That reduction in the clinician's authority occurred because the patient's comments and questions produced a critical mass of interpretive contingencies that the clinician acted on in order to sustain the type of interaction that constitutes a consultation (i.e., obtaining information from a patient and providing information that contributes to treating the patient's symptoms). The nurse and the patient interacted to attend to the screen images, to develop compatible interpretive frames of reference, and to link information in order to produce coherence in the form of process narratives. For the nurse, those interpretation activities included attending to the patient's gestures and movements in regard to the screen images as well as the patient's verbally expressed questions about and interpretations of the images. Such activities added a layer of contingencies encountered by the nurse, which augmented the customary contingencies of observing and interviewing the patient, reading pertinent records and test results, interpreting the patient's responses to questions, and recalling medical knowledge pertaining to those interpretations. This led to the communication patterns that shifted the balance of interpretive contingencies in favor of the patient.

The nurse's attention to the increased set of interpretive contingencies created interactional space for patients to contribute to a pattern of communication that provided them with the opportunity to influence both the topics of the interpretation activity and the forms of expression used to discuss them. The expansive pattern of communication supplanted the professional culture's customary restrictive communication patterns. In contrast, during the biology classes, the teachers applied restrictive communication patterns, which functioned as a form of professional persistence in response to students' digressions. The teachers guided students' interpretation activities toward customary topics, frames of reference, grey boxes, and process narratives. The biology classroom and radiology consultation examples show how a particular balance of participants' interpretive contingencies determines the endurance or change of cultural conventions.

Challenging the Conventions of Professional Culture: Patients' Responses to Visual Information

During the radiology consultations, the contingencies that the nurse encountered included various forms of expression and styles of interaction that patients presented as they interpreted both the images displayed on the computer screen and the nurse's explanation of the images. The following two examples show how the activities of interpreting the medical images affected the balance of contingencies as the nurse adapted her pattern of expression and use of the images for each patient. This resulted in different patterns of communication that provided different information or different expressions of the same information, leading to each patient expressing understanding of certain details of the UFE procedure. In the first case, the patient, P6, often comments on or asks questions related to the computer images or the nurse's explanations. P6 displays a pattern of overlapping the nurse's comments in order to ask digressive questions. In the second case, the patient, P9, often presents minimal or no response to the images and the nurse's explanations.

In the case of P6, during a 2 minute and 34 second representative segment of the consultation, the patient asks questions that request additional information or shift the topic seven times (Transcript Extracts 13.2, 13.3). This creates interpretive contingencies for the nurse: both creative contingencies (answering the questions in ways that apply her expertise to the patient's questions) and administrative contingencies (maintaining the preconceived sequence and topics of the set of images to ensure that the patient receives complete information about fibroids and UFE that is consistent with other consultations).

Transcript Extract 13.2: Clinician Adapting to Patient Assertiveness (P6)

1. N1: (moves right arm toward screen) This is just kind of a nasty picture depicting all the different places /where you could have a/
2. P6: /Wowwwwwwww/
3. N1: fibroid
4. P6: What is that (pointing at the screen) right at the bottom?
5. N1: (clearing throat) anh hammm (moves arm toward screen) These that are on a stalk .
6. P6: Ss
7. N1: like a mushroom stem
8. P6: /Right/
9. N1: /are called/ 'pedunculated.The this one is so bad that it's actually protruding through the cervix into the vagina.You'd know if you had this one.Your doctor would have done a hysteroscopic re/moval/
10. P6: /(smiling, laughing) Hss/
11. N1: of that one. But it's just a picture letting you know what can happen.
12. P6: mmhmm
13. N1: One of the things on the MRI we're looking for is to make sure you don't have a tiny stalk . on . a fibroid because . theoretically if wee . cut off the blood supply here . that fibroid could fall into the abdomen. (P6 nods) That wouldn't be good.We don't wanna do that so . even if on uh some report from s from some . radiologists they'll say that it's um pedunculated (N1 points at screen) like a lot of 'em will call this pedunculated where whereas we call it . exophytic just . (gesturing with hands) going towards the outside but it's so connected to the uterus that it wouldn't . do that it would

Transcript Extract 13.2 (continued)

just shrink back down into the (pointing at screen) (P6 nods) This one probably would too.
14. P6: Hmm/m/
15. N1: /We/'ve never really ssseen . /one/
16. P6: /Detach/ (nodding).
17. N1: detach right but uhm it's just what /all the possibilities/
18. P6: /So when they say/ that fibroids . are . on the . uterine wall externally
19. N1: Exter/nally (nodding)/
20. P6: /do you have/ one in here or no?
21. N1: (leans forward and points at a portion of the screen) That's what this is. This is /(moves hand around part of screen image)/
22. P6: /Oh/ /hh and you just . and you can (P6 points at screen) scrape that/
23. N1: /external. This's called a . This is internal/
24. P6: one off right?
25. N1: This? (moves arm to point at another area of the screen)
26. P6: Yeah.
27. N1: (leaning back in chair) Well . if your gynecologist went in . laparoscopically, (moves arm toward screen) she could cut into the muscle and take that out (P6 nods). The problem being with a lot of fibroids is they can't always get every cell. They can't tell
28. P6: mmhmm
29. N1: and so then the chances of them regrowing is about 45 percent but also that's dependent on your age. So, (clearing throat) hm hhmmmm, so no /they don't/
30. P6: /What's/ dependent on their age? Whether they're gonna regrow?
31. N1: Th the old . fibroids take years to grow so the older you are the less years before menopause you have to grow a new fibroid.
32. P6: (nodding) Okay
33. N1: (nodding) So if you have a 28 year old and you do a myomectomy they really have a 48 percen 45 percent ch/ance of regr/
34. P6: /chance of coming back/ (nodding).
35. N1: owth. . Whereas (gestures with hand) if you're in your 40's /prob'ly/
36. P6: /hmm/
37. N1: drops to more like 10 percent.
38. P6: (nodding) Mm okay.

In this segment of the consultation, the nurse, N1, adapts her explanation to the patient's question about a drawing displayed on the computer screen image. The nurse begins to explain the cross-section of a uterus containing various types of fibroid tumors (Transcript Extract 13.2, lines 1–3). P6 asks a question and points to a particular tumor in the drawing (Transcript Extract 13.2, line 4):

1. N1: (moves right arm toward screen) This is just kind of a nasty picture depicting all the different places /where you could have a/
2. P6: /Wowwwwwwww/
3. N1: fibroid
4. P6: What is that (pointing at the screen) right at the bottom?

The nurse provides an extended explanation related to the part of the drawing at which P6 pointed (Transcript Extract 13.2, lines 5–17). The nurse discusses types and locations of tumors on stalks (Transcript Extract 13.2, lines 5, 7, 9, 11, 13, 15). As the nurse says, 'We've never really ssseen one detach right but uhm it's just what all the possibilities' (Transcript Extract 13.2, lines 15, 17), P6 overlaps 'all of the possibilities', asking, 'So when they say that fibroids are on the uterine wall externally' (Transcript Extract 13.2, line 18). P6 overlaps the nurse's utterance to begin a question that focuses on a particular type of fibroid tumor:

17. N1: detach right but uhm it's just what all the /possibilities/
18. P6: /So when they say/ that fibroids . are . on the . uterine wall externally
19. N1: Exter/nally (nodding)/
20. P6: /do you/ have one in here or no?
21. N1: (leans forward and points at a portion of the screen) That's what this is. This is /(moves hand around part of screen image)/
22. P6: /Oh/ /hh and you just . and you can (P6 points at screen) scrape that/
23. N1: /external. This's called a . this is internal/
24. P6: one off right?
25. N1: This? (moves arm to point at another area of the screen)
26. P6: Yeah.

When the nurse acknowledges attention to the patient's question by repeating P6's use of the word, 'externally', P6 again expresses an overlapping utterance, ‘do you have one in here or no?’ as she asks if any of the tumors in the computer image would be the type she just referred to as ‘on the uterine wall externally’ (Transcript Extract 13.2, lines 18, 19). The nurse answers P6’s question by pointing at one of the tumors in the computer image, and referring to it as ‘external’ (Transcript Extract 13.2, lines 21, 23).

The ensuing interaction shows the nurse continuing to cope with interpretive contingencies introduced by the patient’s digressive questions (Transcript Extract 13.2, lines 21–24). The nurse begins to expand on the topic, types of fibroid tumors, by providing a comparative example. She points at a section of the screen image displaying a variety of tumors, and says, ‘That’s what this is. This is’. P6 acknowledges the nurse’s comment by beginning to say ‘ohhh,’ before the nurse completes her verbal description of the comparison. P6 continues to speak, introducing the topic, treatment of such tumors (‘and you just and you can scrape that’), at the same time that the nurse completes her explanation of tumors presented by the screen image (‘This is external. This’s called a this is internal’), which pertains to the topic, description of the types of tumors. After the nurse says, ‘internal’, P6 completes her question, adding ‘one off right?’ to her preceding utterance, ‘you can just scrape that’. This is another example of the patient’s pattern of interjecting questions at the pace of her own comprehension or interest, rather than trying to synchronize her comments with the nurse’s completion of descriptions or explanations. The presence of the screen images supports this pattern.

At this point in the discussion of the drawing of different types of fibroid tumors, P6 has presented the nurse with the interpretive contingency of choosing to finish her own topic or cut it short in order to address P6’s topic shift. The patient also presents the nurse with the contingency of interpreting a question while talking. The nurse’s clarification request, ‘This?’, accompanied by pointing at the picture of a tumor, shows her using the screen image to reduce those interpretive contingencies (Transcript Extract 13.2, line 25). P6’s response, ‘Yeah’, verifies the nurse’s candidate interpretation of the overlapping topic shift (Transcript Extract 13.2, line 26).

The nurse then provides a description that expands on the patient’s question about scraping off a particular type of fibroid tumor (Transcript Extract 13.2, line 27):

> Well if your gynecologist went in laparoscopically, (moves arm toward screen) she could cut into the muscle and take that out (P6 nods). The problem being with a lot of fibroids is they can’t always get every cell. They can’t tell.

This is an example of the nurse coping with the creative contingencies of recalling and expressing ancillary information, which was not included in her routine explanation of the sequence of images to other patients. The patient applies the ancillary information to resolve the interpretive contingency of creating a process narrative that compares UFE to other procedures for treating fibroid tumors. In addition to describing a medical procedure, the nurse's answer expresses a difference between UFE and a surgical procedure (myomectomy). The latter requires surgical removal of each symptomatic fibroid tumor ('if your gynecologist went in laparoscopically, she could cut into the muscle and take that out'), and has the potential problem of regrowth, because 'they can't always get every cell' (Transcript Extract 13.2, line 27). P6 acknowledges the nurse's explanation, saying, 'mmhmm', and the nurse verbally presents information about regrowth of tumors after surgical removal (Transcript Extract 13.2, lines 28, 29):

> and so then the chances of them regrowing is about 45 percent but also that's dependent on your age.

That information was not included in the image displayed on the screen at the time, although information about regrowth of fibroid tumors after UFE is included later in the presentation as a list of the results of UFE.

After expressing the information about re-growth of fibroids following a myomectomy, the nurse refers to the topic of P6's preceding question ('you just and you can scrape that one off right?' Transcript Extract 13.2, lines 22, 24), by saying, 'so no they don't', indicating that due the chance of tumors regrowing, clinicians do not just scrape off the type of tumor that P6 pointed toward in the computer image (line 29). However, rather than the consultation proceeding with a clinician-directed explanation of the images in the sequence they had been arranged, P6 again presents the nurse with interpretive contingencies by asking another question, which overlaps the nurse's summary conclusion: 'What's dependent on my age? Whether they're gonna regrow?' (Transcript Extract 13.2, line 30).

P6's request for more information about the relation of age to the potential regrowth of fibroid tumors after myomectomy is relevant to her decision about what procedure to select for treatment. The nurse's first mention of age was a qualification concerning the 45% chance of fibroid tumors regrowing after a myomectomy that did not remove every tumor cell (Transcript Extract 13.2, lines 27, 29). The nurse's utterance did not specify whether the 45% chance of regrowth was related to a specific age that was younger, older, or the same as that of P6 ('so then the chances of them regrowing is about 45 percent but also that's dependent on your age', Transcript Extract 13.2, line 29). The patient's questions, 'What's dependent on my age? Whether they're gonna regrow?' (Transcript Extract 13.2, line 30), seek the missing information, which would be useful for creating a recallable process narrative related to the efficacy of surgical removal of fibroid tumors as a treatment. In response to P6's questions, the nurse expresses process narratives detailing how regrowth after surgical removal correlates with age:

> Th the old fibroids take years to grow so the older you are the less years before menopause you have to grow a new fibroid. (Transcript Extract 13.2, line 31)
>
> So if you have a 28 year old and you do a myomectomy they really have a 48 percen 45 percent chance of regrowth. Whereas (gestures with hand) if you're in your 40s prob'ly drops to more like 10 percent. (Transcript Extract 13.2, lines 33, 35, 37)

This provides information that resolves the patient's interpretive contingency related to understanding how age would affect her treatment decision.

The nurse did not postpone dealing with P6's question until the pertinent images would appear. Instead, she immediately responded verbally to P6's question. Rather than de-emphasizing digressions as the biology teachers did, the nurse used the computer images to provide detailed explanations. The clinician provided information, but the patient decided if it was adequate, and, if it was not, continued to interview the clinician. This reversed the discursive roles of patients and clinicians that are common in many consultations.

At this point the patient is setting the topics of discussion. The pattern of expression she has prompted differs from the pattern often noted in medical consultations (cf. Entwistle *et al.*, 2006; Fisher, 1983; Fisher and Groce, 1990; Frankel, 1990; Måseide, 1991; Mishler, 1984; Price *et al.*, 2006; Skea *et al.*, 2004; West, 1984). The patient rather than the clinician shifts topics by overlapping or ignoring utterances. For example, after P6 had established a pattern of overlapping the nurse's explanations when asking questions about the screen images (e.g., Transcript Extract 13.2, lines 17–18, 29–30), the nurse began to expect P6's overlaps. At one point the nurse moved her hand to advance to a different image, but hesitated and pulled her arm away from the computer's mouse pad before P6 gestured or said anything (Transcript Extract 13.3, line 39). This functioned as an anticipation of P6 overlapping or shifting the topic – which is what P6 proceeded to do ('And what after the procedure what's. I read somethinn this weekend that said they only impact their size by 20 percent. Is that accurate?' Transcript Extract 13.3, line 40). The visual information provided an arena for the patient to apply her assertive pattern of digressing from the nurse's topics to ask questions.

During this segment of the consultation, P6 initiated ten linguistic overlaps of the nurse's explanations (Transcript Extracts 13.2 and 13.3, lines 2, 16, 18, 20, 22, 30, 34, 44, 46, 48). The nurse initiated only four overlaps of P6's utterances (Transcript Extracts 13.2 and 13.3, lines 9, 23, 45, 63). The patient's frequent overlapping comments and questions influenced both the topics of discussion and how the nurse presented the visual information. Six of the seven times that P6 shifted the topic of discussion or requested more information she initiated an overlap of the nurse's explanation (Transcript Extracts 13.2 and 13.3, lines 18, 20, 22, 30, 40, 44).

The verbal overlaps of the nurse's topics and explanations by P6 presented the nurse with interpretive contingencies such as:

- Considering whether the initial topic has been adequately explained,
- Considering how to transition to the new topic introduced by the patient,
- Recalling relevant process narratives,
- Formulating a useful explanation.

For example, when the nurse explained a topic previously introduced by P6, the growth or regrowth of fibroid tumors after treatment, P6 presented the comment and question that introduced another topic, i.e., reduction in the size of uterine fibroid tumors after UFE ('I read somethinn . this weekend that said they only impact their size by 20 percent. Is that accurate?') (Transcript Extract 13.3, lines 39, 40). The nurse responded to the question about the accuracy of the information that P6 had read by saying 'no' and 'not really' to indicate that it was not accurate (Transcript Extract 13.3, lines 41, 43). Rather than accepting 'not really' as an end to the discussion of that topic, P6 pressed N1 for more information with another overlapping utterance, 'So what what is the extent of the' (Transcript Extract 13.3, line 44).

Responding to P6's utterance, the nurse began a verbal explanation, 'Generally we're seeing' (Transcript Extract 13.3, line 45), and then decided to advance the computer image to provide visual information, saying 'I'm gonna show you a picture too' (lines 45, 47). Advancing to the next image was a response that provided the nurse with resources to reduce the interpretive contingencies presented by P6's topic shifting questions and comments. The increase in the clinician's interpretive contingencies benefited the patient by focusing the clinician's attention and actions on the patient's immediate concerns, rather than the routine administrative tasks of completing a customary explanation while considering time constraints.

Transcript Extract 13.3

39. N1: Or . the the chances of them growing to the point where it's causing you problems again is . probably even less than that. (moves hand toward computer as if to advance image, but moves it back quickly before advancing the image) Okay /(??)/
40. P6: /And/ what . after the procedure what's. I read somethinn . this weekend that said they only impact their size by 20 percent. Is that accurate?
41. N1: (Shaking her head) No.
42. P6: Okay
43. N1: Not /really/
44. P6: /So what/ what is the extent o/f the/
45. N1: /Generally/ we're seeing . (points right index finger toward screen and moves are toward computer) I'm gonna show y/ou/
46. P6: /Okay/
47. N1: a picture too (P6 looks at the screen and leans toward it) (N1 clicks the mouse twice. Image goes past the one N1 wants, advancing to an image of an MRI of the abdomen with fibroids) Hhho (N1 clicks on mouse once to go back to an image showing two drawings of a uterus with fibroids before and after UFE) (N1 moves arm toward screen) This (leans forward moves arm around screen) . is . let's say this is what the size /of your uterus is now/
48. P6: /Oh wow look at your bladder/ (leaning forward to look at screen).
49. N1: (pointing at image on screen) and so you can see how it impacts the tail/bone here/
50. P6: /mmhmm/
51. N1: (pointing at image on screen) and your bowel r/uns/
52. P6: /mmm/
53. N1: between here and here so you can see /why/
54. P6: /(nods and smiles; looks at N1) pff/
55. N1: um there would be that feeling of fullness or having (P6 nods head) constipation actually having constipation. Pelvic floor pressure. Look at that poor bladder.
56. P6: (exhales) Phhhh
57. N1: (clears throat) Excuse me.
58. P6: (P6 turns toward husband behind N1) (????)
/(P6 laughs)/

Transcript Extract 13.3 (continued)

59. N1: /So (turns toward P6's husband) Frequent urination (N1 turns toward screen)/(P6 turns toward screen) urgency (P6 smiles, turns toward husband, then back toward screen) There are reasons for that.
60. P6: (chuckles)
61. N1: So we we
62. P6: (moves right hand toward screen, pointing index finger and moving it around the drawing) Woo/oww. Look at the difference!/
63. N1: /talk about (looks at P6) 50%. (P6 looks at N1)/ Basically 50% shrinkage. Most women get more than that (P6 nods) . but usually with 50% shrinkage, 90% of the – 90% of the patients have relief of 90% of their symptoms.
64. P6: /(??) (Nods and looks toward screen)/
65. N1: /That's a lot of s . /percentages there, but . does that make sense to you? (points at screen) So it allows your bladder to expand again, and it – look at how much room it gives back to the belly.
66. P6: Wooow. /(looks toward husband)/
67. N1: /So that's that's what we're (N1 moves right hand toward computer) looking at./ (moves hand away from computer) Did that answer that question? (P6 Nods) (N1 moves right hand toward computer) Okay. (N1 advances image)

In the context of the patient's questioning, the presence of the visual information created even more interpretive contingencies for the clinician, i.e.:

- Recalling and expressing information prompted by the patient's comments and questions related to the image on the screen
- Recalling other images that might be pertinent
- Deciding whether advancing or reversing to another image would provide useful information.

In clinical consultations, some patients express assertive styles of interaction similar to that of P6, which challenge the professional culture's common communication patterns of questions and comments initiated by the clinician (cf. Roberts, Moss, Wass, Sarangi, and Jones, 2005: 272–273). In many consultations, when a patient digresses from the clinician's topic, the clinician can resort to the professional culture's routine verbal communication patterns that restrict the agenda of topics about which a patient might inquire (cf. Fisher and Groce, 1990; Price *et al.*, 2006; Skea *et al.*, 2004). However, in the radiology consultations featuring the interactive discussion of images, the clinicians encountered additional interpretive contingencies presented by a patient's verbal and gestural references related to visual information. This resulted in patterns of interaction that supported the patient's understanding of medical information.

Coping with Minimal Patient Responses: Augmenting Explanations

A UFE consultation with another patient, P9, presents a different pattern of interaction in which the patient's responses to the visual information also created interpretive contingencies for the clinician. This pattern also diverged from that noted by many studies. Although P9's verbal and nonverbal responses to the visual information were more subtle and vague than those of P6, they also presented interpretive contingencies that affected how the nurse administered both the consultation interaction and the use of the medical images.

For instance, during one part of P9's consultation, the nurse explained images showing diagrams of a catheter delivering the embolizing agent to fibroid tumors and radiological images showing the blood flow in uterine arteries before and after UFE (Transcript Extract 13.4, 13.5). Nineteen times during this two-minute segment, P9 responded to the nurse with a brief utterance suggesting acknowledgment of what the nurse had just said. Seven of these acknowledgements were overlaps that did not shift the nurse's topic or seek additional information. P9 asked one question that prompted the nurse to shift a topic (Transcript Extract 13.4, lines 4–8). During the nurse's explanation of the screen images, P9 sometimes leaned toward the computer and looked at the screen while providing brief verbal responses, transcribed as variations of 'mm' or 'mmhmm' (Transcript Extract 13.4, lines 10, 12, 14, 18, 28, 32). She nodded during most of her brief utterances (Transcript Extract 13.4, lines 14, 16, 18, 20, 22, 28, 30, 32). Only once during this segment of the consultation did P9 initiate an overlap of the nurse's utterance that prompted the nurse to clarify an explanation (Transcript Extract 13.4, lines 24–32).

Transcript Extract 13.4: Clinician Adapting to Patient's Minimal Verbal Responses (P9)

[Bold text = P9's brief ambiguous utterances; shading = P9's utterances that prompt N1's overlapping utterances]

1. N1: (Advances to photo of catheter, points toward screen) That's the size of (P9 leans toward screen) the catheter we use.
2. P9: And that's gonna be uh the pr when the procedure um . it's (gesturing with hand toward her abdomen) all um

Transcript Extract 13.4 (continued)

3. N1: (Looking at P9, advances to the next image and points at the screen showing a diagram of the uterus with fibroids and a catheter injecting beads into the uterine arteries) (P9 leans forward to look at screen). That's (N1 moves arm toward screen) what goes into the artery here and then (N1 moves arm in circular motion near screen) they thread it around.
4. P9: **Okay**. (Leans back in chair) (N1 reverses the presentation to the previous image of the catheter). How long takes tuh . /proced/
5. N1: /To do this?/
6. P9: ure?
7. N1: About an hour and a half usually.
8. P9: **Wow**. Hour and a half. (nods)
9. N1: Mmhmm (Advances presentation to a diagram of beads flowing through the uterine artery to smaller vessels and a fibroid) So this is just a close up
10. P9: (Leans in close to screen) **Mmhm**
11. N1: (pointing at screen) of that so when we go in the uterine artery then those little beads go in (pointing at screen)
12. P9: **Mmhhm.**
13. N1: to those blood vessels and they just get (pushes on one hand with the other) stuck there at the fibroid
14. P9: **Hm** (nodding) I see.
15. N1: and so then the fibroid (gesturing with hands) doesn't get the blood supply any/more so it /
16. P9: /**Oh**/ (nodding)
17. N1: starves
18. P9: **Mm** (nodding)
19. N1: and it shrinks (clasps hands together).
20. P9: **Hm** (nodding) .... (Leans back in chair) Hm.
21. N1: But the uterus the rest of the uterus gets blood supply (making a circular gesture with arms in front of her waist) from the re/st of the/
22. P9: /**Uhhmm** (nods)/
23. N1: abdomen so it's it/'s okay/
24. P9: /So a/ll (pointing at screen) of fibroids gonna be (gestures by partially closing left hand) sh/rink/
25. N1: /Treated/. (Nodding in agreement) Mmhhm. All of 'em are /treated./
26. P9: /(?okay? or ?I get it?)/

Transcript Extract 13.4 (continued)

27. N1: Doesn't matter how many /or/
28. P9: /(nodding) **mmhmm**/
29. N1: what size.
30. P9: (nodding) **Okay**.
31. N1: or where they're at.
32. P9: (nodding) **Mmhhm**.

P9's minimal response to the visual and verbal information presented the nurse with the contingencies of assessing P9's comprehension and then responding in order to clarify the explanation. An example occurred when P9 expressed a rare overlapping utterance as the nurse described the result of embolization (Transcript Extract 13.4):

15. N1: and so then the fibroid (gesturing with hands) doesn't get the blood supply any/more so it /
16. P9: /**Oh**/ (nodding)
17. N1: starves
18. P9: **Mm** (nodding)
19. N1: and it shrinks (clasps hands together).
20. P9: Hm (nodding) .... (Leans back in chair) Hm.

Following P6's overlapping, 'Oh', the nurse added to 'so it' by saying 'starves' (Transcript Extract 13.4, lines 15–17), and then, after P9 said 'mm' and nodded, the nurse added 'and it shrinks', describing how embolization affects fibroid tumors (Transcript Extract 13.4, lines 18, 19).

However, the brief utterances do not explicitly communicate understanding of the images. P9's variations on 'mmhhm' might suggest acknowledgment of understanding of the nurse's utterances and the images, or they might simply be a display of accountability showing participation in a conversation (cf. McDermott *et al.*, 1978). P9's ambiguous verbal or gestural responses to the combination of images and verbal explanations presented the nurse with additional information to interpret. That contingency resulted from the discussion of images.

Another type of interpretive contingency emerged when the nurse used the images to respond to the patient's utterances and gestures. Twice, the nurse dealt with the contingencies she encountered when P9 expressed ambiguous or minimal comments by advancing to images out of their usual sequence in order to augment verbal explanations. In the first example, P9 presented a comment and gesture (Transcript Extract 13.4. line 2) to which the nurse responded by temporarily advancing to the next computer image in order to elaborate on the preceding images and verbal explanation that had described how a catheter is threaded through the arteries in order to deposit the embolizing agent and stop blood supply to the fibroid tumors in order to shrink all of them:

1. N1: (Advances to photo of catheter, points toward screen) That's the size of (P9 leans toward screen) the catheter we use.
2. P9: And that's gonna be uh the pr when the procedure um . it's (gesturing with hand toward her abdomen) all um
3. N1: (Looking at P9, advances to the next image and points at the screen showing a diagram of the uterus with fibroids and a catheter injecting beads into the uterine arteries) (P9 leans forward to look at screen). That's (N1 moves arm toward screen) what goes into the artery here and then (N1 moves arm in circular motion near screen) they thread it around.
4. [partial]. P9: Okay. (Leans back in chair) (N1 reverses the presentation to the previous image of the catheter).

P9's body movement, comment, and gesture were ambiguous, but their form and inflection combined to suggest a clarification request (Transcript Extract 13.4, lines 1, 2). In relation to the nurse's preceding explanation and the image on the computer screen, P9's gesture of pointing at her abdomen after saying 'that's gonna be', can be interpreted as an attempt to express her interpretation of the preceding visual and verbal information in order to clarify or verify it. The nurse did treat P9's movement toward the screen, comment, and gesture as a request for clarification. The nurse coped with that interpretive contingency by using the sequence of computer images as the basis for recapitulating her preceding explanation of embolization. In order to reiterate and clarify her explanation of how uterine artery embolization affects the blood supply to the fibroid tumors and shrinks them, the nurse advanced the computer to another screen image. She then pointed at parts of the image while explaining it. P9 said, 'Okay', and leaned back in her chair, moving away from the screen image (Transcript Extract 13.4, line 4). Then the nurse returned to the preceding image (Transcript Extract 13.4, line 4). By returning to her customary sequence of images and explanations after the second explanation, she treated P9's 'okay' and leaning back in the chair as indications of comprehension.

In the second example of the nurse advancing images to cope with increased interpretive contingencies (Transcript Extract 13.5, lines 27–50), P9 had expressed a sequence of brief variations of 'mmhmm', while showing interest in the screen image by leaning toward it. She advanced through the sequence of images to an x-ray, which presented, in a different format, information the earlier diagram had displayed (Transcript Extract 13.4, line 3). She explained the image using some different words and gestures than she had before. (Transcript Extract 13.4, line 3). When P9 said, 'Ohhh I see', the nurse returned to the earlier image and continued the prepared sequence of topics (Transcript Extract 13.5, lines 50, 51, discussed in more detail below).

P9's brief utterances and movements suggest her attention to key aspects of the nurse's explanation, but they are ambiguous as indications of understanding. This presents the nurse with the contingencies of quickly considering whether and how to interpret the combination of screen images and patient's utterances/gestures/movements in order to respond appropriately. The nurse's combination of explanatory utterances, advancing the images, and image-related gestures displays the increased interpretive contingencies of attending to the patient's use of the visual information.

At the radiology consultations, although a patient's responses to the visual information increased the clinician's interpretive contingencies, the presence of the medical images also provided the clinician with a resource for resolving those contingencies. The nurse responded to P9's movements in the same way that she had responded to P6's overlapping questions – by providing more information verbally and changing the screen images. The images functioned as external memory for the nurse – i.e., as a convenient set of information relevant to the general purpose of explaining UFE, and as a trigger for recalling process narratives that expanded on and clarified the pictures and text.

During 11 consultations in which the nurse participated, she displayed a pattern of augmenting preceding explanations in response to patients' digressive questions and their movements or gestures related to the screen images. The nurse adapted the form of her explanations to the particulars of a patient's utterances and actions. At P9's consultation, the nurse responded to the increased interpretive contingencies presented by the patient's minimal or ambiguous responses by using the screen images as an anchor for the interaction. She expressed a set of process narratives that combined utterances and gestures related to the images of the embolization procedure and its effects:

- *So this is just a close up (pointing at screen) of that* (Transcript Extract 13.4, line 9)
- *so when we go in the uterine artery then those little beads go in (pointing at screen) to those blood vessels* (Transcript Extract 13.4, lines 11, 13)
- *and they just get (pushes on one hand with the other) stuck there at the fibroid* (Transcript Extract 13.4, line 13)

- *and so then the fibroid (gesturing with hands) doesn't get the blood supply anymore so it starves and it shrinks (clasps hands together)* (Transcript Extract 13.4, lines 15, 17, 19)
- *But the uterus the rest of the uterus gets blood supply (makes a circular gesture with arms in front of her waist) from the rest of the abdomen so it's it's okay* (Transcript Extract 13.4, lines 21, 23).

The nurse presented types of verbal and gestural details that depended on the presence of and mutual attention to the medical images.

Increasing the Clinician's Administrative Contingencies

The shared use of visual, gestural, and verbal forms of expression to explain and clarify medical information leads to a discourse framework that features the patient influencing the agenda of topics and forms of expression by presenting the clinician with interpretive contingencies that are absent from many customary medical consultations. One of these contingencies involves finding ways to incorporate the administrative concerns of the professional culture when patients use their increased authority over the conversational agenda to express interpretations of medical information that diverge from those of the clinician.

An example occurred after the nurse had advanced the screen image and gestured while explaining how UFE shrinks a fibroid tumor (Transcript Extract 13.4):

24. P9: /So a/ll (pointing at screen) of fibroids gonna be (gestures by partially closing left hand) sh/rink/
25. N1: /Treated/. (Nodding in agreement) Mmhhm. All of 'em are /treated./

P9 expresses her understanding by saying, 'So all of fibroids gonna be shrink' (Transcript Extract 13.4, line 24). As P9 utters the 'sh' sound in 'shrink', the nurse immediately responds by saying 'treated' (line 25), overlapping P9's completion of the word 'shrink'. The nurse then repeats the word, 'treated', as she says, 'all of 'em are treated'. When the nurse had said 'and it shrinks' a few seconds earlier (Transcript Extract 13.4, line 19), she was verbally and gesturally explaining a heuristic diagram on the screen, a drawing which showed one fibroid being treated with the embolizing agent. In the context of concerns with consistency and accuracy that are part of the professional culture, P9's subsequent gesture and utterance expressing 'shrink' presented the nurse with the additional contingency of expressing a difference between 'shrink' and 'treat'.

The nurse's emphasis on 'treated' rather than 'shrink' shows two of the administrative interpretive contingencies presented to a clinician by a patient's use of medical terminology when responding to the visual information: 1) concern with the patient's expectations about treatments, 2) concern with risk management (cf. Sarangi and Clarke, 2002). The distinction between 'treats' and 'shrinks' relates to information that the nurse and the images presented at various points in the consultation:

- A single UFE procedure treats all of the patient's fibroid tumors by eliminating their blood supply.
- Statistics about patients treated with UFE indicate that this will often shrink them.
- However, UFE may not shrink all of the fibroids or it may not shrink them enough to relieve symptoms.[39]

The nurse's emphasis on 'treated' relates to specificity and accuracy in regard to the patient's understanding and decision-making. It manages the risk of a patient being misinformed about the outcome of a medical procedure. The nurse's insertion of the distinction between 'treat' and 'shrink' deals with administrative contingencies that are consequences of P9's particular interpretations of and responses to the visual, gestural, and verbal information of the consultation.

A Balance of Interpretive Contingencies that Favors the Patient

The next example shows how the nurse's increased interpretive contingencies and her use of the images and related gestures to cope with them reduced the patient's interpretive contingencies. The nurse explained radiological images showing the uterus, fibroids, and uterine arteries before and after a UFE procedure. The content of the images is not obvious unless someone has been trained to interpret them. During the UFE consultations the nurse explained certain aspects of the images, and monitored patients' responses in regard to their understanding. P9's responses presented the nurse with the interpretive contingencies of assessing if P9's brief ambiguous comments, movements, and gestures indicated understanding, and, if they did not, then elaborating on the explanation to prompt expressions of understanding.

When P9 leaned close to the screen image (e.g., Transcript Extract 13.5, lines 34, 35), she did not express the verbal information showing comprehension of the explanation of UFE that more talkative patients expressed during the radiology consultations (e.g., P6's assertive verbal responses). The nurse again encountered the contingencies of assessing the combination of P9's brief utterances, movements toward the screen, and visual information displayed on the screen (Transcript Extract 13.5). Consequently, the nurse elaborated on the explanation of embolization by advancing to images out of their ordinary sequence, and saying, 'I wanna (pointing at screen) show you this picture now' (Transcript Extract 13.5, line 43). In addition to presenting the patient with more information detailing the embolization procedure, this also provided the nurse with the opportunity to obtain more responses from P9 that would suggest comprehension (Transcript Extract 13.5, lines 43–51).

The nurse began to augment her explanation by advancing the presentation past the next image to an image containing two x-rays placed side-by-side, showing details of uterine arteries before and after an embolization procedure (Transcript Extract 13.5, line 43). In the x-ray made prior to the placement of the embolizing agent, the uterine arteries appear as prominent dark lines. In the x-ray taken after the embolization, those lines do not appear. The nurse points at the x-ray showing the darkened uterine arteries prior to the placement of the embolizing agent as she says, 'So this side there's still the uterine arteries'. Then she points at the other x-ray, saying, 'and this is afterwards. They're gone' (Transcript Extract 13.5, lines 43, 45). In conjunction with the visual and gestural information, the nurse's utterances present the process narratives,

> *Prior to the catheter that is threaded through an artery depositing the embolizing agent, blood flows through the uterine arteries to supply the uterine fibroid tumors*
>
> *After the catheter is threaded through an artery to deposit the embolizing agent, no blood flows through the uterine arteries, stopping the supply to the uterine fibroid tumors.*

P9 again acknowledges this explanation with brief vague responses, variations of 'mm' (Transcript Extract 13.5, lines 44, 46, 48).

Transcript Extract 13.5 [Bold text = P9's brief ambiguous utterances]

33. N1: (Looks at P9, nods, advances to image showing before and after embolization x-rays of uterine arteries) So this is what we're looking at during the procedure.

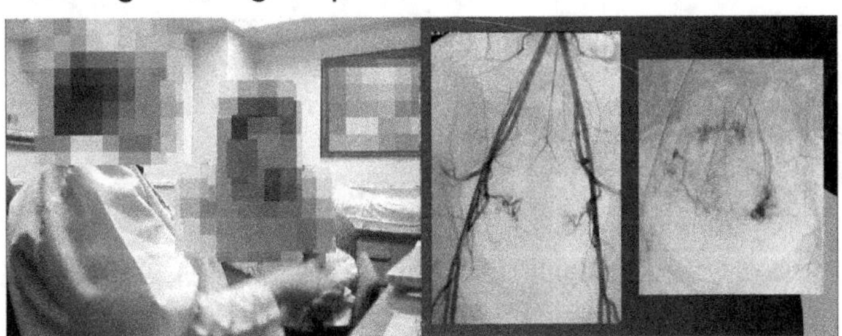

34. P9: (Leans forward to look at screen) **Mmh/hm/**
35. N1: /So/ (Moves arm to different parts of screen image as she speaks)

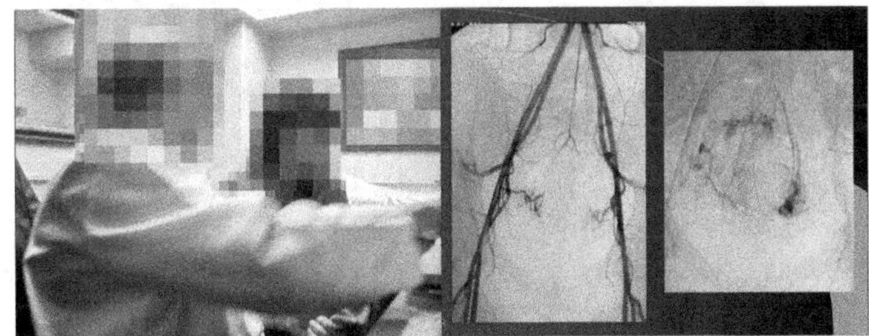

they go into those (P9 leans closer to screen)

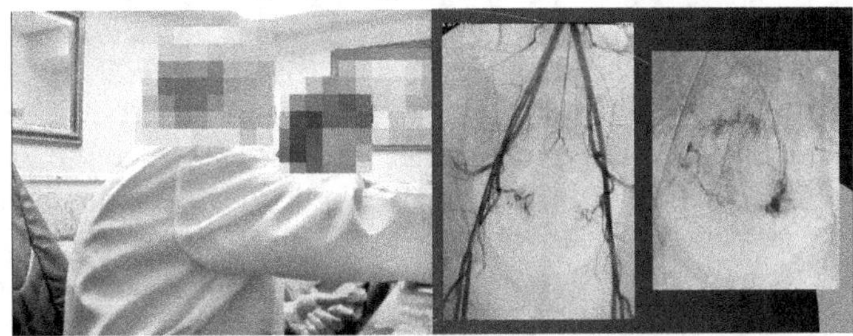

arteries . come down here. These are the uterine arteries here. So he's threads the catheter in there . puts the beads in .

36. P9: **Mmhhm.**
37. N1: comes back around . puts the catheter in here .
38. P9: **Mmhm**
39. N1: puts the beads in . then they take the catheter out.

Transcript Extract 13.5 (continued)

40. P9: **Hm**
41. N1: And so uh (advancing to image of embolizing agent in syringe) whoops (reverses to previous image of uterine arteries, advances again to photo of embolizing agent in syringe). Where'd it go? (mouse clicks; a small inset of a group of embolizing agent particles appears next to the syringe photo).
42. P9: Oh that's some . . /beads./
43. N1: /I'm gonna/ (Briefly advances to a drawing of a single enlarged fibroid with arteries, skips it and advances to next image containing two x-rays showing pre- and post-embolization details of uterine arteries) I wanna (pointing at screen) show you this picture now. So (pointing at screen) this side there's . still the uterine arte/ries and/

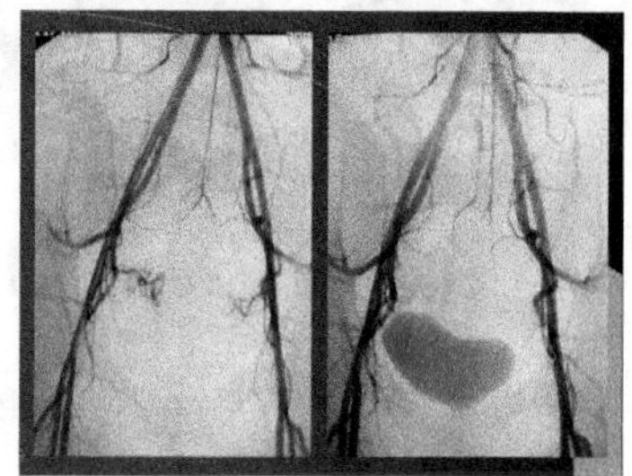

44. P9: /**Mmhhm**/.
45. N1: this is afterwards. They're gone. (looking directly at P9) . .
46. P9: (P9 nods head) **Mm**
47. N1: That's what we're trying . so we're not looking (looks at P9, gestures with hands apart) at your fibroids during the procedure
48. P9: **Mmhm**
49. N1: we're looking at the (brings hands together) blood sup/ply to it./
50. P9: /Ohhh/ I see. (Leans back in chair) . . /**Hmm**/.
51. N1: /Okay/ (Uses computer mouse to return to the earlier image showing two x-rays of the uterine arteries before and after insertion of the embolizing agent.) we'll go back here. So . . .

The nurse continues to explain the images and the UFE procedure. She shifts the frame of reference from description of the actual procedure to an explanation of a clinicians' perspective, by saying,

> That's what we're trying so we're not looking (looks at P9, gestures with hands apart) at your fibroids during the procedure we're looking at the (brings hands together) blood supply to it. (Transcript Extract 13.5, lines 47, 49)

N1's gesture of bringing her hands together resembles a gesture she made earlier when explaining that the fibroid tumors shrink after the embolization procedure blocks the blood flow to the tumors (Transcript Extract 13.4, lines 15–19). At this point, P9 overlaps the end of the nurse's utterance, saying, 'Ohhh I see' and moves away from the computer screen by leaning back in her chair (Transcript Extract 13.5, line 50). After a pause, she utters another 'hmm', concurrent with the nurse saying, 'okay', and backtracking the computer to the image she had skipped. N1's return to the predetermined sequence of the presentation functions as acknowledgment that the patient has understood the explanation. P9's clearer verbal response and movement away from the screen suggest that the nurse's additional visual, verbal, and gestural information resolved the earlier interpretive contingencies of linking the linguistic and visual information.

Subsequently, when the nurse's explanation again reaches the image containing two x-rays placed side-by-side, she does not repeat the explanation, but advances to the following image and related topic. This displays another interpretive contingency faced by the nurse due to the discussion of images – i.e., recalling which information has been covered out of sequence. In the absence of the conventional interview-based pattern of clinician-patient interaction, the discussion of images presented the nurse with the contingencies of interpreting the patient's reactions to the screen images and explanations while managing the sequence of images. During P9's consultation, the patient's brief and vague responses added to those contingencies. The nurse's augmentation of her initial explanation by changing the usual sequence of images functioned as a way of coping with those additional contingencies.

Shifting the Contingencies and the Professional Culture

The preceding examples are representative of how a patient influences the topics and detail of a clinician's explanation of medical information when the discourse framework features discussion of images. The patient's increased authority over the amount of information presented during the consultation is a consequence of the added interpretive contingencies that the clinician manages when dealing with the interactive discussion of images. The immediate cognitive and interactional work that a clinician encounters in such circumstances overcomes some of the professional culture's customary communication patterns – particularly the administrative patterns of deemphasizing or ignoring digressive questions.

Both of the respectively different adaptations by the nurse to P6's frequent topic shifting and to P9's minimal responses affected the nature of professional authority in the consultations. Due to the increased interpretive contingencies encountered by the nurse, the patients guided the patterns of communication and the topics of discussion, even though the approach to presenting and explaining the general topic, 'how UFE works', had been established in advance of any particular patient's consultation by the clinicians who assembled the sequence of images.

A result of such adaptation by the clinician to a patient is the patient's understanding and recall of medical information – displayed by the data analyzed in Chapters One and Nine. The radiology patients' recall of the medical information during the post-consultation telephone discussions correlated with their verbal and gestural interpretation activities during the radiology consultations. Those activities resulted from the changes in the patterns of interaction prompted by the increase in the clinician's interpretive contingencies. Patterns of interaction are fundamental components and expressions of professional culture. When applied for an extended period by a group of clinicians, such changes in patterns of interaction and the resulting shift in the balance of patients and clinicians' interpretive contingencies can also constitute a change in the local production and reproduction of professional culture.

14 Conclusion – Professional Culture: Persistence and Change

The preceding data analysis shows how interaction, cognition, and culture intertwine to shape understanding. It also shows that simply changing technologies and providing visual resources does not lead to understanding. In that context, how does beneficial change occur? The radiology consultations provide an example: visual information resources and new patterns of interaction combine to shift the balance of interpretive contingencies that participants encountered, reducing those of patients and increasing those of the clinician. The work by clinicians to cope with increased contingencies presents each patient with opportunities to use the visual resources in ways that change the conventional discourse framework, producing recallable process narratives that constitute understandings. The shift in the balance of interpretive contingencies functions as an innovative communication pattern that beneficially disrupts the professional culture's customary restrictive discourse framework.

Considering understanding in terms of the development of process narratives, grey boxes, and discourse frameworks shows that an emphasis on particular interpretive contingencies is part of the production and reproduction of professional culture. The use of visual resources during the radiology consultations and the genetics learning activities had different effects in regard to reproducing or changing professional culture. In the consultations, discussion of visual medical information changed the conventional patterns of communication, providing patients with substantial influence over the topics discussed. However, in the classrooms, discussion of visual information related to genetic inheritance did not change the topics or the communication patterns expressed by teachers.

The classroom outcome resulted from the interaction patterns incorporated in the professional culture, which reduced the teachers' administrative contingencies during interpretation activities. Those contingencies included presenting required curriculum, maintaining order during learning activities, and overseeing classroom resources such as computers, task prompts, and lab equipment (Saferstein and Souviney, 1997). The emphasis on grey boxes and the de-emphasis of seeking or applying information about cellular genetic processes functioned as a restrictive management of the interpretation activities by which students developed recallable process narratives. It created a balance of contingencies that supported the teacher's agenda of topics and forms of expression. The absence of cellular process information, the patterns of student-teacher interaction that restrict searching for it, and the emphasis on conventional Mendelian grey boxes combined to guide students toward accepting the grey boxes as a way to reduce interpretive contingencies. That discourse framework, which applied and reproduced the teachers' professional culture, limited the effect of visual resources on changing the conventional interaction patterns. Paradoxically, the reproduction of the traditional professional culture occurred in the context of attempts to avoid a teacher-centered transmission style of teaching – either by T1's Socratic pedagogical approach or T2's recognition of students' questions and comments.

Such outcomes are examples of the local processes of cultural reproduction and adaptation. The professional culture of teachers has adapted to include routinely practiced patterns of interaction that resolve interpretive contingencies presented by students, such as students' attempts to apply or seek information about cellular genetics. Both T1 and T2 provided examples of commonly used elicitation frameworks and short responses, which reduced the administrative interpretive contingencies of dealing with students' digressive comments and questions. Such culturally shaped patterns of interaction restricted searching for cellular process information and reinforced the use of grey boxes.

As in the biology classrooms, the professional culture of clinicians has featured communication patterns, which restrict patients' access to information that would contribute to recallable process narratives. (cf. Anspach, 1993; Fisher, 1993; Fisher and Groce, 1990; Måseide, 1991; Swinglehurst, Greenhalgh, and Roberts, 2012). In contrast, routine discussion of visual medical information during the radiology consultations changed the professional culture for the clinicians involved. The cause of that outcome is also paradoxical, deriving in part from the restrictive communication patterns and the absence of visual information in many conventional clinical consultations. Those aspects of the traditional professional culture not only prevent patients from searching for missing information, but also provide few or no textual or pictorial resources that a clinician could use as grey boxes to fill the information gaps that patients notice and mention. Instead, the professional culture's communication patterns emphasize reliance on verbal expression of medical terms or inattention to patients' questions. Consequently, during the radiology consultations, when patients digressed from the nurse's prepared topics and explanations by mentioning and gesturing toward the medical images, the professional culture had not provided restrictive grey-box related communication patterns that clinicians could apply in order to reassert the customary restriction on patients' information seeking – the clinical professional culture had no analogue to the teachers' communication patterns and discourse framework redirecting students' digressions toward the Mendelian visual and textual grey boxes. Thus, the nurse was faced with additional interpretive contingencies that she alleviated by fully explaining the visual information that the patient had noted.

Dealing with the Endurance of Professional Cultures

Analysis of the radiology consultations provides a model for comprehensively changing clinical consultations to improve patients' understanding and recall of important medical advice. Rather than considering change primarily in terms of client-centered approaches that adjust clinicians' attentiveness and courtesy during professional encounters, recognizing the interrelation of process narratives to interpretation activities, contingencies, discourse frameworks, and grey boxes presents a cooperative patient-clinician approach to understanding. The discussion of visual resources in the radiology consultations provided patients with information that prompted questions, comments, movements, and gestures. In combination with the physical orientation of the patient and clinician to the visual resources, those activities shifted the balance of the participants' interpretive contingencies – creating contingencies for the clinician and decreasing them for the patient. This led to a discourse framework featuring patterns of communication that supported the patients' creation of recallable process narratives. In the local context of the radiology practice, this both reconfigured the cultural conventions of consultations and enhanced patients' understandings of medical information.

Applying the findings of the radiology consultation analysis to high school genetics education indicates that change to the professional culture that fosters the conventional Mendelian curriculum would not result from simply advising teachers to avoid patterns of discussion that de-emphasize students' digressive questions. Rather, it would require changing the classroom discourse framework's standard communication patterns, visual resources, and interpretive frames of reference, which support the traditional Mendelian grey boxes. Providing students with opportunities to apply information about cellular genetic processes would contribute to process narratives that link information about DNA with the appearance of traits across generations.

As the radiology consultations show, technical information is a useful part of the visual and verbal components of a discourse framework that supports the creation of substantive recallable process narratives. The radiology patients did not remember all of the technical information they encountered, but its presence provided them with the opportunity to select certain pieces of technical medical information to link coherently with other information and create recallable process narratives and understandings. In genetics courses, process narrative creation involving cellular genetics information would foster students' achievement in regard to standard institutional curricular mandates, and it would support creation of understandings that meet students' information needs in practical situations they encounter throughout their lives outside of educational settings. Such change would not require students to learn all of the biochemistry involved in trait inheritance. Instead, it would provide them with the type of ancillary information that contributed to the radiology patients' creation of recallable process narratives. In regard to developing a functional understanding of dominant and recessive genes, information about cellular processes would help to resolve interpretive contingencies such as those some of T1's and T2's students expressed.

Biology teachers interacting with many students in a classroom cannot follow each student's particular concerns about genetics information in the way that the radiology nurse attended to the comments and gestures of each patient. However, teachers could reduce the interpretive contingencies, which often complicate students' acceptance and application of Mendelian grey boxes, by incorporating information about cellular genetic processes into lessons featuring conventional visual resources, such as whiteboard diagrams or computer simulations of trait inheritance. In cases such as those analyzed in Chapters Seven and Ten, where some students expressed an interest in absent information or in applying the process narratives developed during earlier lesson units, teachers could attend to those inquiries by following the trail of the students' digressions and supplying missing verbal and visual information. As in the radiology consultations, this would shift the balance of interpretive contingencies, and begin to change traditional communication patterns, reducing the interpretive contingencies students encounter.

Although training contributes to teachers' emphasis on Mendelian grey boxes, their professional culture results from repeatedly mobilizing particular communication patterns during classroom interpretation activities. Organizational constraints, such as standardized tests and curricular requirements, also reinforce the professional culture. However, these influences do not preclude a form and content of explanations that would feature the cellular process information that students seek. A systemic approach to expanding the understanding of genetic inheritance would involve changing components of the traditional discourse framework by:

- Recognizing that Punnett squares and genetics nomenclature are grey boxes,
- Integrating some concepts taught in cellular genetics lesson units with the teaching of genetic inheritance in order to reduce students' interpretive contingencies and to produce process narratives that apply outside of the classroom,
- Revising biology curricula by reducing the emphasis on the Mendel story and Mendel's methods.[40]

Understanding and Interaction

This study has focused on what gets done as tangible interpretation activities produce, reproduce, and change systems of social organization and professional culture. The patterns of interpretation activities in the radiology consultations and the genetics learning tasks show people actively participating in the production of understandings. 'Process' in 'process narratives' does not primarily signify a description of how to do something or how something happens. Instead, it emphasizes the ways that the interpretation activities of producing understandings concurrently engage setting, culture, interaction, and mental operations. Identifying the components of understandings shows how culture is reproduced, and how it can transform when those components are changed.

Comparing the clinical and educational data shows why understandings do not simply result from providing well-designed linguistic explanations and visual resources. During the creation of discourse frameworks and process narratives, the interrelation of interpretation activities and the information resources of particular environments can lead to the reproduction of professional culture that restricts understandings. In contrast, the interpretation activities of the radiology consultations have shown how changes in professional cultures occur that expand understandings. Those changes result from shifting the balance of interpretive contingencies between professionals and clients.

Technological innovations, shifts in economic resources, and the development of new facilities to meet population growth provide opportunities for reconfiguring sets of resources and communication patterns in organizational settings. Recognizing the constraints related to particular discourse frameworks and the use of grey boxes exposes ways to change professional and organizational cultures in order to improve clients' development of useful understandings. Comprehensive change to professional cultures in clinical and educational settings requires identifying the key components of the communication patterns and information resources that affect clients' creation of understandings, incorporating changes to those components during formal and applied aspects of professional training, and then deploying them in routine organizational activities. This approach not only benefits clients' production and subsequent use of understandings, but also contributes to professionals recognizing their clients' information needs.

Endnotes

1 Although aesthetic formulas persist within the culture and social networks of dramatic production and interpretation, meanings that viewers or readers develop in regard to a particular drama vary widely and are subject to a variety of influences other than a text or performance: e.g., personal experiences, settings of reception, discussions with friends, and socioeconomic status often shape interpretations. The referential, semiotic model of representation and meaning may seem to apply within a community of dramatists, actors, technicians, critics, scholars, etc., who have previously developed common interpretive frames of reference by encountering certain explanatory models and commonly used linguistic terms while experiencing the production of theatrical works. However, this approach repeats the mistake of attributing shared understanding to the linguistic terms, themselves, while de-emphasizing the interpretation activities that constitute their use and usefulness. Even within such drama communities the immediate interpretations and evaluations of scripts and theatrical productions differ.

2 Schank and Abelson's monograph is published in a volume that includes chapters by other scholars of cognition, including some who apply the coherence-base reasoning and constraint satisfaction approaches discussed in this and following chapters. Many of those responses challenge Schank and Abelson's emphasis on stories as the primary component of memory (Wyer, 1995). However, in contrast to the process narrative approach to understanding discussed here, the arguments disputing Schank and Abelson's story model continue to emphasize the nature of mental operations, rather than the interrelationship of social, cultural, and material components of the interpretation activities that produce the objects of those mental operations.

3 The study is ongoing at the time of this book's publication. At the time writing began, 12 cases had been recorded and studied.

4 Uterine fibroid embolization (UFE) is also referred to as uterine artery embolization (UAE). UFE is used here because it was the acronym used during the recorded radiology consultations. The procedure is an alternative to more invasive surgical procedures, hysterectomy and myomectomy, for treatment of symptomatic uterine fibroid tumors. Uterine fibroid tumors (also referred to as uterine leiomyomas) are the most common tumors of the female reproductive tract and

are the leading indication for hysterectomy in the United States. Studies have reported the occurrence of uterine fibroid tumors in nearly 70% of white women and more than 80% of black women by age 50 (Baird, Dunson, Hill, Cousins, & Schectman, 2003; Parker, 2007). Common pelvic symptoms of uterine fibroid tumors include bleeding, anemia, pelvic pain, frequent urination, and pelvic pressure (Nevadunsky, Bachmann, Nosher, & Yu, 2001). Medical procedures for treating the symptoms of uterine fibroid tumors include hysterectomy (surgical removal of the uterus) and less drastic procedures, such as myomectomy (surgical removal of the uterine fibroid tumors), and uterine fibroid embolization. UFE blocks the blood supply to the uterine fibroid tumors, which shrinks them and stops or alleviates symptoms. However, hysterectomy has been the most common medical procedure for treating uterine fibroid tumors (Whiteman *et al.*, 2008). The prevalence of hysterectomies as a prescribed treatment for uterine fibroid tumors presents many women with a difficult medical decision that may affect their fertility and quality of life.

5 The nurse and patients refer to the embolizing agent as particles, beads, balls, or spheres. Those terms describe the agent's representation in the diagrams included in the set of medical images viewed during the consultation. The manufacturer calls the particles of embolizing agent 'embospheres®'.

6 Key to transcriptions:

/two words/	Words between slashes overlap words between slashes for following speaker.
.	Each period represents a pause of 0.5 seconds or less.
(?)	Each question mark within parentheses indicates one unclear word.
(?maybe this?)	Parenthesized words between question marks are interpretations suggested by utterances in which parts are indistinct
(laughs)	Words inside parentheses represent the analyst's descriptions of sounds or actions.

7 During consultations, the computer displaying the visual presentation simultaneously recorded the participants interacting and the computer screen at which they looked. The transcript examples are representative of the understandings and interpretation activities related to the discussion of images at the interventional radiology consultations.

8 I have distorted the pictures of the participants taken from the video data in order to protect their privacy. All of the pictures presented in this book showing clinical or educational interpretation activities, computer screen images, and whiteboard images are either still frames taken from video data or, in the case of the images presented during the interventional radiology consultations, from the actual PowerPoint presentation that the patients and clinicians discussed. The original video data and PowerPoint images are in color. The analysis is based on the original color video and images. However, the publisher's guidelines for figures required converting the images to grey scale for the print versions. In order to provide the clarity of the original color images, the author has

sharpened the brightness and contrast of the grey scale images using photographic software. This has not otherwise affected their content in regard to the people, actions, or settings initially recorded.

9 During the post-consultation telephone discussion, P3 also mentioned 'embolizing little balls' when describing diagrams viewed during the consultation (Figure 1.2, Images D, E):

T38 (partial). . . . I knew they had gone into through the through the groin area and they y'know put a catheter in there and everything, but to actually see the catheter in the vein and
T39. Researcher: Ummm
T40. P3: in the y'know in the what's that, vein I guess – it's going through arteries and actually seeing them disperse the . embolizing . little balls

The images had represented the embolizing agent particles in the uterine artery as spheres, and the nurse mentioned that they were drawn larger than the actual particles: "(N1 points at the screen) they're not that big." (Transcript Extract 1.3, line C69).

10 The classroom data analyzed in Chapters Two, Three, and Seven were recorded in a High School biology class, as part of the Community of Explorers Project (National Science Foundation RED-9154815). Chapter Twelve and Appendix A present information about the settings and participants.

11 This discussion expands on Saferstein and Sarangi (2010), pages 165–179.

12 Italics indicate the author's expression of participants' process narratives by paraphrasing sets of transcript segments, quoting transcripts, or incorporating quoted transcript segments with paraphrasing.

13 The software is designed so that each new generation presented after mating two parent rabbits will appear in rows and columns demarcated by a box. The software is set to display 12 offspring in each generation box produced by a particular mating, configured in four columns of three rabbits. Appearing above each generation box is another box containing images of the generations' parents (selected from the previous generations after the first generation).

14 Although the students eventually apply genetics terms, such as 'dominant', and genetics nomenclature to replace or elaborate on 'the same', those terms and nomenclature continue to function as grey boxes for missing information about the cellular and molecular processes by which genes influence the development of the physical characteristics within the bodies of individual organisms. In that sense, 'the same' reverberates through the subsequent interpretation activities of the students, which lead to a mistaken explanation of genetic inheritance based on noting that certain qualities of various generations of offspring are 'the same':

B652. B21: Now, in F1 the children of those parents . . the F1 they all had **the same** pointy ears.
B653. B22: (speaking as he writes) the . children
B654. B21: F1 had **the same** pointy ears.

B655. B22: (speaking as he writes) **the . same**
[Transcript Extract 3.7]

B684. B21: We run 'em and they're **the same** (F1.1 generation of offspring rabbits appears on screen).
B685. T1: As what?
B686. B21: **The same** as (mistakenly points at the floppy-eared male parent in the top row) the male.

B701. B21: And notice their ears are **the same**.

B751. B21: But what if we take two of **the same** though?
[Transcript Extract 3.8]

B786. G21: (referring to B21's use of the software to breed another generation) /Put **the same** kind in/
[Transcript Extract 3.9]

B842. B21: They're the same. Was it every sixth – every sixth to seventh generation that are **the same**, but are they gonna alternate?

B847. B21: (points to the floppy-eared and straight-eared F6 parents) These are **the same**. So they alternate.
[Transcript Extract 3.10]

The development and application of such grey boxes are examined in Part Two.

15 These images and many of those in the remainder of Part One are enlarged sections of still frames made from video data recorded in the VHS format as part of the first study of learning activities. The activities and settings are discernable when viewing the full-sized color images on a video screen. However, fitting the full images to the print format of this book would have reduced them so that relevant parts would not be clear. The enlarged sections resolved that problem, but the still images and enlargement also reduced clarity. To increase the clarity of these enlarged sections as much as possible; the images have been sharpened using photographic software. In other chapters, the still images captured from the video recordings of the second study of learning activities (T2's classes) and the clinical study have been cropped, enlarged, or sharpened in order to fit the print format and improve clarity. This has not otherwise affected the content of the video still frames – the image components are those of the original video recordings. A few images have arrows or circles added to highlight specific movements or gestures.

16 B21's utterance is imprecise: he mentions 'two couples' while pointing at one couple, the two parent rabbits. However, in this instance, B21's pointing at the particular row of two rabbits and the context of the rest of his utterance override his verbal mistake of saying 'two couples', indicating that he meant the two rabbits in the parent couple (Figure 2.7, Row C).

17 Images B-H are presented to show student G21's pointing at various parts of the computer simulation image. Reduction in size in order to fit the printed page has limited the visibility of the computer simulation details, which are visible in the actual video data and described in the accompanying transcript extracts.

18 The following descriptive process narratives contribute to the 'automatically skips a generation' explanation:

B21: /See/ . look! They skipped." (B21 points at floppy-eared F2 rabbit. Then skips his finger up the screen, pointing at another floppy-eared F2 rabbit, a straight-eared F1 rabbit, and, finally, a floppy-eared parent of the F1 generation.)

[Transcript Extract 2.7, line B392]

B22: It looks like every generation it's skipping
R1: It's skipping a generation?
B21: It did on the first time.
B22: And then it did on the second time too

[Transcript Extract 3.2, lines B419-B422]

B21: It skipped.
B22: It skipped a generation.
R1: Oh you mean it doesn't show up in the firs-in that
B22: In the first one it won't show up and then the second one will.

[Transcript Extract 3.2, lines B430-B433]

B21: So then. Then now . they're gonna be floppy. Watch. (7 second pause in talk as he creates another generation from the F3 parents.) See. /Floppy/ (The production of the F4 box reduces all of the generation boxes again, revealing only one row of rabbits in each box. Refers to the mixture of floppy and straight-eared rabbits in the visible row of the F4 box.)
G21: /One./ (May refer to the one floppy-eared rabbit visible in the new generation)
B21: But watch, now they're gonna go back (7 second pause in talk as B21 creates another generation of rabbits). Go back. (4 second pause in talk while they pause wait for the computer to create a new generation) I told you! They skip generations.
B22: They skipped a generation.
R1: Does it ah (?????)
B22: No it doesn't make a difference cause it just automatically skips a generation.
B21: Why though?
B22: (questioning) Hmmm?
G21: So it's no?
B22: It's no, because it doesn't matter which one you put in there. It's always gonna skip a generation.

[Transcript Extract 3.4, lines B442-B451]

19 B21 may have misspoken, saying 'gene' instead of 'generation', or he may have had in mind a single gene model of inherited traits when he said, 'Look . if if it skips a gene then it'll most likely be like this' (Transcript Extract 3.1, line B405). However, the utterance can have another function when considered in the context of the students' interpretation activities. As part of the process of

interpreting information and constructing coherence, B21 may have linked previously expressed words and concepts, which he had not yet completely defined or understood.

In the context of the missing information about the operation of genes, the meaning for the students of the utterance, 'skips a gene', is its syntactical function as a grey box – i.e., a placeholder for missing information about genes that enables the linking of the visual information to form a process narrative. Subsequently, revised as 'automatically skips a generation', it contributes to the students' emphasis on description and de-emphasis of inferences about dominant and recessive genes. 'Automatically skips a generation' continues to function as a grey box. Part Two discusses in detail the syntactical function of grey boxes and their linkage to a setting's information resources.

20 Ambiguous interpretation activities and comments occurred in the context of B21's confusion in operating the simulation, which resulted in a different configuration of the offspring generations, and conflicting interpretations of the screen images by G21 and B22. B21's difficulty in operating the simulation to expand the generation boxes resulted in hiding the F1.1 generation box and expanding the F2.1 and F3.1 generation boxes. B21 then mated two of the F2.1 offspring with different ear shapes, which resulted in the simulation splitting the F3.1 box into two smaller boxes containing partial displays of the F3.1 and F3.2 generations. At this point, B22, who was most distant from the screen said, 'They all have floppy ears'. G21 responded, 'No no-no here' and pointed at a straight-eared F3.2 rabbit at the bottom of the screen. B22 then says, 'Oh', following which G21 emphasized the heterogeneity of the F3.2 offspring by saying, 'Pointy and floppy'. Facing contradictory interpretations of the screen images, B21 and B22 reverted to their recall of previous outcomes of the simulation. B22 continued to apply the previously developed process narrative, saying, 'It looks like every generation it's skipping'. When I briefly intervened, seeking clarification of that comment, which was not consistent with the screen images ('It's skipping a generation?'), B21 and B22 referred to earlier runs of the simulation. B21 said, 'It did on the first time', and B22 added 'And then it did on the second time too. But we put – both of 'em have straight'. The interaction did not clarify what B22 meant by 'both of 'em have straight' (Transcript Extract 3.1, lines B414-B419; Transcript Extract 3.2, lines B420-B422).

B21 then operated the computer to start a new simulation repeating the earlier actions that had led to the previously developed 'skips a generation' process narratives. The ensuing interactions show that this reemphasis on the cognitive ecology of the 'automatically skips' process narratives eliminated from consideration any alternative information related to the recent contradictory simulation outcome. The confounding screen information and ambiguous interpretation activities were replaced with references go the prior simulation outcomes, previously developed process narratives, and a repeat of the earlier use of the computer simulation.

21 When B21 operated the mouse and the keyboard, he often did act on the other students' requests to use the software in particular ways.

22 The software program had a feature that showed a picture of two genes marked as dominant or recessive for each rabbit's ear shape. However, it required the students to mouse click an icon shaped as a microscope, and then to click on a particular rabbit. Neither the teacher nor the task prompt, which he adapted from the software tutorial, explained this feature. This was an intentional omission, because the learning task was based on students replicating a version of Gregor Mendel's research, which did not include knowledge of genes.

23 G21, B21, and B22 subsequently acquired additional information about Mendelian genetics, which they used to develop process narratives that incorporated the teacher's concerns and to cope with the confounding information that had been produced by the computer simulation.

24 The research methods applied during the development of these approaches (e.g., formal logic problems, responses to interview questions, thought experiments, participants' retrospective accounts) play a part in their focus on mental operations. Those methods emphasize linguistically expressed results of interpretation rather than the interpretation activities directed at particular information resources, which led to those results. For example, studies of interpretive contingencies have presented subjects with logic problems, then analyzed and aggregated the answers (cf. Bauer & Johnson-Laird, 1993; D'Andrade, 1989; Johnson-Laird, 2006; Khemlani, et al., 2013). Such research infers the interpretation activities that have led to correct or mistaken answers to logic problems. Consequently, the actual interpretation activities and information resources that are components of explanations and understandings are often submerged by the use and conceptualization of categorical distinctions such as cognitive schemata and mental models.

25 The data analyzed in the preceding and following chapters show that the interpretation activity glossed by restructuring is not just a matter of mentally reassembling words or ideas as if they were building blocks, but consists of reengaging the interpretation activities and resources that contributed to the process narratives developed earlier (e.g., B21's revision of 'automatically skips a generation' from every other generation to every six generations [Chapter Three]). Restructuring not only involves revising or discarding previously developed process narratives, but also changing the interpretive frame of reference and communication format that had developed concurrently with those process narratives.

26 A commonly used example of the selective interpretation categorized as functional fixedness is an experiment called the candle puzzle. Klein and D'Esposito (2007: 177) provide the following description:

> A classic functional fixedness experiment is to provide a subject with a box of matches, a candle, and a tack. The problem is to affix the lit candle to a wall. If the match box itself is seen as one of the objects that can be used in solving the problem, then the solution is readily obtained: empty the box of

the matches; tack the box to the wall, creating a shelf; light the candle with one of the matches; and place the lit candle on the side of the box protruding from the wall. If the subject doesn't see the box as a separate object to be used, but simply as a container for the matches, either the problem will not be solved or it will take materially longer. Hence, the term functional fixedness or mental fixation: a subject is 'fixated' on the function of an object, in this case a match box, and does not consider an alternative use for it. Once the subject is made aware that the box itself may be used in performing the task, it is quickly completed.

27 The term, 'the bedroom', was used in the class to refer to the area of the computer simulation screen where images of two parent rabbits were moved in order to produce a generation of offspring.

28 As mentioned in Chapter Three, the teacher in this example favored a discovery approach to teaching. However, the emphasis on patterns of traits across generations was the same as that of other teachers studied.

29 The data show that students' attempts to use information about cellular genetic processes also complicate teachers' work to focus the students on Mendel's method of studying and explaining inheritance. In response to such complexity, T1 modified the organization of the genetic inheritance curriculum for the academic year following the 'blueprints' example. The 'automatically skips' example discussed in Chapters Two and Three involved T1's revised curriculum. He provided more time for students to work with the simulation and more task prompts. Yet, as the 'automatically skips a generation' interaction showed, an increase in the amount of prompt information and more time to work with the computer simulation did not lead to less complicated interpretation activities.

30 In the clinical research project, I conducted the telephone follow-up discussions so that patients could volunteer explanations of the understandings that they developed during the radiology consultations. Since the objective of the project was to study the relationship of patients' recallable understandings of medical information to the interpretation activities that produced them, my prompts to each patient were general, and did not specify particular topics that had been presented during her radiology consultation. Patients might have individually developed grey boxes or treated visual or verbal information encountered during the consultations as grey boxes without revealing them in their post-consultation telephone discussions. However, even if that were the case, the patients did not display complex interpretation activities related to creating grey boxes during the radiology consultations or the telephone interviews.

31 The utterances 2.17–2.20 resulted from a second telephone call that occurred a few minutes after the first call in which utterances 1.40–1.66 were recorded.

32 The placement of descriptions of gestures and head movements in Transcript Extract 9.2 represents a general model of the degree to which P1 and N1 presented verbal and nonverbal displays of attention to the computer screen images. Transcripts cannot adequately represent the combination of verbal and nonverbal aspects of interaction presented by video data (Saferstein 2004). Text organized

as a sequence of utterances, gestures, and movements does not fully convey the overlap and simultaneity of multiple gestures, head movements, and utterances.

33 My verbal prompt preceding P1's mention of post-procedure complications was: 'So you mentioned those two points [i.e., the particles staying in the end blood vessels and the chance of early menopause]. Wa anything else that stood out about the Power about the information that was in the uh PowerPoint that that you can recall?' I did not mention specific information that had been discussed at the radiology consultation. The patient introduced the recalled information during the telephone discussion.

34 Transcript Extract 10.4 contains the first part of line 45.

35 Punnett squares (Figure 14.1, Row A) are tables used to demonstrate the possible combinations of genes for particular traits that are passed from parents to offspring (Row B), the probability ratio of resulting traits (Row C), and the probability of gene combinations (Row D).

Figure 14.1: Punnett Squares

	G = Green Eyes (Stipulated as Dominant), g = Hazel Eyes (Stipulated as Recessive)			
A	G G G GG GG G GG GG	g g g gg gg g gg gg	G G g Gg Gg g Gg Gg	G g G GG Gg g Gg gg
B	4 green-eyed individuals	4 hazel-eyed individuals	4 green-eyed individuals	3 green-eyed individuals
C	Probability Ratio of Green-Eyed Offspring to Hazel-Eyed Offspring			
	4:0	0:4	4:0	3:1
D	Probability ratio of homozygous dominant to heterozygous to homozygous recessive			
	4:0:0	0:0:4	0:4:0	1:2:1

Alleles for particular traits (e.g., eye color, hair color) are represented by a letter – lower case representing a recessive allele and upper case representing a dominant allele. In the coursework for the biology classes studied, the number of columns and rows in a Punnett square was determined by multiplying the two alleles for a particular trait (a dominant and a recessive) by the number of traits being considered. One parent's alleles for specified trait(s) are placed above the top boarder, with each allele (when considering one trait) or possible combination of alleles (when considering multiple traits) placed above each column (Figure 14.1, Row A). The other parent's set of alleles for trait(s) is placed outside of the left border, with each allele (when considering one trait) or combination of alleles (when considering multiple traits) placed next to one of the rows. Each cell of the table is filled in by selecting the corresponding alleles outside of the intersecting column and row. Cells containing two lower case letters of a particular allele indicate the appearance of recessive traits in offspring (Figure 14.1, Rows A, B). The cells containing one or two upper case letters of particular alleles represent the appearance of dominant traits (Figure 14.1, Row B). The probability of various offspring genotypes and phenotypes occurring can be demonstrated by respectively counting the homozygous dominant (i.e., two upper case letters), homozygous recessive (i.e., two lower case letters), and heterozygous (i.e., one upper case letter and one lower case letter) Punnett square cells, and expressing the outcome as a ratio (Figure 14.1, Rows C, D). The common classroom use of Punnett squares to express inheritance of eye color is heuristic, since eye color is actually affected by multiple genes interacting.

36 **Figure 10.14: Variations of Punnett Squares**

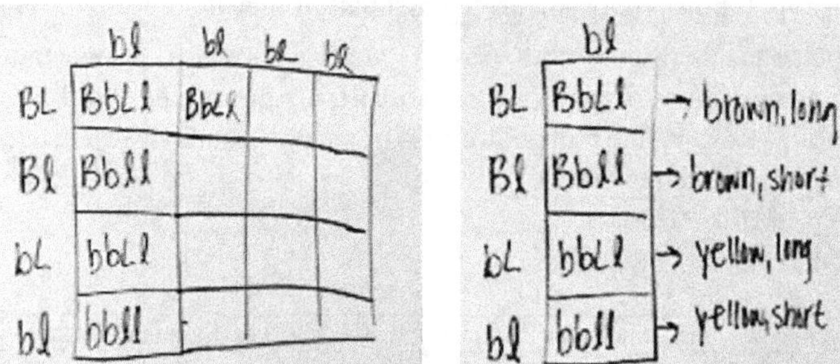

The incomplete Punnett square displayed above left was designed by G33 to calculate the outcome of two different traits in each individual, tail length (L or l) and fur color (B or b) (discussed in Chapter 10). In a case where an individual's displayed traits derive from only recessive alleles (top of table), a Punnett square may be abbreviated to display only one row or column for the recessive trait (above right) – since the ratio of allele combinations for all of the recessive trait rows or columns will be the same (Chapter 10, Transcript Extract 10.13). T2 and G33 discussed this abbreviation when T2 answered G33's question during her work on a genetics problem (Chapter 10, Transcript Extract 10.12). T2 also explained the abbreviated form of a Punnett square when G33 presented her whiteboard diagram to the class (Chapter 10, Transcript Extract 10.13).

37 The data examined here emphasize visual and verbal components of discourse frameworks. However, other modes of expression and perception, such as non-verbal sounds, taste, and touch could also contribute to the interpretation activities that produce and apply discourse frameworks. Those modes of expression could also be applied to grey boxes for missing information.

38 In that context, I considered identifying students with gender-neutral nomenclature, but the common alternatives, such as using forms of 'they' as both singular and plural pronouns, create confusion when discussing both multiple and individual participants in a group. Consequently, I have retained the G1 and B1 nomenclature for female and male teenaged students. However, the linguistic acknowledgment of gender differs from the imposition of gender roles as an analytical frame of reference.

39 Near the end of the set of images discussed with patients are lists of statistics, which present averages of UFE outcomes:

- Expect 50% shrinkage and 90% of symptoms resolved at 12 months in 90% of patients. (image 33 of 48, 'Postprocedure Care')
- Fibroid re-growth & new fibroids less than 10% under age of 40, less than 4% age 40 and older (image 35 of 48, 'Results')
- 'Your fibroids will shrink and quit bothering you … they will not disappear!' (image 37 of 48, 'Results')
- Roughly 50% reduction in VOLUME at six months (image 37 of 48, 'Results')
- Volume = 4/3 × pi × CUBE of radius i.e. a 10mm fibroid going to 8mm = 51% reduction (image 37 of 48, 'Results')

40 High school genetics curricula do adapt to include recent discoveries. Biology courses eventually will include discussion of the relationship between genes, proteins, and traits – some have begun this shift. However, without change in the components of the traditional discourse framework, the emphasis on applying Mendelian nomenclature and Punnett squares as grey boxes for cellular processes will persist, and continue to produce the classroom-specificity of many students' understandings of trait inheritance.

Furthermore, the traditional genetics curriculum's format – teaching a scientific research method by withholding cellular process information and forcing students to reinvent the Mendelian grey boxes – strays from Mendel's actual investigative process and fails when the students simply memorize the ready-made grey boxes. Since the students do not have to develop tabular and computational devices as Mendel did, they do not really replicate his interpretive frame of reference or investigative methods. This attempt to teach simultaneously about research methods and genetic inheritance contributes to the de-emphasis or omission of key information about cellular processes that would contribute to students developing transferable process narratives that are useful outside of the classroom throughout their lives.

Bibliography

Anspach, R. (1993). *Deciding Who Lives: Fateful Choices in the Intensive Care Nursery* 86–111. Berkeley, CA: University of California Press.

Armstrong, D. (1995). The rise of surveillance medicine. *Sociology of Health and Illness* 17 (3): 393–404.

Armstrong, D. (2002). Clinical autonomy, individual and collective: The problem of changing doctors' behavior. *Social Science and Medicine* 55: 1771–1777.

Arnseth, H. C., and Säljö, R. (2007). Making sense of epistemic categories: Analysing students' use of categories of progressive inquiry in computer mediated collaborative activities. *Journal of Computer Assisted Learning*, 23: 425–439.

Baird D. D., Dunson D. B., Hill, M. C., Cousins, D., and Schectman, J. M. (2003). High cumulative incidence of uterine leiomyoma in black and white women: Ultrasound evidence. *American Journal of Obstetrics and Gynecology* 188: 100–107.

Barowy, B., and Laserna, C. (1997). The role of the Internet in the adoption of computer modeling as legitimate High School science. *Journal of Science Education and Technology* 6 (1): 3–13.

Bauer, M. I., and Johnson-Laird, P. N. (1993). How diagrams can improve reasoning. *Psychological Science*, 4 (6): 372–378

Bobrow, D. G., and Norman, D. A. (1975). Some principles of memory schemata. In D. G. Bobrow and A. M. Collins (Eds), *Representation and Understanding: Studies in Cognitive Science* 131–149. New York: Academic Press.

Brown, J. S., and Duguid, P. (2000). *The Social Life of Information*. Cambridge, MA: Harvard Business Press.

Cicourel, A. V. (1973). *Cognitive Sociology: Language and Meaning in Social Interaction*. Harmondsworth: Penguin.

Cicourel, A. V. (1982). Language and belief in a medical setting. In D. Tannen (Ed.), *Georgetown University Round Table on Languages and Linguistics: Analyzing Discourse, Text and Talk* 48–78. Washington, DC: Georgetown University Press.

Cicourel, A. V. (1987). The interpenetration of communicative contexts: Examples from medical encounters. *Social Psychology Quarterly* 50 (2): 217–226.

Cicourel, A. V. (1988). Elicitation as a problem of discourse. In U. Ammon, N. Dittmar and K. Mattheier (Eds), *Sociolinguistics: An International Handbook of the Science of Language and Society* 903–910. Berlin: Walter de Gruyter.

D'Andrade, R. G. (1989). Culturally based reasoning. In A. Gellatly, D, Rogers, and J. A. Sloboda, (Eds) *Cognition and Social Worlds* 132–143. Oxford: Oxford University Press.

Eggly, S. (2002). Physician-patient co-construction of illness narratives in the medical interview. *Health Communication* 14 (3): 339–360.

Entwistle V., Williams, B., Skea, Z., MacLennan, G., Bhattacharya, S. (2006). Which surgical decisions should patients participate in and how? Reflections on women's recollections of discussions about variants of hysterectomy. *Social Science and Medicine* 62: 499–509.

Evans-Pritchard, E. E. (1937). *Witchcraft, Oracles and Magic among the Azande*. Oxford: Oxford University Press.

Fisher, S. (1986). *In The Patient's Best Interest*. Piscataway, NJ: Rutgers University Press.

Fisher, S. (1993). Doctor talk/patient talk: How treatment decisions are negotiated in doctor-patient communication. In S. Fisher and A. Todd (Eds), *The Social Organization of Doctor-Patient Communication* (2nd ed.) 161–182. Norwood, NJ: Ablex.

Fisher, S. (1995). *Nursing Wounds: Nurse Practitioners, Doctors, Women Patients, and the Negotiation of Meaning*. New Brunswick, NJ: Rutgers University Press.

Fisher, S., and Groce, S. B. (1990). Accounting practices in medical interviews. *Language in Society* 19: 225–250.

Frank, M. C., and Ramscar, M. (2003). How do Presentation and Context Influence Representation for Functional Fixedness Tasks? *Proceedings of the 25th Annual Meeting of the Cognitive Science Society*: 1354.

Frankel, R. (1990). Talking in interviews: A dispreference for patient-initiated questions in physician-patient encounters. In G. Psathas (Ed.), *Interactional Competence* 231–262. Lanham, MD: University Press of America.

Frake, C. O. (1980). Plying frames can be dangerous: Some reflections on methodology in cognitive anthropology. In A.S. Dil (Ed.), *Language and Cultural Description: Essays by Charles O. Frake* 45–60. Stanford, CA: Stanford University Press.

Glucksberg, S. (1962). The influence of strength of drive on functional fixedness and perceptual recognition. *Journal of Experimental Psychology* 63: 36–41.

Golden, L., and Hardison, Jr., O. B. (1968). *Aristotle's Poetics* (Translated by L. Golden. Commentary by O. B. Hardison, Jr.). Englewood Cliffs, NJ: Prentice-Hall.

Goldenberg, E. P. (1995). Multiple representations: A vehicle for understanding. In D. N. Perkins, J. L. Schwartz, M. M. West and M. S. Wiske (Eds), *Software Goes to School: Teaching for Understanding with New Technologies* 155–171. New York: Oxford University Press.

Gumperz, J. (1982). *Discourse Strategies: Studies in Interactional Sociolinguistics*. Cambridge University Press.

Heath, Shirley B. (1982). Questioning at home and at school: A comparative study. In G.D. Spindler (Ed.), *Doing the Ethnography of Schooling* 96–101. New York: Holt, Rinehardt and Winston.

Holyoak, K. J., and Simon, D. (1999). Bidirectional reasoning in decision making by constraint satisfaction. *Journal of Experimental Psychology: General*, 128 (1): 3–31.

Hymes, D. (1986). Models of interaction of language and social life. In J. J. Gumperz and D. Hymes (Eds), *Directions in Sociolinguistics: The Ethnography of Communication* 35–71. Oxford: Basil Blackwell Ltd.

Johnson-Laird, P. N. (1983). *Mental Models.* Cambridge, MA, Harvard University Press.

Johnson-Laird, P. N. (2002). Peirce, logic diagrams, and the elementary operations of reasoning. *Thinking and Reasoning*, 8 (1): 69–95.

Johnson-Laird, P. N. (2006). Models and heterogeneous reasoning. *Journal of Experimental and Theoretical Artificial Intelligence* 18 (2): 121–148.

Johnson-Laird, P.N. (2010). Mental models and human reasoning. *Proceedings of the National Academy of Sciences of the United States of America*, 107, (43): 18243–18250.

Johnson-Laird, P. N., and Byrne, Ruth M. J. (2002). Conditionals: A theory of meaning, pragmatics, and inference. *Psychological Review*, 109 (4): 646–678.

Johnson-Laird, P. N., Byrne, R. M. J., and Schaeken, W. S. (1992). Propositional reasoning by model. *Psychological Review* 99: 418–439.

Johnson-Laird, P. N., Legrenzi, P., Girotto, V., and Legrenzi, M. S. (2000). Illusions in Reasoning about Consistency. *Science*, New Series, 288, (5465): 531–532.

Johnson-Laird, P. N., Legrenzi, P., and Legrenzi, M. S. (1972). Reasoning and a sense of reality. *British Journal of Psychology*, 63: 395–400.

Kaput, J. J. (1995). Creating cybernetic and psychological ramps from the concrete to the abstract: Examples from multiplicative structures. In D. N. Perkins, J. L. Schwartz, M. M. West and M. S. Wiske (Eds), *Software Goes to School: Teaching for Understanding with New Technologies* 130–154. New York: Oxford University Press.

Khemlani, S. S., Mackiewicz, R., Bucciarelli, M., and Johnson-Laird, P. N. (2013). Kinematic mental simulations in abduction and deduction. *Proceedings of the National Academy of Sciences of the United States of America*, 110 (42): 16766–16771.

Klein, H. E., and D'Esposito, M. (2007). Neurocognitive inefficacy of the strategy process. *Annals of the New York Academy of Sciences*, 1118: 163–185.

Knorr-Cetina, K. (1999). *Epistemic Cultures: How the Sciences Make Knowledge.* Cambridge, MA: Harvard Edition World.

Lee, H. S., and Holyoak, K. J. (2008). The role of causal models in analogical inference. *Journal of Experimental Psychology: Learning, Memory, and Cognition*, 34 (5): 1111–1122

Marcuse, H. (1969). *An Essay on Liberation*. Boston, MA: Beacon Press.

Måseide, P. (1991). Possibly abusive, often benign, and always necessary: On power and domination in medical practice. *Sociology of Health and Illness* 13 (4): 545–561.

Måseide, P. (2007). Discourses of Collaborative Medical Work. *Text and Talk* 27 (5/6): 611–632.

MacLeod, J. (1987). *Ain't No Makin It: Leveled Aspirations in a Low-Income Neighborhood.* Boulder, CO: Westview Press

McDermott, R. P., Gospodinoff, K., and Aron, J. (1978). Criteria for an ethnographically adequate description of activities and their contexts. *Semiotica* 24: 245–275.

Mehan, H. (1979). *Learning Lessons: The Social Organization of Classroom Instruction.* Cambridge, MA: Harvard University Press.

Mehan, H. (1990). Oracular reasoning in a psychiatric exam. In A. Grimshaw (Ed.), *Conflict Talk* 160–177. Cambridge: Cambridge University Press.

Mishler, E. G. (1984). *The Discourse of Medicine: Dialectics of Medical Interviews.* Norwood, NJ: Ablex.

Molotch, H., and Boden, D. (1985). Talking social structure: Discourse, domination, and the Watergate Hearings. *American Sociological Review* 50: 273–288.

Nevadunsky, N. S., Bachmann, G. A., Nosher, J., Yu, T. (2001). Women's decision-making determinants in choosing uterine artery embolization for symptomatic fibroids. *Journal of Reproductive Medicine* 46 (10): 870–874.

Newman, D. (1990). Using social context for science teaching. In M. Gardner, J. Greeno, F. Reif, A. Schoenfeld, A. diSessa, and E. Stage (Eds), *Toward a Scientific Practice of Science Education* 187–202. Hillsdale, NJ: Lawrence Erlbaum Associates.

Ochs, E. (1992). Indexing Gender. In A. Duranti and C. Goodwin (Eds), *Rethinking Context* 336–358. Cambridge: Cambridge University Press.

Ogbu, John (1991). Immigrant and involuntary minorities in comparative perspective. In M. Gibson and John Ogbu (Eds), *Minority Status and Schooling.* New York: Garland.

Ogbu, John (2003). *Black American Students in an Affluent Suburb: A Study of Academic Disengagement.* Oxford: Routledge.

Östman, L. (1998). How companion meanings are expressed by science education discourse. In D. A. Roberts and L. Östman (Eds), *Problems of Meaning in Science Curriculum* 54–70. New York: Teachers College Press.

Parker W. H. (2007). Etiology, symptomatology, and diagnosis of uterine myomas. *Fertility and Sterility* 87: 725–736.

Pennington, N., and Hastie, R. (1992). Explaining the evidence: Testing the story model for juror decision making. *Journal of Personality and Social Psychology* 62: 189–206.

Perkins, D. N., Crismond, D., Simmons, R., and Unger, C. (1995). Inside understanding. In D. N. Perkins, J. L. Schwartz, M. M. West and M. S. Wiske (Eds), *Software Goes to School: Teaching for Understanding with New Technologies* 70–87. New York: Oxford University Press.

Polanyi, L. (1985). Conversational storytelling: Discourse and dialogue. In T. A. Van Dijk (Ed.), *Handbook of Discourse Analysis* 183–202. London: Academic

Polanyi, M. (1952). The stability of beliefs. *The British Journal for the Philosophy of Science* 3 (11): 217–232.

Polanyi, M. (1958). *Personal Knowledge.* London: Routledge and Kegan Paul.

Polanyi, M. (1967). *The Tacit Dimension.* Garden City, NY: Doubleday and Co.

Poole, D. (1994). Differentiation as an interactional consequence of routine classroom testing. *Qualitative Studies in Education* 7 (1): 1–17.

Price, J., Farmer, G., Harris, J., Hope, T., Kennedy, S., Mayou, R. (2006). Attitudes of women with chronic pelvic pain to the gynaecological consultation: A qualitative study. *British Journal of Obstetrics and Gynaecology* 113 (4): 446–452.

Ranney, M, and Thagard, P. (1989). Explanatory coherence and belief revision in naïve physics, *Proceedings of the Tenth Annual Conference of the Cognitive Science Society* 426–432. Hillsdale, NJ: Erlbaum.

Roberts, C., Moss, B., Wass , V., Sarangi, S., Jones, R., (2005). Misunderstandings: A qualitative study of primary care consultations in multilingual settings, and educational implications. *Medical Education* 39 (5): 465–475.

Rosenthal, J. W. (1996). *Teaching Science to Language Minority Students: Theory and Practice*. Philadelphia, PA: Multilingual Matters.

Rumelhart, D. and Norman, D. (1978). Accretion, tuning and restructuring: Three modes of learning. In. J. W. Cotton and R. Klatzky (Eds), *Semantic Factors in Cognition*. Hillsdale, NJ: Erlbaum.

Rumelhart, D. E., and Norman, D. (1981). Analogical processes in learning. In J. R. Anderson (Ed.), *Cognitive Skills and their Acquisition* 335–359. Hillsdale, NJ: Erlbaum.

Saferstein, B. (1992). Collective cognition and collaborative work: The effects of cognitive and communicative processes on the organization of television production. *Discourse and Society* 3 (1): 61–86.

Saferstein, B. (1994). Interaction and ideology at work: A case of constructing and constraining television violence. *Social Problems* 41 (2): 316–345.

Saferstein, B. (2004). Digital technology and methodological adaption: Text on video as a resource for analytical reflexivity. *Journal of Applied Linguistics*, 1 (2): 197–223.

Saferstein, B. (2007). Process narratives, grey boxes, and discourse frameworks: Cognition, interaction, and constraint in understanding genetics and medicine. *The European Journal of Social Theory* 10 (3): 424–447.

Saferstein, B. (2010). Cognitive sociology. In J. Jaspers, J-O. Östman, J. Verschueren (Eds), *Society and Language Use*. Amsterdam: John Benjamins Publishing Company.

Saferstein, B. (2014). Reasoning with and without reasons: The effects of professional culture and information access in educational and clinical settings. *Journal of Cognition and Neuroethics,* 2 (1): 103–123. ISSN 2166-508, http://www.cognethic.org/jcn/jcnv2i1_Saferstein.pdf.

Saferstein, B., and Oiye, N. (1999). 'The Intersection of Language Community and Gender Roles in Collaborative Learning in High School Science Classes.' Presented at the Society for the Study of Social Problems Annual Meeting, Chicago, 3–7 August.

Saferstein, B., and Sarangi, S. (2010). Mediating modes of representation in understanding science: The case of genetic inheritance. In P. A. Prior and J. A. Hengst (Eds), *Exploring Semiotic Remediation as Discourse Practice* 156–183. Houndmills, Basingstoke: Palgrave Macmillan.

Saferstein, B., and Souviney, R. (1997). Secondary science teachers, the Internet, and curriculum development: The Community of Explorers Project. *The Journal of Educational Technology Systems* 26 (2): 113–126.

Säljö, R. (1998). Learning inside and outside schools: Discursive practices and sociocultural dynamics. In D. A. Roberts and L. Östman (Eds), *Problems of Meaning in Science Curriculum* 39–53. New York: Teachers College Press.

Sarangi, S., and Clarke, A. (2002). Zones of expertise and the management of uncertainty in genetics risk communication. *Research on Language and Social Interaction* 35 (2): 139–71.

Schank, R. C., and Abelson, R. P. (1995). Knowledge and memory: The real story. In R. S. Wyer Jr. (Ed.), *Knowledge and Memory: The Real Story*. 1–85 Hillsdale, NJ: Lawrence Erlbaum Associates.

Simon, D. (2004). A third view of the black box: Cognitive coherence in legal decision making. *University of Chicago Law Review* 71: 511–586. USC Public Policy Research Paper No. 04–10. Los Angeles: University of Southern California Law School.

Simon, D., and Holyoak, K. J. (2002). Structural dynamics of cognition: From consistency theories to constraint satisfaction. *Personality and Social Psychology Review* 6 (6): 283–294.

Simon, D., Snow, C. J., and Read, S. J., (2004). The redux of cognitive consistency theories: Evidence judgments by constraint satisfaction. *Journal of Personality and Social Psychology* 86 (6): 814–837.

Simon, D., Stenstrom, D. M., Read, S. J. (2015). The coherence effect: Blending cold and hot cognitions. *Journal of Personality and Social Psychology*, 2015, 109 (3): 369–394.

Siouta, E., Broström, A., and Hedberg, B. (2012). Content and distribution of discursive space in consultations between patients with atrial fibrillation and healthcare professionals. *European Journal of Cardiovascular Nursing*, published online 11 January 2012. DOI: 10.1177/1474515111430894.

Skea, Z., Harry, V., Bhattacharya, S., Entwistle, V., Williams, B., MacLennan, G., Templeton, A. (2004). Women's perceptions of decision-making about hysterectomy. *British Journal of Obstetrics and Gynaecology* 111: 133–142.

Street, R. L., Jr. (1992). Communicative styles and adaptations in physician-parent consultations. *Social Science and Medicine* 34: 1155–1163.

Street, R. L., Jr., Gordon, H. S., Ward, M. M., Krupat, E., and Kravitz, R. L. (2005) Patient participation in medical consultations: Why some patients are more involved than others. *Medical Care*, 43 (10): 960–969.

Suchman, L. A. (1987). *Plans and Situated Actions.* Cambridge: Cambridge University Press.

Swinglehurst, D., Greenhalgh, T., and Roberts, C. (2012). Computer templates in chronic disease management: Ethnographic case study in general practice. *BMJ Open*, 2:e001754. doi:10.1136/bmjopen-2012-001754

Thagard, P. (1989). Explanatory coherence. *Behavioral and Brain Sciences* 12 (3): 435–502.

Thagard, P. (2006). Evaluating explanations in law, science, and everyday life. *Current Directions in Psychological Science*, 15 (3): 141–145.

Vendetti, M. S., Wu, A., Rowshanshad, E., Knowlton, B. J., and Holyoak, K. J. (2014). When reasoning modifies memory: Schematic assimilation triggered by analogical mapping. *Journal of Experimental Psychology: Learning, Memory, and Cognition*, 40 (4): 1172–1180.

Wason, P. C. (1968). Reasoning about a rule. *Quarterly Journal of Experimental Psychology* 20: 273–281.

West, C. (1984). *Routine Complications: Troubles with Talk Between Doctors and Patients*. Bloomington, IN: Indiana University Press.

Whiteman, M. K., Hillis, S. D., Jamieson, D. J., Morrow, B., Podgornik, M. N., Brett, K. M., Marchbanks, P. A. (2008). Inpatient hysterectomy surveillance in the United States, 2000–2004. *American Journal of Obstetrics and Gynecology* 198 (1): 34. e1–7.

Willis, P. (1977). *Learning to Labour: How Working Class Kids get Working Class Jobs.* Westmead: Saxon House.

WINGS for Learning, Inc. (1991). *Biology Explorer: Genetics*

Winograd, T. (1975). Frame representations and the declarative-procedural controversy. In D. G. Bobrow and A. M. Collins (Eds), *Representation and Understanding: Studies in Cognitive Science* 185–210. New York: Academic Press.

Wyer, R. S. (Ed.) (1995). *Knowledge and Memory: The Real Story*. Hillsdale, NJ: Lawrence Erlbaum Associates.

Appendix A: Research Methods

Data Collection and Analysis

Interventional Radiology Consultations

The primary clinical data were recorded during the period 2008–2012, during a study of clinicians and patients in interventional radiology consultations. The clinical data totaled 13 hours and 39 minutes of video and audio recordings. This total included: 7 hours and 31 minutes of video recordings of 12 consultations (ranging from 26 minutes to 62 minutes), 2 hours 32 minutes of audio recordings of telephone follow-up discussions with patients (ranging from 8.2 minutes to 21.2 minutes), and 3 hours 36 minutes of audio recordings of discussions with clinicians about the consultations. The recording of consultations was conducted following research protocols approved by the pertinent hospital and university institutional review boards. Prior to their consultations, the participants had been informed of the recording of their consultations, received an explanation of the research project as a study of the use of images during consultations, and consented to participate.

The radiology practice had been using the discussion of the images during consultations prior to the study. Each case in the study involved recording a patient-clinician consultation, which involved the discussion of a series of images displayed on a laptop computer placed on a desk in the consulting room. A miniature video camera installed near the computer screen unobtrusively recorded the utterances and actions of the patient and clinician as they discussed treatment of uterine fibroid tumors and uterine fibroid embolization. Simultaneously, screen-capture software installed on the computer recorded what the patient and clinician viewed on the computer screen as they discussed fibroid tumors and UFE. I was not in the consultation room during the consultations. During my subsequent analysis of the recordings, side-by-side synchronization of the recorded interaction and the recorded screen images provided documentation of both the patient-clinician interaction and the particular image to which the participants referred or gestured as they interacted.

I conducted a telephone follow-up discussion with each patient four to eleven days after her interventional radiology consultation. I recorded the follow-up discussions for subsequent discourse analysis and comparison with the consultation recordings. This provided data on patients' recall and understanding of information presented at the consultation. I also conducted and recorded separate follow-up discussions with the clinicians involved in the consultations, during which we reviewed the recordings, and the clinicians commented on the activities during the consultations. These discussions provided information about the clinicians' interpretive frames of reference.

Biology Classrooms

The primary educational research that contributed to this book included video and audio recording of genetic inheritance learning activities during classes in 13 courses taught by seven teachers at eight U.S. high schools, during the period 1992–2002. Two hundred and twenty-three hours of recordings were analyzed in the context of ethnographic observation of classes and in-service activities of science teachers, as well as discussions with teachers and students. The recordings include students' group work, student-teacher discussions, teachers' lectures, oral testing, student classroom presentations, and the author's discussions with students and teachers.

One hundred and fifty-eight hours of the genetics education video data were recorded as part of the author's work on the Community of Explorers project (Phase One of the National Educational Testbed, NSF RED-9154815). The Community of Explorers data collection was not organized as a study of understanding, but as a study of the results of providing teachers with digital technology to foster the collaborative development of curriculum to benefit students (Saferstein & Souviney, 1997). However, the recorded classroom learning interactions of students and teachers contained data, which also opened areas of inquiry transcending the scope of the initial research project. Further analysis of that data provided a basis for comparison with the data collected later in the second classroom study.

The second genetics education study produced 65 hours of video recordings of T2's biology courses and 6 hours of audio recordings of voluntary follow-up discussions with students and discussions with T2 regarding the classes. The introductory lecture and subsequent activities were analyzed in the context of that data.

Recordings and observations were conducted following research protocols approved by the pertinent university institutional review boards, with informed consent obtained from teachers, students, parents, and administrators at the schools where the classroom learning activities were studied. After obtaining consent I observed classes, discussed the classes with the teachers, and then recorded the learning activities. In the first study, I used one video camera to record students working alone and in groups in biology classes at eight high schools. In the second study, a research associate, Nancy Oiye, and I used two cameras during the recording of each class.

Data Analysis

The detailed discussion of data presented in the preceding chapters explicates my discourse analytic approach. It emphasizes attention to linguistic and non-linguistic interaction, the use of material resources in settings, and what gets done by means of the participants' interaction and application of local resources. Chapter 12 presents ethnographic information about the participants in the research and the settings.

The data analysis involved the use of digital video editing software to mark, annotate, and compare video, audio, pictures, and textual data. This included the text on video approach, which places transcript on video in order to sustain emphasis on the actual activities of the participants, rather than on transcripts, which are analytical artifacts (Saferstein, 2004). This approach facilitated examination of participants' attention to visual resources and of the nonverbal components of interaction. It provided constant and immediate access to recorded activities and settings as well as the transcriptions of utterances. It emphasized the multiple components of interaction and setting that were relevant to developing and communicating understandings.

I analyzed the video data that had been transcribed by myself, research assistants, and a research associate in order to identify patterns of interaction. I then sorted the patterns of interaction in the recorded and transcribed data in relation to emergent categories, such as process narratives, grey boxes, discourse frameworks, interpretive contingencies, and interpretive frames of reference displayed by participants. The discussion of data here presents representative examples of the patterns of interpretation activities occurring in the larger data sets. The sorting and categorizing combined the textual descriptions and video images of the recorded activities in tables featuring columns which mapped transcriptions of initial consultation or classroom activities, material resources that featured in the transcribed activities, and follow-up discussions with participants in the recorded activities. The sorting and mapping of the recorded data contributed to systematically compiling and comparing representative examples of significant interpretation activities across cases.

Appendix B: Time P1 looks at screen or nurse during consultation discussion related to SNF

[Bold text indicates gestures and head movements pertaining to P1's process narratives subsequently expressed during post-consultation telephone discussion. Shaded text also pertains to those process narratives. Mention of infection is italicized.]

A	2.5 seconds looking at N1
	505. N1: **(Turns toward screen)** So . **(P1 looks toward N1)** directly (N1 looks toward P1) related to the procedure itself, none, **(P1 nods)** but (N1 looks toward screen) those are the things that we know about.
B	15.2 seconds looking at screen
	505 (continued). N1: (**P1 looks toward screen**) Okay, I (N1 points right hand toward screen) said I'd show (N1 looks at P1) you (**P1 nods**) those slides (N1 looks toward screen and stops pointing) that correlated with those—th this is (N1 movers right hand toward screen) actually (N1 looks at P1) our main concern. (N1 looks toward screen) And it happens in (N1 looks toward P1) less than 5 percent of the patients (**P1 nods**; N1 turns head toward screen) and it's called sloughing a necrotic fibroid. In other words (N1 lifts right and turns both hands palm up) a
C	13 seconds looking at N1
	505 (continued). N1: (**P1 turns to look at N1**) fibroid is (N1 turns both hands over) closer to (N1 moves right hand back and forth) the lining . (**P1 nods.** N1 moves left hand to meet right hand to form a spherical shape) of the uterus and (N1 moves right hand above left hand) it actually (N1 moves right fist down toward left palm) falls (N1 cups right fist with left hand) into the lining (**P1 nods.** N1 raises right fist from left hand) of—or into the center cavity of the uterus. 506. P1: and tries to come out through the cervix 507. N1: Well um eh . of (N1 points right hand at the screen) those
D	2.5 seconds looking at screen
	507 (continued). N1: (**P1 turns head toward screen**) five (N1 moves right hand back to left palm) percent, 95 percent (N1 looks at P1) of them (N1 moves hands away from each other)
E	2 seconds looking at N1
	507 (continued). N1: **(P1 looks at N1)** just get passed in your cycle. 508. P1: Okay.

F	5 seconds looking at screen
	508 (continued). (P1 nods and turns head toward screen) 509. N1: (N1 turns head toward screen and moves right hand in toward screen) That five (N1 looks at P1) percent (N1 moves right hand toward left hand) that's (N1 looks at screen) left over if they get (N1 looks at P1) stuck (P1 nods) there and they (N1 cups right fist with left hand)
G	17.7 seconds looking at N1
	509 (continued). N1: **(P1 looks at N1)** can't . go out, then it's (N1 separates hands) ***gonna set you up for infection***. (P1 nods) So what da we **(P1 smiles)** need to do? You need to (N1 pokes right fingers into left palm, repeats for each of following points) call us. We need to do an MRI right away—bring you in the hospital. I.V. antibiotics. Do an MRI. See what's **(P1 nods)** going on, and we may ask your (N1 clasps hands) gynecologist to do a D&C.
H	17 seconds looking at screen
	510. P1: (P1 Nods; turns toward screen) Okay. (P1 nods 4 times) 511. N1: (N1 Turns head toward screen) Umm so (N1 unclasps hands and moves them toward screen) like I said this (N1 clasps hands on knee) is really our main concern. (N1 moves right hand toward screen) Th--our main concern is that you're (N1 moves right hand toward P1; looks at P1) educated to know . 512. P1: what to look for 513. N1: (N1 nods) what to look for, /and/ 514. P1: /(P1 nods) yeah/ 515. N1: to call us, **(P1 nods)** because (N1 turns head toward screen) we (N1 extends right arm toward computer) think a little bit differently. So, (N1 points right hand at screen) what would you look for (N1 moves right hand away from screen to left hand and looks downward) is . generally it happens weeks to months after the **(P1 nods 3 times)** procedure . if it happens at all. And-so you've been (N1 looks at P1) feelin' pretty good
I	4.2 seconds looking at N1
	515 (continued). N1: **(P1 looks at N1)**. and then all of a sudden you don't feel so good. **(P1 nods)** So, high

J	20 seconds looking at screen
	515 (continued). N1: **(P1 looks toward screen)** fever, foul smelling vaginal drainage, **(P1 nods twice and grimaces;** N1 looks downward; then toward screen) . and cramping. You just (N1 looks at P1) don't feel **(P1 nods five times)** good. Some'n's not right. (N1 turns toward computer) 516. P1: Okay. 517. N1: (N1 moves right hand toward computer) So . um (N1 advances PowerPoint to next image) . (N1 clears throat) . . . A lot of (N1 looks downward). . . gynecologists or any other medical doctors will think ***uterine infection*** . (N1 looks at P1) if they
K	18.3 seconds looking at N1
	517 (continued). N1: ***(P1 looks at N1)*** see these symptoms ***(P1 nods)*** in you. (N1 looks upward) Um . . ***uterine infection*** (N1 looks at P1) is life threatening .
L	2 seconds looking at screen
	517 (continued). N1: (**P1 looks toward screen**) but . . we think a
M	22 seconds looking at N1
	517 (continued). N1: **(P1 looks at N1)** little bit differently. They're thinking ***uterine infection***, and we're thinkin' yeah you've got that fibroid ***(P1 nods 3 times)*** probably sittin' in there. If we get rid of that, then we're okay. **(P1 nods 5 times** as N1 turns head toward screen**)** So . a gynecologist will tend to **(**N1 looks at P1**)** rush you into the operating room and do a hysterectomy **(P1 grimaces and nods 4 times**; N1 looks toward screen**)**. Whereas, we're saying, "Well let's **(**N1 looks at P1**)** just take a look and make sure." We may still recommend a hysterectomy **(P1 nods)**. but that's really . rare . **(**N1 looks toward screen**)**
N	5 seconds looking at screen
	517 (continued). N1: **(P1 looks toward screen)** and so if a D&C will take care of it, then most **(**N1 looks at P1**)** patients will opt . /to do that/
O	.3 seconds looking at N1 [P1 nods and turns when N1 looks at her]
	518. P1: /(P1 nods toward N1;
P	2.5 seconds looking at screen
	518 (continued). N1: (**P1 looks back at screen**) to do a D&C yeah/ 519. N1: We've actually had this happen

<table>
<tr><td rowspan="2">Q</td><td>3.4 seconds looking at N1</td></tr>
<tr><td>519 (continued). NI: (PI looks at NI) to two patients (NI turns head toward PI)
520. PI: (nods head) Okay
521. NI: and came out . did a D&C and everything was fine.</td></tr>
<tr><td rowspan="2">R</td><td>3 seconds looking at screen</td></tr>
<tr><td>521 (continued). NI: (PI nods and turns head toward screen) And they're (NI looks away from PI) they're still glad.</td></tr>
<tr><td rowspan="2">S</td><td>5.3 seconds looking at N1</td></tr>
<tr><td>521 (continued). NI: (PI looks at NI) But at that point if you decide, "I'm done (NI looks at PI) with this, y'know I want a hysterectomy," that's fine too.</td></tr>
<tr><td rowspan="2">T</td><td>5.3+ seconds looking at screen</td></tr>
<tr><td>521 (continued). NI: (PI looks toward screen and nods head 3 times) That's your decision . . (NI turns head toward screen) So it's just so that you're aware and know what to look for. (NI advances to next image)
522. PI:Alright.</td></tr>
</table>

Index

www.ingramcontent.com/pod-product-compliance
Lightning Source LLC
LaVergne TN
LVHW010443080826
844660LV00026B/1202

* 9 7 8 1 8 4 5 5 3 4 3 6 3 *